Now Faith Is

Faith That Works!

By
Steven Lambert, ThD, DMin

Copyright Page

Unless otherwise indicated, Scripture quotations are from The New American Standard Bible (NASB), © 1960, 1962, 1963, 1968, 1971, 1972, 1973, 1975, 1977, 1988; The Lockman Foundation. All rights reserved. Used by permission.

Scripture quotations marked AMP are from the Amplified Bible, Old Testament © 1965, 1987 by the Zondervan Corporation; The Amplified New Testament © 1958, 1987 by the Lockman Foundation. Used by permission.

Scripture quotations marked GNB are from the Good News Bible © 1976 by The American Bible Society. Used by permission.

Scripture quotations marked KJV are from the King James Version of the Bible. Public domain.

This book is authored AI-free.

NOW FAITH IS – Faith That Works!

© Copyright 2023; Steven Lambert, ThD, DMin

All rights reserved under International Copyright Law. Contents and/or cover in whole or part may not be reproduced, stored in any electronic retrieval system, transmitted in any form by any means—mechanical, electronic, photocopying, recording, or otherwise—without prior written permission of the author.

Published by:
Real Truth Publications
8314 Riviera Way
Port Saint Lucie, FL 34986
Email: admin@realtruthpublications.com
Website: https://www.realtruthpublications.com

ISBN 978-1-887915-24-3 (Ingram-LSI Print Version)
ISBN 978-1-887915-30-4 (RTP PDF Ebook Version)
ISBN 978-1-887915-28-1 (Amazon-KDP Print Version)
ASIN: B0CJ9MRJQK (Amazon-Kindle Version)

LCCN: 2023903055

Printed in the United States of America

Contents

	Preface	1
	Introduction	5
1	Saving Faith	9
2	Weak/Feeble Faith	15
3	Effective Faith	27
4	Strong Faith	39
5	Mountain-Moving Faith	57
6	Wonder-Working Faith	73
7	Great Faith	93
8	Faith for Healing and Deliverance	103
9	The Faithless	115
10	Obtaining And Activating Faith	125
11	Building Yourself Up On Your Faith	147
12	The Testing Of Our Faith	171
13	Hindrances To Genuine Faith	199
14	Walking By Faith	247
15	Faith Without Works	265
16	Contending For The Faith	281
17	Falling Away From The Faith	305
18	The Shield of Faith	327
	Epilogue	403
	Other Books By Author	409
	About the Author	420

Salvation Prayer

Salvation Scriptures assuring that *everyone* who believes in the Lord Jesus Christ, that He rose from the dead, and calls upon His Name shall be saved and born again as a new creature in Christ Jesus:

"He who has BELIEVED and has been baptized shall be SAVED; but he who has disbelieved shall be condemned. (Mar. 16:16)

"I am the door; if anyone enters through Me, he will be SAVED...." (John 10:9a)

'AND IT SHALL BE THAT EVERYONE WIIO CALLS ON THE NAME OF THE LORD WILL BE SAVED.' (Acts 2:21)

for "WHOEVER WILL CALL ON THE NAME OF THE LORD WILL BE SAVED." (Rom. 10:13)

But what does it say? "THE WORD IS NEAR YOU, IN YOUR MOUTH AND IN YOUR HEART"—that is, the word of faith which we are preaching, that if you CONFESS WITH YOUR MOUTH Jesus as Lord, and BELIEVE IN YOUR HEART that God raised Him from the dead, YOU WILL BE SAVED; for with the HEART a person BELIEVES, resulting in RIGHTEOUSNESS, and with the MOUTH he CONFESSES, resulting in SALVATION. For the Scripture says, "WHOEVER BELIEVES IN HIM WILL NOT BE DISAPPOINTED." (Rom. 10:8-11)

You MUST be born again. (John 3:6)

Therefore if anyone is in Christ, he is a NEW CREATURE; the old things passed away; behold, new things have come. (2 Cor. 5:17)

And without faith it is impossible to please Him, for he who comes to God must believe that He is and that He is a rewarder of those who seek Him. (Heb. 11:6)

For if we believe that Jesus died and rose again, even so God will bring with Him those who have fallen asleep in Jesus. (1 Thes. 4:14)

If you want to be saved, born again, and become a new creature in Christ Jesus with your past sins erased through the shed blood of Christ, the Lamb of God who took away the sins of the world, pray this prayer out loud in faith with all sincerity, and by faith all of those transactions will take place in your life:

Dear Lord Jesus, I believe you are the only Savior of all mankind. I believe you died on the cross for my sin and then rose again from the dead three days later. I am a sinner. I need the salvation you purchased for me with your shed blood. I'm sorry for all my sin. Please forgive me. I now repent of all my sin and turn to you to help me to walk in newness of Life, leaving sin behind, as best as I can with the help of the Holy Spirit. I ask you to come and live in my heart forever. I receive your salvation and the forgiveness of my sins. Please make me anew, give me a new life in you! Redeem me! Receive me into your Kingdom of Light and deliver me from the kingdom of darkness. Right now, this moment! In your name, I pray! Thank you! By faith I believe I am now born again! AMEN!

Preface

I am a preacher. At the time of the writing of this book, I am in my 47th year of ministry, having begun my ministry only a few months after surrendering my heart and life to Jesus as my Master, Lord, and Savior in January 1976. Ministry in some capacity is all I've known since the age of 28.

Despite this, a few years ago, I realized that though my whole ministry is essentially preaching and teaching about faith in Christ Jesus, and I had taught on the subject of faith many times, I had never written a book about faith, per se, despite having written a dozen or so books. I decided then that it was time that I did write a book on the subject. I wanted it to be simple, uncomplicated, and as non-theological as possible and practical (though theologically correct), which has its challenges for a theologian by training. So, what you are reading or listening to is my best attempt at same. My hope is that it meets the goal and ministers to you in a way that you can easily understand it.

As the title suggests, this book is simply about faith, which is always a *now*-kind of belief, or it is not genuine faith at all. Faith must not be confused with hope. Hope is relegated to the *future*; it is a desire for a favorable future outcome. Faith is *not* about the future, but the *present*. I often say, "Faith is either *now*, or it is *never*!" Faith cannot be activated or effected in the future, but only right *now*. Faith must be appropriated at the present moment when it is being exerted or applied.

Faith comes by hearing, and hearing comes through reading or listening to the Word of Christ.[1] The Rhema-Word of Christ produces real, active, and effectual faith.[2] That is one of the mysterious properties of the Word of God—it produces faith. How it does this, as I said, is to some extent a mystery. It just does!

Ironically—or perhaps not—the time I felt the unction to begin writing this book occurred only a few months prior to my entering into a very strange time in my life that would require me to apply into my own life every ounce of spiritual understanding I had acquired over the best part of five decades. Other than a few brief bouts with the common cold or virus, I had never before experienced significant health problems. In the latter part of 2020, a surgeon surgically removing what he had misdiagnosed as an umbilical hernia discovered what instead was a large malignant tumor in my abdomen. Not a hernia at all! When I finally was seen by an oncologist in January 2021, his words to me were, "Mr. Lambert, I give you four months to live, but I'm going to start you on chemotherapy treatments that we hope will allow you to live longer." At the time I am publishing this book, by God's grace, I've beaten that grim prognosis by more than a year, however.

I have great respect for medical doctors and practitioners. They have invested a lot in obtaining the training they have obtained. Most are extremely dedicated to helping people as best they can, often at great personal sacrifice. The life of a medical practitioner of any sort at any level is a difficult one, requiring much from them personally. I honor them all. Nevertheless, Isaiah the prophet said, "Who hath believed our report."[3] In my own case, I can honestly say the answer to that question is: **ME**! I believe the report of the Lord over the report of medical practitioners every time and all the time! God cannot lie; it is impossible for Him to do so. Human medical practitioners, without meaning or intending to, do speak untruths! They believe what the science tells them, but science does not always tell the ultimate whole truth! It is intrinsically unreliable. That's just its nature.

I believe in medical doctors and science to a point, but I believe in Doctor Jesus, The Great Physician, *more*! Only Jesus knows the ultimate real truth regarding the outcome of any given situation or scenario, including those involving illness. I myself have stood a number of times over gravely ill people laying on hospital beds who doctors said would be dead in hours or not make it through the night, and heard the Lord speaking, prophesying, through my mouth out loud, "You shall LIVE and not die!" Every one of those people not only made it through the night but are alive yet today! Several times the Lord sovereignly arranged a face-to-face meeting with some of these people who told me they know they are alive today because I came into their room at the time they were supposed to die and prayed and prophesied over them. Fascinatingly, each of those people told me that despite being unconscious they heard every word I spoke! Something happened in their spirit—those prophetic words pierced the darkness and despair and changed their thinking to comport with the prophetic decree, causing them to know by faith they would indeed live and not die! And they did! Praise God!

I myself, along with many other people who know about my situation, have prayed and prophesied similar words over me in the last year or so. I thoroughly BELIEVE their decrees! I shall LIVE and NOT die! Though, as the Apostle Paul said, I have had the sentence of death within me,[4] I have decided to live and not succumb to premature death. To die is gain,[5] certainly, for to be absent from the body is to be instantaneously in the Lord's presence,[6] yet for me to continue living would be more fruitful labor on behalf of Christ unto the advancement of His Kingdom in these last days![7] I WANT to live! I WILL live!

All of this has been my efforts at applying the faith that has been produced in me by nearly five decades of not just reading, but diligently studying, the Word of God. It works! I believe! I have faith! It is for the purpose of sharing as best as I can as much as I can with you, the reader and/or listener, what I have come to understand about faith, not only through this latest battle, but the many other trials, troubles, and tribulations I have endured since surrendering my heart and life to Jesus that I have written this book!

I fully believe God will eventually transform my current "*mess*," so to speak, into a "*mess*age"—a testimony of the almightiness of God, for with God NOTHING is impossible!

By the way, also rather ironically, several years ago the Lord prompted me to write and narrate an article-size Kindle book on *Forty Healing Scriptures* in His Word. I obeyed, and they are available on Amazon® as a Kindle book and the audiobook (set to beautiful background music) is available on Amazon® and Audible®. For more information, view the promotional page on this title in the back of this book. Literally hundreds upon hundreds have already downloaded and been blessed by these products.

My sincere and earnest desire is that this book minister to you to help you understand a little better this matter of genuine, biblical, effective faith, and help you to appropriate and activate it in your own life. (It's not really complicated or difficult.) If I accomplish that in the following pages, I will have succeeded in what I set out to do in writing this book. Praise the Lord Jesus!

One final thought. As the human author of this book, I want to fully acknowledge one vital truth. The one thing I, or any human for that matter, cannot supply for this or any book, though I desperately desire it for this book, is: THE ANOINTING!

The mere compiling or scribing of truth does not, cannot, of itself produce the anointing. The anointing is distributed by and comes from "the Holy One" exclusively, who is the three Persons of the Godhead!

> But you have an anointing from the Holy One, and you all know (know all things; KJV). I have not written to you because you do not know the truth, but because you do know it, and because no lie is of the truth.[8]

Thus, I have in my best effort of complete sincerity, earnestness, and humility of heart, as best as I can know it, repeatedly petitioned God that His anointing fall and rest upon this human endeavor!

> Be anxious for nothing, but in *everything* by prayer and supplication with thanksgiving let your requests be made known to God.[9]

I have done the best I know how to do, as inept, frail, and inadequate as my "best" may be, by prayer and supplication with thanksgiving to let my requests be made known to God in this regard. That's all I know how to do. The response is entirely in the hands of God!

Endnotes

1. Rom. 12:3
2. Rom. 10:17; Rhema is the verbalized or spoken Word of Christ.
3. Isa. 53:1
4. 2 Cor. 1:9
5. Plp. 1:21
6. 2 Cor. 5:8
7. Plp. 1:22
8. 1 John 2:20-21
9. Plp. 4:6

Introduction

The primary purpose of this book is to inform believers concerning the various degrees or dimensions of faith that exist. The intent is to help the Body of Christ better understand the "measure"[1] or "degree"[2] of faith God graciously "has allotted to each" believer individually and bestows unto all believers collectively, which allotment carries with it the responsibility by each believer to grow or increase that measure of faith, and how to incrementally expand faith over the course of their walk with God.

The basics of faith, according to the Word of God, are, first: "Faith comes by hearing and hearing by the Word of Christ."[3] Or, it would be correct to restate it this way: "Faith comes by hearing the Word of Christ." In other words, hearing or listening (reading is a form of hearing) to God's written Word, the Bible (the sixty-six books of canonized Scripture), produces faith in the human heart or spirit.

Throughout this book, it is critical to understand that the faith being described is this "spiritual faith" that is authored[4] or originated and given[5] by **God**, is communicated and generated through[6] the Word of God, i.e., Jesus,[7] and must be received by and reside in the believer's Born Again human spirit.[8] So, genuine faith, comes from God, and therefore is a spiritual, not a psychological, mental, intellectual, or emotional matter, for "God is *Spirit*."[9] Thus, genuine faith is of the Spirit, *by* the Spirit, *in* the Spirit, and *from* the Spirit.

With this as our foundation, the next thing we need to understand about genuine faith is that, according to Scripture, there are degrees or dimensions of faith, and it is the responsibility and should be the aspiration of every individual believer to grow or increase the magnitude of his/her faith over the process of time. One passage of Scripture that refers to degrees of faith is Romans 12:3 (AMP): "as God has apportioned to each a degree of faith."

Regarding growing or expanding our faith, notice what the Holy Spirit said through the Apostle Paul concerning Abraham growing strong in faith in God:

> yet, with respect to the promise of God, he did not waver in unbelief but *grew strong in faith*, giving glory to God,[10]

Moreover, demonstrating how vital this matter of believers' faith is, in the subsequent verses the Spirit goes so far as to say God credited Abraham's faith to him as righteousness or rightstanding with God. He does the same to *us* as well:

> Therefore his faith was credited to him as righteousness (rightstanding with God). Now not for his sake alone was it written that it was credited to him, but for *our* sake also—to whom righteousness will be credited, as those who believe in Him who raised Jesus our Lord from the dead—[11]

Next, we need to understand that to accomplish that incremental expansion of faith operating in our life, we must give deliberate attention to increasing the size of our faith, implementing, or applying our faith to particular needs and situations as they occur in our life, and setting specific goals for over time increasing the measure of faith given us by God.

All of this coupled with what I have explained in this volume, I believe are directives of Heaven concerning this vital matter of faith, for "without faith it is impossible to please God,"[12] and the desire to please God is the reason I've written this book and presumably is the reason you are reading it.

Hopefully, when you have come to the end of this book, you will have learned more about the various dimensions of faith, discovered what dimension or dimensions you have been operating in heretofore, as well as gained an understanding of how to progress to the highest dimensions of faith available to believers in this life.

Our ability to walk by faith and not by sight[13] will be a landmark by which to measure our growth and determination to seek out the dimensions of this faith-walk with God.

> For by the grace [of God] given to me I say to everyone of you not to think more highly of himself [and of his importance and ability] than he ought to think; but to think so as to have sound

judgment, as God has apportioned to each a degree of faith [and a purpose designed for service]."¹⁴

Endnotes

1. Rom. 12:3; KJV
2. Rom. 12:3; AMP
3. Rom. 10:17
4. Heb. 12:2
5. Rom. 12:3
6. Rom. 10:17; Acts 3:16
7. John 1:1-4; 1 John 1:1-3
8. Rom. 10:8-10
9. John 4:24
10. Rom. 4:20
11. Rom. 4:22-24; AMP
12. Heb. 11:6; AMP
13. Heb. 11:6; AMP
14. Rom. 12:3

Chapter One

SAVING FAITH

But **without faith**[1] it is impossible to [walk with God and] please Him, for whoever comes [near] to God must [necessarily] believe that God exists and that He rewards those who [earnestly and diligently] seek Him.[2]

The first requirement regarding faith is: one must accept, receive, and activate it to become a *Believer*.

But what does it say? "THE WORD IS NEAR YOU, IN YOUR MOUTH AND IN YOUR HEART"—that is, the word [the message, the basis] of faith which we preach— because if you acknowledge and confess with your mouth that Jesus is Lord [recognizing His power, authority, and majesty as God], and believe in your heart that God raised Him from the dead, you will be saved. For with the heart a person believes [in Christ as Savior] resulting in his justification [that is, being made righteous—being freed of the guilt of sin and made acceptable to God]; and with the mouth he acknowledges and confesses [his faith openly], resulting in and confirming [his] salvation."[3]

The second requirement is: You must be a *Receiver* of the Word.

But to as many as did receive and welcome Him, He gave the right [the authority, the privilege] to become children of God, that is, to those who believe in (adhere to, trust in, and rely on) His name— who were born, not of blood [natural conception], nor of the will of the flesh [physical impulse], nor of the will of man [that of a natural father], but of God [that is, a divine and supernatural birth—they are born of God—spiritually transformed, renewed, sanctified]."[4]

The third requirement is: You must be "an active *doer*" or *operator* or *obeyer* of the Word.

> For if anyone only listens to the word **without obeying it**, he is like a man who looks very carefully at his natural face in a mirror; for once he has looked at himself and gone away, he immediately forgets what he looked like. But he who looks carefully into the perfect law, the law of liberty, and faithfully abides by it, not having become a [careless] listener who forgets but an **active doer** [who obeys], he will be blessed and favored by God in what he does [in his life of obedience]."[5]

Unless a person is a believer, he/she cannot receive, act on, obey, perform, or do the Word of God. This statement can only be explained from a theological perspective, which requires a little foundation-laying, if you will indulge me briefly. I promise that the reward in terms of revelation will be well worth the excursion.

The Tragedy of the Garden of Eden

In the Garden of Eden, God explicitly commanded Adam and Eve not to eat or partake of the fruit of the Tree of the Knowledge of Good and Evil, for if they did, they would "surely die!"[6] The fruit of that Tree was the nature of Satan, the sin nature, carnality. The primary law governing the Kingdom of God is righteousness. Preserving and protecting God's Kingdom from corruption by its occupants—those who God chose to receive into His Kingdom for eternal fellowship or relationship, i.e., the Righteous—required the establishment of another cardinal law governing the Kingdom: "The wages of sin is death,"[7] so that any creature who chose to defy and disobey God, which is *un*righteousness, would die and thereby be purged or removed from the Kingdom. This was the reason God admonished Adam and Eve that if they defied and disobeyed His explicit command not to eat or partake of the fruit of the Tree of the Knowledge of Good and Evil, and did eat or partake of it, they would surely die!

As we know, Adam and Eve *did* defy and disobey God's explicit command and *did* eat or partake of the fruit of the Tree of the Knowledge of Good and Evil, yet curiously we are informed that Adam lived 930 years before he died (ironically, we are not told how long Eve lived),[8] though we are not specifically told how long after the fall it was that he died. Critics of Christianity and the Bible sometimes point to this seeming contradiction in an attempt to discredit Christian beliefs and the Bible. But the fact is that Adam and Eve *did* surely die, instantaneously, the very moment they disobeyed God, but it was *spiritually* not *physically* that they died; that is to say their human *spirit* died, not their human *body*!

Adam and Eve, the progenitors of the human race, were created as SPIRITS—for they were made in the likeness and image of God,[9] and God is Spirit[10]— possessing a SOUL, with the spirit and soul being contained in a human BODY. Since God is Trinity, i.e., three divine Persons in ONE Godhead, creating mankind in His likeness and image required He created Man as a "tripartite-being," meaning consisting of three parts: spirit, soul, and body.[11]

God created Man originally so that their spirit was the "tabernacle" or "temple of God," i.e., the Holy Sanctuary where God dwelt. The human spirit, or heart, was the part of Man that continuously connected them with Almighty God, their Creator and Spiritual Father. Thus, it was the human *spirit* that was the predominant part of Man, which God intended to rule over the human *soul*[12]— which consists of the mind, will, and emotions—and the physical human *body*.

That was the original Creational order of things for human beings. It is both interesting and telling that whenever you hear unregenerate people of the world or even carnal or uninformed believers speak about this tripartite human constitution, they invariably speak of it in the opposite order of how God created Mankind: body, soul, and spirit. But the order the Holy Spirit of God speaks of the three parts of human constitution is the opposite, the proper Creational order, as evidenced by what the Holy Spirit spoke/wrote through the Apostle Paul in his first letter to the Thessalonians:

> "Now may the God of peace Himself sanctify you entirely; and may your *spirit* and *soul* and *body* be preserved complete, without blame at the coming of our Lord Jesus Christ."[13]

The tragic consequence of Adam and Eve's disobedience of God's explicit command not to eat or partake of the fruit of the Tree of the Knowledge of Good and Evil was that they died *spiritually*, in that their human spirit—the Tabernacle or Temple of God—the place where God resided in them, was mortified, or rendered dead and inoperable, because the wages of sin is death; and when their spirit died, as a result of their disobedience, God, who is Zoe-Life, departed their human spirit, rendering it dead and lifeless. Now they were no longer connected with God in their human spirit. Their connection or relationship with God was now only with their soul, which meant they could from then on only relate with God through their mental or intellectual reasoning (carnal mind), their human emotions, and according to their own carnal desires (will). The sad and dire result was that Adam and Eve's—and by extension, Mankind's—connection to God was now reduced to the vastly inferior, corrupted realm of the natural and carnal.

After the fall, God had to speak to them physically or in the natural so that they **heard** His voice with their physical hearing through their physical ears. Prior to the fall, God communicated with Adam and Eve by His Spirit in their human spirit! We see the evidence of that in Genesis 3:8: "They **heard the sound** of the LORD God walking in the garden in the cool of the day, and the man and his wife hid themselves from the presence of the LORD God among the trees of the garden." Whereas, prior to the fall their connection with God was by the Spirit in their human spirit, which meant their communion with God's Spirit was not limited to their physical hearing. This is also the reason that when God called out to them after they had disobeyed, asking, "Where are you?" (v. 9) Adam replied, "I **heard the sound** of You in the garden, and I was afraid because I was naked; so I hid myself" (v. 10).

It is because of this spiritual death that occurred in the Garden of Eden and was passed on to every human being afterward born in the lineage of Adam and Eve that when people are birthed physically they are dead spiritually, as the Spirit indicates in Ephesians 2:1-2:

> And you were dead in your trespasses and sins, in which you formerly walked according to the course of this world, according to the prince of the power of the air, of the spirit that is now working in the sons of disobedience. (NASB)

> And you [He made alive when you] were [spiritually] dead and separated from Him because of your transgressions and sins, in which you once walked. You were following the ways of this world [influenced by this present age], in accordance with the prince of the power of the air (Satan), the spirit who is now at work in the disobedient [the unbelieving, who fight against the purposes of God]. (AMP)

The only antidote to this unspeakably horrible predicament is that every person "*must* be Born Again,"[14] as Jesus told the Jewish elder and teacher Nicodemus, explaining to him that at physical birth people are born physically because human reproduction produces a physical human being, but the human being that is born is born spiritually dead because: "That which is born of the flesh is *flesh* (i.e., carnal nature), and that which is born of the Spirit is *spirit*."[15] Thus, when a person is Born Again, accepting Christ as Savior and receiving Him by His Spirit into their human heart or spirit, their formerly dead human spirit is regenerated or made alive[16] or quickened by the infusion of the Holy Spirit, the third Person of the Godhead.

In the Spirit that transaction is the equivalent of when Jesus was resurrected from the dead: the Born Again person's human spirit that had been dead and dormant is instantaneously quickened or made alive or enlivened; and the moment that occurs that person is resurrected or raised from the dead, and instantaneously seated with Christ in Heavenly places[17] at the right hand of God![18]

Connecting the Dots

Now with all this as our foundation, it is here that I connect it all to our topic of "spiritual faith!" When a person accepts the Lord as his/her Savior, and his/her human spirit is infused with the Holy Spirit, regenerating or quickening his/her human spirit, as a result that spiritual faith God originally embedded at Creation in the human spirit of all mankind is likewise quickened or activated or made operable in the life of that Born Again believer! In other words, at the moment of salvation, when a person receives the Lord Jesus Christ into his/her human spirit or heart, genuine spiritual faith in God, which had been mortified [put to death] with the disobedience of Adam and Eve[19], instantaneously comes alive and becomes active and operable in that person's life.

WOW! That's enough to make an Egyptian mummy jump up and shout, "AMEN!"

This active, alive, operative faith of the Spirit, or "spiritual faith," is what theologians and Bible teachers sometimes refer to as "saving faith." It is "the God-kind of faith" that instantaneously connects the genuinely Born Again believer to the heart/Spirit of God and makes the God-kind of faith operable in his/her life. Whereas previously, prior to being Born Again, any "faith" the unregenerate or non-Born-Again person thought he/she had was in actuality only mental assent or "intellectual faith" and merely the "faith" of dead, lifeless, non-productive religiosity.

With that foundation laid, let us now move on to discuss in the next chapter the category of human beings who do not have this "spiritual faith"—Saving Faith—described in this chapter.

Endnotes

1 To be "without faith" is to be "faithless."
2 Heb. 11:6
3 Rom. 10:8-10
4 John 1:12-13
5 Jas. 1:23-25
6 Gen. 2:17
7 Rom. 6:23
8 Gen. 5:5
9 Gen. 1:26-27
10 John 4:24
11 1 Ths. 5:23
12 Col. 3:15; et al.
13 1 Ths. 5:23; NASB
14 John 3:16
15 John 3:6
16 Eph. 2:1-9; John 3:6,7
17 Eph. 2:6; Col. 3:1
18 Mark 16:19
19 Gen. 2:16-17

Chapter Two

WEAK/FEEBLE FAITH

So faith comes from hearing [what is told], and what is heard comes by the [preaching of the] message concerning Christ.[1]

The Bible indicates there is such a thing as "weak" or "feeble faith." However, the fact that it is mentioned in the Word of God does not mean that it is something God wants, or that those operating in it should be content with. Quite the contrary, the premise of this book is that God wants and even *expects* believers to grow in and increase their faith. Weak or Feeble Faith is better than *no* faith, obviously, but it should be considered merely an "entry level" or "beginner" faith," a starting point of faith. Believers should not be content with weak faith but should be in constant pursuit of growing or increasing their faith.

Acceptance of Those with Weak or Feeble Faith

The Holy Spirit, through the Apostle Paul, instructs believers to *accept* the person who is "weak in faith,"[2] and not be judgmental of or discouraging to such novices in the Lord because their faith is indeed feeble or weak. However, it also indicates believers should be wary of accepting as true or being influenced by the opinions of those who are walking in an entry level or beginner's faith.

In other words, it is important when it comes to spiritual knowledge and understanding that more mature believers make allowances for and extend grace towards those who are new in the Lord regarding the opinions they may express about spiritual matters, because of the very fact that their faith has not yet had the time needed to develop to the extent that it presumably will (or should) over time.

A stellar example of that is found in Paul's admonition to the predominantly Gentile Roman believers regarding their attitude toward believers in their fellowships who believed they should continue to observe the dietary practices mandated by God under the Old Covenant laws:

> As for **the one whose faith is weak**, accept him [*into your fellowship*], but not for [*the purpose of*] quarreling over his opinions. One man's faith permits him to eat everything, while the weak *believer* eats *only* vegetables [*to avoid eating ritually unclean meat or something previously considered unclean*]. The one who eats [*everything*] is not to look down on the one who does not eat, and the one who does not eat must not criticize *or* pass judgment on the one who eats [*everything*], for God has accepted him. Who are you to judge the servant of another? Before his own master he stands [*approved*] or falls [*out of favor*]. And he [*who serves the Master--the Lord*] will stand, for the Lord is able to make him stand.[3]

Notice that Paul describes such people whose level of faith was such that their conscience would not allow them to discard those Old Covenant mandates as "the one whose faith is *weak*." Clearly, these are "feeble faith" believers in Paul's and the Holy Spirit's mind, in that every word evoked in the Bible is God-breathed.[4]

In many other portions of his letters comprising two-thirds of the New Testament, Paul taught that the Old Covenant Laws were now, under the New Covenant of grace and truth in Christ,[5] obsolete[6] and no longer in effect. In fact, Paul revealed in this same Roman letter the Truth that "the righteousness of faith" would be nullified, or made of no effect and void, if God were to base rightstanding (righteousness) with Him on obedience to or observance of the Old Covenant Laws:

> For the promise to Abraham or to his descendants that he would be heir of the world was not through [*observing the requirements of*] the Law, but through the righteousness of faith. [Gen_17:4-6; Gen_22:16-18] If those who are [*followers*] of the Law are [*the true*] heirs [*of Abraham*], then faith [*leading to salvation*] is of no effect *and* void, and the promise [*of God*] is nullified.[7]

Notice also how Paul compares the believer whose faith is free of any obligation to Old Covenant dietary observances: "One man's faith *permits* him to eat everything" contrasted to "the weak *believer*" who "eats *only* vegetables." Clearly, Paul and the Holy Spirit are saying that the faith of the believer that allows him to eat anything and everything he wants without regard to Mosaic Law restrictions is a stronger faith than the faith of the believer who, for religious reasons, eats no meat but only vegetables.

Nevertheless, Paul and the Spirit, instruct that believers who eat everything without observance of Old Covenant limitations, must not "look down on," regard condescendingly, shun, or be contemptuous of "the one who does not eat." And "the one who does not eat must not criticize *or* pass judgment on the one who eats [*everything*], for God has accepted him."

Paul then goes further in this example he selected to ask, "Who are you to judge the servant of another?"—a question that is directed not only to the Roman church at the time, but also to the entire Church for all time. Indeed, who is any believer to think he is right in rejecting or alienating another genuine believer in Christ based merely upon his/her dietary practices—what they eat or don't eat—when God has totally accepted that person based entirely upon their acceptance and profession of faith in the Savior of all Mankind?[8]

Paul concludes this portion of his admonition by indicating that it is "Before his own master"—Jesus—any believer "stands" (has divine approval and favor) "or falls" (has divine disapproval and disfavor), and, indeed, the believer *will* stand, "for the Lord is able to make him stand" before God holy, spotless, and blameless.[9]

The overall truth we should take from Paul's instruction here is that while the faith based purely and entirely on the irrefutable fact of "the summing up of all things in Christ, things in the heavens and things on the earth,"[10] and that Christ Jesus is "the mediator of a *better* covenant, which has been enacted on *better* promises,"[11] which superseded and made the former covenant totally *obsolete, null and void*, is a **stronger** faith than that of those who believe they should still follow the dietary ban of the Old Covenant; nevertheless, possessing and walking in such a faith in no way grants the right to treat with contempt and disdain and be judgmental toward those of feeble or weaker faith who have not yet possessed and are not yet walking in the stronger and higher dimension of faith.

Abel's Strong Faith, Cain's Feeble Faith

> Now the man Adam knew Eve as his wife, and she conceived and gave birth to Cain, and she said, "I have obtained a man (baby boy, son) with the help of the Lord." And [later] she gave birth to his brother Abel. Now Abel kept the flocks [of sheep and goats], but Cain cultivated the ground.[12]

> And in the course of time Cain brought to the Lord an offering of the fruit of the ground. But Abel brought [an offering of] the [finest] firstborn of his flock and the fat portions. And the Lord had respect (regard) for Abel and for his offering; but for Cain and his offering He had no respect. So Cain became extremely angry (indignant), and he looked annoyed and hostile.[13]

Here, in this section, we want to cite another example in the Bible illustrating Strong Faith contrasted to Feeble Faith. In Genesis we read:

> But Abel brought [an offering of] the [finest] firstborn of his flock and the fat portions. And the LORD had respect (regard) for Abel and for his offering; but for Cain and his offering He had no respect. So Cain became extremely angry (indignant), and he looked annoyed and hostile. And the LORD said to Cain, "Why are you so angry? And why do you look annoyed? If you do well [believing Me and doing what is acceptable and pleasing to Me], will you not be accepted? And if you do not do well [but ignore My instruction], sin crouches at your door; its desire is for you [to overpower you], but you must master it."[14]

Inherent in this aspect of the Genesis story is the first mention of the "first-fruits" sacrifice, which is later revealed in Moses' writings to be a mandate from Heaven and a loving Father-God. The first-fruits offering was a demonstration of love for God through the act of sacrifice.

Where we pick up the story Adam and Eve have produced two sons. The firstborn was Cain, who was what we would today call a "farmer": "Cain cultivated the ground." The second-born was Abel, who was a shepherd: "Abel kept the flocks [of sheep and goats]."

It was Cain, the firstborn son, who at some point in his life first brought an offering to the Lord: "And in the course of time Cain brought to the Lord an offering of the fruit of the ground."

Now it is significant that the Bible says specifically that it was "to the Lord" that Cain brought the sacrifice, as opposed to saying to God or Jehovah, because when the Bible makes reference to "the Lord," it is referring to the Lord Jesus Christ, in particular, the "firstborn of every creature" and "Creation,"[15] who at this time, of course, had not yet been manifest on earth as a Man, but who nevertheless was the Lord, because He is Lord eternally. So, in essence, this was the firstborn of the First Adam offering the first-fruits sacrifice to the Only Begotten Son of God and Firstborn of all Creation and the Second Adam, who four millennia later became our Kinsmen Redeemer as He offered Himself up to God as the First-fruits Sacrifice!

Now, we are not told how Cain knew about the first-fruits offering. In fact, this is the first time we hear about anything that happened in the lives of Adam and Eve and their offspring after their removal from the Garden of Eden. We do not know the specific timeframes of the events that occurred following their banishment. We only know Adam knew Eve in intimacy and she gave birth to two sons, Cain and Abel. Subsequently, we never hear another peep from or about Adam in the Genesis story, only from and about Eve. With so little information provided by the Spirit of God through the writing of Moses, we are left to wonder how life was for them after the fall.

The Word of God says in Genesis 3:24:

> So God drove the man out; and at the east of the Garden of Eden He [permanently] stationed the cherubim and the sword with the flashing blade which turned round and round [in every direction] to protect and guard the way (entrance, access) to the tree of life.

God forcefully evicted Man out of Paradise, which was originally Heaven on Earth where God tabernacled or communed with His Mankind Creation in continuous fellowship by the Spirit. With their eviction from the Garden, Adam and Eve became wanderers or nomads upon the Earth, condemned to living under the curses that came upon them as a result of their disobedience and sin instead of the unfathomable superabundant blessings they had previously enjoyed in the Garden in the Spirit.

When Eve is reintroduced after the fall, she appears to be elated at God's blessing her with two sons, and that she regarded them as a great and gracious gift of restoration from God following the severe judgment their disobedience had produced. It would be reasonable to surmise that the bearing and birthing of these two sons generated in Eve a sense of God's forgiveness and pardon emanating out of the Creator's overarching and abiding love.

It appears the first parental pair, Adam and Eve, may have taught their children to honor God by bringing their sacrifices to Him, and the importance of giving one's best to Him. It would be reasonable to surmise that after their banishment from the Garden of Eden, as Adam and Eve began to understand to some degree the severity and extent of their losses resulting from their disobedience of God's Word to them, they began to teach their children about the dire consequences of disobeying God.

Maybe it was that influence, or something else—we are given no information what specifically—that motivated Abel, the second son of the Adamses, at some point to offer God as a sacrifice a portion of the best of his possessions he had to offer, which was the fattiest portions of the first-born of the finest of the flock of sheep he tended. It was a sacrifice because he had to slaughter the sheep in order to offer it to God. The offerings of Cain and Abel are the first mention in the Bible of the "first-fruits sacrifice."

Cain, we are told, "brought to the Lord an offering of the fruit of the ground." Maybe it was some uncooked broccoli or asparagus or turnips or carrots...we don't know specifically what it was except that it was from "the fruit of the ground"—vegetables he had grown in the fields he cultivated. Whatever it was, it came from a stingy, self-centered, sin-corrupted heart, and it was not pleasing to the Lord: "but for Cain and his offering He (the Lord) had no respect (regard)."

It is interesting and worthy of mention that Cain knew his offering was not pleasing and acceptable to the Lord, though we are not told how he knew it. We can only speculate.

Moses also informs us that because he and his sacrifice was rejected by the Lord: "Cain became extremely angry (indignant), and he looked annoyed and hostile." I could easily go off on a tangent here regarding this matter and how representative it is of mankind who essentially throughout human history has reacted with the same anger and hostility to God because they know instinctively that the sacrifice of their own works likewise are not acceptable to God and will not appease His righteous wrath for their extreme waywardness and sinfulness, but I'll resist that temptation. Suffice it to understand that Cain was extremely angry with both the Lord and Abel because he realized his sacrifice would not appease God's righteous wrath toward him due to the sin that permeated his being since Adam and Eve's fall into perdition, though Abel's sacrifice *did* appease and please the Lord, and was regarded by Him as a temporary "covering" unto Abel.

What was the polar difference between the two sacrifices? Cain's consisted of the fruits of **HIS** works or labors, and Abel's consisted of the fruits of **GOD'S** works, because it was a living being, an animal, a sheep, that had a heart that pumped blood through other internal organs required for life, and only God can give life to living beings—i.e., the creatures of the Creation of which the Lord is the Creator! Only a blood-sacrifice, a life for a life, is an acceptable sacrifice to God for atonement of sin, for life is in the blood:

> For the life of the flesh is in the blood, and I have given it to you on the altar to make atonement for your souls; for it is the blood that makes atonement, by reason of the life [which it represents].[16]

When the Lord saw that Cain was angry, He spoke to him, asking him: "Why are you so angry? And why do you look annoyed?" This was an amazing thing when you think about it. This was the Lord of Heaven and Earth, and the only begotten Son of God, God the Son, who is the only acceptable sacrifice, whose human blood had to be shed and who had to die to appease the righteous wrath of God for man's sinfulness, speaking to the firstborn son of the first Adam, the first human being, who was the one who disobeyed God and as a result died spiritually, who was asking Cain this question! Astounding!

It was the Lord who had every right to be righteously angry and annoyed with Cain, who was so spiritually bereft that he thought an offering of dead, lifeless vegetables that had no blood of life coursing through them, could possibly be adequate to appease the righteous wrath of God! The Lord knew only His willingness for the ultimate act of humility-obedience of laying aside His deity and coming to earth and to be born as a human being, having the appearance or likeness of a man,[17] to become our Kinsmen Redeemer and the Ultimate Sacrifice, could ever be sufficient to appease the righteous wrath of God! HE, the Lord, was the One who had every right to be totally and completely offended by Cain's utter narcissism and spiritual emptiness to essentially compare the Creator of the Universe to vegetables—broccoli, carrots, cabbage!

> By faith Abel offered to God a more acceptable sacrifice than Cain, through which it was testified of him that he was righteous (upright, in right standing with God), and God testified by accepting his gifts. And though he died, yet through [this act of] faith he still speaks.[18]

In the carnality of his sin-corrupted heart, Cain possessed only *Feeble Faith*, very weak in the sight of God. This degree of faith would only allow Cain to offer to God a sacrifice consisting of the produce of his labors in tilling the ground to cultivate vegetables for food. God can't be pleased with a faith based only on self-works, even though "faith without works is dead (useless)."[19]

God forewarned Cain that if he did not do what was right and righteous, sin was crouching at the door, lying in wait to seize upon his sinful thoughts and attitudes, motivating him to do evil.

> "If you do well [believing Me and doing what is acceptable and pleasing to Me], will you not be accepted? And if you do not do well [but ignore My instruction], sin crouches at your door; its desire is for you [to overpower you], but you must master it."

Sinful thoughts of murderous jealousy and rage against his blood-brother, Abel, did indeed overpower Cain, instead of him mastering it, with the result that Cain slew Abel.[20] Cain's rage was really against *God* because God had rejected his sacrifice, which he took as God rejecting him personally; but he could not avenge his anger against God, so he directed it toward Abel, and killed him.

It wasn't *Abel* who rejected Cain's sacrifice but *God*! But the murderous competitiveness he harbored in his heart against his brother caused Cain to be enraged at Abel because Abel's sacrifice was acceptable to God. That same competition produces jealousy and hatred in the hearts of multitudes today, including those in ministry against fellow ministers. Yet, the Word of God clearly and unequivocally warns that: "Everyone who hates his brother is a *murderer*; and you know that no murderer has eternal life abiding in him."[21] Jealousy, which is in essence competition, unabated and unrepented of, will preclude the holder thereof from obtaining Eternal Life and everlasting fellowship with God! That is an irrefutable fact!

Peter's Feeble Faith

Another example of Feeble Faith in the New Testament is recounted in Matthew 17. The Roman government had established a two-drachma or denarii (two days' wages), so-called "Temple Tax" to be paid by the Jews. When the tax-collectors came to Capernaum, where Jesus and the disciples were living, they confronted Peter as the group's leader, inquiring as to his rabbi's policy regarding the tax and His intention to pay it. Of course, the disciples' rabbi was Jesus.

Peter's knee-jerk reaction, though he really had no idea what Jesus thought about the tax and his policy or intention regarding paying it, was to answer on Jesus' behalf that, oh, yes, his teacher believed in paying the tax and would be paying it. He made this commitment despite knowing the group did not possess the requisite two drachma in the treasury to pay the tax. He now faced a dilemma for which he had no answers or solutions. When Peter went to the home where the group was staying, Jesus, knowing by the Spirit what had taken place, immediately spoke to Peter about the incident upon his arrival before Peter could say a word about it.

> When they arrived in Capernaum, the collectors of the half-shekel [temple tax] went up to Peter and said, "Does not your teacher pay the half-shekel?" Peter answered, "Yes." And when he came home, Jesus spoke to him first, saying, "What do you think, Simon? From whom do earthly rulers collect duties or taxes, from their sons or from strangers?" When Peter said, "From strangers," Jesus said to him, "Then the sons are exempt [from taxation]. However, so that we do not offend them, go to the sea and throw in a hook, and take the first fish that comes up; and when you open its mouth, you will find a shekel. Take it and give it to them [to pay the temple tax] for you and Me."[22]

As an aside in examining this story, it's important to point out that in paying the Temple Tax, Jesus did not pay tribute taxes to Rome but only to Solomon's Temple, the icon of Jewish worship.

His entire life before being called, anointed, and appointed by the Lord, Simon Peter's occupation was that of a commercial fisherman. Fishing was a way of life to Peter, a life he inherited from many previous generations of fisherman, as well as the way he earned his living to provide for himself and his family. He and his brother Andrew were the first two disciples Jesus chose as He was walking by the Sea of Galilee and saw the pair casting their fishing nets into the sea.[23] It's certainly understandable that Peter, along with Andrew, were the first two men Jesus chose to be His followers, in that he possessed atypical characteristics. He was bold to the point of being brash and impetuous at times, physically strong, headstrong, strong-willed, and a warrior-type.

It was an easy task for Peter to go fishing for the Master, per His instructions. Nevertheless, when Peter caught that fish that had a coin in its mouth just as Jesus prophesied, doubtless, his faith instantaneously soared from being "*feeble* faith," to being "*great* faith!" (We examine the category of "Great Faith" in Chapter Seven). Likely Peter never forgot this miraculous act of supernatural provision. When Jesus instructs us to go, say, do, and believe in what in the natural seems to be the impossible, and we obey Him, *we* can expect to experience supernatural provision and events of various types and dimensions in *our* lives as well!

We can only wonder what Peter's thoughts might have consisted of during the span of events described in the course of a few verses in Matthew 16 when he was first "promoted," so to speak, in that Jesus changed his name from Simon to Petros, (the Rock) and told him He will give him the keys of the Kingdom of God (verses 13 through 20), and then shortly afterward rebuked him and addressed him as "Satan" in verses 21 through 23. This speaks to how quickly even followers of Christ can go from operating "in the Spirit" to jumping headlong into the flesh!

Can you imagine now, in his trip to the sea to catch that one prophesied fish, he might have thought: "Lord, I don't want to be rebuked for my lack of faith or be addressed as Satan again. Hope I do this right this time."

Many other things could have been in his thoughts that day as well. Likely nothing though could have prepared him for this giant leap of faith that manifested during the familiar act of going fishing he had done so many countless times before. Certainly, Peter had caught massive amounts of fish during his life, but nothing had ever manifested on any of his previous fishing trips like what manifested this day.

He went to the seashore as Jesus instructed him to, and threw his line out, and immediately the one particular prophesied fish bit on the bait. Upon reeling it in, lo and behold, Peter saw something shiny in the mouth of that fish—a silver coin! "How can this be," he must have thought to himself? How is it that I catch *one* fish, and *that* fish has in its mouth a coin the value of which is sufficient to pay the Temple Tax owed to the government? Unbelievable! Yet, Jesus knew this supernatural event was going to occur because He had prophetically decreed it,[24] and Peter learned from this event to expect the unexpected and believe the unexplainable when Jesus spoke it.

Now, the funds needed to pay the Temple Tax were supernaturally provided, demonstrating to Peter once again that Jesus was the Son of God and God the Son! With this event, Peter's faith advanced to another level.

Jesus had instructed Peter: "Take it and give it to them [to pay the temple tax] for *you* and *Me*." With these words Jesus was signifying He assumed personal responsibility for this collective financial obligation of the disciples as a ministry team. The message embedded in this incident is that Jesus will provide the means, even if it has to be by supernatural means, to faithful disciples today who labor on His behalf and in His stead in genuine God-appointed ministry. Jesus Himself declared the laborer is worthy of his wages.[25] God pledges by His Word to supply according to His riches in glory by Christ Jesus the financial needs of every legitimate minister and ministry commissioned by Him![26] Metaphorically, ministers yet today are required to depend upon coins or miracle money in the mouths of fish they have caught.

Again, the takeaway from this story for all believers is to always expect the unexpected and unexplainable when Jesus commands you to go and do something on His behalf! As your Master, He is also your financier! It is *His* responsibility to supply all that is needed to fulfill your assignment He has called you to perform! And He'll do it according to HIS riches in glory, as opposed to our limited means here on Earth!

Endnotes

1   Rom. 10:17
2   Rom. 14:1
3   Rom. 14:1-4; bold added
4   2 Tim. 3:16
5   John 1:17
6   Heb. 8:13
7   Rom. 4:13-14
8   1 Tim. 4:10
9   Eph. 1:4, 5:27; Col. 1:22; 2 Pet. 3:14
10 Eph. 1:10
11 Heb. 8:6
12 Gen. 4:1-3
13 Gen. 4:4-5
14 Gen. 4:4-7
15 Mat. 1:25; Luke 2:7; Rom. 8:29; Col. 1:15; Col. 1:18; Heb. 11:28; Heb. 12:23
16 Lev. 17:11
17 Plp. 2:6-8
18 Heb. 11:4
19 Jas. 2:20; KJV
20 Gen. 2:8
21 1 John 3:15
22 Mat. 17:24-27
23 Mat. 4:18
24 Job 22:28
25 Luke 10:7
26 Plp. 4:19

Chapter Three

Effective Faith

For in the gospel the righteousness of God is revealed, both springing from faith and leading to faith [disclosed in a way that awakens more faith]. As it is written and forever remains written, "THE JUST and UPRIGHT SHALL LIVE BY FAITH."[1]

What is Effective Faith? Webster Dictionary states *effective* means: "producing a decided, decisive, or desired effect."

We can extrapolate this to mean that Effective Faith, produces a decided, decisive, or desired effect. In other words, a decided, decisive, or desired effect is produced as a result of a person applying genuine faith to a given situation or scenario.

The God-Kind of Faith

According to the above-cited scripture, Effective Faith is the faith "the just and upright...live by!" Effective Faith is the God-Kind of faith!

And Jesus answered saying to them, "Have faith in God. (Lit., Greek: Have the faith OF God; i.e., the God-Kind of Faith.) "Truly I say to you, whoever says to this mountain, 'Be taken up and cast into the sea,' and does not doubt in his heart, but believes that what he says is going to happen, it will be granted him. "Therefore I say to you, all things for which you pray and ask, believe that you have received them, and they will be granted you."[2]

So, what is the God-kind of faith?

The God-Kind of Faith Is Creative

The God-Kind of faith is creative faith. It creates by speaking, verbalizing, saying, decreeing, declaring, professing what it desires to come into being or to manifest in the natural realm.

> In the beginning God **CREATED** the heavens and the earth. The earth was formless and void, and darkness was over the surface of the deep, and *the Spirit of God was moving* over the surface of the waters. Then God **SAID**, "Let there be light"; and there was light.[3]

Nine times in Chapter One of Genesis, the Book of the Beginnings, God SAID, verbalized, decreed what He was desiring to come into being or to manifest in the natural realm.[4] God released His creative power by SPEAKING, calling into being that which did not yet exist in the natural realm, calling those things which be not as though they were![5]

The Word of God created everything that was created in the beginning. The Word of God became flesh—Jesus Christ, the Creator of the Cosmos is also its Savior!

> In the beginning was the WORD, and the Word was WITH God, and the Word WAS God. He was IN THE BEGINNING with God. All things came into being through Him, and apart from Him nothing came into being that has come into being.[6]

> And THE WORD became flesh (Christ Jesus), and *dwelt among us* (i.e., in a human body), and we SAW His glory, glory as of the ONLY BEGOTTEN from the Father, full of grace and truth.[7]

The God-Kind of Faith is The Faith of Abraham

> For this reason it is by FAITH, in order that it may be in accordance with grace, so that the promise will be guaranteed to all the descendants, not only to those who are of the Law, but also to those who are of **the faith of ABRAHAM**, who is the father of us all, (as it is written, "A FATHER OF MANY NATIONS HAVE I MADE YOU") in the presence of Him whom he believed, even God, who gives life to the dead and calls into being that which does not exist. In hope against hope he *believed*, so that he might become a father of many nations according to that which had been spoken, "SO SHALL YOUR

DESCENDANTS BE." *Without becoming weak in* **faith** he contemplated his own body, now as good as dead since he was about a hundred years old, and the deadness of Sarah's womb; yet, with respect to the promise of God, he did not waver in unbelief but grew strong in faith, giving glory to God, and being fully assured that what God had promised, He was able also to perform.[8]

(As it is written, I have made thee a father of many nations,) before him whom he believed, even God, who quickeneth the dead, and **calleth those things which be not as though they were.**[9]

(as it is written, "A FATHER OF MANY NATIONS HAVE I MADE YOU") in the presence of Him whom he BELIEVED, even God, who gives life to the dead and CALLS INTO BEING THAT WHICH DOES NOT EXIST.[10]

The Abraham-kind of faith, which, as stated, is also the God-Kind of faith, is a faith in accordance with *grace,* so that the promise will be *guaranteed*! It is the kind of faith that *calls into being* that which has not previously existed in the natural realm! It is the kind of faith that in *hope against hope believes*! It is the kind of faith that *contemplates* the undeniable facts, does not *deny* them, and yet is not *weakened* by those facts, does not *waver* in unbelief because of them, but rather *grows* strong despite them, giving *glory* to God, being *fully assured* that what God *promised,* He is able also to *perform*!

Now faith is the ASSURANCE of things hoped (faith is not hope, but the assurance of things hoped for) for, the CONVICTION of things not seen. For by it (faith) the men of old gained approval.[11]

The God- and Abraham-kind of faith, as stated previously in this volume, is a NOW kind of faith. Faith is a NOW thing. Faith is always *now* or its *never* (or it's *not*). Now faith is the *assurance* of things hoped for in the spirit realm until it is manifest in the natural realm. Faith is the *conviction* of things not yet manifest in the natural realm (i.e., seen or perceived with the natural senses). Conviction, by dictionary definition, is a fixed or firm belief; the state of being convinced. Men of old gained approval from/with God by the faith they demonstrated and walked in; the same is true for believers today. Favor with God makes all things to which we have applied our unwavering faith possible and ultimately fait accompli (a done deal)!

In the ensuing chapters we will be examining four different kinds or levels of faith: Strong Faith, Mountain-Moving Faith, Wonder-Working Faith, and Great Faith. Each of those levels are subcategories of this overarching category of the God-Kind of faith.

Let's take a look at a few stories of individuals in the Bible, who walked in Effective Faith.

The Four Lepers and Their Effective Faith

In Chapter Seven of Second Kings, we find a poignant story of four unnamed men afflicted with the highly contagious and deadly disease called leprosy. And if that was not dire enough circumstances for these men, the entire land of Samaria was stricken with a severe famine,[12] causing many to die of starvation and driving some Samaritans to extreme measures to avoid it.

Leprosy laws restricted lepers from coming within what was regarded to be the contagion range of twenty paces of other people, violation of which was punishable by death by stoning. Most cities of the region banned lepers within their walls. Ad hoc leper colonies or camps formed outside of many cities as a means of self-preservation.

Well aware of the inevitable death sentence this dread disease had pronounced upon them, in the interim, this group of four lepers take stock of their situation and conclude they have only two choices left to them with respect to self-preservation: death by stoning if they enter the city or death by starvation if they did not.

"Now four men who were lepers were at the entrance of the [city's] gate; and they said to one another, "Why should we sit here until we die? If we say, 'We will enter the city'—then the famine is in the city and we will die there; and if we sit still here, we will also die. So now come, let us go over to the camp of the Arameans (Syrians). If they let us live, we will live; and if they kill us, we will only die."[13]

In essence, their predicament symbolizes the predicament all humans are in: we're all going to die someday, for "it is appointed unto men once to die,"[14] so we might as well do what we can to live life well and productively while we're alive, and avoid doing anything that would shorten our life unnecessarily. Of course, for the believer, living life is far more than simply existing or shortening our life, it is choosing to live abundant life that Jesus Himself stated He came to give every human being who will receive Him as their personal Lord and Savior.[15]

The point is: we can all understand these four lepers' apparent thinking: We're lepers with a death sentence on us anyway, so why just sit here and die without at least trying to do something to prolong or preserve our lives as much as possible, as opposed to resigning ourselves and succumbing to dying an agonizing slow death by starvation?

Having considered their options, the decision these condemned men made was something akin to exercising Effective Faith, in the form of them taking a chance on entering into the Syrians' camp.

Upon entering the camp, to their utter amazement, they discover the camp is completely deserted, without one man in it:

> So they got up at twilight to go to the Aramean camp. But when they came to the edge of the camp, there was no one there. For the LORD had caused the Aramean army to hear the sound of chariots, and the sound of horses, the sound of a great army. They had said to one another, "The king of Israel has hired against us the kings of the Hittites, and the kings of the Egyptians, to come [*and fight*] against us." So the Arameans set out and fled during the twilight, and left their tents, horses, and donkeys, *even left* the camp just as it was, and fled for their lives.[16]

The lepers entered one tent and ate and drank of the food and drink they found there, and then took all the silver and gold and clothes they found left behind in the tent, carried it outside of the camp and hid it in their own camp. Subsequently—likely after observing a while longer to see if the Aramaeans returned—they reentered the camp and plundered another tent of its valuables and secreted that haul of bounty as well.

Shortly afterward, however, they realized they now faced a dilemma. If the army and king of Israel somehow learned they had discovered and had knowledge of this huge treasure trove of abandoned booty but kept it to themselves and didn't report it to them, they would surely punish them for it. So, they went to the gates of the city and called to the city gatekeepers and reported to them their find, who in turn reported it to the king's household.[17]

Eventually, the people of Israel went to the Arameans camp and plundered its abandoned valuables. It would appear that the moral of the story of the four lepers is that in exercising Effective Faith in the midst of the dire and deadly circumstances that beset them through no fault of their own they secured for themselves a trove of valuable life-sustaining goods as well as contributed to the improvement of the lives of an entire nation from the booty obtained from the defeat of an adversary that had been set on their annihilation by war. As the saying goes, "To the victor goes the spoils."

In the case of this real historic incident, this all occurred as the result of supernatural divine intervention in which God caused the Aramaean army that greatly outnumbered the Israelite army to hear the sound of chariots, horses, and of a great army that terrified them to the extent of causing them to abandon everything and flee for their lives:

> For the LORD had caused the Aramean army to hear the sound of chariots, and the sound of horses, the sound of a great army. They had said to one another, "The king of Israel has hired against us the kings of the Hittites, and the kings of the Egyptians, to come [*and fight*] against us." So the Arameans set out and fled during the twilight, and left their tents, horses, and donkeys, *even left* the camp just as it was, and fled for their lives.[18]

No doubt, what the Aramaeans heard was the sound of the angelic army described in the previous chapter that the Lord had opened up the eyes of Gehazi to see in answer to Elisha's prayer for same when he was frightened by the sight of the Aramaean army surrounding the city.[19] Elisha allayed the fear of his servant by saying, "Do not be afraid, for those who are with us are more than those who are with them."[20]

This story was recorded in the Bible for us believers living in these last days as an example[21] to symbolize the battle believers wage against "our adversary, the devil,"[22] who in ourselves and on our own, is a far too formidable foe, being of the angelic class, for us mere humans. Nevertheless, as *redeemed* humans, believers have been enabled to defeat the devil and his armies of demons in our lives through the supernatural intervention of the Spirit of the Lord who resides in our hearts and whose supernatural dunamis-power Spirit-baptized believers are empowered to operate in spiritual warfare against our adversary.

When believers invoke the name of Jesus, "the name which is above every name,"[23] to which every other name in Heaven and Earth must bow and submit,[24] including the devil and his imps, the "sound" of that name and of the hordes of angelic armies He commands causes an indescribable terror in the devil's camp that compels them to immediately flee to preserve themselves,[25] leaving all they have been possessing and guarding[26] behind.

We serve an awesome God! Many purporting Christians forget, if they ever really knew, just how awesome He really is! The devils, however, *never* forget! In this respect, believers would do well to know what the devils know!

Effective Faith of Four Friends of a Paralytic

Another illustration of Effective Faith in action are the four unnamed men who loved and cared for their paralytic friend, which story is recorded in the second chapter of Mark. They had such a strong desire for him to be healed that they destroyed the roof of another family's house where Jesus was ministering (which presumably they afterward rebuilt or compensated the homeowner for its rebuilding).

These men heard that Jesus had returned to and was ministering at his current hometown of Capernaum. The house Jesus was teaching in was so crowded with those who had come to hear and receive ministry from Him that these four men had to carry this paralyzed man lying on his pallet to the roof, remove it, and let the man down with ropes attached to the corners of his pallet so that Jesus could minister to him.

> Jesus returned to Capernaum, and a few days later the news went out that He was at home. [Mat_4:13] So many people gathered together that there was no longer room [*for them*], not even near the door; and Jesus was discussing with them the word [*of God*]. Then they came, bringing to Him a paralyzed man, who was being carried by four men. [Mat_9:2-8; Luk_5:18-26] When they were unable to get to Him because of the crowd, they removed the roof above Jesus; and when they had dug out an opening, they let down the mat on which the paralyzed man was lying.[27]

We're told nothing about these men other than that there were four of them; not their names, or their relationship to the paralytic. We don't know if they were relatives, friends, neighbors, or anything about their relationship to the man. We *can* properly presume, though, based on what they were willing to do and *did* do for this paralytic, that these men were themselves special, that they had a special love and compassion for this man with respect to his current condition of being paralyzed, and that they had a special faith—Effective Faith—toward God and Jesus to believe that if they just got Him to Jesus, he would be healed. We can also presume they brought him to the house where Jesus was because they had heard of the stir that was being "noised abroad"[28] about Jesus and His supernatural ministry of miracles, healings, and deliverance from demons that had been taking place in the region.

The faith of these men in removing the roof and letting him down on ropes to the floor below to receive ministry from Jesus—James indicated was genuine faith verified by works or actions[29]—was Effective Faith in order to have resulted as it did in the man's healing and recovery from his paralysis:

> When Jesus saw their [active] faith [springing from confidence in Him], He said to the paralyzed man, "Son, your sins are forgiven. But so that you may know that the Son of Man has the authority *and* power on earth to forgive sins"—He said to the paralyzed man, "I say to you, get up, pick up your mat and go home." And he got up and immediately picked up the mat and went out before them all, so that they all were astonished and they glorified *and* praised God, saying, "We have never seen anything like this!"[30]

This, indeed, was Effective Faith in action, and what happened is what happens when Effective Faith is put into action or activated. In fact, all of what occurred during Jesus' three-and-a-half-year ministry was genuine revival, and when real revival hits, hearts are changed, crowds gather, faith for the miraculous grows, and mighty works of the Lord happen.

But whenever revival is taking place and faith is being established, there will always be the unbelieving religious naysayers and scorners showing up and attempting to discredit the move of God. Jesus encountered them:

> But there were certain of the scribes sitting there, and *reasoning* in their hearts, Why doth this man thus speak blasphemies? who can forgive sins but God only?[31]

Enter religion operating by carnal reasoning. The intellectual religionists will always try to make the Word of God of none effect. This kind of religious reasoning is always a product of carnal, i.e., fleshly, unspiritual, thinking. Carnality and faith can never run on the same track. Carnality will negate faith every time. Effective Faith, however, when it is in operation, always prevails over and negates or obliterates carnal reasoning.

> Immediately Jesus, being fully aware [of their hostility] and knowing in His spirit that they were thinking this, said to them, "Why are you debating and arguing about these things in your hearts? Which is easier, to say to the paralyzed man, 'Your sins are forgiven'; or to say, 'Get up, and pick up your mat and walk'? But so that you may know that the Son of Man has the authority and power on earth to forgive sins"—He said to the paralyzed man, "I say to you, get up, pick up your mat and go home."[32]

Jesus told these intellectual religionists essentially that their unbelief was a *heart* issue. The paralytic was totally healed, had taken up his pallet, and walked home, as Jesus directed him. But, these self-exalting and egotistical religionists of the day were so jealous and angered at the attention and adulation Jesus was receiving as the Son of God and long-awaited Messiah, diverting it all away from them, and the authority and power He was manifesting, that they were hysterically and desperately trying to find or conjure up some kind—*any* kind—of reasons to "rein Him in," restrict Him, take the spotlight off Him and His ministry, and negate the effect He was having on the people. But, Jesus, being God the Son, always knew the evil and evil thinking that was in their religion-permeated hearts.[33]

We can just imagine what it was like when the former paralytic's four friends and him made their way to his home? They must have been ecstatic with immeasurable joy at the miracle their actions of faith had produced. Faith-motivated action mixed with Effective Faith is what it takes to produce an explosion of miracles.

Many of us are staunchly believing God that one day, prior to the rapture of the saints, we will witness and have a part in an extended period of time when God will be freely and generously wielding through us miracles of this sort and "greater works" Jesus promised believers would one day perform because He went to the Father and is seated at His right hand where He evermore liveth to make intercession on behalf of the saints.[34] Hallelujah!

When this happens, it will be Effective Faith that is at work in individual believers and thus in the collective Ekklesia that Jesus is building!

Endnotes

1 Rom. 1:17
2 Mark 11:22-24
3 Gen. 1:1-3
4 Gen. 1:3, 6; 9: 11, 14, 20, 24, 26 29
5 Rom. 4:17
6 John 1:1-3; caps added for emphasis
7 John 1:14
8 Rom. 4:16-21; emphases added
9 Rom. 4:17; KJV; emphases added
10 Rom. 4:17; NASB
11 Heb. 11:1-2
12 2 Kgs. 6:25

13 2 Kgs. 7:3-4
14 Heb. 9:27
15 John 10:10
16 2 Kgs. 7:5-7
17 2 Kgs. 7:10-11
18 2 Kgs 7:6-7
19 2 Kgs. 6:15-17
20 2 Kgs. 6:16
21 Rom. 15:4; 1 Cor 10:11
22 1 Pet. 5:8
23 Plp. 2:9
24 Plp. 2:10
25 Jas. 4:7
26 Luke 11:21
27 Mark 2:1-4
28 Luke 1:65; KJV
29 Jas. 2:17-18
30 Mark 2:5,10-12
31 Mark 2:6-7
32 Mark 2:8-11
33 John 2:24-25
34 John 14:12; Heb. 7:25

Chapter Four

STRONG FAITH

"Now faith is the **assurance** (title deed, confirmation) of things hoped for (divinely guaranteed), and the **evidence** of things not seen [the **conviction** of their reality—faith comprehends as fact what cannot be experienced by the physical senses]. For by this [kind of] faith the men of old gained [divine] approval."[1]

The writer of Hebrews reveals in this verse three vital truths regarding genuine faith:

1. it is the **assurance** or **confirmation**, or other versions render the word as "**substance**," of things hoped for;
2. it is the **evidence** or **conviction** of the reality of things not seen, or perceived, by the physical senses;
3. the operation of **this kind** of faith—i.e., genuine spiritual faith—by "men of old" gained those men the approval and favor of God.

As stated in previous chapters, this is the kind of genuine faith, or spiritual faith, that we are referring to throughout this volume. In this chapter, we are going to talk about this faith being applied in an unusually strong and bold way. It is this degree or dimension of faith that produces the favor and approval of God. In other words, God really likes it when we live our lives walking in and applying this kind of faith to circumstances and in situations that arise during our life.

King David—A Stellar Example of Strong Faith

One of the greatest examples of *Strong Faith* in the Bible comes to us in the story of a mighty man of God named David, who went from being a lowly shepherd boy tending his father's sheep, to becoming the king of, initially Southern Israel, then later, all of Israel. It is important to remember that David's kingship was only the second in the history of the nation, following Saul's reign.

David possessed many righteous attributes and godly character, as well as demonstrated many God-given talents. He was bold as a lion, cunning as a fox, strong as a bear, and a mighty military warrior of exceeding courage and fearlessness in battle.

What made David such an exemplary leader and man of God was his unfaltering Strong Faith in Jehovah-God. Considering that no one then, living in the Old Covenant era, *prior* to the Cross of Christ, could be Born Again and infused with the Holy Spirit or immersed in the Spirit as believers are under the New Covenant *after* Christ's substitutionary sacrifice, the testimony of David stands as an incredible record of monumental personal dedication to Jehovah God.

A thoughtful reading of the seventy-three Psalms written by David alone readily reveals a sense of his extraordinary spiritual depth, his unmatched personal knowledge of God, as well as his personal relationship and interaction with God in a dispensation when the Holy Spirit could not come *into* the hearts of worshipers to abide, but only *upon* them sporadically and transiently.

No doubt the primary factor for all of who David was and His great achievements as the leader of his nation, which is so poetically and accurately summed up in Samuel's rebuke of Saul when he presumed to himself offer the burnt offering instead of the high priest, and that the man God would appoint to replace Saul was "a man after" God's "own heart,"[2] was that David was a *worshiper*, an extremely passionate worshiper! This is what produced the Strong Faith he possessed and applied throughout his extraordinary 70-year life.

In order to make the case for the topic of the chapter, however, we first need to review some background of the lead-up to David's ascension to power as Israel's second king following the reign of Saul.

The first instance of a human king over Israel, that of David's predecessor, turned out in the end not to be a good experience at all for the nation. This was the 42-year reign of Saul who was anointed and coronated king at the age of 30 and ruled until his death at the age of 72. Saul was ungodly, wicked, and corrupt, and thus set a horrible precedent for kings for the entire history of ancient Israel.

From the time God supernaturally delivered the Hebrews from Egypt where they had been captives and slaves for 430 years,[3] Israel was a truly theocratically ruled nation, meaning that Jehovah-God was their ultimate Ruler (King, Governor), albeit through human surrogates, beginning with Moses, then Joshua, followed by the Judges, and culminating with the last judge and first ruling prophet, Samuel.

God Himself raised up, anointed, and appointed Samuel the prophet to be his human representative to the nation of Israel. Though the exact span of his life and tenure as prophet over the nation is a matter of sharp disagreement by scholars and historians, it was most likely approximately 67 years, from the age of 13 to his death at the age of 80. Samuel was the last of the Judges and the first of the prophets (sometimes referred to as "the major prophets") who were God's *spiritual*, though not *political*, leaders over the nation.

When Samuel "was old,"[4] though scholars estimate he was only around 52 years old at that time, we are told he appointed his two sons, Joel and Abijah, as his deputies over certain regions of the nation. However, unfortunately, they did not inherit (not that such can be) the spiritual attributes, morality, and integrity of their father, but were corrupt, and misused their power for their own gain:

> His sons, however, did not walk in his ways, but turned aside after dishonest gain and took bribes and perverted justice.[5]

This maltreatment and malfeasance by Samuel's sons, in time, appears to have incited an insurrection of the people, who pressed their tribal leaders to confront Samuel, and demand he appoint a king to be their ruler, like all the other nations of the world existing at the time had as their rulers. The corruption of the succeeding generation of the last of God's ruling and judging prophet generated in the minds of the people what they regarded to be a blight on God's system of governance through human prophetic surrogates, which made them believe they were justified in demanding a ruler who was like *them*, and who would therefore think like and represent *them*, rather than like *God* as the prophets were, who thought like and represented God.

We find the same concept driving political elections in free nations of the world yet today, wherein the people vote to elect leaders who are like *them* and represent *them* and *their* thinking, beliefs, and morals, rather than leaders who will lead the nation and its people into godliness and righteousness, which is what is best for the society of all nations.

When Israel cried out to Samuel the prophet, who was the de facto human leader appointed by God to represent Him and His authority over the nation, and were clamoring for a king, a singular autocrat, like all the other nations, Samuel was greatly displeased by their brazened insolence toward God.[6] So he prayed to the Lord, inquiring what he should do. God shocked Samuel with His response, and, in a sense, it is shocking to all who are students of God and His ways yet today; though in another sense, it is not at all surprising:

> The LORD said to Samuel, "Listen to the voice of the people in regard to all that they say to you, for they have not rejected you, but they have rejected *Me* from being King over them. Like all the deeds which they have done since the day that I brought them up from Egypt even to this day—in that they have abandoned (rejected) Me and served other gods—so they are doing to you also. So now listen to their voice; only solemnly warn them and tell them the ways of the king who will reign over them."[7]

Again, remember, to this point Israel did not have a human political ruler, but were ruled over only by God Himself through His chosen human surrogates, though in the entire history of the nation since they were delivered out of Egypt, as God said in His response to Samuel, they rebelled against Him and everything He commanded them.

Nevertheless, Samuel told the people God's answer: that a human king would be appointed over them, but he also told the people the prophetic future of what all that king and his successors would do to them and how he and the succession of kings that would follow would constantly oppress them.

> Nevertheless, the people refused to listen to the voice of Samuel, and they said, "No, but there shall be a king over us, so that we too may be like all the nations [around us], that our king may judge [and govern] us and go out before us and fight our battles." Samuel had heard all the words of the people and repeated them to the LORD. And the LORD said to Samuel, "Listen to their request and appoint a king for them." So Samuel said to the men of Israel, "Go, each man to his own city."[8]

Subsequently, the Lord led Samuel to appoint and anoint as king a man named Saul who was the son of "a mighty man of influence and wealth" named Kish of the tribe of Benjamin, the smallest of all the twelve tribes:

> There was a man of [the tribe of] Benjamin whose name was Kish the son of Abiel, the son of Zeror, the son of Becorath, the son of Aphiah, a Benjamite, a mighty man of influence and wealth. Kish had a son named Saul, a choice and handsome man; among the sons of Israel there was not a man more handsome than he. From his shoulders and up he was [a head] taller than any of the people.[9]

Saul began his reign in 1052 BC. Many years into the reign of Saul and after committing a number of misdeeds for which Samuel rebuked him, Samuel was grieving over having appointed Saul as king, though it was God that had commanded him to do so, and God spoke to Samuel:

> The LORD said to Samuel, "How long will you grieve for Saul, when I have rejected him as king over Israel? Fill your horn with oil and go; I will send you to Jesse the Bethlehemite, for I have chosen a king for Myself among his sons."[10]

Finally, the Lord's patience with Saul and his constant rebellion ran out, and He commanded Samuel to appoint another king to replace Saul, though it took twenty-two years for Samuel's prophecy that the Lord had chosen another man and anointed him king in Saul's place to come entirely to pass.

God sent Samuel to the house of Jesse in Bethlehem, the city where Jesus Christ, the Messiah, would be born hundreds of years later, to anoint the new king of Israel. While working as a humble shepherd boy tending his father's sheep, at the age of fifteen, David, the one who Samuel had told Saul that the Lord had sought who had a heart after His,[11] was chosen over all his seven older brothers and was anointed by the Lord through Samuel to become king of Israel.

At Jesse's house, where they had gathered to partake of the sacrificial meal, each one of the seven older sons of Jesse were paraded one by one before Samuel. Concerning each one, Samuel said, "The LORD has not chosen this one either." Puzzled, the prophet asked Jesse if all his sons were present:

Jesse had seven of his sons pass before Samuel. But Samuel said to Jesse, "The LORD has not chosen [any of] these." Then Samuel said to Jesse, "Are all your sons here?" Jesse replied, "There is still one left, the youngest; he is tending the sheep." Samuel said to Jesse, "Send word and bring him; because we will not sit down [to eat the sacrificial meal] until he comes here." So Jesse sent word and brought him in. Now he had a ruddy complexion, with beautiful eyes and a handsome appearance. The LORD said [to Samuel], "Arise, anoint him; for this is he."[12]

David's family apparently regarded him the "runt of the litter," so to speak, maybe because he was the youngest child and was born so many years after his siblings. But as God explained to Samuel as he was considering Eliab, the oldest son of Jesse, man looks at the outward appearances when choosing their leaders, but God looks at men's hearts for the required attributes of leadership in His kingdom:

But the LORD said to Samuel, "Do not look at his appearance or at the height of his stature, because I have rejected him. For the LORD sees not as man sees; for man looks at the outward appearance, but the LORD looks at the heart."[13]

This had been the problem with the people's choice of Saul as their first king: he looked the part, being relatively tall and possessing other characteristics of his outward appearance that made him stand out from the rest, but his heart was filled with a range of evil characteristics rooted in insecurity and inferiority that resulted in him being an evil, dominating, controlling, self-centered, self-aggrandizing, and oppressing leader. These inward characteristics eventually drove him to the idolatry of witchcraft and seeking the counsel of a witch, on account of which God subsequently killed him.[14]

The Lord was looking for someone with Strong Faith in Him. We know David had this Strong Faith by his adventures in the field recorded in Scripture. With the courage and direction given him by the Lord, David had killed a bear and a lion. We don't know if David had told his family any of these things, but he told King Saul, before he slew Goliath.[15] David's Strong Faith is apparent within the passionate poetic prose comprising the seventy-three Psalms he authored, much of which he composed while worshiping God alone in the fields as he tended his father's sheep and while in exile evading Saul's death threats.

Ziklag—David Displays Strong Faith

In First Samuel 30, we find this mighty warrior, David, who had come home to be with his family after fighting battle after battle with his army against the Philistines. Upon arrival, he learns that the Amalekites had raided, plundered, and burned Ziklag to the ground, absconding with all their possessions that had value and abducting everything that had breath, including their people and their animals.

> Now it happened when David and his men came [home] to Ziklag on the third day, [they found] that the Amalekites had made a raid on the Negev (the South country) and on Ziklag, and had overthrown Ziklag and burned it with fire; and they had taken captive the women [and all] who were there, both small and great. They killed no one, but carried them off [to be used as slaves] and went on their way. When David and his men came to the town, it was burned, and their wives and their sons and their daughters had been taken captive. Then David and the people who were with him raised their voices and wept until they were too exhausted to weep [any longer]."[16]

Not only was everything of value stolen by the Amalekites, but the people and perhaps some of his army were blaming David and rising up against him with such vehemence that they were speaking of stoning him to death.

> Further, David was greatly distressed because the people spoke of stoning him, for all of them were embittered, each man for his sons and daughters.[17]

Nevertheless, David stood strong and courageous in the face of this extreme adversity, drawing upon his previous experiences of looking to the Lord for help when confronted with overwhelming adversity and encouraged himself with remembrances of the Lord's past deliverances, as he wrote so passionately and eloquently in one of his Psalms:

> "I will lift up my eyes to the hills [of Jerusalem]— From where shall my help come? My help comes from the LORD, Who made heaven and earth."[18]

Though such adversity would have been withering and even paralyzing to most men, David strengthened and encouraged himself in the Lord, and inquired of the Lord regarding what action He would have him to take in response against the enemy who had perpetrated this barbarous act against the people of God:

> But David felt strengthened and encouraged in the LORD his God. David said to Abiathar the priest, Ahimelech's son, "Please bring me the ephod." So Abiathar brought him the ephod. David inquired of the LORD, saying, "Shall I pursue this band [of raiders]? Will I overtake them?" And He answered him, "Pursue, for you will certainly overtake them, and you will certainly rescue [the captives]."[19]¶

The Lord answered David's inquiry, directing him to pursue the enemy and promising that they would overcome them and recover all that the enemy had stolen, all of which happened. While David's and Israel's enemies had let down their guard and were doubtless celebrating their conquest with a victory party, David and his army attacked them unawares and took back everything that belonged to them. The enemy was defeated, and victory belonged to Israel and David because he possessed and exercised Strong Faith, believing and trusting God in all things despite adversity's appearances.

Again, as stated before, all these stories recorded in the Bible were written for *us*—believers living in these last days—as an example to *us*,[20] representing the spiritual warfare believers are required and commanded to wage against "our adversary, the devil,"[21] to recover all that he has illegally stolen from us as the master-marauder of all that God intended for us to possess both in the natural and the spiritual realm. We must utilize "the weapons of our warfare (that) are not of the flesh, but divinely powerful for the destruction of fortresses."[22] The weapons of our warfare are *spiritual* weapons of the Spirit that we engage the enemy with in "good warfare"[23] to overcome the enemy and win the victories Jesus has already obtained for us when He soundly and utterly defeated the devil at Calvary and the empty tomb!

Whatever you are going through as you read this, whether it's family, or your friends, boss, or co-workers turning against you, remember where your help comes from! Run to God, run to his Word, pursue the very heart of God with Strong Faith, believing all things work together for the good to them that love God and are called according to His purposes!

And we know [with great confidence] that God [who is deeply

concerned about us] causes all things to work together [as a plan] for good for those who love God, to those who are called according to His plan and purpose.[24]

Strong Faith of Saul of Tarsus

Our next example of Strong Faith comes from the New Testament, and concerns another man named Saul, who became the Apostle Paul. The story of Saul begins in Acts 9. Saul had previously been the number one enemy of the new church (ekklesia, Gr.) that was developing after Jesus was taken from the Earth. The disciples of the early church went out to spread the gospel in obedience to Jesus's mandate,[25] which angered the nascent religious leaders so vehemently that they were paying bounty hunters to find and arrest them and turn them over to the Roman government for execution. Luke describes this time as a "great persecution"[26] that arose against the early church in Jerusalem.

This great persecution against the church then headquartered in Jerusalem did not stop the spreading of the Good News gospel of Christ, however, but only served to fuel its increase further:

> The word of God kept on spreading; and the number of the disciples continued to increase greatly in Jerusalem, and a great many of the priests were becoming obedient to the faith.[27]

No doubt, when "a great many of the priests were becoming obedient to the faith," this was something that the demon-possessed Jewish religionists simply could not stand idly by and allow to happen without taking some action to counter this, to them, dangerous, spread of the Word of God that was taking place in the environs of Jerusalem.

In retaliation, a group of religionists rose up to oppose Stephen, who at that time was merely a deacon in the Jerusalem church, and not one of the apostles who were its primary leaders, began to gain a lot of attention because of the great signs and wonders the Lord was performing through him:

> And Stephen, full of grace and power, was performing great wonders and signs among the people. But some men from what was called the Synagogue of the Freedmen, including both Cyrenians and Alexandrians, and some from Cilicia and Asia, rose up and argued with Stephen. But they were unable to cope with the wisdom and the Spirit with which he was speaking. Then they secretly induced men to say, "We have heard him

speak blasphemous words against Moses and against God." And they stirred up the people, the elders and the scribes, and they came up to him and dragged him away and brought him before the Council. They put forward false witnesses who said, "This man incessantly speaks against this holy place and the Law; for we have heard him say that this Nazarene, Jesus, will destroy this place and alter the customs which Moses handed down to us." And fixing their gaze on him, all who were sitting in the Council saw his face like the face of an angel.[28]

Stephen is often recognized as being the first martyr of the Jerusalem church by the hands of his own countrymen. Stephen responded with the longest sermon recorded in the Bible, rebuking the Israelites for their long history of disobedience to God and all He commanded them, which sermon he culminated by declaring:

> "You men who are stiff-necked and uncircumcised in heart and ears are always resisting the Holy Spirit; you are doing just as your fathers did. "Which one of the prophets did your fathers not persecute? They killed those who had previously announced the coming of the Righteous One, whose betrayers and murderers you have now become; you who received the law as ordained by angels, and yet did not keep it."[29]

This was too much truth for this angry mob of murderous religionists to handle, so, "Now when they heard this, they were cut to the quick, and they began gnashing their teeth at him."[30]

> But Stephen, being full of the Holy Spirit, gazed intently into heaven and saw the glory of God, and Jesus standing at the right hand of God; and he said, "Behold, I see the heavens opened up and the Son of Man standing at the right hand of God."[31]

While gazing intently into heaven, Stephen saw the glory of God and Jesus standing at the right hand of God giving him a standing ovation for his boldness in preaching truth to power even in the face of these murderers who proceeded to stone him to death for what they considered blasphemy, but in actuality was Truth from God Himself, spoken through Stephen's mouth!

> But they cried out with a loud voice, and covered their ears and rushed at him with one impulse. When they had driven him out of the city, they began stoning him; and the witnesses laid aside

their robes at the feet of a young man named Saul. They went on stoning Stephen as he called on the Lord and said, "Lord Jesus, receive my spirit!" Then falling on his knees, he cried out with a loud voice, "Lord, do not hold this sin against them!" Having said this, he fell asleep.[32]

As he was dying, with his last breath (reminiscent of Jesus on the Cross of Calvary) Stephen implored the Lord that this sin not be impugned against these individuals who were participants in the unspeakable crime of murder against an innocent man whose only "crime" was worshipping the King of Kings and Lord of Lords, preaching the Gospel, and performing many mighty miracles in His stead, as he was instructed to do by the Lord Himself.

One of the things that makes Stephen's forgiveness of these murderers' crime against him so significant was that one of the participants in this heinous act was none other than a man named Saul (who later became the Apostle Paul), who stood watching the whole event while actually tending to the outer garments that those doing the actual stoning had removed to carry out the dastardly deed.

> But they shouted with loud voices, and covered their ears and together rushed at him [considering him guilty of blasphemy]. Then they drove him out of the city and began stoning him; **and the witnesses placed their outer robes at the feet of a young man named Saul.**"[33]

Saul was a firsthand eyewitness of this horrifying incident and heard the fiery Spirit-inspired testimony of Stephen as he was dying. He also heard Stephen's incredible prayer of forgiveness and petition to the Lord that this blatant and deliberate sin be not charged against the participants. It was this forgiveness and petition for God's forgiveness that released Saul from his personal guiltiness that allowed him to be able to later experience the incredible personal encounter he experienced with the resurrected and ascended Lord Jesus Christ Himself on the road to Damascus.

In Chapter Nine of the Book of Acts, we read that as Saul was traveling to persecute other Christians, he had an encounter with the heavenly realm. Suddenly there was a light from heaven flashing all around him so brilliantly that it blinded him and literally knocked him off his high horse to the ground, and out of the light came a voice calling his name twice:

> As he traveled he approached Damascus, and suddenly a light from heaven flashed around him [displaying the glory and majesty of Christ]; and he fell to the ground and heard a voice [from heaven] saying to him, "Saul, Saul, why are you persecuting and oppressing Me?" Now get up and go into the city, and you will be told what you must do."[34]

Saul was literally blinded by the brilliance of the light and this phenomenal encounter with King Jesus. Those accompanying him, led him by the hand into the city of Damascus, where he fasted and prayed before the Lord for three days, no doubt engaging in much self-examination, meditation, and repentance. The Lord Jesus then sent a believer named, Ananias, to lay hands on and pray over Saul to receive back his physical sight as well as spiritual sight via the Baptism in the Holy Spirit. As a result of Ananias's prayer, Saul received both!

Saul had become blinded to the Truth by all the teaching and training he had experienced in his life, having been taught for years and years as a Pharisee under the tutelage of one of the most revered teachers in Israel, Gamaliel.[35] As a result, Saul became blinded by the deceitful religious doctrines of men, blinded by hatred for the non-compliant Gentiles, blinded by a murderous spirit[36] stemming from that hatred.

But on the Road to Damascus, revelation came to Saul[37] so that Jesus, the Head of the Church, could use him for the next phase of setting the captives free. His mission was to preach the Gospel of Christ to the Gentiles for them to know and understand that Jesus loved them and died and rose again for them also. Relative to his mission of being sent to the Gentiles and his identification with the Gentiles, the former Hebrew of Hebrews,[38] Saul, began to be known also by the Gentile version of his name, Paul.[39]

The life of Paul is a standout example of Strong Faith, believing Jesus was the Messiah of Israel and Savior the whole world had been waiting on for so long.

Timothy and His Strong Faith

Timothy, the hand-picked protégé of the Apostle Paul, like Abraham, "did not waver in unbelief but grew strong in faith, giving glory to God"[40] and in grace under the personal tutelage of Paul. Presumably, he came to understand that in order to face the challenges and strong pull of the world, he had to apprehend this Strong Faith in Jesus Christ alone and no one else, as he mimicked the example of his mentor, Paul.

Paul encouraged his followers to emulate him and his walk with God: "Therefore I exhort you, be imitators of me."[41] One of his students who did exactly that, apparently, was Timothy, to the extent that Paul at some point began having Timothy accompany him on many of his ministry excursions, calling Timothy his "fellow worker,"[42] "my beloved and faithful child in the Lord,"[43] "my true child in the faith,"[44] "my son,"[45] and "my beloved son," [46] and even sending Timothy in his stead as his representative to places where he himself was unable to go, because he had utmost confidence in Timothy that he would teach exactly what Paul taught in every church he ministered to:

> For this reason I have sent to you Timothy, who is my beloved and faithful child in the Lord, and he will remind you of my ways which are in Christ, just as I teach everywhere in every church.[47]

Titus and His Strong Faith

There were also others who emulated Paul as he mentored them, such as Titus, for example. Paul was so assured of Titus' faithfulness to him and his doctrines and "ways" he taught the Gentile churches where he ministered that he instructed Titus to remain on the Isle of Crete after he departed as his surrogate or stand-in to "set in order" the groups of followers to whom Paul had ministered by appointing elders in every city as Paul had directed:

> For this reason I left you in Crete, that you would set in order what remains and appoint elders in every city as I directed you,[48]

As an important aside, setting in order what remains by appointing elders is what takes a group of rag-tag disciples comprising what is basically a "fellowship group" that will eventually dissolve to nothing if spiritual leadership is not appointed to become a local church, providing that spiritual leadership is the role of Fivefold Ministry elders.[49]

Regarding Titus, Paul said something that is important to our subject matter in this book, i.e., faith, in that he identified Titus as, "my true child in a common *faith*." Paul was celibate and never married or fathered children, so those he mentored that he fondly regarded as his sons or children, he meant *spiritual* sons or children. And, as we see in this reference to Titus, Paul's mentoring produced a "common faith" in those he mentored. It was common to them because it was engendered by the doctrines and "ways" that Paul extruded from the Word of God and passed along to his disciples, which then in turn, produced in them "like precious *faith*,"[50] as the Apostle Peter referred to it, or "a *faith* of the same kind as ours" the NASB renders it.

All Believers Must Obtain and Walk in Strong Faith

It is incumbent upon every believer today as well to know foundationally that nothing has changed in regard to obtaining such Strong Faith, that it comes only through complete devotion and dedication to Christ Jesus as Master, Lord, and Savior. The challenges facing today's believers in the world we presently live in, differ substantially and are exponentially more powerful than those the Apostle Paul's protégés faced in their day, but that is all the more reason that believers today must obtain and exercise this level of Strong Faith in their lives. Doing so carries the potential to propel every believer to the status of "uber-conqueror" Paul talked about in Romans 8:37 that enables us to "overwhelmingly conquer" every trial, trouble, and tribulation Satan throws at us!

What About You?

What about you? What areas of your life needs Strong Faith applied to it? Do you have Strong Faith to believe revival can start in your heart, your church, your tent, your family?

Do you have a desire to produce Strong Faith in your life as David did, who was rejected by family, friends, loved ones, and rulers, yet had faith to believe God was with him to pursue and possess all things God willed for him to pursue and possess?

The Apostle Paul, who was formerly a murderer of Christians, had Strong Faith propelling him toward his destiny to go into all the world to save the lost after he had a personal encounter with Jesus. Both of these men believed the Word of God and the prophecies spoken to them, and it all produced Strong Faith in their hearts that manifested in extraordinary acts of faith and valor in their lives.

What about you? Is Strong Faith operating in your life to pursue and possess all things God wills for you to pursue and possess? It can be, if you will follow the pattern set by the heroes of faith mentioned in this chapter. However, there are two things you must provide to the process yourself, and that is, first, *desire*! No one else can give you the desire to possess Strong Faith or any of the levels/degrees of faith addressed in this book; it must come from you! But, if you *do* have the desire to possess Strong Faith and the other levels/degrees of faith, the next thing you must also provide for the process to work in your life is: pursuit. **The *proof* of genuine desire is *pursuit*!** Unless and until you are actively pursuing the desire to possess, your desire is not real, nor will it manifest or materialize your purported desire in your life.

As an example, have you ever said to yourself or even out loud when you heard someone playing a musical instrument proficiently, "Boy, I sure wish I could play (that instrument) like that! Well, except for the most extraordinarily rare cases in which that person is some sort of a savant or prodigy, the inordinate proficiency he/she demonstrates is the product of a lot of hard work and, as the saying goes, practice, practice, practice, and more practice, over an extended period of time. That kind of proficiency—at any endeavor—doesn't just "happen," rather it requires extreme dedication and discipline and *desire*! So then is your exclamation about *wishing* you could play the instrument like that person really true? *Not really*, if you are not willing to dedicate yourself and put in the required dedication, discipline, and desire. It could be rightly said that this is essentially what distinguishes mere *wishing* and genuine *desire*.

Ask for the Help of the Helper

I strongly believe, because I've seen it happen in my own life, that if you have a desire for something that you are willing to do what it takes to obtain it, whatever that may be, even though you may be beset with weaknesses that unabated could hinder the process of obtaining it, if you will go to Abba Father in genuine sincerity and humility and ask Him to help you with the process of obtaining what it is you want to manifest in your life, He will! After all, surely this is a legitimate kind of need Jesus was referring to when He said to His disciples—then and now—that though He would soon be leaving the Earth to ascend into Heaven to retake His rightful place at the righthand of God, He and the Father would send the Helper (Paracletos; Gr.) in His stead:

> "But I tell you the truth, it is to your advantage that I go away; for if I do not go away, the Helper will not come to you; but if I go, *I will send Him* to you."[51]

There are four passages in the Gospel of John wherein Jesus referred to the Helper, whom He identifies in one of those passages[52] as "the Holy Spirit" and "the Spirit of Truth" in another,[53] and it is interesting that in one of them (above) Jesus says HE will send the Helper,[54] in another He says HE will send the Helper *from* the Father:

> "When the Helper comes, whom *I will send* to you *from the Father*, that is the Spirit of truth who proceeds from the Father, He will testify about Me,[55]

In another He says the FATHER will send the Helper in Jesus' name:

> "But the Helper, the Holy Spirit, whom the Father will send in My name, He will teach you all things, and bring to your remembrance all that I said to you,[56]

and in another He says He will ask the Father to give His disciples the Helper.[57]

> "I will ask the Father, and He will give you another Helper, that He may be with you forever;"[58]

What is the significance of these different statements concerning the Helper, the Holy Spirit, the Spirit of Truth? My view is that it is to demonstrate that the Father, the Son, and the Holy Spirit—the Three Members of the triune Godhead—while separate and distinct as divine Persons—"Hear, O Israel: The LORD our God *is* **ONE** LORD:"[59]—yet are one or united in essence and purpose. While three separate and distinct Persons, yet They are ONE in all that They are and do. As the American Pledge of Allegiance says, "...one nation under God, *indivisible*...."—the triune Godhead is three *indivisible* Persons. A plethora of Scriptures, too many to delve into here, prove the Personhood of each Member of the Godhead—Father, Son, and Holy Spirit—as opposed to three "manifestations" or "roles."

The point is: the entire Godhead will work in tandem in every way to help you obtain the highest levels of faith that you have a sincere and earnest desire to obtain in your life! Hallelujah! Praise God forever!

Endnotes

1. Heb. 11:1-2; AMP
2. 1 Sam. 13:13-14
3. Ex. 12:40
4. 1 Sam. 8:1
5. 1 Sam. 8:3
6. 1 Sam. 8:6
7. 1 Sam. 8:7-9
8. 1 Sam. 8:19-22
9. 1 Sam. 9:1-2
10. 1 Sam. 16:1
11. 1 Sam. 13:14
12. 1 Sam. 16:10-12
13. 1 Sam. 16:7
14. 1 Chr. 10:13
15. 1 Sam. 17:32-37
16. 1 Sam. 30:1-4
17. 1 Sam. 30:6
18. Psa. 121:1-2
19. 1 Sam. 30:6-8
20. Rom. 15:4; 1 Cor 10:11
21. 1 Pet. 5:8
22. 2 Cor. 10:4
23. 1 Tim. 1:18, KJV
24. Rom. 8:28
25. Mat. 16:15
26. Acts 8:1
27. Acts 6:7
28. Acts 6:8-15
29. Acts 7:51-53

30 Acts 7:54
31 Acts 7:55-56
32 Acts 7:57-60
33 Acts 7:57-58
34 Acts 9:3-4,6
35 Plp. 3:5
36 Acts 9:1
37 Gal. 1:12; 2:2; Eph. 3:3
38 Plp. 3:5
39 Acts 13:9
40 Rom. 4:20
41 1 Cor. 4:16
42 Rom. 16:21
43 1 Cor. 4:17
44 1 Tim. 1:12
45 1 Tim. 2:18
46 1 Cor. 4:17; 16:10; Plp. 2:19; 1 Ths. 3:2
47 1 Cor. 4:17
48 Tit. 1:5
49 Acts 2:28; 1 Pet. 5:1-3; Plp. 1:1; Eph. 4:11; 1 Tim. 5:17; 1 Pet. 5:5
50 1 Pet. 1:1; KJV
51 John 16:7
52 John 14:26
53 John 15:26
54 John 14:26
55 John 15:26
56 John 14:26
57 John 14:16
58 Ibid.
59 Deu. 6:4

Chapter Five

MOUNTAIN-MOVING FAITH

"Jesus replied, "Have faith in God [constantly]. I assure you and most solemnly say to you, whoever says to this mountain, 'Be lifted up and thrown into the sea!' and does not doubt in his heart [in God's unlimited power], but believes that what *HE says* is going to take place, it will be done for him [in accordance with God's will]."[1]

In this incident recorded in the Gospel of Mark, Jesus is teaching his disciples how to have *Mountain-Moving Faith*. He was commanding them to literally speak to metaphorical mountains and believe, without doubting, that whatever THEY say will be done for them in accordance with God's will. In this story Jesus is traveling with His disciples and becomes hungry. He and His disciples passed by a fig tree and saw its leaves blooming, which portended it to be fruitful with figs, but it was not. The tree was a hypocrite in that it portended to be something it wasn't and to have something it didn't!

The very next day, Jesus took the disciples by the tree again, and now the tree had withered from the roots up. The disciples were astonished at this. Jesus told them that they could perform miracles like this as well if only they would have faith in *God*, or the original language infers "the *God-kind* of faith."

It wasn't a coincidence that Jesus took them by the Fig Tree the next day. Jesus wanted them to know by this illustration the power a believer's spoken word accompanied with the God-Kind of faith in which there is no doubt and a belief that what the believer SAYS is going to happen, can and will produce this Mountain-Moving Faith that brings into being what the believer says. Our words spoken in believing faith void of doubting produces an environment in which supernatural occurrences happen. Jesus was not merely showing off the power He had as a Son of God to perform miracles, rather He was teaching the disciples—then and now—that Born Again, Spirit-baptized believers have at our disposal supernatural dunamis-power to effect miracles.

A Key to Effecting Mountain-Moving Faith

Jesus went on to explain a little further the key to effecting Mountain-Moving Faith: "Therefore I say to you, all things for which you pray and ask, *believe* that you have *received* them, and they will be granted you."[2] The King James Version says, "and you shall have them." He was emphasizing that when you pray and ask for certain things to happen or needs to be supplied, at the time you are praying, believe that you <u>have</u> *received* them—at that moment when you pray—and when you pray that way you shall have/receive what you have prayed and asked for.

Jesus was indicating, in other words, that it was not a surprise to Him to see the next day that the fig tree had withered from the roots up because when He cursed the tree for its hypocrisy, He expected then for it to wither and die as a result of what He spoke to it. He used the incident as a teachable moment to teach the disciples how to implement the God-Kind of faith, in which whatever you say happens.

Another Key to Mountain-Moving Faith

After telling the disciples what He told them, He immediately added that there was yet another requirement for Mountain-Moving Faith to operate: *forgiveness*. In the subsequent verses, Jesus explained:

> For this reason I am telling you, whatever things you ask for in prayer [in accordance with God's will], believe [with confident trust] that you have received them, and they will be given to you. Whenever you stand praying, if you have anything against anyone, forgive him [drop the issue, let it go], so that your Father who is in heaven will also forgive you your transgressions and wrongdoings [against Him and others]. [But if you do not forgive, neither will your Father in heaven forgive your transgressions."][3]

On the surface, it seems like an out-of-place aside for Jesus to address the matter of forgiveness as an addendum to His discussion about faith. But, it certainly is not at all, for faith can only operate in the life of those walking in genuine forgiveness. Creative miracles, signs and wonders, and supernatural healing will only manifest where genuine forgiveness is manifest! To state it in the negative, faith fails wherever there is unforgiveness!

The Many Effects of Unforgiveness

Most every war in human history was initiated out of an offense taken by someone or a collective of someones who refused to merely forgive!

Myriad divorces have occurred because either or both spouses refused to simply forgive! (This is not to say that there are not just and even biblical causes for divorce.) Multitudes of children have been forced to grow up with the expansive pain of losing one or both parents to the alienation of divorce. Countless numbers of grown children around the world today remain estranged from parents and siblings long into their adulthood due to the breakup of their families occurring at the most formative and vulnerable years of their youth.

Prevailing unforgiveness in the form of longtime grudges, blackballing, and shunning, producing relational estrangement and alienation, is one of the primary factors precluding widescale flow of supernatural miracles in churches, denominations, ecclesial networks, and various church streams today. Sometimes it is collective unforgiveness resulting in division and schisms, and sometimes it is bitterness and strife by individuals against other individuals.

The clear and unambiguous principle inherent in the Mark 11:2-26 passage is that God cannot forgive any individual their transgressions against Himself if that individual wills not to forgive anyone else of their trespasses against themselves. And make no mistake about it, forgiveness is a matter of an individual's *will*, his/her volition. It is a choice one makes individually and inwardly.

Why is Forgiveness So Hard

Certainly, it begs the question: Why is forgiveness such a difficult thing to do, especially in the world we live in today? For various reasons, genuine, heartfelt forgiveness is a difficult, and for myriads of people, a virtually impossible choice to make, without the help of the Helper, the Holy Spirit.

Much of the reason for that lies in the fact that our flesh, which is the enemy of our soul, driven or impelled as it is by our carnal (fleshly) mind, or unredeemed intellect, which the Apostle Paul told us is "*enmity against God*," i.e. set against the mind and will of God the Spirit who dwells within Born Again believers:

> For they that are after the flesh do mind the things of the flesh; but they that are after the Spirit the things of the Spirit. For to be carnally minded is death; but to be spiritually minded is life and peace. **Because the carnal mind is enmity against God**: for it is not subject to the law of God, neither indeed can be. So then they that are in the flesh cannot please God. But ye are not in the flesh, but in the Spirit, if so be that the Spirit of God dwell in you. Now if any man have not the Spirit of Christ, he is none of his.[4]

At the top of the list of reasons for forgiveness being such a difficult thing to walk in is *pride*.

> And He was saying, "That which proceeds out of the man, that is what defiles the man. "For *from within, out of the heart of men*, proceed the evil thoughts, fornications, thefts, murders, adulteries, deeds of coveting and wickedness, as well as deceit, sensuality, envy, slander, **PRIDE** and foolishness. "All these evil things proceed from within and defile the man."[5]

In one of his Psalms, David implored God, "Let not the foot of *pride* come upon me."[6] Reflecting the attitude of God, in Proverbs, he stated, "The fear of the LORD is to hate evil; **Pride** and arrogance and the evil way And the perverted mouth, I hate."[7]

In Psalm 75, out of the experience of fiery trials, David warns:[8]

> "I said to the boastful, 'Do not boast,' And to the wicked, 'Do not lift up the horn; Do not lift up your horn on high, *Do not speak with insolent pride*.'" For not from the east, nor from the west, Nor from the desert comes exaltation; But God is the Judge; He puts down one and exalts another.[9]

Mustard Seed Faith Is Mountain-Moving Faith

> When they came to the crowd, a man came up to Jesus, falling on his knees before Him and saying, "Lord, have mercy on my son, for he is a lunatic and is very ill; for he often falls into the fire and often into the water. "I brought him to Your disciples,

and they could not cure him." And Jesus answered and said, "You unbelieving and perverted generation, how long shall I be with you? How long shall I put up with you? Bring him here to Me." And Jesus rebuked him, and the demon came out of him, and the boy was cured at once. Then the disciples came to Jesus privately and said, "Why could we not drive it out?" And He *said to them, "**Because of the littleness of your faith**; for truly I say to you, **if you have faith the size of a MUSTARD SEED, you will SAY to this mountain, 'Move from here to there,' AND IT WILL MOVE; and nothing will be impossible to you.**[10]

In this instance, the disciples were unsuccessful in casting out the demon possessing the man's son. Though many people do not want to put the blame for faith failures on the the seeker or petitioner, Jesus expressly stated the cause of their failure was "the size of their faith." Apparently, the disciples' faith was smaller than a mustard seed with respect to their ability to cast the demon out. In their question to Jesus as to the reason for their failure, the disciples admitted they could not drive the demon out. Ostensibly, they invoked the command for the demon to come out, but it did not come out because, according to what Jesus said, the disciples' faith was inadequate to drive the demon from the boy.

Yet, what Jesus said at the end of this exchange with the disciples is paramount: that if our faith is at least the size of a mustard seed and we boldly speak what we want to happen unto the mountain opposing us, "*nothing* will be impossible to you."

Jesus unequivocally and unambiguously stated during this incident as it occurred that Mustard Seed Faith is Mountain-Moving Faith! In particular, in this incident, He referred to the "size" of faith—that if it was only (at least) the size of a mustard seed when verbalized it will remove the *figurative* "mountain" it is spoken to.

Figurative language *is* sometimes used in the Bible, though that does not mean that, as many agnostic or atheistic purporting "theologians" theorize, particularly regarding the supernatural occurrences recorded in it, the majority of the record it chronicles is figurative, or allegorical, or metaphorical, or even mythological. It is not! Nonetheless, it is important to understand that Jesus was indeed using the term "mountain" in the instances He evoked the term recorded in the

Gospels as a figure of speech. He was not referring to a literal physical mountain. Undergirding that assertion is the fact that there is no record in the Gospels in which Jesus Himself as a Man or in His human form ever moved a literal mountain by speaking to it.

Hence, Jesus set no precedent for believers to emulate to move literal mountains by speaking to them but rather in the incidents recorded in the Gospels in which He evoked the concept of moving mountains[11] it was each time an adverse *circumstance* or *situation* He was likening to a mountain. Jesus often spoke in parables and allegorically during His fleshly ministry on Earth to illustrate the truths He was communicating.

Thus, moving mountains by speaking to them in faith believing is referring to *metaphorical* mountains—trials, troubles, problems, difficulties, afflictions, hindrances, obstacles—standing in the believer's way, precluding him/her from going where he/she believes he/she should be going or obtaining something or an outcome that he/she should, in the general will of God, be obtaining. The Lord holds no expectations of believers that their faith can move literal mountains! That is important to understand, otherwise Satan, the accuser of the brethren,[12] can constantly accuse us of and condemn us for not having the kind and quality of faith God expects us to have and operate in. It's *circumstances*, not landscapes, that we exert our faith toward by declaring, decreeing, pronouncing, verbalizing it, expecting the circumstances to change as a result!

Abraham & Sarah's Encounter with Mountain-Moving Faith

In the Seventeenth Chapter of Genesis, Abram and Sarai receive a prophetic word from Heaven that they would conceive a son when Abraham was 99 years old and Sarah was 90 years old. According to the natural, such would be an extreme, unheard of, rarity, to put it mildly.

> And the LORD brought Abram outside [his tent into the night] and said, "Look now toward the heavens and count the stars—if you are able to count them." Then He said to him, "So [numerous] shall your descendants be." Then Abram believed in (affirmed, trusted in, relied on, remained steadfast to) the LORD; and He counted (credited) it to him as righteousness (doing right in regard to God and man)."[13]

Can you even imagine God speaking to you in such a phenomenal way? Showing you a firmament filled with innumerable twinkling stars lighting up the Heavens, and informing you that out of your bosom shall proceed offspring as numerous as these stars?

The Lord then went on to say:

> "As for Me, behold, My covenant is with you, And [as a result] you shall be the father of many nations. "No longer shall your name be Abram (exalted father), But your name shall be Abraham (father of a multitude); For I will make you the father of many nations. I will make you exceedingly fruitful, and I will make nations of you, and kings will come from you."[14]

This prophetic mandate from God to Abram is supernatural to the nth degree. God declares to Abram he will be a father to many nations at a time when he had not yet fathered *one* child in the natural. God required Abram to operate in Mountain-Moving Faith in order to see himself as God saw him. A person perceiving only what can be perceived in the natural realm could not even begin to wrap his mind around this seemingly impossible prospect. How could such a thing possibly happen! Only almighty Jehovah could put the action to this faith and bring it into being!

> Then God said to Abraham, "As for Sarai your wife, you shall not call her name Sarai (my princess), but her name will be Sarah (Princess). I will bless her, and indeed I will also give you a son by her. Yes, I will bless her, and she shall be a mother of nations; kings of peoples will come from her."[15]

Look carefully at this poignant, mindboggling prophetic word from God to Abram! First, let's consider their name changes. Why did God change their names? Presumably, it was because their walking in this new mandate from Heaven required they totally abandon their past, leaving behind their old wineskin theologies, mind-sets, and thinking. They now had a new covenant filled with kingly or regal perspective encompassing a global vision that they must now embrace, assimilate, and transition into.

Can you even imagine Abraham going back to his tent to inform Sarah of this new destiny given by Jehovah? He even had to tell Sarah they were going to conceive and birth a baby boy at their advanced ages. What Mountain-Moving Faith they both had to now walk in in order to receive this word as factual reality.

Then God said to Abraham, "As for Sarai your wife, you shall not call her name Sarai (my princess), but her name will be Sarah (Princess). I will bless her, and indeed I will also give you a son by her. Yes, I will bless her, and she shall be a mother of nations; kings of peoples will come from her." Then Abraham fell on his face and laughed, and said in his heart, "Shall a child be born to a man who is a hundred years old? And shall Sarah, who is ninety years old, bear a child?" And Abraham said to God, "Oh, that Ishmael [my firstborn] might live before You!" But God said, "No, Sarah your wife shall bear you a son indeed, and you shall name him Isaac (laughter); and I will establish My covenant with him for an everlasting covenant and with his descendants after him. As for Ishmael, I have heard and listened to you; behold, I will bless him, and will make him fruitful and will greatly multiply him [through his descendants]. He will be the father of twelve princes (chieftains, sheiks), and I will make him a great nation. [Gen 25:12-18] But My covenant [My promise, My solemn pledge], I will establish with Isaac, whom Sarah will bear to you at this time next year."[16]

Yet, somehow, along with the promise came the Mountain-Moving Faith to accept as fact this prophetic word form God's mouth that would shape the destiny of not only the nation of Israel, but also many Arab nations far into the future.

The Mountain-Moving Faith of Two Women Warriors

The next story of Mountain-Moving Faith is recounted in the book of Judges. In Chapter Four, we find two Warriors of Valor, Deborah and Jael, who were both women.

Deborah was a prophetess and judge of Israel, and the wife of Lappidoth. For Deborah to be used by God as she was, including to be appointed a judge over Israel, was a divine exception and accommodation, a departure from the norm of political power and governing authority resting with men only, necessitated by the disobedience of Israeli men to take their proper place of rule and military leadership.

We are told little about Deborah's rise to becoming a judge of Israel. Presumably, it was a result of the extraordinary faith and trust she placed in Jehovah as the Almighty God and Ruler over the affairs of the nation of Israel. The nation of Israel had been extremely disobedient to

God in a multitude of ways. They loved their lustful sins and following after other gods. As a result, at this time, they had been in bondage to the foreign nations surrounding them and their despotic rulers for decades.

> Then the LORD raised up judges who delivered them from the hands of those who plundered them. Yet they did not listen to their judges, for they played the harlot after other gods and bowed themselves down to them. They turned aside quickly from the way in which their fathers had walked in obeying the commandments of the LORD; they did not do as their fathers. When the LORD raised up judges for them, He was with the judge and He delivered them from the hand of their enemies all the days of the judge; for the LORD was moved to pity by their groaning because of those who oppressed and afflicted them.[17]

The Lord raised up judges to deliver diminutive Israel from the superior military power of the surrounding nations who oppressed and afflicted them because He was moved to pity by their groaning! During the days of the judges, God delivered Israel from the oppressing hand of their enemies.

> But it came about when the judge died, that they would turn back and act more corruptly than their fathers, in following other gods to serve them and bow down to them; they did not abandon their practices or their stubborn ways. So the anger of the LORD burned against Israel, and He said, "Because this nation has transgressed My covenant which I commanded their fathers and has not listened to My voice, I also will no longer drive out before them any of the nations which Joshua left when he died, in order to test Israel by them, whether they will keep the way of the LORD to walk in it as their fathers did, or not." So the LORD allowed those nations to remain, not driving them out quickly; and He did not give them into the hand of Joshua.[18]

Because the people of Israel were so blatantly disobedient and obstinate, each successive generation acting more wickedly than the previous, the anger of the Lord burned hot against them, and to discipline them He determined not to drive out the enemy nations surrounding them any longer as He had done through Joshua before he died, "in order to test Israel by them, whether they will keep the way of the LORD to walk in it as their fathers did, or not." He allowed those nations to remain, "not driving them out quickly," not giving "them into the hand of Joshua" to defeat and subdue them.

So instead of dispossessing the occupying nations from the land God had apportioned unto Israel, He allowed a contingent of the Philistines, Canaanites, Hittites, Amorites, Perizzites, Hivites, and the Jebusites to remain in the land. Instead of having the land to themselves, the Israelites had to share the land with the idolatrous peoples of these foreign nations. This was not God's intent, but He allowed it, to test them to see if the now extant generations of Israelites would repent of their gross wickedness and idolatry and return to Jehovah God, who had so miraculously delivered them from the oppression of their Egyptian captors and led them to this land flowing with milk and honey.

> They (the nations God allowed to remain) were for testing Israel, to find out if they would obey the commandments of the LORD, which He had commanded their fathers through Moses.[19]

But they did not repent. They continued to disobey God's explicit command not to intermarry with the godless peoples of the nations surrounding them and cease from serving their false gods:

> and they took their daughters for themselves as wives, and gave their own daughters to their sons, and served their gods.[20]

So, in order for the nation to survive and be preserved (remember, this was the nation Jehovah had chosen from whom to bring forth the Messiah, so therefore it had to be preserved), it was necessary for the Lord to "teach war" to this now extant generation of Israelites.

> only in order that the generations of the sons of Israel might be taught war, at least those who had not experienced it previously.[21]

To summarize what transpired over the subsequent decades, "Then the anger of the LORD was kindled against Israel," because:

> The sons of Israel did what was evil in the sight of the LORD, and forgot the LORD their God and served the Baals and the Asheroth.[22]

This compelled the Lord to give Israel into the hands of Cushan-rishathaim. the king of Mesopotamia, to whom they were subservient for eight years.[23]

Then, when the Israelites cried out to the Lord after living under the severe oppression of the king of Mesopotamia, the Lord again had mercy and raised up another mighty warrior-judge, Othniel, to deliver them and give the nation rest from oppression for forty years:

> When the sons of Israel cried to the LORD, the LORD raised up a deliverer for the sons of Israel to deliver them, Othniel the son of Kenaz, Caleb's younger brother. The Spirit of the LORD came upon him, and he judged Israel. When he went out to war, the LORD gave Cushan-rishathaim king of Mesopotamia into his hand, so that he prevailed over Cushan-rishathaim. Then the land had rest forty years. And Othniel the son of Kenaz died.[24]

Incredibly, after the death of Othniel, the succeeding generation "again did evil in the sight of the LORD," requiring the Lord to again consign Israel to the subjugation of a foreign nation and its king, Eglon, the king of Moab, who the Lord Himself actually "strengthened" in order to bring it about. Eglon elicited as allies the descendants of Ammon and Amalek to fight against and defeat Israel, gaining and maintaining dominance over the nation for eighteen years.[25]

Yet again, when the Israelites cried out to the Lord after that period of oppression, the Lord once again raised up another judge, Ehud, the son of Gera, from the tribe of Benjamin.[26] By way of a plot of intrigue and deceit, Ehud killed Eglon, the Moabite king, and with the supernatural help of the Lord was then able to defeat the Moabites, thereby liberating Israel from the clutches of oppression by a foreign nation once again, bringing rest to the nation for the next eight years.[27]

Following those eight years of peace, God sent another judge named Shamgar, the son of Anath, about whom we are told little except that he "struck down six hundred Philistines with an oxgoad" and that he "also saved Israel."[28]

Subsequently we are told another twenty-year period of severe subjugation under a foreign power ensued, again at the hand of the Lord for Israel's disciplining because the nation remained obstinate and rebellious against the Lord, refusing to obey His commandments, and continuing to serve the foreign gods of the nations with whom their lives were inextricably linked as a result of intermarriage.

> Then the sons of Israel again did evil in the sight of the LORD, after Ehud died. And the LORD sold them into the hand of Jabin king of Canaan, who reigned in Hazor; and the commander of his army was Sisera, who lived in Harosheth-hagoyim. The sons of Israel cried to the LORD; for he had nine hundred iron chariots, and he oppressed the sons of Israel severely for twenty years.[29]

It is at this interval that we first hear of Deborah, who was a judge over Israel instrumental in delivering Israel from subjugation to the Canaanites and their king, Jaban, with the result that under her protracted leadership the land of Israel "was undisturbed for forty years." I am citing the story of Deborah as an example of Mountain-Moving Faith, though I suppose it could be cited as an example of just about any of the other kinds and degrees of faith addressed in this book. So, my choice to do that is purely subjective on my part. Notwithstanding, certainly, Deborah exhibited a level or degree of faith during her career as a judge of Israel that was extraordinary and inordinate, at any rate.[30]

> Now Deborah, a prophetess, the wife of Lappidoth, was judging Israel at that time. She used to sit [to hear and decide disputes] under the palm tree of Deborah between Ramah and Bethel in the hill country of Ephraim; and the Israelites came up to her for judgment.[31]

One day, apparently at the prophetic leading of the Lord, Deborah summoned Barak, the commander of Israel's army, and gave him a directive she declared was a command of the Lord, the God of Israel, to confront in battle Sisera, the commander of Jabin's army, whom the Lord, she further declared, had given into Barak's hands.

> Now she sent word and summoned Barak the son of Abinoam from Kedesh-naphtali, and said to him, "Behold, the LORD, the God of Israel, has commanded, "Go and march to Mount Tabor, and take with you ten thousand men [of war] from the tribes of Naphtali and Zebulun. I will draw out Sisera, the commander of Jabin's army, with his chariots and his infantry to meet you at the river Kishon, and I will hand him over to you." Then Barak said to her, "If you will go with me, then I will

go; but if you will not go with me, I will not go."³²

Deborah's response was that she would surely go with him but that the credit for the elimination of Sisera would not go to him but to a woman:

> She said, "I will surely go with you; nevertheless, the honor shall not be yours on the journey that you are about to take, for the LORD will sell Sisera into the hands of a woman." Then Deborah arose and went with Barak to Kedesh.³³

Do you see the favor and Mountain-Moving Faith Deborah is carrying here? Why the Faith? The army of Israel had been in bondage to the ruler of Jabin, who withheld iron from them so that they could not make battle weapons required for fighting. Thus, their Mountain-Moving Faith was all they had, but the reality was that their faith was all they needed to allow God to act on their behalf. As Jesus said, all things are possible with God:

> Looking at them, Jesus said, "With people [as far as it depends on them] it is impossible, but not with God; for all things are possible with God."³⁴

To sum this story up, Jabin's army, led by Sisera; was over-taken by Barak, just like it was told by Deborah. God had given Israel the victory. The impossible became possible because God used strong warriors—in this case, led by a female warrior—who possessed Mountain-Moving Faith.

Working in tandem with Deborah was another woman, Jael. She was wife of Heber the Kenite, who proved also to be a fierce warrior. She was in her tent that was located in the vicinity where Sisera fled on foot when the battle became intense. Thinking her tent was the dwelling of an ally, Sisera ran to it.

> But Sisera fled on foot to the tent of Jael, the wife of Heber the Kenite, because there was peace between Jabin the king of Hazor and the house of Heber the Kenite. Jael went out to meet Sisera, and said to him, "Turn aside, my lord, turn aside to me! Have no fear." So he turned aside to her [and went] into the tent, and she covered him with a rug.³⁵

Sisera asked Jael for a drink of water, and she gave him drink, and he laid down to recoup.

And he said to her, "Please give me a little water to drink because I am thirsty." And she opened a skin of milk and gave him a drink; then she covered him. And he said to her, "Stand at the door of the tent, and if any man comes and asks you, 'Is there anyone here?' tell him, 'No.'"[36]

Weary from the intense battle, letting down his guard for a brief moment, Sisera mistakenly presumed Jael was an ally and thus willing to conceal him from the army of Israelites because she called for him to come into her tent. But he was very mistaken in his presumption. When he fell asleep from exhaustion, Jael ruthlessly drove a tent peg through his head, killing him instantly:

> But Jael, Heber's wife, took a tent peg and a hammer in her hand, and came up quietly to him and drove the peg through his temple, and it went through into the ground; for he was sound asleep and exhausted. So he died. And behold, as Barak pursued Sisera, Jael came out to meet him and said to him, "Come, and I will show you the man whom you are seeking." And he entered [her tent] with her, and behold Sisera lay dead with the tent peg in his temple.[37]

This woman's Mountain Moving Faith, love, and honor of Jehovah, as was also the case with Deborah, worked to save the Children of Israel from hegemony by their enemy as God delivered the nation from otherwise certain defeat.

Again, these historical Old Testament accounts are conveyed to us who are living in these last days as an example and for our instruction[38] to encourage us to attain for ourselves the kind of faith these heroes and heroines of old obtained and walked in so that in accordance with prophecy in the latter days them who know their God shall do great exploits.[39]

Endnotes

1. Mark 11:22-23
2. Mark 11:24
3. Mark 11:24-26; AMP
4. Rom. 8:5-9; KJV
5. Mark 7:20-23
6. Psa. 36:11a
7. Pro. 8:13
8. While authorship of Psalm 75 is attributed in the title to Asaph, most scholars and O.T. historians agree that David was likely the actual author who expressed it in the presence of Asaph, who was in essence David's poet-laureate, penning David's rapturous extemporized musical expressions in prose or lyrical form.
9. Psa. 75:4-7
10. Mat. 17:14-20
11. Mat. 13:31; 17:20; Mark 4:31; Luke 13:19; 17:6
12. Rev. 12:10
13. Gen. 15:5-6
14. Gen. 17:4-6
15. Gen. 17:15-16; AMP
16. Gen. 17:15-21; AMP
17. Jdg. 2:16-18
18. Jdg. 2:19-23
19. Jdg. 3:4
20. Jdg. 3:6
21. Jdg. 3:2
22. Jdg. 3:7
23. Jdg. 3:8
24. Jdg. 3:9-11
25. Jdg. 3:12-14
26. Jdg. 3:15

27 Jdg. 3:16-30
28 Jdg. 3:31
29 Jdg. 4:1-3
30 Jdg. 5:31
31 Jdg. 4:4-5
32 Jdg. 4:6-8
33 Jdg. 4:9
34 Mark 10:27
35 Jdg. 4:17-18
36 Jdg. 4:17-18
37 Jdg. 4:21-22
38 1 Cor. 10:11
39 Dan. 11:32

Chapter Six

WONDER-WORKING FAITH

to another [wonder-working] faith [is given] by the same [Holy] Spirit, and to another the [extraordinary] gifts of healings by the one Spirit;[1]

The kind and level of faith alluded to here is rare and rarely attained. It is a dimension of faith that generates what is referred to in the New Testament as "signs and wonders," supernatural occurrences so extraordinary so as to astonish, amaze, bewilder, and cause receivers and witnesses to marvel. These are utter miracles without earthly and intellectual explanation that leave no doubt they are performed by God alone through human vessels!

It was for this dimension of faith that Peter and John, along with their companions, prayed after they were miraculously released from the jail cell in which they were cast by the Sanhedrin Counsel, which prayer immediately produced such a sign and wonder of supernatural origin with supernatural effect:

> "And now, Lord, take note of their threats, and grant that Your bond-servants may speak Your word with all confidence, while You extend Your hand to heal, and **signs and wonders** take place through the name of Your holy servant Jesus." And when they had prayed, the place where they had gathered together was shaken, and they were all filled with the Holy Spirit and began to speak the word of God with boldness.[2]

There are many examples in the Bible of individuals who attained this Wonder-Working Faith and thereby performed mighty signs and wonders. We examine in this chapter some of the more outstanding examples in the Bible.

The Wonder-Working Faith of Moses

Certainly, among the most extraordinary examples of Wonder Working-Faith is the mighty miracles performed by/through Moses. Depending on how they are characterized and listed, there were a minimum of 25 miracles that transpired during the Exodus of the Israelites under the leadership of Moses, each of which qualified as a sign and wonder. When miracles occur, they occur due to the faith of *someone*. These miracles occurred, I believe, as a result of Moses' faith. The following is a list of those 25 miracles in chronological order.

1. Turning the Nile into blood (Exo. 4:9; 7:14-24; Psa. 78:44; 105:29).

2. The plague of frogs (Exo. 8:1-6; Psa. 78:45; 105:30).

3. The plague of lice (Exo. 8:16-19; Psa. 105:31).

4. The plague of flies (Exo. 8:20-31; Psa. 78:45; 105:31).

5. The plague of murrain of livestock (Exo. 9:1-7).

6. The plague of boils (Exo. 9:8-11).

7. The plague of hail (Exo. 9:13-25; Psa. 78:47-48; 105:32-33).

8. The plague of locusts (Exo. 10:1-20; Psa. 78:46; 105:34-35).

9. The plague of darkness (Exo. 10:21-29; Psa. 105:28).

10. The plague of the death of the firstborn (Exo. 11-12; Psa. 78:51; 105:36; 135:8; 136:10).

11. The cloud and the fire (Exo. 13:21-22; 40:34-38; Neh. 9:12, 19; Psa. 78:14; 105:39; 1 Cor. 10:1-2,6,11).

12. The parting of the Red Sea (Exo. 14:21-31; Psa. 78:53; 106:9,11,22; Heb. 11:29).

13. The healing of Marah's bitter waters (Exo. 15:22-27; Num. 33:8).

14. The provision of manna (Exo. 15:6-15; Num. 11:1-9; Jos. 5:11-12; Neh. 9:15; 20; Psa. 78:20; 105:40; see also John 6:22-59).

15. The provision of quail (Exo. 16:8, 11-15; Num. 11:31-34; Psa. 78:26-30; 105:39-42).

16. The smitten rock (Exo. 17:1-9; Psa. 78:16-17; 105:41).

17. The victory over the Amalekites (Exo. 17:8-16; Num. 13:29;

14:25; Deu. 25:17-19; Psa. 83:7).

18. The miracles at Sinai (Exo. 19:16-25; Deu. 4:5; 5:7-22; 9:8-11; Psa. 68:8; Heb. 12:18-21).

19. The punishment of Nadab and Abihu (Lev. 10:1-7; Num. 3:1-4; 26:61; 1 Chr. 24:2).

20. The fire at Taberah (Num. 11:1-3; Deu. 9:22; Psa. 78:21).

21. The infliction of Miriam with leprosy (Lev. 13:46; Num. 12; 20:1; Deu. 24:8-9).

22. Judgment upon Korah and sons (Num. 16; 26:9-11; Psa. 106:17).

23. The budding of Aaron's rod (Num. 17; Heb. 9:4).

24. The bronze serpent (Num. 21:4-9; 2 Kgs. 18:4; John 3:14; 1 Cor. 10:9).

25. The provision of drinking water (Num. 21:13-18).

It could well be said that all these miracles were the product of Wonder-Working Faith! One through ten transpired while the Israelites remained in captivity under the unrelenting, obstinate grip of Pharoah and the Egyptians. It was not until all of these recompenses were exacted upon the Egyptians that Pharaoh began to relent and finally allow Israel to go free.

> Now it came about at midnight that the LORD struck all the firstborn in the land of Egypt, from the firstborn of Pharaoh who sat on his throne to the firstborn of the captive who was in the dungeon, and all the firstborn of cattle. Pharaoh arose in the night, he and all his servants and all the Egyptians, and there was a great cry in Egypt, for there was no home where there was not someone dead. Then he called for Moses and Aaron at night and said, "Rise up, get out from among my people, both you and the sons of Israel; and go, worship the LORD, as you have said. "Take both your flocks and your herds, as you have said, and go, and bless me also."[3]

Finally, when sudden and unexplainable death began to strike the households of the Egyptians, including Pharaoh's, and there was a great outcry throughout Egypt, Pharaoh "rose in the night, he and all his servants and all the Egyptians," summoned Moses and Aaron, and commanded them and all the sons of Israel to depart from their nation and worship the Lord, taking all their flocks and herds of animals with them, and adding an incredibly audacious selfish request that Moses and Aaron bless *him* also in the name of Jehovah as they went!

The twelfth of those miracles was the parting or dividing of the Red Sea for the Children of Israel. When their trek led them to the Red Sea with Pharaoh and his armies in hot pursuit, the Israelites, who numbered more than two million including all the men, women, and children, were stopped dead in their tracks, not able to go forward due to the depth of the Red Sea, nor to go backwards with the armies of Pharaoh in dogged pursuit of them. Once again, Moses did not falter in his faith, but rather his Wonder-Working Faith, ostensibly motivating him, he boldly commands the people to not be afraid and to take their stand against the situation they were now in, in order to witness the salvation of the Lord that He would accomplish for them that very day!

> Then Moses said to the people, "Do not be afraid! Take your stand [be firm and confident and undismayed] and see the salvation of the LORD which He will accomplish for you today; for those Egyptians whom you have seen today, you will never see again. The LORD will fight for you while you [only need to] keep silent and remain calm."[4]

The story of the outcome and how God delivered the Israelites is renowned! As it turns out, God did not lead the nation to the Red Sea in order to destroy *them*, but rather to destroy Pharaoh and his entire army! The Red Sea miraculously parted with the raging waters standing straight up as a wall on each side, and the entire nation of two-million people crossed over the seabed of the great sea on *dry ground* with all their possessions, including their livestock they were transporting with them.

> The angel of God, who had been going before the camp of Israel, moved and went behind them; and the pillar of cloud moved from before them and stood behind them. So it came between the camp of Egypt and the camp of Israel; and there was the cloud along with the darkness, yet it gave light at night. Thus the one did not come near the other all night. Then Moses stretched out his hand over the sea; and the LORD swept the sea back by a strong east wind all night and turned the sea into dry land, so the waters were divided. The sons of Israel went

through the midst of the sea on the dry land, and the waters were like a wall to them on their right hand and on their left.[5]

What a sight this must have been! The angel of God that had been going before them suddenly moved to their rear and stood behind them! The dark cloud that had been hovering over them was replaced with brilliant light flooding the path before *them* but somehow simultaneously darkened the path of the Egyptians following behind them. Then Moses stretched out his hand over the sea, and the waters miraculously divided!

It boggles the mind to imagine two million people with all their possessions crossing the Red Sea one-by-one on totally dry ground void of muck and mire! Not one person, animal, or transport vehicle was bogged down in the seabed as they crossed over to the other side! And, to think all this occurred because Moses' faith was so powerfully manifest that he was able to persuade the people to resist and reject fear and dismay, and instead trust God explicitly to deliver them! I believe this demonstrates how that faith, even this level of Wonder-Working Faith, is "transferable" when it is activated and operated through even one believer!

> Now these things happened to them as an example, and they were written for *our instruction*, upon whom the ends of the ages have come.[6]

> For whatever was written in earlier times was written for *our instruction*, so that through perseverance and the encouragement of the Scriptures we might have hope.[7]

Innumerable are the times over the centuries, especially in the 19th and 20th Centuries, when this Wonder-Working Faith was transferred through one man or woman to an entire assembly of people that produced such an atmosphere of faith that a massive number of miracles, signs, wonders, miracles, and supernatural healings transpired under the anointing in meetings during that period! Such was the case in the ministry career of Smith Wigglesworth, who became known as, "The Apostle of Faith," and others, such as Maria Woodworth-Etter, John G. Lake, Lester Sumrall, Oral Roberts, William Branham, A.A. Allen, Jack Coe, Kathryn Kuhlman, T. L. Osborn, and a host of lesser known miracle-working and healing evangelists.

In the case of the Israelites, when they obeyed the word of the

Lord uttered through Moses to fear not, remain calm, and watch and see what God was about to do, God fought their battle for them and delivered them from their fierce enemy! What a lesson this is for all believers today! The believer's battle is the "good fight of faith!"[8] God Himself supplies the victory in the battles of life for believers who fight that good fight of faith!

The Wonder-Working Faith of Elijah

The prophet Elijah lived from c. 900BC to c. 849BC and performed sixteen miracles during his lifetime. As with Moses, each of the miracles God performed in the life of Elijah can be considered a sign and wonder. They were signs to demonstrate that Jehovah God was working in and through the prophet, and that the prophet was a surrogate spokesman of God. They were a wonder to demonstrate conclusively that God alone was the source of these supernatural occurrences performed through a human vessel. The following are the miracles performed in Elijah's life, listed in chronological order.

1. Pronounced/decreed a drought (1 Kgs. 17:1,7);
2. Fed by ravens sent by God (1 Kgs. 17:4-6);
3. Pronounces perpetual flow of flour and oil for the Widow of Zarephath (1 Kgs. 17:8-16);
4. Revives/raises the Widow's son from the dead (1 Kgs. 17:17-24);
5. Prays down fire from Heaven consuming the sacrifices on Mount Carmel where all of Israel had gathered to witness a contest between 450 prophets of Baal and 400 prophets of the Asherah who were sustained by Jezebel against Elijah and Jehovah God, wherein the God who answered by fire was demonstrated to be the true God (1 Kgs. 18:19-40);
6. Decrees rain, ending the three-year draught he had previously decreed (1 Kgs. 18:41-45);
7. Outruns Ahab and his soldiers traveling by horse-drawn chariots to Jezreel (1 Kgs. 18:46);
8. God sustains the prophet for 40 days and nights with baked cakes and water brought to him by an angel twice (1 Kgs. 19:8);
9. Pronounces judgment on Ahab (1 Kgs. 21:17-24);
10. Diverted judgment from Ahab to his son, Ahaziah, which Elijah pronounced upon Ahaziah, in person, when he was instructed by

"the angel of the Lord" to go with the third captain and his squad of fifty soldiers Ahaziah sent to seize Elijah and take him to the king [2 Kgs. 1:15-17] (1 Kgs. 21:28-29);

11. Pronounces judgment on Jezebel (1 Kgs. 21:20-24; 2 Kgs. 9:30-37);
12. Calls down fire from heaven that consumes the first captain and his squad of fifty soldiers sent by King Ahaziah to seize Elisha and bring him to the king (2 Kgs. 1:10);
13. Calls down fire from heaven that consumes the second captain and his squad of fifty soldiers sent by King Ahaziah to seize Elisha and bring him to the king (2 Kgs. 1:12);
14. Divides the waters of the river (2 Kgs. 2:8);
15. Taken up alive (raptured) by a whirlwind on chariots of fire (2 Kgs. 2:11);
16. Pronounces judgment upon Jehoram via written letter he sent to him before being taken up (2 Chr. 21:12-15).[9]

The Purpose of the Record of These Miracles

What extraordinary Wonder-Working Miracles these events were! They truly set Elijah the prophet apart in a very distinguishable way. But it's important to understand that these miracles were not God showing off His power through a prophet; they are far more than that. Each event, while undeniably miraculous, had a specific and higher purpose regarding the nation of Israel and its future at the time. Moreover, they were all a part of the ancient record of the things that "happened to them (Israel) as an *example*, and they were written for our *instruction*, upon whom the ends of the ages have come."[10]

> For whatever was written in earlier times was written for our *instruction*, so that through perseverance and the encouragement of the Scriptures we might have hope.[11]

Both of these cited Scriptures indicate that there was a purpose for the miracles and miraculous events that occurred in Old Testaments times, and that purpose is that they would be instructive examples to the believers who would be living when "the ends of the ages have come." Those believers are US—you and I—who are living right now in the Twenty-First Century! Without any doubt, at least to those who understand the significance of eschatological events predicted in

Scripture, the time we are living in right now is the end-times! We are that generation "upon whom the ends of the ages have come." This is an unequivocal and irrefutable fact!

It would behoove us then, and the onus is upon us then, to seek revelation from the Lord, the Head of the Church, as to what He wants the end-times Ekklesia to understand about these instructional examples. They did not occur to simply "wow" us and inspire us to say, "now isn't that something!" No, there's more to it than that. In some ways, the *why* of these events being a part of the biblical record is more important than the *what* of them.

I believe we can expect to see similar miracles and wondrous acts to be repeated in the Twenty-First Century. I believe God is looking for a people, who will comprise the End-Times One-Third Remnant Church, who the Lord has brought through refining fires to refine them as silver is refined and test them as gold is tested:

> "And I will bring *the third part* through the fire, Refine them as silver is refined, And test them as gold is tested. They will call on My name, And I will answer them; I will say, 'They are My people,' And they will say, 'The LORD is my God.'"[12]

In this last hour before the return of Christ in the clouds in the air, the Body of Christ must come to the unequivocal understanding that not everyone who claims to be a "Christian" is truly a genuine Born Again believer; not every ecclesial entity that purports to be a part of the genuine Ekklesia Jesus is building[13] is truly a part of it! It's time to drop all the unbiblical altruistic sentimentality about Heaven and who all is going to be there. Only the *Redeemed* will be there—the Redeemed Saints of God—those that have truly been washed in the Blood of the Lamb! No impostors will be there! There's no fooling the Almighty and All-Knowing God! God knows who are His children! And who are the Redeemed Saints of God? Those whose human spirits have been genuinely regenerated by the infusion of the Holy Spirit,[14] which is verified by the evident manifestation of the "fruit of the Spirit."[15]

The world more or less believes Heaven is some sort of a *nirvana*[16] where everyone goes when they die. Of course, such foolishness is completely unscriptural, not to mention nonsensical. Heaven is a place—a place where God is, lives, and where His Presence permeates the entire place. It is not just some ethereal state of consciousness. It is real, in ways that are unexplainable. It is material and substantial; yet it is spiritual. Perhaps we could say that everything there has spiritual substance. This is proven by what the Scripture writers who experienced it and came back to earth to reveal what the Lord allowed them to reveal to us described.

It is also verified by the fact that when the Resurrected Christ appeared unto particular disciples, they recognized Him, though in some cases not immediately. His resurrected form was the same as His bodily form absent the fleshly substance. In His resurrected body, He was able to walk through locked doors and walls, appear to the 120 disciples in the Upper-Room on Resurrection Evening, be recognized by them, and converse with them.

In His resurrected body, He was able to stand on the shore and call out to Peter and his fishing companions asking them whether they had caught any fish, and the disciples could eventually recognize Him, which, we are told, was "the third time that Jesus was manifested to the disciples, after He was raised from the dead."[17]

In His resurrected body, He was able to appear "in a different form" to two of His disciples as they were walking on the road to Emmaus, though "their eyes were prevented from recognizing Him" as being Jesus, until He once again shared the communion meal with them, "Then their eyes were opened and they recognized Him," but He then immediately vanished from their sight.[18]

None of these supernatural events are hocus-pocus or Jesus playing with the disciples some version of hide-and-seek. Far from it! God is showing us in these events things He wants us to know about the spirit realm, the Kingdom of God, and the Kingdom of Heaven. I expect similar occurrences to take place here in the last days we are living in—events that will far exceed anything we have seen previously.

Why? Because we are entering into a period of time in which Heaven and the Presence of God is being brought so near to us that there will be brief, fleeting, moments when the temporal realm will be incurred by the spirit realm with flashes of the Glory of God (the tangible manifestation of the Presence/Essence of God) so as to be seen by the eyes of men. These will be astonishing occurrences! They will shake people witnessing them to their core! They will leave no doubt that there is an Almighty God who is so far above Mankind and His Creation in a multiplicity of ways that are inscrutable and inexplicable!

Human words fail when we try to use them to explain spiritual things:

> Now we have received, not the spirit of the world, but the Spirit who is from God, so that we may know the things freely given to us by God, which things we also speak, not in words taught by human wisdom, but in those taught by the Spirit, combining spiritual *thoughts* with spiritual *words*. But a natural man does not accept the things of the Spirit of God, for they are foolishness to him; and he cannot understand them, because they are spiritually appraised. But he who is spiritual appraises all things, yet he himself is appraised by no one.[19]

Unfortunately, though, there will continue to be charlatans who will introduce counterfeit miracles and displays of purported supernatural power. So, the Body of Christ needs to be much more on the alert than in recent years and learn to "test the spirits to see whether they are of God!"

> Beloved, do not believe every spirit, but *test the spirits* to see whether they are from God, because many false prophets have gone out into the world.[20]

The Wonder-Working Faith of Elisha

Another person in the biblical account who manifested this level of Wonder-Working Faith as well was the humble servant and successor of Elijah, is Elisha.

Before Elijah's rapture into Heaven, Elisha began to pursue a closer relationship with him. Apparently, of all "the sons of the prophets," Elisha had the closest relationship with Elijah. It appears that was so because Elisha pursued Elijah and the relationship he had with him; certainly not vice versa. This is made clear by Elijah's responses to Elisha, that were W.C. Field's-like, "Get away, my boy, you bother me." This is an important point in the area of relationships between Fivefold Ministers, especially the prophetic pantheon; the *lesser* must pursue relationship with the *greater*, not the other way around, for "without any dispute the *lesser* is blessed by the *greater*."[21] Less inveterate Fivefold Ministers should not expect more inveterate Fivefold Ministers to pursue them!

The Sons of the Prophets

The term "sons of the prophets" appears eleven times in First (once) and Second Kings (ten times). Information about this group's origins and development is limited. Ostensibly, the term referred to a cadre of "prophets-in-training," who originally were mentees and students of Elijah the prophet, and comprised a prophetic order or guild of some sort who lived together in a monastical community. The word "sons," did not imply familial descent from a prophet, but only to the mentor-mentee relationship, similar to the Apostle Paul calling some of his mentor-protégés, such as Timothy and Titus, his *spiritual* "sons," though they were not his biological offspring. Somewhere along the line, references by historians and commentators to this community of prophet-trainees as a "school of the prophets" emerged, despite that term not appearing in the Bible. Several indirect Old Testament references to a band or group of prophets affirm these prophetic communities existed and continued to exist throughout Israel's monarchy.[22] Evidence that these prophetic guilds were recognized and given some degree of deference in Israel is inherent in Amos' disavowal of special pedigree, saying that he himself was neither a prophet nor a "son of a prophet," i.e., a member of a prophetic order.[23]

> There were several different guilds or branches of the same guild located at various places: (1) at Bethel (2 Kings 2:3), (2) at Jericho (2:5), (3) at Gilgal (4:38), (4) in the hill country of Ephraim (5:22). Yet they were all "ruled" by the same prophet whom they called master (2:3,5). When the master died or was taken, as Elijah was, one of the guild members took his place as the new master. The promotion had to be recognized by the guild members, and the test was whether the new master had the powers of the old master (2:8, 14) and whether the spirit of the old master rested on the new master (2:15). The guild may have lived in a monastic community. They erected community buildings (6:1ff.) and shared a common table (4:38-44). Yet some were married (4:1ff.). Some of their work was done at the command of the master (4:38; 9:1), and often they sought his approval before doing something (2:16-18; 6:1ff.). Yet they could act on their own (1 Kings 20:35).[24]

When Elijah was taken up alive to Heaven in his own private "rapture," Elisha was recognized as his successor, having satisfied the prerequisites to be thus recognized by the other "sons of the prophets" delineated in the above citation. In the course of time, these prophets came to Elisha with a complaint that their living quarters complex had become too small (presumably as a result of their growing families, as some were married and had families, indicating they were not celibate, nor required to be).

> Now the sons of the prophets said to Elisha, "Behold now, the place before you where we are living is too limited for us. "Please let us go to the Jordan and each of us take from there a beam, and let us make a place there for ourselves where we may live." So he said, "Go." Then one said, "Please be willing to go with your servants." And he answered, "I shall go." So he went with them; and when they came to the Jordan, they cut down trees. But as one was felling a beam, the axe head fell into the water; and he cried out and said, "Alas, my master! For it was borrowed." Then the man of God said, "Where did it fall?" And when he showed him the place, he cut off a stick and threw it in there, and made the iron float. He said, "Take it up for yourself." So he put out his hand and took it.[25]

Trees lining the banks of the nearby Jordan River would be the source of wood needed to build the new residences. Apparently, a beam was formed from the thick trunk of one of those tall trees as the main anchor to which the other parts of the structure were attached. It was sort of a "Habitat for Humanity" communal project they all worked on together.

One day, while hewing a tree, the iron axe-head wielded by one of the prophets flew off the handle into the coursing river waters. This was especially stressing to the prophet because the axe was borrowed. In distress, the prophet called out to Elisha for help, exclaiming that the axe was borrowed. Elisha asked where the axe-head had fallen, cut a stick from one of the trees, and threw it into the river at the spot where it had fallen in "and made the iron float," the passage declares. Common knowledge says that wood (a stick from a tree) normally does not make iron float! Somehow, it appears, the properties of a magnet to draw up that axe-head from the river bottom was infused into this wooden stick through the "double-portion" of the prophetic anointing Elisha had received via Elijah's prophetic pronouncement upon him! That, while on the surface may seem somewhat insignificant, *was a miracle*! It was a miracle because it was *supernatural*—an occurrence that superseded the natural. It was a miracle the prophet needed because the axe was a valuable tool that would be rendered useless and valueless, if the head was irretrievably lost, because he did not have the means to replace it!

Much speculation regarding the explanation of this scientifically unexplainable occurrence by analysts of the text has transpired over the centuries. Of course, atheistic and agnostic analysts and commentators who purport that much of the Old Testament accounts are Jewish mythology or lore, adamantly claim it didn't happen at all! Those of us who believe that every word of the closed canon of Scripture is God-breathed[26] and that it is impossible for God to lie or tell an untruth,[27] know better, of course! This event happened! What believers should want to know is HOW this miracle happened and what can be drawn from the incident to apply to our understanding of Miracle-Working Faith. As I have indicated throughout this book, God gave us these Old Testament events as examples and instruction to teach us concerning the operations and ways of God so that we can replicate these supernatural occurrences in our lives today!

My conclusion is that this event is recorded in Scripture to show us that the prophetic anointing, and more specifically, the double-portion prophetic anointing can be the source of phenomenal supernatural miracles—Wonder-Working Miracles! It's not abracadabra, it's the ANOINTING! Hallelujah. God is well able to confer upon His genuine prophets a measure of the anointing that allows such extraordinary miracles to transpire. The Church needs to begin to believe for this level of the anointing and these kinds of inscrutable miracles to occur now in these last days we are living in! With God ALL things are possible! "Jesus said unto him, *If thou canst believe*, **all things are possible** to him that *believeth*."[28]

The Miracles of Elisha

The following is a chronological list of miracles performed through Elisha's double-portion anointing. In response to Elijah's question concerning what Elisha wanted him to do for him, was for a double-portion of Elijah's anointing. Elijah responded that Elisha had asked for a "hard" or "difficult" thing, but that if he were to see him being raptured into heaven, his request would be granted him. Of course, we know

Elisha was there with Elijah when the angel band came to take him up and Elisha eye-witnessed the entire event. When Elijah's mantle floated down to the ground (anointings are not needed in Heaven), he immediately picked it up and struck the waters of the Jordan, crying out, "Where is the God of Elijah?" Notice he did not ask where is the *anointing* of Elijah, but rather where is the *God* of Elijah, from whom all anointings flow! When he struck the waters of the Jordan, they immediately dried up as he had seen Elijah do once before, and he walked across the Jordon to the opposite banks on dry ground!

This was truly a miracle after the same manner as Moses had also parted the Red Sea and Elijah had parted the Jordan! It was the first of thirty-two miracles that were performed through the prophetic anointing upon Elisha—precisely *double* the miracles performed through Elijah! The last miracle that occurred through Elisha's anointing, number 32, occurred after he was dead and buried when an unnamed man was, apparently inadvertently, buried in his grave, and was revived from the dead when his dead body touched Elisha's bones! Talk about "that great gittin' up morning!" Glory!

Elisha received exactly what he had requested of Elijah, even though Elijah had said he was asking for a "hard" or "difficult" thing. With God *all* things are possible, and nothing is impossible to or with God, so Elijah's statement was not referring to the degree of difficulty on the part of God, but rather to the degree of difficulty in terms of the personal "cost" of what he was requesting. Every believer has been given an anointing from the Holy One, but the greater the magnitude of the anointing severally bestowed upon us, the greater the personal cost. History proves this to be so with some of God's greatest spiritual generals, from ancient times to the present.

The following table is a delineation of the thirty-two miracles Elisha performed during his lifetime with the scripture citing in which they are described.

#	Miracle	Scripture
1	Jordan River Dried up	2 Kgs. 2:13-15
2	Purification of water	2 Kgs. 2:19-22
3	Bears fulfill pronounced curse	2 Kgs. 2:23-25
4	Water filling ditches without rain	2 Kgs. 3:16-20
5	Defeat of Moabites	2 Kgs. 3:18-27
6	Optical illusion and confusion	2 Kgs. 3:21-23
7	Increase of widow's oil	2 Kgs. 4:1-7
8	Healing of Shunammite woman's barrenness	2 Kgs. 4:12-17
9	Resurrection of Shunammite woman's son	2 Kgs. 4:18-37
10	Stew made edible	2 Kgs. 4:38-41
11	Bread multiplied to feed 100 men	2 Kgs. 4:42-44
12	Naaman's healing and conversion	2 Kgs. 5:1-19
13	Discernment of Gehazi's lie	2 Kgs. 5:20-26
14	Gehazi infected with Naaman's leprosy	2 Kgs. 5:27
15	Causing iron axe-head to float	2 Kgs. 6:1-7
16	Revealing war secrets	2 Kgs. 6:8-10
17	Revealing war secrets	2 Kgs. 6:10-11
18	Revealing war secrets	2 Kgs. 6:12
19	Spiritual eyes of Elisha's servant opened	2 Kgs. 6:13-17
20	Blinding of the Syrian army	2 Kgs. 6:18
21	Capture of Syrian army	2 Kgs. 6:19
22	Healing the Syrian army of blindness	2 Kgs. 6:20-23
23	Foreknowledge of the king's acts	2 Kgs. 6:32-33
24	Miracle producing utterance	2 Kgs. 7:1
25	Miracle producing utterance	2 Kgs. 7:2,9-20
26	Confusion among the Syrians	2 Kgs. 7:3-8
27	Pronouncement of 7 years of famine	2 Kgs. 8:1-2
28	Miracle producing utterance	2 Kgs. 8:7-11
29	Miracle producing utterance	2 Kgs. 8:12-15
30	Miracle producing utterance	2 Kgs. 9:1-15
31	Miracle producing utterance	2 Kgs. 13:14-19
32	Man revived after touching Elijah's bones	2 Kgs. 13:20-21

The Story of Jairus' and Wonder-Working Faith

In the New Testament synoptics there are numerous stories we could categorize as involving the gift of Wonder-Working Faith. One of those outstanding accounts is the incident that took place at the house of a synagogue official named Jairus.

> When Jesus had crossed over again in the boat to the other side, a large crowd gathered around Him; and so He stayed by the seashore. One of the synagogue officials named Jairus came up, and on seeing Him, fell at His feet and implored Him earnestly, saying, "My little daughter is at the point of death; please come and lay Your hands on her, so that she will get well and live." And He went off with him; and a large crowd was following Him and pressing in on Him.[29]
>
> While He was still speaking, some people came from the synagogue official's house, saying [to Jairus], "Your daughter has died; why bother the Teacher any longer?" Overhearing what was being said, Jesus said to the synagogue official, "Do not be afraid; only keep on believing [in Me and my power]." And He allowed no one to go with Him [as witnesses], except Peter and James and John the brother of James. They came to the house of the synagogue official; and He looked [with understanding] at the uproar and commotion, and people loudly weeping and wailing [in mourning]. When He had gone in, He said to them, "Why make a commotion and weep? The child has not died, but is sleeping." They began laughing [scornfully] at Him [because they knew the child was dead]. But He made them all go outside, and took along the child's father and mother and His own [three] companions, and entered the room where the child was. Taking the child's hand, He said [tenderly] to her, "Talitha kum!" —which translated [from Aramaic] means, "Little girl, I say to you, get up!" The little girl immediately got up and began to walk, for she was twelve years old. And immediately they [who witnessed the child's resurrection] were overcome with great wonder and utter amazement. He gave strict orders that no one should know about this, and He told them to give her something to eat."[30]

Jairus came to Jesus broken and overwhelmed with the prospect of his daughter dying. His only hope was Jesus healing her. Some of the guests at Jairus' house were faithless and were adamantly telling Jairus that his daughter was dead, and were pressing him to stop troubling Jesus with the matter because it was now beyond all hope. Jesus, however, operated on the basis of the ruler's expressed faith to perform the required miracle that would save his daughter's life. Jesus exclaimed with all authority that his daughter was *not* dead but only asleep (perhaps, meaning in a coma). By faith, Jesus was able to look past the situation as it appeared in the natural to see *life* rather than *death*. It was Wonder-Working Faith in operation that produced this miraculous result. When Jairus' twelve-year-old daughter responded to Jesus' command to "get up," she awoke from her sleep, rose up and began to walk, causing great wonder and amazement to charge the atmosphere producing faith in many of those present to believe!

In this case, Jesus had not allowed many of those discouraging people to accompany Him, because of their unbelief, but only Peter, James, and John. There's a principle at work here that we need to recognize. In times when Wonder-Working Faith is required, it may be necessary to be discriminant regarding who accompanies us, to ensure that doubt and unbelief does not prevail in the atmosphere.

When you need a miracle in your life, it's critical that you separate yourself from naysayers, scorners, the doubting, and the unbelieving! Do all you can to surround yourself with believers who have faith in God's unchanging and unfailing Word to agree with you for the supernatural intervention needed in your life. Jesus said, it only takes two or three believers standing in agreement for what you are praying for to be done by the Father because where two or three believing are gathered together in His Name He is present by the Spirit:

"Again I say to you, that if two of you agree on earth about anything that they may ask, **it shall be done for them by My Father who is in heaven.** "For where two or three have gathered together in My name, I am there in their midst."[31]

Notice also in this story that when Jesus came to Jairus' house it was filled with commotion and an uproar with people weeping and wailing in mourning. *Unbelief is often very noisy and loud because it is based in fear!* In those days and in that culture, as strange as it seems to us today in our culture, people were hired as paid mourners, because there was an insidious belief that the louder and more intense the mourning was when someone died, the noise would somehow reach

Heaven and move God to raise the person from the dead. Of course, that is not at all how it works. God's ears are attuned to genuine faith professed by someone verbalizing their faith in Him and His limitless supernatural power.

Contrastingly to the scenario in Jairus' house, when genuine faith is in operation, there is a staid calmness and steady quiet as believers turn their attention to calling upon Almighty God with whom *nothing* is impossible! There is no panic where the Spirit of the Lord is present and in operation! Loud shouting is not required for genuine faith to work. The power is not in the shouting, but in the *anointing*! Commotion and uproar, and loud weeping and wailing, while such as that is often manifest when the Spirit of the Lord begins to move in an assembly, is more due to unbelief, fear, and presence of the demonic on the part of the unredeemed than it is the presence of the Lord and genuine faith upon the redeemed!

Summing Up

We have examined in this chapter some biblical instances of Miracle-Working Faith in order to help us to build our faith to believe for this level or degree of faith operating in our individual lives and the collective Ekklesia that Jesus is building. In the next chapter we turn our attention to the level of degree of faith that could well be termed, "Great Faith."

Endnotes

1   1 Cor. 12:9; brackets part of source text
2   Acts 4:29-31
3   Exo. 12:29-32
4   Exo. 14:13-14; AMP
5   Exo. 14:19-22
6   1 Cor. 10:11
7   Rom. 15:4

8   1 Tim. 8:12

9   Some historians propound that the letter Elijah wrote and sent to Jehoram was received by him after Elijah was taken up.

10   1 Cor. 10:11

11   Rom. 15:4

12   Zec. 13:9

13   Mat. 16:18

14   John 3:6

15   Gal. 5:22-23

16   A place or state characterized by freedom from or oblivion to pain, worry, and the external world; https://www.dictionary.com/browse/nirvana

17   John 21:1-14

18   Mark 16:12; Luke 24:13-32

19   1 Cor. 2:12-15

20   1 John 4:1

21   Heb. 7:7

22   1 Sam. 10:5ff;19:20; 1 Kgs. 18:4,19; 22:6; 2 Kgs. 23:2; Jer. 26:7,8,11

23   Amos 7:14; Amos was a farmer

24   https://www.biblegateway.com/resources/encyclopedia-of-the-bible/Sons-Prophets

25   2 Kgs. 6:1-7

26   2 Tim. 3:16

27   Num. 23:19

28   Mark 9:23; KJV

29   Mark 5:21-24

30   Mark 5:35-43; AMP

31   Mat. 18:19-20

Chapter Seven

GREAT FAITH

And when Jesus was entered into Capernaum, there came unto him a centurion, beseeching him, And saying, Lord, my servant lieth at home sick of the palsy, grievously tormented. And Jesus saith unto him, I will come and heal him. The centurion answered and said, Lord, I am not worthy that thou shouldest come under my roof: but speak the word only, and my servant shall be healed. For I am a man under authority, having soldiers under me: and I say to this man, Go, and he goeth; and to another, Come, and he cometh; and to my servant, Do this, and he doeth it. When Jesus heard it, he marvelled, and said to them that followed, Verily I say unto you, I have not found so GREAT FAITH, no, not in Israel. And I say unto you, That many shall come from the east and west, and shall sit down with Abraham, and Isaac, and Jacob, in the kingdom of heaven. But the children of the kingdom shall be cast out into outer darkness: there shall be weeping and gnashing of teeth. And Jesus said unto the centurion, Go thy way; and as thou hast believed, so be it done unto thee. And his servant was healed in the selfsame hour.[1]

This now famous incident involving the Roman Centurion is one of the most outstanding and poignant examples in the Bible of a person who exhibited "great faith!" For Jesus Himself to so identify and declare is remarkable! Not only did He recognize this Roman soldier's faith as being *great*, but He also declared He had not seen such a level or degree of faith with any Israelite, who if anyone, you would think would be the people who would demonstrate great faith.

Why was the Centurion's faith great? Essentially, it was because his faith was centered on Jesus' authority. One thing this man had come to understand as a commander in the Roman Army was how authority works; namely by giving commands. He said he was "a man under authority, having soldiers under me" and exercising that authority he would tell a man to go somewhere, and he would go or to another come and he would come, or do this or that, and he would do it. This is how authority works, the Centurion was telling Jesus.

He actually was telling the Son of God that it was not necessary for Him to walk all the way to where the Centurion's house was—for Jesus had said to him, "I will come and heal him"—but rather, because he believed Jesus possessed ultimate authority, all He had to do was "SPEAK THE WORD ONLY, and my servant shall be healed!"

When you read the story, you can almost hear Jesus' astonishment at what the Centurion was saying! His great faith seemed to stop Jesus in His tracks much like the incident involving the woman with an issue of blood who touched the hem of Jesus' priestly garment in faith, having previously professed that if she but touched the hem of his garment she believed she would be healed.[2] When the woman touched Jesus's garment in faith believing, Jesus felt healing virtue flow out of Him and the woman was instantaneously healed! She went from being an anonymous woman to being a *somebody* when Jesus declared, "*Somebody* touched Me!"[3]

As a result of the Centurion's declaration, Jesus told him to go his way and as he had believed "so be it done unto thee." His servant was healed in that very same hour, we are told.

So moved was Jesus by this Centurion's great faith that He even contrasted it to the agnosticism of "the children of the kingdom," i.e., the Israelites, who He said, due to their lack of faith and unbelief in Him, "shall be cast out into outer darkness: there shall be weeping and gnashing of teeth." For this man to have faith of this magnitude was absolutely incredible! Where did it come from? We can only attribute it as being "the measure of faith"[4] that God has dealt or distributed to everyone who believes!

The Great Faith of a Canaanite Woman

There is another incident recorded in the gospels that happened during the earthly ministry of Jesus, which is that of the Canaanite woman who came to Jesus imploring Him to heal her daughter who she had come to believe was possessed with a demon.

> Jesus went away from there, and withdrew into the district of Tyre and Sidon. And a Canaanite woman from that region came out and began to cry out, saying, "Have mercy on me, Lord, Son of David; my daughter is cruelly demon-possessed." But He did not answer her a word. And His disciples came and implored Him, saying, "Send her away, because she keeps shouting at us." But He answered and said, "I was sent only to the lost sheep of the house of Israel." But she came and began to bow down before Him, saying, "Lord, help me!" And He answered and said, "It is not good to take the children's bread and throw it to the dogs." But she said, "Yes, Lord; but even the dogs feed on the crumbs which fall from their masters' table." Then Jesus said to her, "O woman, your faith is great; it shall be done for you as you wish." And her daughter was healed at once.[5]

The Canaanites were the descendants of Ham, the son of Noah, more specifically, the grandson of Noah, Canaan. They occupied the land of Canaan, where God led Abraham to settle after leaving his father and place of origin. God chose to fulfill His promise to Abraham to bless him and make him a father of many nations in Canaan land.

> "I will make you into a great nation, and I will bless you; I will make your name great, and you will be a blessing. I will bless those who bless you, and whoever curses you I will curse; and all peoples on earth will be blessed through you."[6]

God deliberately, purposefully chose a land occupied by people who were hostile to the Lord to give to Abraham and his progeny as an inheritance. The Canaanites worshiped many different false gods, and their culture was steeped in abominable practices like child sacrifice and cult prostitution. As a result, they were cursed by God:

> "'Cursed be Canaan! The lowest of slaves will he be to his brothers.' He also said, 'Praise be to the LORD, the God of Shem! May Canaan be the slave of Shem.'"[7]

To gain control of this land that was "flowing with milk and honey" as their inheritance required the Israelites dispossess its original inhabitants. God commanded them:

"However, if it does not make peace with you, but makes war against you, then you shall besiege it. When the LORD your God gives it into your hand, you shall strike all the men in it with the edge of the sword. Only the women and the children and the animals and all that is in the city, all its spoil, you shall take as booty for yourself; and you shall use the spoil of your enemies which the LORD your God has given you. Thus you shall do to all the cities that are very far from you, which are not of the cities of these nations nearby. Only in the cities of these peoples that the LORD your God is giving you as an inheritance, you shall not leave alive anything that breathes. **But you shall utterly destroy them**, the Hittite and the Amorite, the Canaanite and the Perizzite, the Hivite and the Jebusite, **as the LORD your God has commanded you**, so that they may not teach you to do according to all their detestable things which they have done for their gods, so that you would sin against the LORD your God."[8]

God further instructed Israel to utterly annihilate the nations living in the expanded land of Canaan, to make no covenants of peace with them, to show them no mercy at all, to not intermarry with them, to destroy their altars of worship, cut down the tree groves they worshiped, and burn the graven images of their idols:

When Jehovah your God shall bring you into the land where you go to possess it, and has cast out many nations before you, the Hittites, and the Girgashites, and the Amorites, and the Canaanites, and the Perizzites, and the Hivites, and the Jebusites, seven nations greater and mightier than you, and Jehovah your God shall deliver them before you, you shall crush them, completely destroy them. You shall make no covenant with them nor show mercy to them. Nor shall you make marriages with them. You shall not give your daughter to his son, nor shall you take his daughter to your son. For they will turn away your son from following Me, so that they may serve other gods. So the anger of Jehovah will be kindled against you and will destroy you suddenly. But you shall deal with them in this way: you shall destroy their altars and break down their images, and cut down their groves and burn their graven images with fire. For you are a holy people to Jehovah your God. Jehovah your God has chosen you to be a special people to Himself above all people that are upon the face of the earth.⁹

So, the Canaanites were an utterly cursed people who the Israelites were to detest and have no dealings with.¹⁰ And that is what makes this incident involving the Canaanite woman so remarkable. For this woman to dare to even speak to Jesus, a Jew, demonstrated incredible audacity on her part. Where that audacity came from is anyone's guess, but perhaps it was partly due to the fact that it was Jesus who decided to go into the region of Tyre and Sidon, which were both located within the boundaries of Canaan. Again, that region was considered to be off limits to Israelites because it was a cursed land. So great was the contempt for the Canaanites that even Jesus evoked the term the Israelites called them, "dogs!" Nonetheless, Jesus went there, by His own decision, on His own accord, no doubt against the strong protestations of His followers.

Why did He go there? Well, we know one thing: He *never* did anything on his own initiative, but only did what He saw and heard the Father doing.¹¹ He was always "led by the Spirit," to do what He did and said and where He went.¹² It seems apparent, as was the case with so many other incidents during Jesus' fleshly ministry, that the Father had heard the despairing cries of this Canaanite woman and had led Jesus to go to that area where what subsequently occurred occurred. It was preordained that Jesus would have this exchange with the Canaanite woman and her demon-possessed daughter would be delivered.

Obviously, this was a matter of divine mercy and grace! What precipitated it? Jesus revealed that it was because of this Canaanite woman's *great faith*!

Her great despair prompted her to cry out, "Have mercy on me, Lord, Son of David; my daughter is cruelly demon-possessed!" How did she know that Jesus was the Lord and a descendant of David? It is likely that it was partially due to the extraordinary miracles, signs, and wonders she had witnessed in following after Jesus during His ministry. Who else could possibly perform these supernatural feats? But, as with the case of the Centurion, it must be attributed in part also to "the measure of faith"¹³ that God has bestowed unto everyone who believes! Faith is not of ourselves but rather "the gift of God."¹⁴ No one can believe unless God gives him/her the gift of faith to believe! Thank God He freely and generously bestows that gift of faith unto its recipients! Those who refuse to believe do so by their own obstinacy and rebellion. Their unbelief is their own and the evil spirits by which they are influenced!

What was it that so moved Jesus to compassion for this woman and her daughter? Surely, part of the reason is how she was crying out for *mercy*! Jesus was filled with mercy and compassion—to such an extent that the Bible indicates it was only mercy and compassion that would move Him to do anything![15] Nothing moves the heart of God like a cry for mercy with faith!

The disciples were demanding that Jesus send her away because of her repeated heart-piercing outcries. But Jesus did not send her away, but actually answered her, saying: "I was sent *only* to the lost sheep of the house of Israel," indicating His mission was limited to the lost of Israel—Jews. But she just would not be denied and bowed down at the feet of Jesus, imploring Him to help her!

Still Jesus' answer was: "It is not good to take the *children's* bread and throw it to the **dogs**." It seemed like such a cruel and harsh thing for the Son of God to say to this poor woman who was begging for Jesus to help her. But we know that Jesus was full of compassion, so it was not that He was being hard and uncompassionate. We can only speculate that Jesus was testing her resolve and the legitimacy of her faith.

Again, with inordinate tenacity and audacity, the woman's response to Jesus was: "Yes, Lord; but even the dogs feed on the crumbs which fall from their masters' table."

Wow! Who would even have the presence of mind in such a public exchange with the Son of God to make such a bold, audacious statement? Why wasn't she terrified of speaking in that courageous way to a Jew who was not just any Jew but the Son of God and the long-awaited Messiah? Again, the answer can only be that it was God-given **great faith** that rose up in her, driven by the desperate need for her daughter to be delivered!

Great Faith of Those Enshrined in the Faith Hall of Fame

Hebrews 11 delineates and describes the acts of numerous Old Testament characters who exercised extraordinary **great faith** during their lifetimes. The chapter essentially establishes what could be referred to as a "Faith Hall of Fame," a la such enshrinement entities as: the NFL, MLB, NBA, NH, IFHOF Halls of Fame, devoted to memorializing elite career achievers in each of those professional sports leagues, along with similar entities associated with the vast network of subordinate national and international collegiate and precollegiate sports conferences and associations. Of course, such halls of fame are by no means limited to the sports realm; a nearly boundless number of similar entities exist relative to many other fields of endeavor from music to journalism to education to entertainment, to...you name it.

The list of those receiving mention by name in the Faith Hall of Fame include such Old Testament Saints as: Abel, Enoch, Noah, Abraham, Sarah, Isaac, Jacob, Esau, Joseph, Moses' parents, Moses, inhabitants of Jericho, Rahab the harlot, Gideon, Barak, Samson, Jephthah, David, Samuel, and by appellation, the (O.T.) prophets. Each of these individual's accomplishments are amply described in Scripture and well-known to Bible students, thus time and space to examine each of them individually here is unnecessary, but the irrefutable fact that each of them accomplished great exploits through the exercise of **great faith** certainly makes this cast of uncommon characters worthy of mention in the context of this chapter. The author (and the Holy Spirit, who inspired this memorialization of these elite achievers of acts of faith) said of them:

> who *by faith* conquered kingdoms, performed acts of righteousness, obtained promises, shut the mouths of lions, quenched the power of fire, escaped the edge of the sword, from weakness were made strong, became mighty in war, put foreign armies to flight. Women received back their dead by resurrection; and others were tortured, not accepting their release, so that they might obtain a better resurrection; and others experienced mockings and scourgings, yes, also chains and imprisonment. They were stoned, they were sawn in two, they were tempted, they were put to death with the sword; they went about in sheepskins, in goatskins, being destitute, afflicted, ill-treated (men of whom the world was not worthy),

wandering in deserts and mountains and caves and holes in the ground. And all these, *having gained approval through their faith,* did not receive what was promised, because God had provided something better for us, so that apart from us they would not be made perfect.[16]

The following is a listing, according to the text, of the mighty acts those of the Hall of Fame performed *by faith*:

- conquered kingdoms;
- performed acts of righteousness;
- obtained promises;
- shut the mouths of lions;
- quenched the power of fire;
- escaped the edge of the sword;
- from weakness were made strong;
- became mighty in war;
- put foreign armies to flight;
- they (Moses and Israelites) passed through the Red Sea as though they were passing through dry land; and the Egyptians, when they attempted it, were drowned.

Among the afflictions and trials these Faith Giants suffered *by faith* yet persevering in faith were:

- (Moses) refused to be called the son of Pharaoh's daughter, choosing rather to endure ill-treatment with the people of God than to enjoy the passing pleasures of sin, considering the reproach of Christ greater riches than the treasures of Egypt; for he was looking to the reward; left Egypt, not fearing the wrath of the king; for he endured, as seeing Him who is unseen; kept the Passover and the sprinkling of the blood, so that he who destroyed the firstborn would not touch them;
- women received back their dead by resurrection;
- others were tortured, not accepting their release, so that they might obtain a better resurrection;
- others experienced mockings and scourgings, yes, also

chains and imprisonment;
- they were stoned;
- they were sawn in two;
- they were tempted;
- they were put to death with the sword;
- they went about in sheepskins, in goatskins, being destitute, afflicted, ill-treated;
- (men of whom the world was not worthy) wandering in deserts and mountains and caves and holes in the ground.

The reward they received for their exploits by faith:

And all these, having gained approval through their faith, did not receive what was promised, because God had provided something better for us, so that apart from us they would not be made perfect.

Once again, let us be reminded that God provided us this record regarding what these people had to endure in order to inherit the promises as an example to us living in the Last Days with respect to the cost of genuine faith! Let us be sure to take it to heart and pledge our lives to living our lives and everything we do in the course of our lives *by faith*!

Would to God that those comprising the End-times Remnant Church that Jesus is building, "upon whom the ends of the ages have come,"[17] would aspire to achieve great exploits on behalf of Christ and His Kingdom in this hour as part of the overall process of the accomplishment of the end-times purposes and plans of God! God only knows what would happen if that were to occur!

Summing Up

To this point we have identified and examined the various levels and degrees of faith delineated in Scripture. From here forward, we will contemplate some other matters relative to faith and what we need to do to ensure that we are cooperating and comporting with the workings of the Holy Spirit, as our Helper in all spiritual things, that will allow *Faith That Works* to operate freely and fully in our lives.

Endnotes

1. Mat. 8:5-13
2. Mat. 9:21
3. Luke 8:46
4. Rom. 12:3
5. Mat. 15:21-28
6. Gen. 12:2-3
7. Gen. 9:25-26
8. Deu. 20:12-18
9. Deu. 7:1-6; MKJV
10. Cf., John 4:9
11. John 8:28; cf., John 5:30; 8:42; 10:18; 11:51; 12:49; 14:10; 16:13
12. Mat. 4:1; Luke 4:1
13. Rom. 12:3
14. Eph. 2:8
15. Mat. 20:34; Mark 1:41
16. Heb. 11:33-40
17. 1 Cor. 10:11

Chapter Eight
FAITH FOR HEALING AND DELIVERANCE

Do you need physical or psychological healing? Millions do. In this chapter I offer a brief summary of what God says in His Word concerning healing and deliverance, how to appropriate faith for same, and thereby manifest it in your life.

If you need healing in your life—spiritual, physical, or psychological—I encourage you to diligently and faithfully follow the instructions offered herein to allow the healing virtue of Jesus the Healer to flow into your life.

If you are not well–psychologically or physically–you really have nothing to lose—following the instructions herein will not harm you in any way—and you have everything to gain! Try it!

God's Highest Desire And Will Is For Your Total Wellness

> Beloved, I wish *above all things* that thou mayest prosper and be in health, even as thy soul prospereth.[1]

Nothing is of greater priority and importance to God than your prosperity, or complete wholeness in every part of your life—financially, physically, psychologically, and spiritually.

In the account of Jesus' encounter with the Roman Centurion, Jesus responded to the Centurion's plea for Jesus' help, saying, "I *will* come and heal him."

> And when Jesus entered Capernaum, a centurion came to Him, imploring Him, and saying, "Lord, my servant is lying paralyzed at home, fearfully tormented." Jesus said to him, "I *will* come and heal him."[2]

Notice the word, "will." Jesus, being the Son of God and God the

Son, as well as the Word made flesh, never speaks idly, nor does He equivocate. Unlike humans, He always speaks precisely what He means and means precisely what He speaks. In invoking the word, "will," Jesus was stating unequivocally that it was/is His will to heal! And since God is no respecter of persons, meaning, He does not favor some over others, whatever God/Jesus speaks to one person in the Bible we can safely apply that statement to ourselves as well, unless there is some specific, identifiable, obvious reason in the context of a particular circumstance that it cannot be. Rare are those exceptions, however. We can safely deduce from this and other passages of Scripture that it is indeed *always* the will of God to heal those who call upon Him in faith.

Some denominations have indoctrinated their devotees going back to the 1800s to always add the phrase, "if it be thy will" at some juncture in the prayer they pray for someone, especially when it comes to prayer for healing. You might as well not pray at all if you add that phrase to your prayer, because Scripture makes it clear in several places that God only answers prayer that is prayed in accordance with His will.[3] Certainly, the Holy Spirit "intercedes for the saints *according to the will of God*" only.[4] The fact is, it would be literally impossible for God to do anything or answer any prayer that is contrary to His will! Moreover, injecting that phrase into a prayer is a faith killer! It utterly undermines any faith that either the pray-er or the pray-ee has or is trying to exert in the matter. This matter of the necessity to know what the will of God is on a matter and to pray in accordance with His will is precisely what the Apostle Paul was alluding to in his letter to the Roman church when he said:

> In the same way the Spirit also helps our weakness; for we do not know how to pray as we should, but the Spirit Himself intercedes for us with groanings too deep for words;[5]

Another incident that proves the point that Jesus, the Healer, Jehovah-Rapha, is always willing to heal—the incident of Jesus cleansing a leper who came to Him imploring Him to heal him—is recorded in three of the four gospels.[6] In Matthew's synoptic, this incident is recorded as transpiring just prior to the Roman Centurion incident.

> When Jesus came down from the mountain, large crowds followed Him. And a leper came to Him and bowed down before Him, and said, "Lord, if You are *willing*, You can make me

clean." Jesus stretched out His hand and touched him, saying, "**I am** *willing*; be cleansed." And immediately his leprosy was cleansed.[7]

Jesus' response reverberates with the same identifying words Jehovah-God spoke to Moses when he asked Him who shall he tell the Israelites sent him when he went to them declaring that Jehovah-God sent him as the human deliverer through whom He would deliver them from their four-and-a half centuries of unspeakably oppressive bondage under the cruel mastery of pharaoh and the Egyptians. God's response was: "Tell them '**I am** who **I am**' sent you!" This revelation came in the infamous encounter of Moses with Jehovah in the incident of the burning bush when Moses had endured forty years of banishment to the backside of the wilderness.

> Now Moses was pasturing the flock of Jethro his father-in-law, the priest of Midian; and he led the flock to the west side of the wilderness and came to Horeb, the mountain of God. The angel of the LORD appeared to him in a blazing fire from the midst of a bush; and he looked, and behold, the bush was burning with fire, yet the bush was not consumed. So Moses said, "I must turn aside now and see this marvelous sight, why the bush is not burned up." When the LORD saw that he turned aside to look, God called to him from the midst of the bush and said, "Moses, Moses!" And he said, "Here I am." Then He said, "Do not come near here; remove your sandals from your feet, for the place on which you are standing is holy ground." He said also, "I am the God of your father, the God of Abraham, the God of Isaac, and the God of Jacob." Then Moses hid his face, for he was afraid to look at God. The LORD said, "I have surely seen the affliction of My people who are in Egypt, and have given heed to their cry because of their taskmasters, for I am aware of their sufferings. "So I have come down to deliver them from the power of the Egyptians, and to bring them up from that land to a good and spacious land, to a land flowing with milk and honey, to the place of the Canaanite and the Hittite and the Amorite and the Perizzite and the Hivite and the Jebusite. "Now, behold, the cry of the sons of Israel has come to Me; furthermore, I have seen the oppression with which the Egyptians are oppressing them. "Therefore, come now, and I will send you to Pharaoh, so that

you may bring My people, the sons of Israel, out of Egypt." But Moses said to God, "Who am I, that I should go to Pharaoh, and that I should bring the sons of Israel out of Egypt?" And He said, "Certainly I will be with you, and this shall be the sign to you that it is I who have sent you: when you have brought the people out of Egypt, you shall worship God at this mountain." Then Moses said to God, "Behold, I am going to the sons of Israel, and I will say to them, 'The God of your fathers has sent me to you.' Now they may say to me, 'What is His name?' What shall I say to them?" God said to Moses, "**I AM WHO I AM**"; and He said, "Thus you shall say to the sons of Israel, '**I AM** has sent me to you.'"[8]

There are so many implications concerning God and who He is in this divine conversation of Moses with God that it would literally require another whole book to even begin to explain it all. So obviously I cannot do that here, but what I will say is that the overall theme of what God is saying here, not only to Moses, but to everyone in human history who will ever read the story, which is that the Omnipotent and Almighty Jehovah God, with whom all things are possible and nothing is impossible, is everything we as subservient mere humans need Him to be to us in every situation and circumstance of life we will ever encounter. If we will call upon Him for every scenario we face in life, He is and will be the God who is more than enough—Jehovah-Shaddai!

God Himself used this Hebrew word, Shaddai, when He identified Himself to Abraham:

> Now when Abram was ninety-nine years old, the LORD appeared to Abram and said to him, "I am *God Almighty* (El-Shaddai); Walk before Me, and be blameless. "I will establish My covenant between Me and you, And I will multiply you exceedingly."[9]

God went on in this encounter with Abraham to declare that He would establish His covenant not only with Abraham, but also with Abraham's descendants in perpetuity as an everlasting covenant:

> "I will establish My covenant between Me and *you and your descendants after you throughout their generations* for an *everlasting* covenant, to be God to you and to your descendants after you."[10]

The exceedingly Good News is that this, of course, means that God's everlasting seven-fold covenant extends also to every Born Again believer that ever lives! In that covenant, the promises of which are delineated in Psalm 91, God pledges to:

1) **Deliver you and protect you.** "For he will deliver you from..." (v. 3). "There shall no evil befall thee, neither shall any plague come nigh thy dwelling. For he shall give his angels charge over thee, to keep thee in all thy ways" (v. 10-11).

2) **Set you on high.** "...I will set him on high, because he hath known my name" (v. 14).

3) **Answer you when you call on Him.** "When he calls to me, I will answer him..." (v. 15a).

4) **Be with you in trouble and deliver you.** "I will be with him in trouble; I will rescue him..." (v. 15b).

5) **Honor you.** "...and honor him" (v. 15b).

6) **Satisfy you with long life.** "With long life I will satisfy him..." (v. 16a).

7) **Show you, His salvation.** "...show him my salvation." (v. 16b).

Indeed, our God—El-Shaddai—is *more* than enough! He is not the barely-get-by God or the God of just enough. Rather, He is El-Shaddai, the God who is *more* than enough—the God without limitations! Throughout the Old Testament, account after account demonstrates El-Shaddai reveals Himself over and over in the lives of men and women: leaders, prophets, priests, and kings, but also to farmers and lowly shepherds. In supernatural and superfluous ways, He delivers them, provides for them, and saves them. Unfortunately, though, many today relegate God's work to the past or to those who they think were "special" or more worthy than they. Many surmise that God only did those things back in the Old Testament times and He doesn't do those things today. But God declares in Malachi 3:6 that He IS God and He changes not! What He was, He still is! What He still is, He always has been and always will be! He is, always has been, and always will be El-Shaddai, the God who is *more* than enough, who is able to abundantly supply every need we will ever have "according to His riches in Glory by Christ Jesus!"[11] Hallelujah! Praise His Holy Name!

Healing Is Inherent in God's Nature

By nature, God is the ultimate and supreme Healer! Healing is just part of who He is! He declares in Exodus 15:16: "For I am the LORD who **heals** you." This passage in the original language of Hebrew identifies the Lord (the preincarnate Christ Jesus) as Jehovah-Rapha, the Lord who heals you, which is one of the many names He consigns to Himself in Scripture.

One of the greatest and most comprehensive volumes ever written on this topic is, *Christ The Healer*, written by the late F.F. Bosworth (1877-1958), and first published in 1924, that has sold well over half-a-million copies. His late son, Robert, published a revised edition in 2008 that he also narrated. The books and audiobook are available on Amazon and other retail distributors. They all are well worth your time and money.

Divine Healing Requires Faith in the Lord Jesus Christ

This divine promise of healing from the Lord comes with one caveat, however: You must *believe* upon the Lord Jesus Christ as your personal Savior in your heart and confess that belief with your mouth!

> They said, "Believe in the Lord Jesus, and you will be saved (lit., delivered, healed, restored), you and your household."[12]

Divine Healing Requires Profession of Faith in the Lord Jesus Christ

> But what does it say? "THE WORD IS NEAR YOU, IN YOUR **MOUTH** AND IN YOUR **HEART**"—that is, the word of faith which we are preaching, that if you confess with your mouth Jesus as Lord, and believe in your heart that God raised Him from the dead, you will be saved; for with the heart a person believes, resulting in righteousness, and with the mouth he confesses, resulting in salvation (lit., healing, restoration, deliverance). For the Scripture says, "WHOEVER BELIEVES IN HIM WILL NOT BE DISAPPOINTED."[13]

Divine Healing is Part of Relationship with God

The healing God wants to effect in the lives of His Human Creation is embedded in the eternal relationship He seeks with them. Jesus is the door or gateway into that relationship, which is activated by believing upon Him:

> "I am the door; if anyone enters through Me, he will be saved,

and will go in and out and find pasture."[14]

Jesus said to him, "I am the way, and the truth, and the life; no one comes to the Father but through Me."[15]

Jesus Christ IS The Word of God

It is vital to understand that the Word of God is Jesus Himself.[16] Alternately, the obverse of that statement is also true: Jesus Himself *is* the Word of God. Thus, to receive and believe the Word of God is to receive and believe upon Jesus Christ.

Effective Faith Comes By Hearing The Word of God

So faith comes from hearing, and hearing by the word of Christ.[17]

There is only one way God prescribes in His Word to appropriate effective faith—faith that works in your life—that is, through hearing (reading is a form of hearing) the Word of God. The Word of God heard produces effectual faith!

God's Power Is Contained/Manifest/Resident In His Rhema-Word

Hebrews 1:3 speaks of "the WORD of His (God's) POWER!" This is alluding to the fact that all of God's POWER is resident or contained in His WORD! God created the entire Creation by verbalizing, speaking, His WORD!

Three words are used in the New Testament in the original language that are rendered "word" in English. One of those words is *graphe*, which refers to the written Word, the words as they appear in the Bible. The *Graphe*-word, i.e., the written Word of God, is not in itself active, or animated, activated, alive, and thus has no power to produce anything. It becomes active, alive, animated, activated when it is spoken or verbalized by a human-being on Earth, transforming it from the *graphe* to the *Rhema*-Word.

It is the *Rhema*-Word of God that is active, animated, activated, alive,[18] and has the power to produce what it says, to bring into being on Earth the words it contains.

For the word of God is **living** and **active** and sharper than any two-edged sword, and piercing as far as the division of soul and spirit, of both joints and marrow, and able to judge the thoughts and intentions of the heart.[19]

When the *Rhema*-Word of God *is* spoken, verbalized, all of God's creative POWER is released to perform what it says, and God said His Word shall not return unto Him void without accomplishing the purpose for which it was sent.[20] Moreover, He declares that He is WATCHING OVER His Word to PERFORM it or bring it into being.[21]

The very reason God has given us sixty-six books containing His Word is for us to *speak* it, *verbalize* it, *declare* and *decree* it—and thereby **ACTIVATE** it on Earth and in our lives!

Return To The Lord And Decree God's Word Over Your Life

Indeed, God promises in His Holy Word that anyone who will return to the Lord, He will restore them and their relationship with Him, and that when those who have so returned decree a thing that is predicated on and congruous with the Word of God, that which they have decreed and declared will be established or manifest or come to pass![22]

That is a mindboggling and amazingly powerful promise from the Almighty God who cannot lie![23]

God Sent His Word To Heal Those Who Trust In Him From Illness

I am the LORD who **heals** you."[24]

He sent His word and **healed** them, And delivered them from their destructions.[25]

That is why He sent His Word (the Son of God/God the Son Himself) to **HEAL** you! Remember what I said earlier: Jesus Himself **IS** the Word of God and the Word of God **IS** Jesus! The living Word of God is not just words printed on paper, but the Word of God is a Person, the Second Member of the triune Godhead—God the Son, the Son of God!

Healing Is Included In The Finished Work Of Christ On The Cross

Healing—of every sort and kind of illness, i.e., anything that is not wellness—was purchased for us by Jesus when He surrendered His physical life on the cross at Calvary.

> But He was wounded for our transgressions, He was bruised for our iniquities; The chastisement for our peace (lit., total well-being) was upon Him, And by His stripes we *are* **healed**.[26]

> and He Himself bore our sins in His body on the cross, so that we might die to sin and live to righteousness; for by His wounds

you *were* **healed.**[27]

Positionally, in the Spirit realm, healing is a done deal! Christ's last words on the Cross were: "It is finished!" Healing was included in that finished work of Christ on that old-rugged cross, for in so dying for us and in our stead, He redeemed us from the curse of law (death), having taken on and become that curse for us and in our stead:

> Christ hath redeemed us from the curse of the law, being made a curse for us: for it is written, Cursed is every one that hangeth on a tree:[28]

This is why the prophet Isaiah in his Messianic prophecy, looking ahead hundreds of years to the cross, prophesied, "by His stripes (the 39 lashes with which Jesus was savagely brutalized) we **are** healed," and the Apostle Peter, looking back upon the substitutionary death of Christ on the Cross at Calvary, which he witnessed firsthand, declared "by His wounds you **were** healed."

Healing Is A Done Deal

Healing is a *fait accompli*—an accomplished fact—a done deal! It is indeed a finished work! It is a present possession of every genuine and sincere believer in Christ who will gaze upon the finished work of Christ purchased on that old-rugged Cross raised up on that hill called Golgotha, the Hill of the Skull, more than 2,000 years ago, where our complete and whole redemption was purchased by the shed blood of Christ as He laid down His life as the Ransom for us all!

Faith Without Works Is Dead

Though all I have said thus far about faith, God's Word, and divine healing is true, nevertheless, there is one other truth that is absolutely vital for you to understand in order to activate all these truths in your life: Faith without the kind of works or actions that verifies your belief in God's promises will do you absolutely no good at all and will not work for you. God declares in James 2:26 that faith without works is useless and dead, ineffectual, lifeless, and powerless. The Expanded Bible version renders the verse this way:

> Just as a person's body that does not have a spirit [the force of life that animates the body[29]] is dead, so faith that does nothing [without works] is dead!

Another version paraphrases the verse, saying essentially that faith that is merely rhetorical and does nothing to convert the profession of faith into real actions, produces nothing, and is not real or genuine faith. Real faith, then, or effective faith, is productive; it *produces* what it *professes*. That's why it is critical to not only read the Word of God, in this case, passages about healing, but also to *hear* them, really hear them, and then speak them—converting those written or graphe-words to effective rhema-words, verbalized words—in order to produce healing in your life.

I will expand much more on this matter of faith without works being dead in Chapter Fifteen.

For those not accustomed to any of these principles, it all may sound far-fetched or like some kind of hocus-pocus or even metaphysical mumbo-jumbo, but it's not, not by a long shot! In fact, it is entirely consistent with what God Himself instructs in His very own, God-breathed Word. And He Himself testifies concerning His Holy Word:

> All Scripture is inspired by God (lit., God-breathed) and profitable for teaching, for reproof, for correction, for training in righteousness;[30]

Conclusion

In this chapter we have examined faith for healing and deliverance. In the next chapter we take a look at the sort of individuals who possess little or no operable faith in God at all, those who we will call, "The Faithless."

Endnotes

1 3 John 1:2

2 Mat. 8:5-7

3 1 John 5:14-15, e.g.

4 Rom. 8:27

5   Rom. 8:26
6   Mat. 8:3; Mark 1:41; Luke 5:13
7   Mat. 8:1-3
8   Exo. 3:1-14
9   Gen. 17:1-2
10 Gen. 17:7
11 Plp. 4:19
12 Acts 16:31
13 Rom. 10:8-11
14 John 10:9
15 John 14:6
16 Rom. 10:17
17 c.f., John 1-14; 1 John 1:1-3
18 c.f., Heb. 4:12
19 Heb. 4:12
20 Isa. 55:11
21 Jer. 1:12; cf., Ezk. 12:25
22 Job 22:28
23 Num. 23:19
24 Exo. 15:26
25 Psa. 107:20
26 Isa. 53:5
27 1 Pet. 2:24
28 Gal. 3:13
29 Gen. 2:7
30 2 Tim. 3:16

Chapter Nine

THE FAITHLESS

The focus of this chapter is the ilk of human beings who lack the types of faith described in previous chapters, which means they are either *atheists* (those who assert there is no God [though God calls such people "fools"[1]]), or *agnostics* (those who maintain they do not know if there is a God, i.e., a divine being, who is the Creator of all things), or they are *religious devotees* (those who practice some form of false, antichrist religiosity made up of only the false "faith" of mental assent or acknowledgement of the existence of an impersonal and unknowable God to whom they ascribe some form of religious homage, but with whom they have no direct and personal relationship). Every false religion known to mankind is part of this last category. All three ilk of unsaved, unregenerate are those I refer to in this chapter and book as "*The Faithless.*"

There are many references in the Bible to "*The Faithless,*" that is, people—individuals, groups, and even whole nations—who did not respond to God in true or saving faith, or who rejected Him and His dealings with them, or who refused to believe what He said to them, i.e., His Word. And, of course, there are multitudes of such non-believing people living in the world today as well. In fact, people who study such things tell us that there are more than six billion people alive today who have never so much as heard the name of Jesus, who is the only begotten Son of the only true God and the Creator of the Cosmos! Since, those six billion have never heard the name of Jesus, that means they have not been "saved by grace through faith," because that comes about, as we discussed in the previous chapter, when a person accepts Jesus as their personal Savior and Lord in their heart and confess that with their mouth.[2]

The Faithless Israelites

The people at the center of "His Story" that comprises the Old Testament books of the Bible is the Hebrews, or Israel, whose arch-patriarch was Abraham. The Book of Exodus recounts the story of the faithless acts and behavior of the Children of Israel during their forty-year trek in the desert after God had supernaturally delivered them from 430 years of slavery in Egypt that God punished them for their centuries of stubborn disobedience of His Laws. The Spirit of God informs us twice in the New Testament that the account of Israel's long history of disobedience was written (primarily by Moses) and recorded in the Bible as instruction and examples to last-days believers.[3] Despite having witnessed firsthand many supernatural acts of God during their deliverance process, the two-million plus Israelites, as a nation, remained "Faithless Ones."

Moses, who was Hebrew by birth and adopted and reared by an Egyptian Pharaoh, was the man God had supernaturally birthed, prepared, and anointed and appointed at the age of eighty to lead the Israelites out from their captivity into a territory in Canaan God had designated for the Jewish people to possess and occupy forever. The Bible calls it the "Promise Land," and describes it as a land of supernatural abundance "flowing with milk and honey."

When the exact time for the Hebrews' deliverance out of Egypt had finally come, Jehovah God, in a pitched battle between good and evil, openly displayed His great majesty and mighty power over the false gods of Egypt in the form of ten supernatural plagues He orchestrated upon the Egyptians—one for each of the ten false gods the Egyptians worshiped—wreaking severe devastation and ultimately massive loss of life. But, during all the decimation God wrought, the lives of the Hebrews were miraculously spared, and God showered them with multiple manifestations of His love, provision, and protection. Yet, despite God's demonstration of His abundant lovingkindness toward the Hebrews, throughout the Book of Exodus, we see the Children of Israel, continually murmuring and complaining about God, His provision for them, and the leaders He appointed over them. They never understood that God's ways of caring for them during this wilderness period were all designed to produce faith in their hearts toward Him.

In Chapter 14, we read about the mightiest act of all in the story of the Israelites' deliverance—the crossing of the Red Sea. When Pharaoh and the Egyptians realized the people who had served them as slaves more than four centuries had departed Egypt, Pharaoh reversed his decision to let the Children of God go and pursued them with all the Egyptian armies unto the Red Sea. With the Red Sea before them and the Egyptian armies in hot pursuit behind them, Moses cried out to God as to what he should do, and the Lord instructed him to stretch out his hand, holding his staff toward the Sea. When he did, God supernaturally parted the waters of the sea and congealed the water into a towering wall of water. With Pharaoh's armies speedily closing in upon them, as soon as the last Israelite crossed safely through the watery tunnel on dry ground, God released the wall of water, drowning Pharaoh and his armies with 600 chariots and horses in the Red Sea.

The Bible tells us that following this great and miraculous deliverance by Jehovah God, Moses led the Israelites in singing a new song celebrating the triumphant victory God had orchestrated over their former captors, while Miriam, the sister of Aaron, led the women in jubilant singing and dancing extolling Jehovah for the glorious victory as well.[4] Though, in the very next verses we see the Israelites' ecstatic rejoicing and exultation of Jehovah for His mightiness was quickly replaced with murmuring and complaining as Moses led them from the Red Sea three days into the Wilderness of Shur and ultimately to the waters of Marah that were too bitter to drink, and the people grumbled at Moses in fear and unbelief, charging that he and his God had brought them out to the wilderness so that they would all die. The sad part of the story of the faithless Israelites is that out of two million plus people, despite all they had seen and encountered of God's supernatural deliverance and provision for them during their trek through the wilderness, only *one* man persevered and persisted in believing and trusting faith in God—the man Moses.

Throughout their forty-year wilderness trek which was in actuality only an eleven-day journey from Egypt to their final destination, Jehovah God repeatedly demonstrated by His many mighty displays of supernatural power His superabundant and unfailing love for the Hebrews, yet their persistent faithless professions continued, and constant murmuring and complaining finally cost them entrance into the Promise Land that "flowed with milk and honey!"

Ultimately, out of the estimated four million people the nation grew to following their deliverance from Egypt forty years prior, when they finally arrived at their final destination, only two men of the original estimated two million entered into the Promise Land. All the rest perished in the wilderness, due to their obstinate and persisting unbelief![5] Sadly, by an odd twist of fate, even the one man who remained faithful to God and did not succumb to unbelief and fear, Moses, also was not allowed to enter in, but only allowed to view the expansive and fertile geography of the Promise Land remotely from atop a mountain where he died.

The Faithless Disciples

In the now infamous story when Jesus instructed the disciples to obtain a boat in which they could all cross over to the other side of the Sea of Galilee, we find the Twelve were "Faithless Ones" as well.

"On that (same) day" that Jesus had fed the multitudes after following Him around the countryside for three days as He was ministering to the sick, demonized, and needy, "when evening had come," He said to the twelve disciples, "Let us go over to the other side (of the Sea of Galilee)."[6]

After launching the boat, no doubt exhausted from the previous days of ministering to the multitudes who came out to see Him, Jesus went to sleep on the sailor's cushion (a leather cushion reserved for the captain of the boat to lean on as he directed the navigation of the boat). While He slept, a fierce hurricane-force storm suddenly encompassed the sea surrounding the boat. The disciples, most of whom were professional fishermen who had navigated this expansive lake many times before, became terrified, and woke up the Master, and were asking Him with the anger of terror if He "cared" that they were all in the process of perishing! Jesus stood up, rebuked the storm, and commanded peace to come to the atmosphere. He then rebuked the disciples and angrily asked *them* why it was that they had no faith but only fear? At this point, having seen the authority He had just asserted over the winds and waves, the text indicates, they wondered who this *Man* who they had been following for some time now really was, "that even the wind and the sea obey Him?"[7]

Isn't it strange that these very disciples had witnessed many miracles, signs, and wonders walking right beside Jesus? Incredibly, despite their firsthand observations walking and fellowshipping with Jesus for many days and possibly months at this point, their degree of faith was so limited so as to be non-existent when their lives were on the line, or at least so they had determined, due to Satan successfully blinding their minds and hearts[8] to being able to really know who Jesus was, that He was not merely a Man, but truly was the Son of God and God the Son!

Still today, we find among purporting disciples of Jesus, those who are at times "Faithless Ones," living in as much fear, doubt, and unbelief as the original disciples. That's why it's important that each of us test or examine ourselves, as the Spirit commands us, to determine the degree or dimension of faith we are walking in: "Test yourselves to see if you are in the faith; examine yourselves!"[9]

Those Beside the Road

In the Parable of the Sower, Jesus identified the first category of four categories of hearers of the Word of God, as being "those who are beside the road."

> **Mark 4:4, 15**
> 4 and it came about that as he was sowing, some seed fell beside the road, and the birds came and ate it up.
> 15 And these are the ones who are beside the road where the word is sown; and when they hear, immediately Satan comes and takes away the word which has been sown in them.

The description of "those who are beside the road" is another way of referring to "Faithless Ones." Jesus described them as being "beside the road" because, according to verse fifteen, they rejected the Word when they heard it, and thus remained beside the road of Eternal Life, unsaved. Luke's account of the same parable makes this even more evident that "those beside the road" represents the unbelieving and unsaved:

> And those beside the road are those who have heard; then the devil comes and takes away the word from their heart, so that they may not believe and be saved.[10]

Like the other three categories of hearers in the parable, this category *did* hear the Word. Sowers of the Word, particularly evangelists, sow the Word of God as the Divine Seed of God upon those who are *beside the road*, that is, the unsaved, unbelievers, those who are not Born Again, exhorting them to accept the Gospel and to receive Jesus.

Praise God that the Word *is* sown on those beside the road, otherwise no one would ever be saved. Everyone who is saved, was once *not* saved but responded appropriately to the Good News Gospel of Christ when it was presented to them by someone sowing the Word.

God sees to it that the Word of God is sown as a seed upon the unbelieving in order that they might be saved by receiving the Word as the Divine Seed of God that it is. But, once the Seed has been sown, the burden of the results of what takes place in the lives of the hearers of the Word shifts to the hearers! The hearers determine what happens once the Word is sown, and it is no longer the burden of the sowers.

In the case of those Jesus was describing in the Parable of the Sower, which is representative of billions of humans who have heard the Word of God over the six millennia since the Garden of Eden but rejected it, their hearts were hardened against the Word, and they rejected it and the Savior it preaches. As a result, the Seed remained on the surface of the hard ground of their hearts, making it prey to Satan's evil birds that came and snatched it up.

In other words, when the Seed of the Word was not "received implanted"[11] in the good soil of acceptance[12], Satan dispatched evil spirits, which Jesus figuratively referred to as "birds," to take it away. As Jesus said, just as soon as they hear the Word without receiving it, "*immediately* Satan comes and takes away the word which has been sown in them."[13] Satan does this to prevent the hearers from being able to meditate upon the Word any further, and thus preclude any subsequent acceptance of it.

The tragedy is that the "road" in the parable which these people were beside is the "road" of Eternal Life. There is only *one* "road" or "way" to Heaven. Jesus Christ is *the* Way, *the* Truth, and *the* Eternal Life; no one comes to the Father except by Him.[14] His Life, resident within and manifest through true believers, is the only thing that makes them acceptable unto God and qualified for attaining unto the glory of Heaven: "Christ in you, the hope of glory."[15] However, this first category of hearers in the parable, "Faithless Ones," rejected the Word, and as a result remained *beside* the road of Eternal Life—lost and undone without God forever.

Jesus is the Way to Heaven and eternal fellowship with God. He is the gate unto Eternal Life, "and few are those who find it,"[16] even though the call to salvation is extended to "whoever will call upon the name of the Lord."[17] Salvation is a free gift to all those who will accept the Gospel as they hear it, and believe upon the Lord Jesus Christ, receiving Him as Savior and Lord.

Now, there is "another way," a way that seems right unto man, but the final destination of which is death and destruction.[18] The people of the world who refuse to repent and receive the Gospel of Salvation travel this broad and wide, no restraints, licentious, "everything goes" road. But, unfortunately, it leads straight to Hell's unquenchable fires of eternal judgment.[19] The only "exit ramp" off that road is the Lord Jesus Christ.

It is a life or death matter that every hearer of the Word accepts and obeys it, and thereby gets up on the road of Eternal Life, instead of remaining beside it. Hearing alone is not enough. Every hearer must fully accept the Word, receive it implanted in the good soil of a believing heart, and get up on the road of Eternal Life by obeying it.

For a more in-depth explanation regarding the four categories of hearers of the Word Jesus spoke about in The Parable of the Sower, please read my book (and listen to the audiobook), THE MYSTERY OF THE KINGDOM, *Bearing Kingdom Fruit*, which is available through our publishing company, *Real Truth Publications*. The website is: RealTruthPublications.com.

In closing out this chapter, it is imperative to recognize one vital matter regarding faith. God Himself, by the inspiration of the Holy Spirit, expressly informs us that without faith it is impossible to please God:

> And without faith it is impossible to please Him, for he who comes to God must believe that He is and that He is a rewarder of those who seek Him.[20]

So the two requisites to pleasing God are that one must firstly believe that He "is" or that He exists, and, secondly, that He is a "rewarder" of those who seek Him. The rewards that God bestows upon genuine believers throughout their lifetime here on Earth and in the after-life in Heaven and eternal fellowship with God are virtually innumerable, unfathomable, and unexplainable! But it is God who distributes them to us according to His own will and not by any works or merit of our own. All that we have done to allow God to pour them out upon us in abundance is to *believe* upon Him, *receive* Him into our heart and consciousness, and *accept* Him as our Lord, Master, and Savior. When we do, He lavishes us with "every spiritual blessing in the heavenly places in Christ,"[21] and "everything pertaining to life and godliness":

> seeing that His divine power has granted to us everything pertaining to life and godliness, through the true knowledge of Him who called us by His own glory and excellence. For by these He has granted to us His precious and magnificent promises, so that by them you may become partakers of the divine nature, having escaped the corruption that is in the world by lust.[22]

When we are pleasing to God, as a result, we enjoy full and unfettered fellowship with Him *now*, in this life, and will continue to be throughout all eternity! Jesus came in order to give us the Zoe-life of God in abundant measure.[23]

In this chapter, we looked briefly at those who are without faith, whom we called, "The Faithless." Next, we examine the vital matter of how we, as Born Again believers, go about obtaining and activating effective faith in our personal lives.

Endnotes

1. Psa. 14:1; 53:1
2. Rom. 10:8-10
3. Rom. 15:4; 1 Cor. 10:11
4. Exo. 15:1-21
5. Heb. 3:16-19
6. Mark 4:35
7. Mark 4:41
8. 2 Cor. 4:4
9. 2 Cor. 13:5
10. Luke 8:12
11. Jas. 1:21
12. Mark 4:20
13. Mark 4:15
14. John 14:6, italics added
15. Col. 1:27
16. Mat. 7:14
17. Rom. 10:13
18. Pro. 14:12; 16:25
19. Mat. 7:13
20. Heb. 11:6
21. Eph. 1:3
22. 2 Pet. 1:3-4
23. John 10:10

Chapter Ten

OBTAINING AND ACTIVATING FAITH

We come now to one of the most important aspects of this matter of faith, conclusive teaching elucidating how it is that a genuine Born Again believer obtains, activates, and implements "the measure of faith" that God so freely bestows upon "whosoever will."

First of all, inherent in what I just said, is the first key. As Jesus told Nicodemus, "You must be born again!"[1] It all begins there—the specific moment when a person recognizes that Jesus is the Savior, repents from his/her sin, and asks Jesus to come by way of the indwelling Holy Spirit to live in his/her human spirit or heart. As discussed previously, that is the moment of regeneration, redemption, and salvation. It happens with the infusion of the Holy Spirit into the person's human spirit, which was previously "dead in (his/her) trespasses and sins":

> And you *were* DEAD in your trespasses and sins, in which you formerly walked according to the course of this world, according to the prince of the power of the air, of the spirit that is now working in the sons of disobedience. Among them we too all formerly lived in the lusts of our flesh, indulging the desires of the flesh and of the mind, and were by nature children of wrath, even as the rest. But God, being rich in mercy, because of His great love with which He loved us, even when we were dead in our transgressions, made us alive together with Christ (by grace you have been saved), and raised us up with Him, and seated us with Him in the heavenly places in Christ Jesus, so that in the ages to come He might show the surpassing riches of His grace in kindness toward us in Christ Jesus. For by grace

you have been saved through faith; and that not of yourselves, it is the gift of God; not as a result of works, so that no one may boast. For we are His workmanship, created in Christ Jesus for good works, which God prepared beforehand so that we would walk in them."[2]

Jesus began His conversation with Nicodemus by saying that unless a person is born again he/she "cannot see (perceive) the kingdom of God."[3] Moreover, He said, "Truly, truly, I say to you, unless one is born of water and the Spirit he cannot *enter* into the kingdom of God."[4] Here, He is referring to water baptism for the forgiveness of sins[5] and the infusion of the Living Waters of God, the Holy Spirit, into the penitent person's human spirit at the moment of rebirth, wherein the born again person becomes "a *new* creature" in Christ, "the old things passed away; behold, all things have become *new*!"[6]

The divine promise of God bestowing "the measure of faith" comes with one caveat: You must *believe* upon the Lord Jesus Christ as your personal Savior in your heart and confess that belief with your mouth!

> They said, "Believe in the Lord Jesus, and you will be saved (lit., delivered, healed, restored), you and your household."[7]

> But what does it say? "THE WORD IS NEAR YOU, IN YOUR **MOUTH** AND IN YOUR **HEART**"--that is, the word of faith which we are preaching, that if you confess with your mouth Jesus as Lord, and believe in your heart that God raised Him from the dead, you will be saved; for with the heart a person believes, resulting in righteousness, and with the mouth he confesses, resulting in salvation (lit., healing, restoration, deliverance). For the Scripture says, "WHOEVER BELIEVES IN HIM WILL NOT BE DISAPPOINTED."[8]

"Everything pertaining to life and godliness"[9] is embedded in the eternal relationship God seeks with His Redeemed Children. Jesus is the door or gateway into that relationship, which is activated by believing upon Him:

> "I am the door; if anyone enters through Me, he will be saved, and will go in and out and find pasture."[10]

> Jesus said to him, "I am the way, and the truth, and the life; no one comes to the Father but through Me."[11]

The Author and Finisher of Our Faith

As indicated earlier, faith begins with God distributing or bestowing it upon a person.[12] Unless God initiated that bestowment no one could have faith in Him at all! The author of the book of Hebrews stated that Jesus is "the author and finisher of faith."[13] Again, this passage further corroborates that faith begins with God Himself (Jesus is the Son of God and God the Son). He gives us the capability to believe in Him. He authors faith.

Jesus also is the "finisher" of our faith. This is likening what He does in our life to the refining work of a carpenter or woodworker. Throughout our life here on earth, God is constantly refining our faith to make it into what it needs to be to produce in and through us what He desires to produce. Indeed, production of what God desires to produce in our lives should be what our lives consist of, though few people ever come to this realization during their lifetimes. I'll talk more on this refining process in the next chapter.

How Faith Comes

So faith comes from hearing, and hearing by the word of Christ.[14]

There are no shortcuts to obtaining genuine faith. Allow me to repeat what I said in the Introduction. The basics of faith, according to the Word of God, are, first: "Faith comes by hearing and hearing by the Word of God." Or, it would be correct to restate it this way: "Faith comes by hearing the Word of God." In other words, hearing or listening (reading is a form of hearing) to God's written Word, the Bible (the Sixty-six books of canonized Scripture), produces faith in the human heart or spirit. As I stated in the Preface, the Rhema-Word of Christ produces real, active, and effectual faith.[15] That is one of the mysterious properties of the Word of God—it produces faith. How it does this, well, as I said, is a mystery. It just does! When we read or listen to it, somehow faith is generated in our heart. Praise God!

Let me also reiterate here what I said in the Introduction that the faith being described throughout this book is this "spiritual faith" that is authored[16] or originated and given[17] by **God**, is communicated and generated through[18] the Word of God, i.e., Jesus,[19] and must be received by and reside in the believer's Born Again human spirit.[20] So, *genuine* faith, comes from God, and therefore is a *spiritual*, not a psychological, mental, intellectual, or emotional matter, for "God is *Spirit*."[21] Thus, genuine faith is *of* the Spirit, *by* the Spirit, *in* the Spirit, and *from* the Spirit. No one can believe or have faith with or through the mind or intellect. Neither can you believe God or the Word of God with your soulish human emotions. It just doesn't work that way!

Emotionalism is NOT spirituality! Don't confuse the two! That's exactly what all religion is based upon—*emotionalism*. The Bible does not preach or promulgate *religion*, but rather *relationship* with God through the Son of God, Jesus Christ! Jesus did not come to Earth to start a new religion. Rather, He came to die a substitutionary death as our Kinsman Redeemer to restore relationship between a Holy God and fallen, apostate Mankind. Satan is the master-religionist! He is the one who invented religion.

What is the religion Satan invented? Humanism! Which is actually a derivative of Satanism because it proposes and promulgates another way to rightstanding with God other than through Christ Jesus. Humanism and all religion, at bottom, is really self-righteousness because it purports fallen Man can achieve or obtain righteousness or holiness or even divinity through self-effort, self-awareness, self-understanding, self-exaltation.

Genuine Faith is a Matter of the Heart

"...for with the HEART man believes...."[22]

All the false religions of the world have one thing in common, they attempt to achieve righteousness (rightstanding) with God (whoever/whatever divinity is in that religion) through the mind/intellect. The fact is: no matter how sincere and how hard a person tries, he/she cannot believe or produce genuine faith with his/her mind. It's an impossibility! True belief/faith is generated and resides in the heart, i.e., the human spirit, and "even that not of yourselves, for it (faith) is the gift of God!"

Biblical faith, on the other hand, is centered on the Word of God, not on the unreliable whims of human reasoning. It places Jesus, who is "the word made flesh," at the absolute center of everything having to do with rightstanding and relationship with God in the here and now and in the ages to come!

Genuine Faith Overcomes the World

For whatever is born of God *overcomes the world*; and this is *the victory that <u>has</u> overcome the world—our* FAITH.[23]

Born Again believers are "born of God!" This is reminiscent of what Jesus said in His conversation with Nicodemus.[24] He stated explicitly and directly to him, "Truly, truly, I say to you, *unless one is* BORN AGAIN he cannot SEE *the kingdom of God*."[25] Obviously, if one cannot see or perceive the Kingdom of God, he cannot enter into it because he does not see or perceive a pathway and entranceway or door to it. And Jesus also stated categorically twice that He alone is the DOOR into the Kingdom of God![26]

To Nicodemus' somewhat argumentative response, "How can a man be born when he is old? He cannot enter a second time into his mother's womb and be born, can he?"[27]—Jesus answered:

"Truly, truly, I say to you, unless one is born of water and the Spirit he cannot enter into the kingdom of God. "That which is born of the flesh is flesh, and that which is born of the Spirit is spirit. "Do not be amazed that I said to you, 'You must be born again.' "The wind blows where it wishes and you hear the sound of it, but do not know where it comes from and where it is going; so is everyone who is born of the Spirit."[28]

"You **must** be born again!" The word "must" connotes something one is *bound* or *compelled* to do, an imperative requirement, something that is not optional but rather a necessity. All that is exactly why Jesus invoked the word "must." It is not something that is optional, but rather absolutely imperative, required. That is, to see, perceive, and enter into the Kingdom God! To do that, one MUST be born again, regenerated by the infusion of the Holy Spirit into one's dead, lifeless, human spirit! There is no other way! Religion won't and can't make it happen! Procuring intellectual knowledge, regardless of volume or quantity, won't and can't make it happen! Only being regenerated by the Holy Spirit can cause a person to be born again!

Regarding the matter of overcoming the world, Jesus stated:

"These things I have spoken to you, so that *in Me* you may have *peace. In the world* you have *tribulation*, but take courage; *I* have *overcome the world*."[29]

What I believe He wants us to take from this statement is that because *He* has overcome the world, *we* share in that victory, because what *He* is, *we* are, what *He* has attained, *we* have attained, and what *He* possesses, *we* possess as Joint-Heirs with Him:

> The Spirit itself beareth witness with our spirit, that we are the children of God: And if children, then *heirs*; *heirs* of God, and *joint-heirs* WITH CHRIST; if so be that we suffer with him, that we may be also glorified together.[30]

In common law, an heir is a person who inherits all the property of a deceased person, as by descent, relationship, will, or legal process.[31] In the case of the collective Body of Christ, all believers are "joint-heirs" with Christ in that we all have inherited from Christ Jesus, pursuant to His death, our spiritual heredity, or spiritual DNA, from Him, by means of our spiritual communion/relationship with Him, by the Last Will and Testament He published in His Word, and the legal process that transpired in the spirit realm when He died in our stead, being wounded for our transgressions, bruised for our iniquities, chastised for our peace, and whipped with the vicious stripes on His back that purchased our physical, mental, emotional, and spiritual healing![32] Being joint-heirs is actually a mathematical miracle, because it does not mean that the inheritance is divided and distributed equally or by designated percentage to the heirs, but rather that each heir is given the full 100% of the inheritance!

Through inspiration of the Holy Spirit,[33] the Apostle Paul informed us that without any equivocation or limitation we (believers in Christ) have already—now, in the here and now, in *this* life—been blessed "with *every* spiritual blessing in the heavenly places in Christ."[34] These spiritual blessings are not relegated to the so-called, "afterlife," as some people refer to it. We do not have to wait until we get to Heaven to possess these spiritual blessings; we've already been blessed with them now. They've been bestowed upon us already, *now*! This is by virtue of the fact that the benefactor died and had proscribed and published a Last Will and Testament (The Bible)! Praise God! We need to do all we can to live in and walk in these manifold blessings *now*! Otherwise, it would be tantamount to being notified that someone has deposited a million dollars into our bank account, and ignoring that notification and acting as if it isn't true, so that we live as if we are poor and maybe even destitute, though in reality, we are actually rich! Tragically, that is exactly how a lot of believers are living, as if they are spiritually poor, when in actuality, they are spiritually rich, and they never make any withdrawals on the spiritual riches stored in their spiritual bank account!

Overcoming the world entails conquering, surmounting, taking dominion or triumphing over the various attacks, troubles, trials, tribulations, and adversity with which we are assailed by our common "adversary, the devil,"[35] who the Apostle Paul identified as "the god of this world"[36] and "prince of the power of the air,"[37] Jesus identified three times as "prince of the world,"[38] and even the Pharisees and scribes knew and identified as "the prince of the devils."[39] Peter informs us that our "adversary, the devil, prowls around like a roaring lion, seeking someone to devour."[40] The King James Version says Satan walks around on the Earth "seeking whom he MAY devour." The word "may" is a term of permission. So, this scripture is saying that Satan is looking for those who will give him permission to devour them, whether tacitly, ignorantly, or passively, instead of offensively resisting him, as James tells us we must do in order to make him flee from us.[41]

We are also warned to give the devil NO PLACE or opportunity[42] to usurpingly insert himself and his cohorts in our lives. The devil is a complete rebel and has no sense of justness or rightness or fairness; if you give him even an inch of place or opportunity in your life, he will do everything he can and stop at nothing to take the proverbial mile!

The Key to Activating Effective Faith

Asking, I believe, is the primary key to believers activating Effective Faith in their lives. The word "ask" appears 63 times in 61 verses in the New Testament (NASB). Some of the most astounding and important statements Jesus made during His fleshly ministry that were memorialized in the four Gospels had to do with *asking* either Him or the Father to do or provide something for or to us.

In Bible parlance, generally speaking, the word *ask* is the equivalent of and entails requesting, petitioning, or requisitioning. Overall, taking into account all the instances in which the word *ask* is used in the New Testament, especially, it is essentially God telling or really *commanding* believers to request, petition, or requisition something of or from Him, i.e., to supply or provide something of which He is the supplier or provider; or to supplicate or entreat Him to do something the believer wants/needs Him to do that only He can do. In other words, it's much like the term used in the military or business enterprises, "put it in writing," or "submit a requisition," or petition a court, for example, to intervene in some situation and order someone or some entity to do something they have not done and should do, meaning, make the request or supplication or requisition in whatever formal means is required by policy, practice, or law.

Bottom-line, the formal request is the *trigger* that initiates the process for the provision of what is being requested to be supplied to the asker, requester, supplicant, or petitioner. Moreover, unless and until the formal request is submitted, the needed provision cannot and will not be supplied no matter how legitimate, critical, and even desperate the need. Our desperation does not move God; it's only *our* FAITH and *his* COMPASSION[43] that moves Him to act on our behalf.

This is exactly what God is conveying in His Word to believers regarding petitioning or asking Him to supply the many and varied needs believers have throughout the course of their lives on Earth! Essentially, God has put His policy and procedure in writing—in His Word—regarding how to obtain or receive the immeasurable provisions He is so ready, willing, and able to supply to us, if we will but ask Him for it!

In one passage, He expressly identifies what is being asked for in prayer and supplication is "requests":

> Be anxious for nothing, but in everything *by prayer and supplication with thanksgiving* let your *requests* be made known to God.[44]

Notice the specificity and forthrightness of the language: "let your requests *be made known* to God." There is no hint of timidity or tenuousness or requirement to cower or beg in those words. It's essentially a command! "Let your...." And it is that same forthrightness and forcefulness that is inherent in every passage of Scripture wherein the word "ask" is invoked. It is reminiscent of the Nike® slogan: "Just Do It!" That is precisely what God is communicating to believers in the usage of the word *ask* or its equivalent in Scripture.

Remember, this is God saying this to whoever will believe Him! It is not, as some religious-minded critics complain, the lowly petitioner presumptuously, blasphemously, irreverently, and arrogantly *prevailing* upon God, demanding that He do something that He is not already predisposed to do! Nothing even close to that! When believers do exactly what God tells them in His Word to do, that is not presumption or blasphemy or arrogance or irreverence, but *obedience*—something that such carnal religious-minded critics will never understand!

And to whom does the passage say to let your requests be known? GOD! That's right, God Himself! It is God telling us in His Word to go directly to Him and let our requests be made known to HIM! So, put that in your spiritual pipe and smoke it, devil, and all your cohorts! You see why I say that some of the most astounding divine statements in the Bible have to do with informing believers what to do regarding their needs—ASK GOD! Put in a requisition to GOD!

Yet, the devil is constantly saying to people, "Oh, don't trouble God for such things! He's too busy! He doesn't care about things like that; those are things you yourself have to deal with. Don't you know how silly and stupid you sound to God talking to Him about such mundane things? You need to talk to God about *spiritual* things only, not material things, and things about Heaven or the afterlife, not about things on Earth in this life! Don't be so carnal and worldly! If you talk to God about those kinds of things, it will just show Him how unspiritual and carnal and silly and immature you are, and you'll be a disappointment to Him!"

I could give a Biblical response to every single one of those statements by the devil attempting to discourage or dissuade people from praying and petitioning God for their legitimate needs, because, believe me, there is a scripture to counter each and every one of those inane and insane arguments. However, time and space will not allow that in this volume.

In Hebrews, the Holy Spirit, through the book's author, goes so far as to instruct or command believers to come unto God's Throne with *boldness* as opposed to *abashedly* or *coweringly*: "Let us therefore come *boldly* unto the throne of grace, that we may obtain mercy, and find grace to help in time of need.[45] The Greek word rendered "boldly" by the translators is a word loaded with meaning and implications. It connotes bluntness, straightforwardness, forthrightness, frankness, outspokenness, confidence, audaciousness, and assuredness. It certainly is conveying that when we come unto God's Throne of Grace our attitude should not be one of cowering or cringing in fear of Him, as if He may respond to us in an austere or angry demeanor, but rather that—

because of what Jesus has accomplished on our behalf as our Kinsmen Redeemer in reconciling us to God and removing the enmity between us and God—we should come unto Him with audacious assuredness that as our loving Heavenly Father He happily welcomes us, eagerly receives us into His presence, and attentively listens as we present our petitions, supplications, and requests to Him! This whole procedure is what is known as "prayer"!

All this is also reflected in Jesus' response to one of His disciple's request, "Lord, teach us to pray!"[46] His response was, "When you pray,"[47] "pray this way, Our Father..."[48] which He continued with what is best known as, "The Lord's Prayer," but would be more accurately titled, "The Believers' Prayer," because the Lord told the disciples that this was the "way" or general template for how to pray unto the Father. Notice Jesus did not say, "IF you pray" but "WHEN you pray.

It is evident by how it happened that He conveyed this prayer to the disciples that He did not intend this to be a verbatim *form* or *liturgical* prayer, but rather a model or template, indicating the general attitude believers should have, along with some general issues, though by no means limited to these particular ones, while petitioning our common Heavenly Abba-Father in prayer.

Jesus also made this clear in His remarks prefacing the prayer:

"When you pray, you are not to be like the hypocrites; for they love to *stand* and *pray* in the *synagogues* and on the *street* corners so that they may be *seen* by men. Truly I say to you, they have their reward in full. "But *you,* when *you* pray, go into your inner room, close your door and *pray to your Father* who is in secret, and your *Father* who sees what is done in secret will reward you. "And when you are praying, do not use meaningless repetition as the Gentiles (lit., heathen, unredeemed, non-believers) do, for they suppose that they will be heard for their *many words*. "**So do not be like them;** for *your Father KNOWS* what you need *before* you *ask* Him."[49]

What Jesus said here is very vital to the matter of prayer and the faith we are enjoined to exert when we are praying, all of which is part and parcel to our topic in this volume. Some people, particularly those functioning in some form of public ministry, relish and become very exercised by *public* praying. I've known or witnessed some preachers who seem to suddenly "come alive" when they take the platform, even more when cameras are rolling, and routinely engage in some excruciatingly long discourse in the form of what they are presenting as "prayer" by sporadically inserting some phrase along the lines of "Father," "Father God," "and Lord," et cetera, forcing people to stand there at their seats for fifteen, twenty, or more minutes, waiting for him to mercifully end his platitudinous monologue with the customary, "in Jesus' name, Amen!"

By the time he's finished his invocational "prayer," the audience is already mentally exhausted and know that what they were just compelled to endure was not even the sermon or message for the day, and that that is yet to come! No wonder there's often a mad dash by some in the audience for the restrooms after such a long religious-sounding oration!

Usually, the content of such "prayers" is essentially extemporaneous preaching of a variety of topics the preacher wants to address that particular day that are too numerous or complex to compile a sermon around, so he touches on them in his prefatory "prayer"!

Friends, I'm sorry, but that *ain't* prayer, and it's certainly by no means *effectual* prayer! That's a *performance*, and a very deceitful one at that! While those who engage in such may seem on the surface to be very pious and righteous (and that's exactly the impression they are trying to evoke) to the naïve or undiscerning, it is *neither*! Again, this, by any definition, is not "prayer"! This is a form of backdoor (usually cowardly) "preaching,"—and sometimes nagging, murmuring, complaining, or criticizing—in the form of false prayer! They have things they want to say but they can't muster the courage to say them openly and directly, so they infuse them into a "prayer". This is what is known as pulpit bullying—weaponizing their leadership position into a "bully-pulpit" to castigate people indirectly or lob verbal grenades at scenarios and events that anger them!

All such public discourse is worthless and meaningless because the speaker is not even addressing God but rather the audience with all this specious, convoluted, and rambling oratory! It certainly is not effectual fervent prayer of a righteous man, but rather ineffectual and inane soliloquies that go no further than ceiling of the room in which they are evoked! They are unequivocally not heard by God, that's for sure!

"The *effectual fervent* prayer of a righteous man availeth much,"[50] James informed us through inspiration of the Holy Spirit. Thus, it would certainly behoove every believer to know what makes prayer *fervent* and *effectual* (effective). Some seemingly pious evocation purported by the evoker to be "prayer," if it is not *effective*, is not really prayer, by definition, but rather inane religious mumbo-jumbo and gobbledygook that is a complete waste of time because it will result in absolutely nothing coming from God! In fact, God does not even *hear* such empty religious incantations, and thank God He doesn't!

Synchronization with God and His Will

Martin Luther profoundly quipped, "Prayer is not overcoming God's reluctance, but laying hold of His willingness." When you believe prayer is your fleshly (and futile) warring to try to overcome God's reluctance in a matter, prayer becomes a laborious and loathsome thing you force yourself to do with reluctance, as opposed to understanding prayer is *two-way* communication in communion with God to determine what *His* will is in the matter, and then praying in accordance with *His* will. John gave us invaluable elucidation regarding prayer, i.e., that God only *hears* prayer that is in accordance with *His* will and those are the prayers that He always answers:

> This is the confidence which we have <u>before Him</u>, that, if we *ask anything* according to HIS *will*, He *hears* us. And if WE KNOW that He *hears* us in *whatever we ask*, we KNOW that we have the *requests* which we have *asked* from Him.[51]

So many people take out of context God's promise to "give you the desires of your heart," passing over the condition that precedes that portion of the verse—"Delight yourself in the Lord!"[52] God will give you the desires of your heart, but He will also take you through some processes that will dramatically and forever change YOUR desires to make them coincide with HIS desires. When *our* desires are synced up with *His* desires, we can, indeed, ask what we want, and it shall be granted us. Effective prayer essentially is asking, petitioning, requesting, for God to *perform* what He has already *promised*! We essentially speak forth His Word! His Word IS His WILL, and His Will is His Word. When we speak His Will it comes into being or comes to pass. That's why both Joshua and David declared that not one word of all God's good promises have ever failed![53]

God's Word is fail-safe. When we have determined God's *Word* on a matter, we have determined His *Will* on the matter as well, and when we speak forth that Word declaring or announcing His Word or even merely repeating His Word back to Him in prayer—two-way conversation with Him—we are inviting His intervention and the application of His promises! That kind of prayer is a sure thing!

Prayer Changes Things!

Prayer brings about change! Prayer prepares the hearts of God's people for the manifestation and fulfillment of His purpose and plans! Mainly and primarily, the change that prayer brings about ultimately is change in *people*. And then changed people become agents for bringing about change where it needs to occur.

No Substitute For Prayer

There is no substitute for prayer. One great preacher on the subject of prayer once wrote, "It is as if God can do nothing unless and until someone first *asks* Him." Ask, seek, knock—this is the process the Lord has decreed that allows His intervention into the affairs of men.[54] He has established forever the principle of free will, and it governs everything upon the Earth. He will not violate it, no matter what; He simply cannot. But, when we ask, He will! "*All* things, *whatsoever* things you ask *in prayer believing*, you *shall* receive." That's as close to carte blanche as it gets, Folks! Our asking gives Him the "permission" or the "opportunity" to do it! But He cannot do it until and unless we ask!

A detrimental mindset that besets us all at times is the presumption that whatever God *wants* to do He *can* and therefore, we presume, *will* do! After all, He can do *whatever* HE *wants*, He's God! Right? *Wrong*! Bad theology! He can only do what WE *want* and ASK Him to do! "The HEAVENS are the heavens of the Lord; But the EARTH He has given to the SONS OF MEN!"[55] *Human* governmental authority in the affairs of men on this planet is sacrosanct! Even His *Word* believers must announce, apply, and assert, over the affairs of men, and everything that transpires on this planet that is not otherwise governed by a God-set and immutable law.

Most Powerful Weapon

Prayer is the most powerful weapon believers possess, yet the enemy makes it seem like the most difficult to wield, and even the most ineffectual. But that is deception! As cited previously, God's Word says, "The effectual and fervent prayer of a righteous man availeth much!" Interpretation? Prayer works! Is it difficult? About as difficult as pondering the next thought that wistfully and effortlessly flutters through your mind. The only thing difficult about prayer is overriding one's flesh that resists us with all its got doing it!

Though thousands of books have been written on the topic, the matter of prayer boils down to this: Prayer is *two-way* communication between people and God. Prayer is conversation with God. But, beyond that, God's highest intent is that prayer would be *communion* or *fellowship* with God. Like the old gospel song says, "Just a little talk with Jesus makes it right!"

Anyone Can Pray

And anyone can pray effectively if he/she prays in faith believing. It is impossible to have faith for and believe for what is wrong, ungodly, and incongruous with the Word of God, for His Word is His will. Neither will you have true faith (for faith is a gift from God) and believe for those things that are not from, of, or inspired by God. That's why it is not as big a deal as some critics of the Gospel make it out to be that God said, "*All* things, *whatsoever* things you ask for in faith believing, you shall receive." He could not have possibly meant for that to be taken literally, they allege. But He meant *exactly* what He said, and said *exactly* what He meant. He always does!

Eighteenth Century English poet and hymnodist, William Cowper, wrote: "Satan trembles when he sees the weakest Christian on his knees." Jailed Paul and Silas praying and singing at midnight caused Hell and earth to shake, breaking open their prison-cell door, setting the two abused and unjustly incarcerated prisoners free![56]

Renowned revivalist and primary founder of Methodism, John Wesley, said, "God does nothing except in response to believing prayer. Prayer is where the action is!"

A.J. Gordon, founder of Gordon College and Cornwell Theological Seminary, speaking of the utter requirement of prayer, stated: "You can do more than pray *after* you have prayed; but you can never do more than pray until you *have* prayed."

Emptying Yourself

Today, too many professing believers petition God to fill them up with everything He's got before they've agonized in prayer to empty themselves out of all they've got!

> "Have this attitude in yourselves which was also in Christ Jesus, who, although He existed in the form of God, did not regard equality with God a thing to be grasped, but emptied Himself, taking the form of a bond-servant, and being made in the likeness of men."[57]

Before the Son of God was manifest in the form of a human, wonder of all wonders, He EMPTIED HIMSELF (one of the great mysteries of God) of His deity for the duration of His existence in the form of a "Man." But after being baptized in water by John the Baptist in the Jordan River and then Baptized in the Holy Spirit, the Word of God says,

> And Jesus being FULL OF THE HOLY GHOST returned from Jordan, and was led *by the Spirit* into the wilderness.[58]

Everyone is full of something...usually *themselves* more than anything else! The burden of every believer must be to EMPTY him/herself and implore God to FILL him/her with the Holy Ghost so that he/she will be "FULL OF THE HOLY GHOST!"

Many people's problem is they are too full of themselves to be full of the Holy Spirit! Regular sessions in the "prayer closet" until you "pray through" sincerely petitioning the Lord to show you some of the junk inside that you need to be emptied of will result in much purging over time.

"Men may spurn our appeals, reject our message, oppose our arguments, despise our persons, but they are helpless against our prayers," said Sidlow Baxter.

Agonizers in Prayer

"The genuinely anointed and appointed Man of God receives the fire-fraught messages that burn the ears of the nominally-believing and the hearts of the unrepentant out of hours spent agonizing prostrate at the altar long before he stands behind any form of pulpit," stated the late Leonard Ravenhill. To paraphrase Leonard Ravenhill, the ecclesiastical realm today is filled with myriad of *organizers* but few **agonizers**!

If more of God's people—"those who are called by (His) name"—fervently pursued a degree in "Knee-ology" fewer of any other kinds of degrees would be needed, and the Church would be more empowered and in every way more powerful on the Earth!

Let us therefore come boldly unto the throne of grace, that we may obtain mercy, and find grace to help in time of need.[59]

The world is FILLED with needs, but God never responds to needs; He responds to the petitions of believing saints! God is not an interloper and never intervenes uninvited and unsolicited in the affairs of men; He only responds and acts when believers ask Him in audacious and believing prayer!

The great preacher and seminary professor, Charles Spurgeon, said it all when he said, "I would rather teach one man to *pray* than ten men to *preach*."

Your Personal Garden of Gethsemane Experience

Eventually and inevitably at some juncture in your personal Christian sojourn with God, you will experience and thenceforth experientially identify with the Son of God's most intense period of agonizing in prayer, Gethsemane. The word literally means "oil-press," referring to the final destiny and destination of olives judged worthy to make the grade for pressing out to produce what to this day is considered the finest and best oil known, *Olive Oil*.

Gethsemane was an olive-tree orchard populated also with various varieties of wildflowers that contemporary locals called a *garden*, located fittingly at the foot of the Mount of Olives, or Mt. Olivet, the very place where Jesus will return and literally stand at His physical return to Earth with the Saints to establish and commence His thousand-year Millennial Reign upon the Earth! The Mount of Olives is the place from which the risen Lord ascended on a cloud of innumerable angels into Heaven in the actual eyesight of the Apostles of the Lamb on the Day of Ascension, for which reason the mount or hill is also known as the Mount of Ascension.

But before the Messiah's agonizing purchase of mankind's salvation on Golgotha, before His triumphant resurrection from the dead, three days later, before His bedazzling and awesome Ascension into Heaven to sit down on His Throne of Rulership, preceding all of that on the eve before His "Passion," as some call it, there was Gethsemane, the place where our Lord and Savior literally agonized in prayer to such an extent that great drops of blood, a medical condition known clinically as, hematidrosis, in which extreme anxiety causes the blood vessels to constrict to the point of rupture, passing blood into the sweat glands, resulting in sweat mixed with blood pressing through the skin—excreted through His skin.

Gethsemane is where the battle was won, where the choicest of all Olives met its glorious destiny, where the Son of God, knowing the trauma and ultimate tumult He was about to suffer as our Kinsmen Redeemer to purchase our redemption by paying the ransom for sin, thrice declared resolutely to His Father, "Nevertheless, not *My* Will, but *Thine* be done."

Gethsemane is the Place Where the Battle of Flesh vs. Spirit is Waged

Yet, during that indescribable all-out war for the souls of men our Lord Jesus single-handedly waged in that garden, the three men He had hand picked to accompany Him to this place of agony, slept through it all, unable to crucify their flesh long enough to intercede with the Lord, "even for one hour," the Lord said, though He had come out of the garden a total of three times to each time find them fast asleep and too groggy to even respond to His sorrowful laments of utter bewilderment and disappointment.

Sometimes it will be in the hours we are facing the most horrendous struggles of our lives, that we will find our own professed closest friends, loved ones, and colleagues fast asleep on the careless cushions of their own self-centeredness outside our Garden of Gethsemane, unable to defeat their flesh long enough to "bear (our) burdens, and so fulfill the law of Christ [Love],"[60] as Scripture commands, in prayer with us. In our Gethsemane crisis in life, we will find it to be the most lonely and alone moments of solitude with the Lord.

Maybe this painful abandonment by others is by divine design, because being alone with the Lord, and with only the Lord at and on our side, is when we discover that the Lord at and on our side is *enough*, and *more* than enough, because He is El Shaddai, the God who is more than enough, who abundantly supplies our every need, even at the neediest, most agonizing precipices of our life! Gethsemane, the birthing room, the "valley of Baca,"[61] the place of sheer agony, is the place where we come to total reliance on the Lord, plus no one else, and we resign our present and future to His Will, and not our own. Gethsemane is the place where we truly come to know our God in the sweetest fellowship and communion of all!

Vocalization of God's Will

So, prayer is a vital key to implementing everything that God desires to do on this planet, within or without of the Church. Knowing God's will is not enough to implement it. His will must also be *vocalized*! Effective prayer is essentially the vocalization of God's Word/Will. We ask; He moves! We ask; He moves! That's the process! That is fervent and effectual prayer of righteous people "who know their God!"[62]

Praying the New Thing into Existence

While time and space will not permit me to go deeply into this matter that I have addressed somewhat in other writings and publications and will be fleshing out more in upcoming books I am writing, it is vital that all this concerning prayer and intercessory prayer be applied to the "new things" that God is moving the End-times Church that Jesus is building into—the new *paradigm*, the new *dimension* of the Spirit. It is not enough for prophets to prophetically *reveal* the "secret counsel" of God, which is a requisite from God for the manifestation of His will.[63] It's not enough for *teachers* to *teach* about it! It's not enough for *preachers* to *preach* about it! It's not enough for apostles to be sent with the apostolic tip-of-the spear, pioneering dimension and measure of the Spirit to bring these things into existence for the first time. The people of God must also PRAY IT—PRAY IT INTO EXISTENCE! There is no substitute for prayer!

Pray What the Prophets Prophesy

Surely the Lord GOD does nothing Unless He reveals His secret counsel To *His servants the prophets*. A lion (*The Lion of the Tribe of Judah*) has roared! Who will not fear? The Lord GOD has spoken! Who can but *prophesy*?[64]

Confirming the word of His *servant*, And performing the purpose of His *messengers*.[65]

What the prophets are foretelling and forthtelling of the purposes and plans of God will not come about or manifest in the natural realm apart from the intercessory praying of the saints! Again, God's people must *pray* what God's prophets *say*! Intercessory prayer regarding any matter is an exercise that unites and unifies the intercessors and brings them into agreement with God's stated purposes and plans—an absolutely critical part of the process of manifesting in the natural the spiritual plans and purposes of God where it can be of real effect to bring about real change. What the Apostle Paul as a spiritual father spoke from his heart to Timothy, his protégée in the Lord, and is now a part of canonized Scripture, is God-breathed admonition to every believer, including every Pentecostal/Neo-Pentecostal believer:

> This COMMAND I entrust to you, Timothy, my son, IN ACCORDANCE WITH THE PROPHECIES previously made concerning you, *that by THEM you may fight the good fight*, KEEPING FAITH and a GOOD CONSCIENCE, which some have rejected and suffered shipwreck in regard to their faith.[66]

Prophesied events do not just happen on their own, automatically, just because they have been prophesied. Prophecy, above all else, is a revelation of the will, the desires, of God. Prophecy (i.e., extrabibilical prophecy) is not *inevitable*, but rather an *invitation* to accept and get into agreement with it in order for it to be fulfilled. Prophesy shows us the target, the objective, but it can only be acquired by fighting the good fight of faith—spiritual warfare—over it! We must take what has been prophesied and steep it in intense and continuous believing prayer, if we are to see it come into being in the natural realm!

The prophesying is only the *first*, and really the *easiest*, step in a two-step process. The next step is the nurturing, the watering, the de-weeding, the cultivating of, the coming into agreement with the word—that manifests through warfare in prayer. When God uses one of His surrogate spokesmen (prophets) to SAY it, then the saints of God must PRAY it, in order for it to come to pass!

In this chapter, we took a good look at the processes involved in obtaining and activating the various levels and degrees of faith God has freely and graciously bestowed upon us. We now turn our attention to the matter of building ourselves up on our most holy faith as God instructs us to do.

Endnotes

1 John 3:7
2 Eph. 2:1-10
3 John 3:3
4 John 3:5
5 Mat. 3:11; 26:28; 24:47; Mark 1:4; Luke 3:3,16; John 1:26; Acts 5:31; 10:43; 13:38; 26:18; Col. 1:14.
6 2 Cor. 5:17
7 Acts 16:31
8 Rom. 10:8-11
9 2 Pet. 1:3
10 John 10:9
11 John 14:6
12 Rom. 12:3
13 Heb. 12:2
14 Rom. 10:17
15 Rom. 10:17; Rhema is the verbalized or spoken Word of Christ.
16 Heb. 12:2
17 Rom. 12:3
18 Rom. 10:17; Acts 3:16
19 John 1:1-4; John 1:1-3
20 Rom. 10:8-10
21 John 4:24
22 Rom. 10:10
23 1 John 5:4
24 John 3:1-21
25 John 3:3
26 John 10:7,9
27 John 3:4
28 John 3:5-8

29 John 16:33
30 Rom. 8:16-17; KJV
31 https://www.dictionary.com/browse/heir
32 Isa. 53:5
33 2 Tim. 3:16
34 Eph. 1:3
35 1 Pet. 5:8
36 2 Cor. 4:4
37 Eph. 2:2
38 John 12:31; 14:30; 16:11
39 Mat. 9:34; 12:24; Mark 3:22
40 1 Pet. 5:8
41 Jas. 4:7
42 Eph. 4:27
43 Mat. 9:36; 14:14; 20:34; Mark 1:21
44 Plp. 4:6
45 Heb. 4:16, KJV
46 Luke 11:1
47 Ibid.
48 Mat. 6:9
49 Mat. 6:5-8
50 Jas. 5:16
51 1 John 5:14-15
52 Psa. 37:4
53 1 Kgs. 8:56; Josh. 21:45
54 Mat. 7:7
55 Psa. 115:16
56 Acts 16:25
57 Plp. 2:5-7
58 Luke 4:1

59 Heb. 4:16

60 Gal. 6:2

61 The valley of Baca: "How blessed is the man whose strength is in You, In whose heart are the highways to Zion! Passing through the valley of Baca they make it a spring; The early rain also covers it with blessings. They go from strength to strength, Every one of them appears before God in Zion." (Psa. 84:5-7) "The Valley of Baca" is only mentioned this one time in the Bible. In Hebrew, Baca means bewailing, weeping, mourning, agonizing lamentation. Though it was an actual physical place located in Palestine, it is evoked by the Psalmist as a symbol for a once-in-a-lifetime "crisis-valley" that many people pass through sometime in their life relative to an agonizingly painful experience they have suffered, usually an unspeakably painful loss. But, thankfully, we can draw from the verse that we pass through this valley of weeping and mourning, and its sorrows may last for "the night," however long that night of darkness might be, once we have passed through it, it will yield uncommon strengthening and blessing and renewal because we drew our strength from the Lord in whom was our strength and not ourselves to make it through, and the conclusion of the matter is communion with the Lord Himself.

62 Dan. 11:32

63 Amos 3:8

64 Amos 3:7-8; italics added

65 Isa. 44:26a; this passage is saying that God confirms the word of His prophetic servants, the prophets, and performs the purposes of God proclaimed by God's prophetic messengers, the prophets.

66 1 Tim. 1:18-19

Chapter Eleven

Building Yourself Up On Your Most Holy Faith

But you, beloved, *building yourselves up on your most holy faith, praying in the Holy Spirit*, keep yourselves in the love of God, waiting anxiously for the mercy of our Lord Jesus Christ to eternal life.[1]

The Apostle Jude teaches us in this passage that once we have obtained and begun to operate in what he (and the Holy Spirit) calls *"your most holy faith,"* there is yet something more we must do, which is to build ourselves up ON our faith, and the way that is accomplished is by "praying in the Holy Spirit."

Jude is telling us that we actually "edify" or build ourselves up on our most holy faith when we pray in the Spirit. The word translated "build up" in the Greek (epoikodomeō) means to build upon, construct, build up, reinforce, expand, edify, and metaphorically to embolden or empower, to "charge up" as a battery is charged up, by infusing or charging it with electrical power. The passage is saying that Spirit-baptized Born Again believers charge ourselves up with dunamis-power (the power that comes through the Baptism in the Holy Spirit)—we build ourselves up or spiritually edify ourselves—when we pray in the Holy Spirit. Evidenced by the specific people to whom the letter is addressing—"But you, *beloved*"—this spiritual edification capability is exclusive to Born Again Spirit-baptized believers. The term, *"beloved,"* refers to "Christians," i.e., believers.

We are told, as alluded to many times in this volume, that "Faith comes by hearing, and hearing by the Word of God."[2] But we actually *build ourselves up ON* that faith that has come, when we *"pray in the Holy Spirit,"* which, according to First Corinthians 14:14, occurs only when we are praying in *tongues*: "For if I *pray in a <u>tongue</u>*, my *spirit* prays, but my mind is unfruitful."

Moreover, First Corinthians 14:4 is a correlating passage to verse 20 in Jude, for it says, "One who speaks in a *tongue* <u>EDIFIES</u> himself." The Greek word rendered "speaks" is "laleō," which according to Strong's Expository Dictionary is: "A prolonged form of an otherwise obsolete verb; to *talk*, that is, *utter* words: - preach, say, speak (after), talk, tell, utter." Thayer's Dictionary defines the word thusly: 1) to utter a voice or emit a sound; 2) to speak, 2a) to use the tongue or the faculty of speech, 2b) to utter articulate sounds; 3) to talk; 4) to utter, tell; 5) to use words in order to declare one's mind and disclose one's thoughts, 5a) to speak."

The reason I cite these definitions is some Bible teachers and expositors—primarily those who espouse Cessationism and those who oppose the "manifestation(s) of the Spirit for the common good,"[3] i.e., the "charismata" or "gifts of the Spirit"—mistakenly purport that this portion of Scripture is talking about speaking in tongues as a prophetic message in a worship assembly, and therefore must be interpreted in order to be orderly and proper. On the contrary, this passage is *not* alluding to a prophetic utterance in an assembly of believers, but rather a verbalization by a believer in a tongue that is unknown to the verbalizer. The primary usage of tongues—and the most common one—is *praying* in the Spirit, as the First Corinthians 14:4 verse specifies. And First Corinthians 14:2 specifies the purpose of praying in the Spirit, that is, praying in a *tongue*, as personal spiritual edification, building oneself up, spiritually:

> For one who speaks (prays out loud, orally, utters) in a tongue does **not** speak to **men** but to **God**; for no one understands (i.e., bystanders in hearing range), but *in his spirit* (not orally as a message to others, but internally in the pray-er's spirit, to himself) he speaks (utters) mysteries. *(Parenthetical explanations added.)*

In this passage is revealed vital revelation rarely recognized: that speaking or praying in *tongues* is direct communication *to* and *with* God, in which we are actually speaking *mysteries* in *our* spirit. A mystery is something that is not commonly understood. But these mysteries that are being uttered in our spirit are *mysteries* that can be interpreted, in some cases, through another gift of the Spirit operating in tandem with tongues, which is the *interpretation of tongues*.[4] And, when we have *tongues* plus *interpretation of tongues*, we then have *prophecy*.[5] Tongues and interpretation of tongues spoken in a public forum is each one half of prophecy.

When a public message from God to someone or a group of people is spoken in tongues, interpretation of the message in tongues is required in order for the hearers/recipients to be able to understand it. But public prophecy is not always the purpose of such praying in the spirit coupled with an interpretation of the message in a language known or understood by the recipients. Many times—in fact, most of the time—God intends such prophetic utterances to be for the person(s) praying in the Spirit, rather than as a message for the entire assembly gathered. In other words, most of the time the prophetic utterance(s) in tongues that come forth while people are praying and praising in a public forum are for the benefit of the people praying and praising in the Spirit, i.e., in unknown tongues, *not* for the entire assembly: "let him speak to *himself* and to *God*."[6] Certainly, this is the case when a believer is praying and praising in tongues *privately* and not in a public meeting.

Tongues, it is important to understand, are an expression of the Holy Spirit, *not* the believer speaking. Tongues are an outflow of the Holy Spirit, the Third Member of the Godhead, *not* the believer who is speaking it forth. Genuine tongues bypass the intellect of the believer as an unfiltered, mentally unprocessed message from God Himself!

As with the 120 and then 3,000 more on the Day of Pentecost, the believer provides the vocalization, but the substance of the vocalization, comes from the Holy Spirit: "And *they* were all filled with the Holy Spirit and (they) began to speak with other tongues, **as the Spirit was giving them utterance.**"[7] The believer yields his/her tongue to the Holy Spirit, who provides the substance of the utterance.

It was *they*, the disciples, who "began to speak with other tongues." They surrendered and submitted their tongue, which is one of the great benefits of the Baptism in the Holy Spirit—the ability to surrender and submit your tongue under the lordship of Jesus Christ. *They themselves* began to speak. And what they were speaking was exultations of God in a language unknown to them, as the *Spirit* was giving them utterance. It was the Spirit who was giving them the *substance* of what they were uttering, but it was *they* who were doing the *speaking*, using their speech faculties to speak the Spirit's utterances with which He filled their mouths.

And what they were speaking was not vain babble and gibberish, as some anti-tongues teachers allege "tongue-talkers" are engaging in, but rather the Bible explicitly says that those who were standing by *heard* them speaking in *languages* that they themselves understood. Yet they also understood that these people did *not* themselves understand those languages and dialects in which they were speaking, indicating that this was a supernatural working of the Holy Spirit as a *sign* to those that were unbelievers[8]—a *sign* that clearly testified of the supernatural power of God being poured out upon these believers in Christ.

One of the points I'm making that I don't want to be lost in all this discussion is that *sometimes*, not every time, but *sometimes*, during our personal prayer and praise in tongues, God will convey a message to us directly that comes in the form of tongues and then, if we ask for it, the Holy Spirit will follow that message with the interpretation into a language we understand. So, we actually can receive prophecy from God *within ourselves* (our spirit), as we pray in the Holy Spirit (i.e., in tongues), and then allow the Holy Spirit to give us the interpretation of the message in tongues that we are verbalizing in the language we are praying in. Oftentimes, when we do that, God will reveal mysteries to us—things that He wants to communicate to us—direction, guidance, and instruction from the Holy Spirit.

> For one who speaks in a *tongue* does not speak to <u>men</u> but to <u>God</u>; for no one understands, but *in his spirit he speaks **mysteries***. But one who <u>prophesies</u> *(speaks in a language the hearers understand)* speaks to men for edification and exhortation and consolation. One who speaks in a *tongue* edifies *himself*; but one who <u>prophesies</u> edifies the *church*.[9]

Praying, praising, worshiping in tongues is a catalyst or an opening of the door into the spirit-realm. It is a "dynamo of the Spirit," as Jude expressed it in the original language in verse twenty of his letter cited at the beginning of this chapter.

Certainly, in this last hour when we are besieged on every front with so much adversity, troubles, trials, tribulations, perplexities inuring from this world system, which is under the rulership of Satan, its god and arch-ruler, we each have an enormous need to build ourselves up on our most holy faith, praying in the Holy Spirit, that is, praying in *tongues*, as much and as often as is practicably possible!

Another reason *tongues* are so important in the lives of believers is that it is genuine *spiritual* prayer, according to First Corinthians 14:14, for there Paul says, "If I pray in a *tongue*, my *spirit* prays." Thus, biblically speaking, the only way to really "pray in the *Spirit*," as it is often referred to, is by praying in *tongues*. The only way we can really know that the Holy Spirit is praying through our human spirit—which is light-years better than us praying on our own out of our finite, flawed, and woefully inadequate intellect—is when we are praying in a *tongue*, according to this verse.

Moreover, Romans 8:26 indicates that "praying in *tongues*" is actually the Holy Spirit in the role as the *paracletos*, as He is called in the Greek—*paracletos*, the One who comes along side and takes hold with, the word literally means. Jesus called Him, "The Helper."[10] The Helper actually is praying or interceding through us when we are praying in the Spirit (in tongues).

And, in the next verse, we see that another reason for, or benefit of, praying in tongues is that the Holy Spirit is praying through us in the *perfect will of God*, and according to the mind, the thinking, the understanding, the knowledge, the wisdom of God.

So also, Romans 8:1-6 tells us that through *tongues*, when we are praying in *tongues*, the Holy Spirit, The Helper, is helping us with our *weakness*—our human frailties, our human spiritual inabilities and inadequacies that come from being merely human, or that are inherent in our human essence and estate. The Holy Spirit helps us with those weaknesses, especially in our spiritual activity of prayer in the Spirit and prays through us in the perfect will of God (for, He "knows what the mind of the Spirit is"), though *we* do *not* know with certainty through our own intellect and reasoning what the will of God is in a particular situation in regard to a particular matter or matters:

> In the same way **the Spirit also helps our *weakness*; for we do not know how to pray as we should,** but **the Spirit Himself *intercedes* for us** with groanings too deep for words; and He who searches the hearts knows what the mind of the Spirit is, because **He intercedes for the saints *according to the will of God*.**[11]

It is important to understand that "intercedes for the saints" means both on behalf of the saints and "for" them in the sense of providing the substance of the prayer—the petition or supplication—that is in accordance or agreement with the perfect will of God.[12]

How Does One Receive This Gift of Tongues?

If you have been tracking with what I've communicated so far and you do not have this gift of tongues operating in your life already, you are likely thinking right now along the lines of: "Okay, if all this is true, then how do I receive this gift of tongues so that I can build myself up on my faith by "praying in the Spirit," which according to what has been said here, is praying in tongues?"

That is an excellent question, and I am so glad you are asking it! As concisely and clearly as I can, I will do my best to answer it! Some of what I write is taken from or based on what I wrote in my book devoted to more thoroughly answering that question: *DUNAMIS! Power from on High*! You can learn more about the book on the promotional pages at the end of this book or my publishing company website at: https://realtruthpublications.com/catalog-store/dunamis/.

Every Born Again believer in Christ receives the gift of tongues by the same means all of the nine charismata gifts, or "the manifestation(s)[13] of the Spirit," are bestowed, which is the Baptism in the Holy Spirit.

> Now on the last day, the great day of the feast, Jesus stood and cried out, saying, "If any man is *thirsty*, let him come to Me and *drink*. He who believes in Me, as the Scriptures said, 'From his innermost being will flow *rivers of living water*.'" But this He spoke of the *Spirit*, **whom those who believed in Him were to receive**; for the Spirit was not yet given, because Jesus was not yet glorified.[14]

First, it is important to understand that Jesus spoke these words on the last day of "the great day of the feast," which is referring to the final required Jewish feast in each calendar year: The Feast of Tabernacles or Booths. This is important because that feast was always symbolic of the Day of Pentecost that would occur fifty days after Jesus' resurrection.

Jesus is speaking in this discourse of a *spiritual* thirst for *spiritual* empowerment that is available to all Born Again believers, and is received by spiritually "drinking" or ingesting it into the Born Again believer's redeemed and regenerated human spirit. In the next sentence, He specifies that this empowerment is given exclusively to *believers* with the words: "He who *believes* in Me." He continues to explain specifically where this empowerment will be infused in a human believer: "his innermost being," which is the human heart or spirit. The remaining clause indicates this empowerment will "flow" as a stream of water flows, and that the stream that will be flowing shall consist of "living water," which is the Water of the Holy Spirit. It is also important to notice that He uses the plural form of "river"—"river*s*"—regarding the living water that will flow out of the vessel of a Born Again believer.

The working of the Holy Spirit Jesus is describing here is what is known as "the Baptism in the Holy Spirit." Jesus Himself,—the *Prototype* of the Sons of God[15]—that is, our *Model* for all spiritual things—was the first human to receive the Baptism in the Holy Spirit, when He was baptized by John in water in the Jordan River, which was the spiritual inauguration of His public ministry. It was for this event that John was appointed by God as the forerunner who would identify the Messiah, the Lamb of God. That day John identified Him for the first time:

> The next day he saw Jesus coming to him and said, "Behold, the Lamb of God who takes away the sin of the world! "This is He on behalf of whom I said, 'After me comes a Man who has a higher rank than I, for He existed before me.' "I did not recognize Him, but so that He might be manifested to Israel, I came baptizing in *water*." John testified saying, *"I have seen the Spirit descending as a dove out of heaven, and He remained upon Him.* "I did not recognize Him, but He who sent me to baptize in *water* said to me, '*He* **upon** *whom you see the Spirit descending and remaining* **upon** *Him, this is the One who baptizes in the Holy Spirit.'* "I myself have seen, and have testified that this is the Son of God."[16]

Interestingly, John repeated this identification of Jesus as the Messiah the next day:

> **Again** the next day John was standing with two of his disciples, and he looked at Jesus as He walked, and said, "Behold, the Lamb of God!" The two disciples heard him speak, and they followed Jesus.[17]

The Significance and Importance of John-the-Baptist's Ministry

John-the-Baptist's unorthodox, unique, and unprecedented forerunner ministry burst forth suddenly, unexpectedly, and dramatically, to say the least:

> Now in the fifteenth year of the reign of Tiberius Caesar, when Pontius Pilate was governor of Judea, and Herod was tetrarch of Galilee, and his brother Philip was tetrarch of the region of Ituraea and Trachonitis, and Lysanias was tetrarch of Abilene, in the high priesthood of Annas and Caiaphas, the word of God came to John, the son of Zacharias, in the wilderness. And he came into all the district around the Jordan, preaching a baptism of repentance for the forgiveness of sins; as it is written in the book of the words of Isaiah the prophet, "THE VOICE OF ONE CRYING IN THE WILDERNESS, 'MAKE READY THE WAY OF THE LORD, MAKE HIS PATHS STRAIGHT. 'EVERY RAVINE WILL BE FILLED, AND EVERY MOUNTAIN AND HILL WILL BE BROUGHT LOW; THE CROOKED WILL BECOME STRAIGHT, AND THE ROUGH ROADS SMOOTH; AND ALL FLESH WILL SEE THE SALVATION OF GOD.'" So he began saying to the crowds who were going out to be baptized by him, "You brood of vipers, who warned you to flee from the wrath to come? "Therefore bear fruits in keeping with repentance, and do not begin to say to yourselves, 'We have Abraham for our father,' for I say to you that from these stones God is able to raise up children to Abraham. "Indeed the axe is already laid at the root of the trees; so every tree that does not bear good fruit is cut down and thrown into the fire."[18]

In bringing forth John's ministry, God ingeniously, if you will, circumvented or bypassed every existing authority structure and system at the time—civil and religious—which demonstrates this is the reason the Holy Spirit inspired Luke to set the scene as He did. Luke specified that regarding the extant *civil* government in place at the time, a) Tiberius Caesar was in the fifth year of his monarchical reign over the Roman Empire; b) Pontius Pilate was governor of Judea; c) Herod was tetrarch of the region of Galilee: d) Herod's brother, Philip, was tetrarch of the region of Ituraea and Trachonitis, and e) Lysanias was tetrarch of the region of Abilene. Regarding the *religious* authority hierarchy in place at the time, John's ministry emerged during the high priesthoods of Annas and Caiaphas.

This circumvention of the existing "authorities," emphatically illustrates that while God in His Word categorically states that "Every *person* is to be in subjection to the governing (civil) authorities," yet the reason for that is "For there is no authority except from *God*, and those which exist are established by *God*." [19] All authority whether on earth, i.e., civil, in the heavenlies, or in the Spirit realm, ultimately originates with God, for He, and He alone, IS the ultimate authority and therefore ultimate source of legitimate authority! So, because God is the ultimate authority of the universe, He has the authority and can legally and legitimately exercise that authority to do whatever He desires to do, including bypassing or circumventing existing authority structures to institute whatever He desires to institute—i.e., His purposes and plans. In this case it was the forerunner ministry of John-the-Baptist.

What God was about to do could not inure from any of the existing systems of the world or any human agency, but rather it had to be the direct work of God Himself! God was establishing a completely new order of things! That new order is known as "The Kingdom of God" on Earth! And the King of that Kingdom (every kingdom must have a king) is King Jesus, the King of Kings and Lord of Lords!

The activation of John-the-Baptist's ministry required that God even intervene in the circumstances of John's birth, in that his father, Zacharias, was a priest born into the division of Abijah of the tribe of Levi, whose wife, Elizabeth, was of the female descendants (daughters) of Aaron, the brother of Moses, the original high priest:

> In the days of Herod, king of Judea, there was a *priest* named Zacharias, of the division of Abijah; *and he had a wife from the daughters of Aaron*, and her name was Elizabeth. They were both righteous in the sight of God, walking blamelessly in all the commandments and requirements of the Lord. But they had no child, because Elizabeth was barren, and they were both advanced in years. Now it happened that while he was performing his priestly service before God in the appointed order of his division, according to the custom of the priestly office, *he was chosen by lot* to enter the temple of the Lord and burn incense. And the whole multitude of the people were in prayer outside at the hour of the incense offering. And an angel

of the Lord appeared to him, standing to the right of the altar of incense. Zacharias was troubled when he saw the angel, and fear gripped him. But the angel said to him, "Do not be afraid, Zacharias, for your petition has been heard, and your wife Elizabeth will bear you a son, and you will give him the name **John**. "You will have joy and gladness, and many will rejoice at his birth. "For he will be great in the sight of the Lord; and he will drink no wine or liquor, and he will be filled with the Holy Spirit while yet in his mother's womb. "And he will turn many of the sons of Israel back to the Lord their God. "It is he who will go as a **forerunner** before Him in the spirit and power of Elijah, TO TURN THE HEARTS OF THE FATHERS BACK TO THE CHILDREN, and the disobedient to the attitude of the righteous, so as to make ready a people prepared for the Lord." Zacharias said to the angel, "How will I know this for certain? For I am an old man and my wife is advanced in years." The angel answered and said to him, "I am Gabriel, who stands in the presence of God, and I have been sent to speak to you and to bring you this good news. "And behold, you shall be silent and unable to speak until the day when these things take place, because you did not believe my words, which will be fulfilled in their proper time." The people were waiting for Zacharias, and were wondering at his delay in the temple. But when he came out, he was unable to speak to them; and they realized that he had seen a vision in the temple; and he kept making signs to them, and remained mute. When the days of his priestly service were ended, he went back home. After these days Elizabeth his wife became pregnant, and she kept herself in seclusion for five months, saying, "This is the way the Lord has dealt with me in the days when He looked with favor upon me, to take away my disgrace among men."[20]

The system for annually choosing priests from the "sons" or male descendants of Levi to perform the sacerdotal temple duties was "by lot" by rotation in which eligible priests—those who had not previously served—drew some sort of markers, a certain one of which was the marker that identified the priest chosen to serve in that capacity. Even here we see the providential intervention of God, in that the lot fell upon the exact person God had ordained to serve in the priestly role of the burning of the incense at this, the most crucial intersection in Creation history! There could be no variance here; rather at this very particular time, everything, every detail of the particulars of this circumstance, would be, *had* to be, exactly perfect!

God had chosen a certain man, whose wife was a certain woman of the progeny of Aaron, the first High Priest, who would give birth to a certain male child that was not just an ordinary or common male but was a prophet, a prophet who was "more than a prophet."[21] And the ministry of *this* prophet would be that of a *forerunner*, to prepare the way for the coming or the manifestation of the long-awaited Messiah!

This prophet would in fact be the cousin of that Messiah!

This prophet's mother, who was a bloodline descendant of Aaron, Moses' brother, would be the blood-aunt of the Messiah's biological mother!

This prophet's biological father would be from the bloodline of the division of Abijah of the tribe of Levi (the tribe of Israel's *priests*)!

This prophet would be the prophesied "Elijah to come!"[22]

Everything that God needed to be perfectly aligned for this, the most momentous moment in Creation history, was indeed in all aspects perfectly aligned!

Even the child's name that God had ordained for this child-prophet who would be procreated through this priest and his priestly wife could not be left to their whim, but rather had to be designated by God Himself, for the name of the child bore the description of his calling and ministry: to be the forerunner to prepare the way for and identify the Messiah, "the Lamb of God who takes away the sins of the world," who at precisely the "right time"[23] in Creational history would die for the ungodly to redeem "whosoever" will receive and believe upon Him.

Notice the passage states that John came: "preaching a baptism of repentance for the forgiveness of sins." His Spirit-anointed, fiery, soul-piercing, preaching moved his Hebrew hearers to the Godly sorrow that leads to repentance,[24] which repentance was required in order to receive forgiveness from God of their personal sins and trespasses, as it is for everyone who seeks forgiveness of and fellowship with God. Penitents who came to this juncture of real repentance, John would baptize in the iconic waters of the Jordon River, the symbol of the Jewish nation's passing through in their exodus from their former bondage of slavery to the Egyptians into the freedom of the Land of Milk and Honey, Beulah Land, The Promised Land, the territory illicitly occupied by the trespassing Canaanites, Canaan, which territory God had set aside and designated for the Israelites to inhabit as an inheritance as the descendants of Abraham.

The spies Moses sent out at the command of the Lord to survey the territory when the Israelites finally arrived there after forty years of wandering in the wilderness, reported that "the Canaanites are living by the sea and by the side of the Jordan." Canaan consists of the territory west of the Jordan River bounded on the west by the "Great Sea,"[25] known today as the Mediterranean Sea. God Himself described to Moses the exact borders demarcating the territory of the Promised Land:

> Then the LORD spoke to Moses, saying, "Command the sons of Israel and say to them, '**When you enter the land of Canaan, this is the land that shall fall to you as an *inheritance*, even the land of Canaan** according to its borders. 'Your southern sector shall extend from the wilderness of Zin along the side of Edom, and your southern border shall extend from the end of the Salt Sea eastward. 'Then your border shall turn direction from the south to the ascent of Akrabbim and continue to Zin, and its termination shall be to the south of Kadesh-barnea; and it shall reach Hazaraddar and continue to Azmon. 'The border shall turn direction from Azmon to the brook of Egypt, and its termination shall be at the sea. 'As for the western border, you shall have the Great Sea, that is, its coastline; this shall be your west border. 'And this shall be your north border: you shall draw your border line from the Great Sea to Mount Hor. 'You shall draw a line from Mount Hor to the Lebo-hamath, and the termination of the border shall be at Zedad; and the border shall proceed to Ziphron, and its termination shall be at Hazar-enan. This shall be your north border. 'For your eastern border you shall also draw a line from Hazar-enan to Shepham, and the border shall go down from Shepham to Riblah on the east side of Ain; and the border shall go down and reach to the slope on the east side of the Sea of Chinnereth. 'And the border shall go down to the Jordan and its termination shall be at the Salt Sea.

This shall be your land according to its borders all around.'" So Moses commanded the sons of Israel, saying, "**This is the land that you are to apportion by lot among you as a possession, which the LORD has commanded to give to the nine and a half tribes.** "For the tribe of the sons of Reuben have received theirs according to their fathers' households, and the tribe of the sons of Gad according to their fathers' households, and the half-tribe of Manasseh have received their possession. "The two and a half tribes have received their possession across the Jordan opposite Jericho, eastward toward the sunrising."[26]

Though the Hebrews were the inheritors and owners of the entire Land of Canaan in that Jehovah had given it to the Hebrew Patriarch, Abraham, they never to this day completely conquered and dispossessed the Canaanites from the territory. Circa 1250 BC the united Kingdom of Israel was established when the Israelites prevailed upon the prophet Samuel and ultimately Jehovah God to appoint them a king, a human monarch, "like all the (other) nations,"[27] who would rule as the singular potentate over the nation.[28] The originally united kingdom that was established in Canaan, following the death of Solomon, became a divided kingdom, consisting of the northern Kingdom of Israel and the southern Kingdom of Judah.

The Significance of Canaan and Significance to this Book

Now why would God communicate to Moses the exact borders of Canaan and ensure that those details were included in His-Story, the record of which comprises what would later be known as the Bible? Moreover, why are these details important to a book such as this one, the transcending subject of which is the matter of *faith*? Both good questions.

Regarding the first question, the Apostle Paul, who authored two-thirds of the canonized New Testament books, gave us the most concise yet comprehensive answer, centuries later:

Now these things happened to **them** as an *example*, and they were written for **our** *instruction*, upon whom the ends of the ages have come.[29]

For whatever was written in earlier times was written for our *instruction*, so that through *perseverance* and the *encouragement of the Scriptures* we might have hope.[30]

In the first passage above, Paul is saying that the entire Old Testament was written by the prophets and prophetic scribes who wrote it, with all its typology and symbolism, for instruction, teaching, direction, particularly for those who would be living during "the ends of the ages." No previous generation fits this description more than those of us who are living right now in the Twenty-First Century! Without any doubt or equivocation whatsoever, the Twenty-First Century is the end of the end of the ages! The Twenty-First Century is the Eschatological Century! All the eschatological events delineated particularly in the book of Revelation, the *last* book of the Bible, will transpire in the Twenty-First Century! That is irrefutable! And there is nothing in Scripture, including the hermeneutical patterns set in it, that provides good cause or justification for the order in which those events are delineated in Revelation to be viewed as anything other than chronological.

In the second passage quoted above, Paul reveals something additional about the instruction the Old Testament record provides believers, especially end-times believers, which is what he terms, "perseverance and the encouragement of Scriptures." There's some spiritual *something*, an intangible, mysterious quality, or property, of the writings of the Old Testament, that when read, studied, pondered, assimilated, generates perseverance and encouragement of the Spirit in Born Again believers! It just does! How, is part of the mystery, perhaps part of "the mystery of the kingdom"[31] to which Jesus alluded.

Regarding the second question previously posed of why the details of the borders of Canaan Land God communicated to Moses is important for a book ultimately about faith, the New Testament book of Hebrews provides the most concise yet comprehensive definition of faith in all of Scripture: "Now faith is the *assurance* of things *hoped* for, the conviction of things not seen."[32] Couple that with the likewise concise and comprehensive scripture that reveals how faith comes—"So *faith* comes from *hearing*, and hearing by the *word of Christ*"[33]—we see that the *hope* Paul said is generated in believers through assimilating the Old Testament writings is part and parcel, in fact a required element, of genuine faith—the assurance of things hoped for.

That means, faith is not just ethereal, random, and non-specific, but rather faith has a target—"the things hoped for." Faith is not hope; but hope is elemental to faith. Hope is the target, the objective, of faith. Hope *defines* the target, the objective, of faith! Faith has a focus! Metaphorically speaking, faith is not like firing a shotgun in the hope that you hit something with the expansive spray of shrapnel contained in shotgun shells. Rather faith is like firing a long-rifle or handgun that you've trained upon, aimed at, a very specific, narrow, focused, target—a bullseye! Hope is what defines the bullseye or objective; faith is what causes the objective to manifest!

In mapping out the perimeters of the Promised Land, God was providing the Israelites a target. This territory was their bullseye. Occupying and establishing the Jewish nation in this geographical territory was the objective the Hebrew people were to focus all their efforts on, for Jehovah God had given it to them as an inheritance as the descendants of Abraham!

Connecting It All

Now to connect all this with the matter of the Baptism in the Holy Spirit, we need to return to the scene at the Jordan River in which John-the-Baptist was baptizing Jesus, the Holy Spirit in the form of a dove descended from Heaven and remained *upon* Jesus as a visible sign John could see of the Holy Spirit baptizing or immersing Him in the Spirit. Just as John immersed Jesus in the waters of the Jordon River (which also bore vital meaning) when He came to John asking him to baptize Him, as he had done for untold numbers of repentant Jews who accepted the preaching of John to prepare the way for the coming Messiah. When he baptized them in the Jordan River, he didn't merely "sprinkle" them with water as with infant baptism in the Catholic Church and some Protestant traditions as well, but rather he would totally *immerse* them in the water, with the person going all the way down under the water from head to foot, symbolizing the killing of the "old man" and the resurrection unto new life of the "new creation in Christ,"[34] as they rose or emerged from their "drowning."

Initially, John resisted Jesus' request, saying, he needed *Jesus'* baptism; meaning, he needed to be baptized in the Holy Spirit. And he was right, John *did* need that baptism, though, curiously, we are never told if he ever received it, and there is no record that John performed any miracles or supernatural works that would inure from the Baptism in the Holy Spirit. From this experience of receiving the Baptism in the Holy Spirit Himself, Jesus then became the Baptizer in the Holy Spirit. He could not have given anyone else anything He Himself had not received from God. As a recipient, He became an authorized giver or bestower of this glorious gift of the Baptism in the Holy Spirit! Ever since that day, Jesus has been bestowing that Baptism unto those who would follow His stated simple instructions of receiving! (See the next to last section of this chapter for those instructions.)

This entire discourse is in contrast to the discourse He had with the Samaritan women at Jacob's Well that occurred two or three years earlier at the beginning of Jesus public ministry. In that conversation, He also invokes the metaphor of "living water," but with the distinction that it would become in the recipient, "a WELL of water SPRINGING UP to Eternal Life"—in contrast to a stream of water "flowing" out to others.

> "If you knew *the gift of God* and who it is who says to you, 'Give Me **a drink**,' you would have asked Him and He would have given you **living water**." She said to Him, "Sir, You have nothing to draw with and the well is deep, where then do You get that living water? You are not greater than our father Jacob, are You, who gave us the well and drank of it himself and his sons and his cattle?" Jesus answered and said to her, "Everyone who drinks of *this water* (i.e., the water that is in the well that you [the Samaritan woman] are referring to, the *physical water*) will thirst again; but whoever **drinks of the water that I will give him** shall never thirst; but the water that I will give him will become in him **a well of water *springing up* to ETERNAL LIFE**." *[Parenthetical explanation and emphases added]*

Do you see it? Jesus' description here in this incident of the living water He is alluding to is that it is "a *well* of water"—"a well of water *springing up* to eternal life." A *well* of water is an enclosed *container* of water, a vessel in which the water is enclosed; it *contains* water, it *holds* water! There is no natural "flow" of water in a well, due to gravity; rather, without some form of plumbing or ducts form a stream, it must be drawn up with some sort of container, like a bucket. That's why the woman replied to Jesus, "You have nothing to draw with." Jesus replied that this "well of water" He was talking about was *"the gift of God"* that would *spring up* to **Eternal Life**. So, what He is alluding to here in this conversation with this woman at Jacob's Well is the gift of **salvation**—i.e., Living Waters of the Holy Spirit unto **Eternal Life**—which is the spiritual transaction of *regeneration* that happens when a person is born again, as Jesus told Nicodemus everyone who desires to inherit eternal life "must be."[35]

What Jesus is describing here is the work of the Holy Spirit in *regeneration* or *spiritual rebirth*, or the moment of salvation, in which we are "...saved...by the washing of *regeneration* and *renewing* by the Holy Spirit."[36] This working of the Holy Spirit can also be referred to as the *infusion* of the Holy Spirit.

The distinction regarding the two different functions or operations of the same Holy Spirit (there is only one) Jesus makes in these two different discourses is critical! Many expositors and Bible teachers—mostly those who do not recognize or believe in the Baptism in the Holy Spirit—mistakenly posit that Jesus is speaking about the Holy Spirit's (Living Water) role in salvation. What I am pointing out is that such a position is obviously (when all Scripture is taken into account) incorrect. In the discourse with the Samaritan woman at Jacob's Well (which also is of vital import) Jesus is speaking about Eternal Life, while in the other Jesus is talking about not a WELL or container of water but "RIVERS of living water" that "flow" as does a stream of water. The former speaks of this living water "springing UP unto Eternal Life," and the latter speaks of the living water FLOWING OUT! The distinction could not be clearer!

But, as we shall see next, there is another or adjunct working of the Holy Spirit in the life of the regenerated, or Born Again, believer, which is the work of the Holy Spirit in the *Baptism or Immersion* in the Holy Spirit.

The Work of the Spirit in the Baptism in the Holy Spirit

To set the stage for this discussion, we need to start with Jesus' specific instruction to the early disciples some days after His resurrection:

> "And, behold, I am sending forth the promise of My Father upon you; but you are to stay in the city until you are clothed with power from on high."[37]

Mirroring that record, Luke goes on to state that Jesus gathered together His original disciples, and,

> He commanded them not to leave Jerusalem, but to *wait* for what the Father had promised, "Which," He said, "you have heard of from Me; for John baptized with water, but you shall

be baptized with the Holy Spirit not many days from now."[38]

And then verse eight of the same chapter says:

"but you will receive power when the Holy Spirit has come upon you; and you shall be My witnesses, both in Jerusalem, and in Judea and Samaria, and to the remotest part of the earth."

Then, the story picks back up in Acts 2:1-4 saying:

And when the Day of Pentecost had come, they were all together in one place. And suddenly there came from Heaven a noise like a violent, rushing wind, and it filled the whole house where they were sitting. And there appeared to them *tongues as of fire* distributing themselves, and they rested on each one of them. And they were all filled with the Holy Spirit *and began to speak with other **tongues***, as the Spirit was giving them utterance.

And the verses following indicate that when this sound occurred, the crowd that was gathered together and witnessing this supernatural phenomenal event were bewildered because each one of them was hearing these original disciples, who had been filled with the Holy Ghost, speaking in their own languages, and they knew these disciples did not know or understand their language.

And verses 12 and following say:

And they continued in amazement and great perplexity, saying to one another, "What does this mean?" But others were mocking and saying, "They are full of sweet wine." But Peter, taking his stand with the eleven, raised his voice, and declared to them: "...these men are not drunk, as you suppose, for it is only the third hour of the day; but *this is (that* which the Prophet Joel had spoken and prophesied so many hundreds of years before): 'And it shall be in the last days,' God says, 'That I will pour forth of My Spirit upon all mankind (upon all mankind); and your sons and your daughters shall prophesy, and your young men shall see visions, and your old men shall dream dreams; even upon My bondslaves, both men and women, I will in those days pour forth of My Spirit and they shall prophesy.'"

And then, Peter, continuing his momentous sermon on that Day of Pentecost, says, in verse 32:

"This Jesus God raised up again, to which we are all witnesses.

Therefore having been exalted to the right hand of God, and having received from the Father the promise of the Holy Spirit, He has poured forth this which you both see and hear." *(Then, picking up in verse 37)* Now when the crowd heard this, they were pierced to the heart, and said to Peter and the rest of the apostles, "Brethren, what shall we do?" And Peter said to them, "Repent and let each of you be baptized in the Name of Jesus Christ for the forgiveness of your sins *(that's talking about water baptism)*. And you shall receive THE GIFT OF THE HOLY SPIRIT *(this refers to the Baptism in the Holy Spirit)*. **For the promise is for you and your children, and for all who are far off, as many the Lord our God shall call to Himself."**

Receive the Baptism in the Holy Spirit

The Baptism in the Holy Spirit and Fire is available to every believer who will turn to the Lord Jesus Christ as their Savior and simply call upon Him, and *ask* Him to receive of this great baptism in the Living Waters of God. As indicated numerous times previously, God desires that ALL believers receive the Baptism in the Holy Spirit with the initial evidence of *tongues*. According to First Corinthians 14, verses 5, 14, and 15, ALL believers should pray and sing in the Spirit, that is, to say *in tongues*. The Apostle Paul tells us in First Corinthians 14:14 that praying in a *tongue* is praying in the *Spirit*. And praying in tongues comes through the Baptism in the Holy Spirit.

The Holy Spirit, through the Apostle Peter, told us, in the passage we looked at previously, that this promise of the Spirit is for *you*, and for your *children*, even for as many as be afar off, meaning those who are yet far away from God and alienated from Him by the great chasm of sin and personal trespasses. All you have to do is come to God, repent of your sin, request His forgiveness that He is so eager to extend, and then *ask* Him for this great Baptism in the Holy Spirit, and Jesus said, "You SHALL receive power after that the Holy Ghost is come upon you."

I encourage you to reach out right now to receive the Baptism in the Holy Spirit, won't you? Jesus promised to give the Holy Spirit to everyone who asks Him for it. That's all you have to do—you merely have to *ask* Him to receive of the Holy Spirit. The Bible says, "*Ask*, and it will be given unto you; seek and you shall find; knock and the door will be opened to you."[39] James said, "You do not have because you do not ask."[40] Indeed, Jesus specifically talks about this with regard to the Holy Spirit, the Baptism in the Holy Spirit:

> So I say to you, **ask**, and it will be given to you; *seek*, and you will find; *knock*, and it will be opened unto you. For **everyone** (everyone, everyone, everyone) who asks, receives; and he who seeks, finds; and to him who knocks, it will be opened. Now suppose one of you fathers is asked by his *son* for a **fish**; he will not give him a **snake** instead of a **fish**, will he? *(He is contrasting Satan's kingdom to God's kingdom. Satan's kingdom being represented by a **snake**, and God's kingdom being represented by a **fish**.)* Or if he asks for an **egg**, he will not give him a **scorpion**, will he?" *(Again, the two kingdoms being contrasted; God will not give you something from **Satan's** kingdom when you are asking Him earnestly and diligently to receive something from **His** Kingdom.)* If you then, being evil, know how to give **good gifts** to your children, how much more will your heavenly Father give **the Holy Spirit** to those who **ask** Him?[41]

And, then, in John 7:37-38 and Isaiah 55:1, we see that anyone who is thirsty for the Holy Spirit need only to come to Jesus, and *drink* of the water of the Holy Spirit, that is, receive it by *faith*. It's truly just that easy. Out of fear, or unbelief, or self-condemnation people, are often so intimidated about merely asking Jesus for the Baptism in the Holy Spirit, but it really is as simple as drinking from a glass of water! He's not holding back; He has no desire to hold back! He's eager to baptize you in the Spirit right now—whenever you *ask* Him!

After all this information I've provided about the Baptism in the Holy Spirit, I would be totally remiss if I did not take it to the next step and invite you to receive this Baptism or Immersion in the Spirit. So, right now I want to help you to receive the Baptism in the Holy Spirit. And, you know, you can!—right where you are right now. If you are a believer in the Lord Jesus Christ, and you have been *regenerated* by the Holy Spirit coming to live on the inside of you, to take up residence on the inside of you, in your heart, you are a candidate for the Baptism in the Holy Spirit. This is what you have been looking for! This is what you have a need for! This is what you have been lacking—the *power of God*, operating in your life.

It is so simple! All you need to do is to ask Jesus, and then simply *drink in* the Holy Spirit. If you earnestly desire to be totally immersed in the Rivers of Living Water of the Holy Spirit, you can be immersed in those Waters right now, wherever you are at this moment!

Lift both hands to Heaven, and pray this prayer with me; say it out loud with me right now. Go ahead!

Dear Lord Jesus, I have believed upon You as my Lord and Savior, and the Holy Spirit already lives within me. I know I am already saved. But John the Baptist testified You were the Baptizer in the Holy Spirit! I ask You now to *baptize* me in the Holy Spirit, and clothe me with power from on High. I receive this Baptism now by faith.

Now, friend, to drink—drink out of a glass of water—you must open your mouth. So, open your mouth right now, get ready to drink. Jesus said, if you are thirsty, come and ask Him, and drink. Now take in a deep breath right now, drink in the Breath of the Holy Spirit; receive by faith.

Father, I ask You in Jesus' Name that you baptize these readers and listeners with the Baptism in the Holy Ghost and Fire!

Now, go ahead, beloved, drink in the Holy Spirit—take three deep breaths right now as if you are drinking water—drink in the Spirit, the Breath of God!

Oh, Holy Spirit, fall upon them now as you fell upon the Gentile believers gathered at Cornelius' house, I pray, in Jesus' Name!

Now just receive the Holy Spirit's baptism by faith; it is not by works that you receive it. It comes just the same way that you got saved—you received Jesus by *faith*—now receive the Baptism in the Holy Spirit by *faith*. You will begin to sense a bubbling forth, a sensation from your innermost being, somewhere in the region of your belly, for Jesus said, "out of your *belly* shall flow rivers of living water." For that is where your human spirit is located, somewhere behind your belly.

Open your mouth, begin singing and speaking the praises of God in the utterances that the Holy Spirit gives you from within. You must *allow* Him to use your *tongue*. Surrender your *tongue* to Him, right now. Don't be concerned if only a few sounds that you do not understand come forth initially. Just speak them forth in faith, abandoning pride and self-consciousness. Remember: tongues are words in languages *you* do not understand, but *God does*!

Conclusion

Everything contained in this chapter is about receiving the Baptism in the Holy Spirit, which is the means by which a Born Again believer receives all nine of the Charismata, or Gifts of the Spirit. One of those nine gifts is the gift of tongues, or the ability to pray and speak in languages you do not know by learning them. The manifestation of these tongues is supernatural, not natural. It is by the usage, operation, or manifestation of these tongues that a believer builds himself up on his most holy faith, per the scriptures quoted herein.

Endnotes

1 Jude 1:20-21
2 Rom. 10:17
3 1 Cor. 12:7
4 1 Cor. 12:10
5 Ibid.
6 1 Cor. 14:28
7 Acts 2:4
8 1 Cor. 14:22
9 1 Cor. 14:2-4; parenthetical explanation added
10 John 14:16,26; 15:26; 16:7
11 Rom. 8:26-27
12 See also: Rom. 12:2
13 1 Cor. 12:7
14 John 7:37-39
15 See Rom. 8:28; the Greek word translated as "firstborn," prōtotokos, means prototype. Jesus was the prototype—original model—of the Sons of God.
16 John 1:29-34
17 John 1:35-37
18 Luke 3:1-9; Caps part of the text indicating quote from Old Testament Scripture.
19 Rom. 13:1; parenthetic explanation added
20 Luke 1:5-25
21 Mat. 11:9; Luke 7:26
22 Mat. 11:14; Mal. 4:5-6
23 Rom. 5:6
24 2 Cor. 7:9-10
25 Num. 34:6
26 Num. 34:1-15

27 1 Sam. 8:5
28 1 Sam. 8:1-9
29 1 Cor. 10:11
30 Rom. 15:4
31 Mark 4:11
32 Heb. 11:1
33 Rom. 10:17
34 2 Cor. 5:17
35 John 3:3-8
36 Tit. 3:5
37 Luke 24:49
38 Acts 1:4-5
39 Mat. 7:7
40 Jas. 4:2
41 Luke 11:9-13

Chapter Twelve

THE TESTING OF OUR FAITH

The *testing* of our faith produces endurance:

> Consider it all joy, my brethren, when you encounter various trials, *knowing that the testing of your faith produces endurance*. And let endurance have its perfect result, so that you may be perfect and complete, lacking in nothing. Blessed is the man who perseveres under trial; for once he has been approved *(or, passed the test, margin)*, he will receive the crown of life, which the Lord has promised to those who love Him.[1]

Endurance is persevering in believing faith in the face of great difficulty. One dictionary defines endurance as: the fact or power of enduring or bearing pain, hardships, etc; the ability or strength to continue or last, especially despite fatigue, stress, or other adverse conditions; stamina; lasting quality; duration; something endured, as a hardship; trial.

The above cited passage tells us that enduring through trials will eventually and ultimately produce a "perfect result," which is that the believer who endures will be perfect (i.e., spiritually mature), complete, and lacking in nothing. You can't get much more of a perfect result than that!

It is an undeniable fact that God allows our faith to be tested, tried, to prove the veracity and quality of it! But it is also an undeniable fact that it is not God Himself who brings the adversity into our lives that tests, tries, proves the veracity and quality of our faith. Rather, Satan is the one who authors the adversity.

The Holy Spirit made it clear who our adversary is, "Be of sober spirit, be on the alert. YOUR ADVERSARY, *the devil*, prowls about like a roaring lion, seeking someone to devour."[2]

In order to be able to understand many of the questions of life with definitiveness and complete confidence, a believer must settle the issue once and for all at the very core of his/her spirit. *God* is NOT the believer's adversary. The adversary, Satan, is the one who authors and brings forth adversity. The matter of the source of adversity is a huge issue in life as we experience the many forms of adversity of which life consists. As long as you are alive on this planet, you will experience adversity. I know that is not a very comforting word, especially if you are going through adversity right now, but it is nonetheless the truth.

No one is impervious to adversity—believer or unbeliever. It is unfortunate that sometimes in altar calls preachers seem to paint a picture that when you surrender your heart to Jesus, then all your troubles and life's difficulties will be over and you will experience heaven on earth. Lay-believers often follow that example and paint the same picture to people they are encouraging to give their life to the Lord, as well. But that simply is not the true Gospel. The Bible *never* says that! It just is not in the contract, not even the fine print, though we may all wish it was.

The question is: why do these trials, troubles, and tribulations come into believer's lives?

Well, actually there are definitive answers in the Bible to that question, and I will be offering some of those answers herein. But, if you want, or more accurately need, to know those answers now, I highly recommend you get your copy of my book, *Mystery of the Kingdom*, which is available both in print and e-book form, as well as Kindle and audiobook for immediate download to your computer or other reading device. Some of what I will be writing here are excerpts from that book. In fact, there is one whole chapter in that book dealing with the answers to that question. Let me say, though the critics and cynics won't believe anything I say, my reference to that book is really not at all a promo for the book. Rather, I know there are people reading this book who really do desperately need answers to the burning questions of life such as this, many of whom are going through some sort of fiery trial right now. And I know that what I wrote in that book can be extremely helpful in times of turmoil and tribulation such as that.

But I will offer here the short answer to this crucial question as to why trials, troubles, and tribulations sometimes come into believer's lives? In fact, Peter himself wrote a succinct answer to that question in his first epistle:

> Beloved, do not be surprised at the fiery ordeal among you, WHICH COMES UPON YOU FOR YOUR TESTING, as though some strange thing were happening to you; but to the degree that you share the sufferings of Christ, keep on rejoicing, so that also at the revelation of his glory, you may rejoice with exultation. If you are reviled for the name of Christ, you are blessed, because the Spirit of glory and of God rests upon you.[3]

I highly recommend that readers read the immediate context of this verse, i.e., verses 12 to 19. Then read the expanded context, which is the entire chapter four. Then, the full extent of what Peter is talking about is even better understood when connected with the full context of the entire epistle, especially the chapters that precede the cited verse.

Indeed, the entire epistle is addressed to believers who have been scattered abroad following what historians refer to as the Diaspora or Dispersion who are suffering greatly in the Great Persecution that drove most of the early church members out of Israel into the surrounding regions and countries. Peter wrote the letter to encourage the scattered and severely persecuted believers to remain faithful to God and Christ during this time of great persecution and distress they were going through. Masses of these early believers were facing death and extreme social oppression if they were able to escape death as a result of being a follower of Christ. By inspiration of the Spirit, Peter wrote to encourage the faithful to focus on the surpassing hope of the "inheritance" they would receive in heaven rather than the agonizing sufferings they were being made to endure on earth. What these believers suffered makes our present "sufferings" pale by comparison into virtual nothingness. Myriads of these ordinary humans just like you and me were martyred by unspeakable manners of death yet remained faithful to the name of Christ to their last breath, refusing to recant their trust in that Name. In the opening portion of his letter Peter writes:

> Blessed be the God and Father of our Lord Jesus Christ, who

according to His great mercy has caused us to be born again to a living hope through the resurrection of Jesus Christ from the dead to obtain an *inheritance* which is imperishable and undefiled and will not fade away, *reserved in heaven for you*, who are protected by the power of God through faith for a salvation ready to be revealed in the last time. In this you greatly rejoice, even though now for a little while, if necessary, you have been distressed by various **TRIALS**, THAT THE PROOF OF YOUR FAITH, being more precious than gold which is perishable, even though **TESTED BY FIRE**, may be found to result in praise and glory and honor at the revelation of Jesus Christ; and even though you have not seen Him, you love Him, and though you do not see Him now, but believe in Him, you greatly rejoice with joy inexpressible and full of glory, obtaining as the outcome of your faith THE SALVATION OF YOUR SOULS.[4]

This last part is what God is after through the "fiery trials" he allows Satan to bring into our lives—"the salvation of your souls." When a believer is born again through genuine repentance and faith in Christ and the salvation He purchased on the Cross of Calvary, his/her spirit is instantaneously regenerated and restored to the condition in which the human spirit existed before Adam sinned. That transpires through the spiritual transaction of the Holy Spirit coming to take up residence in that person's human spirit. Jesus made this clear when He said, "that which is born of the [Holy] Spirit is [the human] spirit."[5]

The human spirit is redeemed, restored, and regenerated at the rebirth or new birth experience. But, the soul, comprised of our mind, will, and emotions, is not automatically, instantaneously, and fully "saved" or restored at the rebirth, but is in the *process* of being saved or sanctified throughout our life after we are born again.[6] The Word of God is implanted in our heart as the Seed (lit., "sperma"; Gr.) of God, in our human spirits, which is "ABLE" to "save" or "sanctify" our soul, but it is not automatic or instantaneous. Rather, that sanctifying process occurs gradually as we yield ourselves to the sanctifying working of the Holy Spirit in our lives.

Thus, when we are born again, our *spirit* is saved, but our *soul* is not, completely, instantaneously, but it is in the process of *being* saved throughout our life on Earth. The trials that come in our lives come to test, and therefore prove, refine, and purify our faith and in turn *us*; i.e., our soul. That's the "tested by fire" part Peter referenced. Satan is the adversary of believers, but it is critical to understand that he cannot do anything that God disallows him to do, because God is still sovereign. Greater is He who is in us than he who is in the world.[7] Satan cannot do anything God does not permit him to do. The "fiery trials" come to test or purify our faith, and thereby purge us of ungodly elements in our lives that defile us. The value of silver and gold increases as it is tested in the refining fiery furnace and purified of its impurities. God allows those who are part of the remnant church to be taken through the fire in order to "Refine them as silver is refined, and test them as gold is tested,"[8] which is by a refining process that consists of "six, yea, seven times through the fire."[9] So, it is likely that true believers will go through multiple refining fires in their lives, with the result of each being more purity.

So, when we are encountering fiery trials that come to test or purify our faith, we should heed the words of the Apostle Paul, "Be on the alert, *stand firm* in the FAITH, act like men, be strong."[10] "(W)ith respect to the promise of God," do not "*waver* in unbelief but *gr(o)w strong* in FAITH, *giving glory* to GOD!"[11]

The Testing of Simon Peter's Faith

There is a great example of how this all works in the incident transpiring not long before Jesus' crucifixion when Jesus prophesied to Simon Peter about impending testing in his life. Jesus warned Peter, "Simon, Simon, Satan has demanded permission (from God) to sift you like wheat."[12]

I'm sure Peter had the same thought occur to him that does to us when we find ourselves in a "fiery trial" authored by the adversary—why didn't Jesus merely pray for him and foil the plot of Satan that He foresaw in the Spirit. But the truth was that He couldn't, because as He stated to Peter, Satan had "demanded permission" from God to sift him. God's prosecuting attorney demanded to try Peter because there were some defiling sinfulness concealed in Peter's "hidden parts" or "innermost being" that gave "the accuser of the brethren" legal right to bring him up on charges and sift him like wheat.

Sifting is a purging process to separate the grain (the usable part) from the chaff (the unusable part). What Jesus foresaw was a "fiery trial" that was necessary for Peter's purging of the fear of man, faithlessness, treachery, and self-centeredness that lay hidden in his heart and was spiritually defiling him. But Satan and all the fiery trials he authors in our lives, are only a tool in the hands of God. If we will respond properly to the purging process of the Spirit, which is by humbling ourselves, admitting our faults, and allowing godly sorrow to produce genuine repentance in us,[13] then we, like Peter, receive genuine pardon and exoneration of the Spirit.

Instead of praying to remove the trial that was coming, which would have only foiled the purposes of God, Jesus told Peter, "**but I have prayed for you**, and when you have turned again, strengthen your brothers."[14] Instead of praying for removal of the fiery trial that was coming for Peter's purging and purification, Jesus prayed for and prophesied something of far greater value—Peter's repentance—and then charged him to strengthen his fellows with the spiritual empowerment he attained as a result of the purging process. And, in the end, Peter did precisely what Jesus prayed and prophesied, for that very reason—because He prayed and prophesied it—which is precisely what especially prophetic believers must learn to do in their relationships with and attitudes toward their fellows. The Apostle Paul described what Jesus did and what we are supposed to do in following His example this way:

> Brethren, even if a man is caught in any trespass, you who are spiritual, restore such a one in a spirit of gentleness each one looking to yourself, lest you too be tempted. Bear one another's burdens, and thus fulfill the law of Christ. For if anyone thinks he is something when he is nothing, he deceives himself. But let each one examine his own work, and then he will have reason for boasting in regard to himself alone, and not in regard to another. For each one shall bear his own load.[15]

God is saying here that it is not spiritual to judge and condemn believers who trespass against God's Word, even when they are CAUGHT in their trespasses, but rather true spirituality is demonstrated in attitudes and deeds reflective of the premise of restoration in which the manner of approach is a spirit of gentleness or meekness accompanied by self-examination and circumspection. Otherwise, we open ourselves up to likewise be tempted by Satan with the SAME sin, or another sin.

Afflictions and Persecutions

Mark 4:6,17
6 And after the sun had risen, it was scorched; and because it had no root, it withered away.
17 and they have no firm root in themselves, but are only temporary; then, when affliction and persecution arises because of the word, immediately they fall away.

Nowhere has God promised believers a rose garden. Some people have a confused understanding of what Jesus meant when He said, "I came that they might have life (*zoe*, Gr.), and might have it abundantly."[16] The Greek word translated "life" in this passage is not a reference to physical existence on Earth, per se. That word "zoe," is actually the word God uses in Scripture for spiritual life; that is, the Eternal Life. Jesus *did* come to bring us that Life in overflowing abundance. In the same regard, the Apostle Peter even said, "His divine power has granted to us everything pertaining to life (*zoe*) and godliness."[17]

The Abundant Life Jesus came to give every true believer is the Eternal Life, *His* Life, which indwells every true, Born Again (there is no other kind) believer, in the person of the Holy Spirit. God spares nothing in giving believers that Life. He pours His Life into us in abounding superfluity, which is what the Greek word Jesus used that is translated "abundantly" means. It means that Jesus came to give us His Life in overflowing measure. It means we have exceedingly more than we will ever need to utilize in any circumstance.

That is the Abundant Life Jesus was talking about. He was not referring to our span of physical existence in this present world. He was not saying that our existence in this world would be so "abundant" so as to be absolutely free of any negative or adverse circumstances. No, such a euphoric state of utopia will never exist on planet Earth in the present age.

Much to the contrary, Jesus forthrightly declared, "In this world you will have tribulation."[18] The Apostle Paul said, "Through MANY tribulations we must enter the kingdom of God."[19] Life in this present world is full of tribulations.

The Abundant Life of Jesus is abundant with nothing but "goodness and righteousness and truth."[20] Nevertheless, our physical existence in this present world is inevitably abundant with "the sufferings of Christ": "The sufferings of Christ are ours in abundance."[21] Especially in these last days in which we live are our lives full of tribulations and difficulties, something which the Spirit of God predicted: "But realize this, that in the last days difficult times will come."[22]

Now all these admonitions concerning tribulation are directed to *believers*. Believers are not impervious to tribulations. No one who lives in this present world on planet Earth is impervious to tribulation. It comes with the territory, as they say. In fact, the real truth is that believers may be the target of more adversity than unbelievers. It's just that believers have the wherewithal to overcome every adversity. This was the essence of what the Apostle Paul wrote to the young minister Timothy, who had learned greatly under the tutelage of Paul, not only from his extraordinary revelation knowledge, but also from his exemplary life, which was replete with afflictions and persecutions:

> But you followed my teaching, conduct, purpose, faith, patience, love, perseverance, *persecutions and sufferings*, such as happened to me at Antioch, at Iconium and at Lystra; what *persecutions* I endured, and out of them all the Lord delivered me! And indeed, all who desire to live godly in Christ Jesus **will be** *persecuted*.[23]

Under the inspiration of the Holy Spirit, Paul declared that *everyone* who sincerely desires to live godly in Christ Jesus in this world will indeed be persecuted. Believers, the Born Again children of God, are the only ones who are "in Christ Jesus." Paul said all believers "who desire to live godly" will be persecuted. He didn't say they "*might be.*" He said they "*will* be" persecuted. It is not even required that a believer be entirely perfected in godly living in order to be persecuted, necessarily, but just have the "desire" to live godly in Christ Jesus.

The more conformed into the Image of Jesus[24] and less conformed to the world[25] a believer becomes, the more persecution he will experience in this world through those who are not conformed into His Image, who walk "according to the course of this world, according to the prince of the power of the air."[26]

"Yes, but we should not 'believe' for persecution," some say today, "because if we do, then we will be sure to get it."

My friend, my Bible says if you desire to live godly in Christ Jesus, you "**will be** persecuted," whether you are "believing" for it or not.

Jesus foretold His death, burial, and resurrection many times. He told the apostles that He would be mocked, spit upon, and beaten. Were all those things fulfilled because He made a "bad confession" and was "believing" for it? Jesus forewarned the apostles they would be mistreated, persecuted, and even killed for the sake of the Gospel. Were those things, including the eventual martyrdom of those great men, fulfilled because they were "believing" for it? Did the great Apostle Paul experience all the afflictions and persecutions he experienced, which he enumerates seemingly endlessly in Second Corinthians 11:23-28, because he was "believing" for them? How absurd!

It is when someone who purports to be a believer is *not* being persecuted and afflicted with adversity that I begin to seriously wonder why not! God's Word says, "**all** who desire to live godly in Christ Jesus **will be** persecuted." I say let God be true and every man a liar.[27] Anyone who is *not* being persecuted to some degree, had better do some checking to see how he is doing in the godly living department.

Defining Affliction and Persecution?

Generally speaking, the term "affliction" in the Bible connotes adverse circumstances or conditions, such as, trouble, trial, difficulty, grief, hardship, anxiety, and the like. Bodily and mental sickness, disease, and pain are also forms of affliction. These physical afflictions, however, were borne by Jesus Christ on the cross at Calvary, and by His stripes we were healed.[28] Nevertheless, those who have not yet received that revelation, continue to be afflicted. Even knowledgeable believers, though, are not impervious to the enemy's attempts to afflict physically, only they must offensively resist him, and refuse to passively accept and receive infirmities Jesus "took" (*vicariously bore*) and diseases Jesus "carried away" (*removed*) at Calvary.[29]

"Persecution," on the other hand, usually refers to adversity brought against a person or group of persons by another person or group of persons. Persecution can range from subtle contrariety to repression to oppression to physical harm and abuse, and all the way to outright murder.

Affliction and persecution would also be included in what the Bible terms "tribulation." We have already seen several Scriptures concerning the fact that our lives in this world will be intrinsically laden with tribulations. Most of us, however, may not be able to readily identify with the term "tribulations" until it is rendered as its literal meaning—"pressures."

Most people can readily identify with having "pressures" in their lives. Understanding that "tribulation" is "pressure" makes it easier to understand what Jesus meant when He said that "in this world" we would have "tribulations." He meant that during the course of our lives we would often experience a variety of "pressures." Nearly every day of our lives, especially in this hectic, fast-paced modern era, we are inundated with pressures of various types and degrees, just as Jesus predicted.

Who Authors Affliction and Persecution?

Contrary to many religious ideologies, the Word of God attributes authorship of all adversity to the "adversary," Satan: "Your adversary, the devil, prowls about like a roaring lion, seeking someone to devour."[30] It is totally unscriptural to purport, however, that God cannot, has not, or does not inflict various forms and degrees of temporal judgments and disciplinary actions on individuals, groups, and even whole nations. God can, has, and does anything He pleases in agreement with His Word. He is Sovereign. Nevertheless, pure adversity void of redeeming value is only attributable to Satan.

Satan is the adversary of everyone, but especially of believers. He hates God and His entire Creation, especially "the apple of His eye"—His redeemed children. Now Satan cannot harm God in any way, so he has mounted a vicious, never-relenting battle against all of God's Creation, and especially against his arch-nemesis, the Church, which consists of genuinely born again believers.

When Adam committed high treason against God in the Garden of Eden, he handed over to Satan the dominion and surrogate lordship of this world which God had delegated unto the Sons of Men (Adam's progeny).[31] Thereby, Satan became "the god of this world,"[32] "the ruler of the world."[33] By virtue of Man's fall into perdition, Satan now had rulership over the elements and order of this world. The entire Creation became enslaved to the effects of his unrighteous nature: corruption.[34] From that moment on, the entire creation eagerly awaited the manifestation of the redeemed Sons of God, true believers, who would resist, oppose, and arrest Satan and his adverse works through the authority given them by the Lord Jesus Christ "over all the power of the enemy."[35]

Satan has the power in the present age to inflict adversity upon those who do not resist him. He never ceases in his evil and adverse works, some of which are to: steal, kill, destroy, deceive, harass, hinder, depress, oppress, possess, tempt, accuse, pervert, blind, captivate, torment, confuse, condemn, provoke, afflict, corrupt, and persecute.

But, praise God, the very purpose of Jesus Christ's appearance was: "that He might destroy the works of the devil."[36] And, He *has* destroyed the works of the devil, but it is up to the redeemed to execute that destruction, at least in their own personal regard, through the authority Jesus has delegated to them.

Satan is the adversary, who is *against* us, but God is **FOR** us. David said, "This I know, that God is for me."[37] If he didn't know anything else, he knew one thing—that his God was *for* him, and **not** *against* him. If a believer does not know anything else, he needs to know one thing for sure—God is *for* him, and **not** *against* him.

Satan authors adversity, but God authors good! God is forever trying to bring good into our lives. The Bible says, "every good thing bestowed and every perfect gift is from above, coming down from the Father of Lights."[38] In the verse preceding that verse, God specifically warns us not to be deceived concerning that fact. Yet so many people *are* deceived because they have bought the devil's lie that God is the one who is bringing all the bad or adversity into people's lives. But that is only a vicious lie, under which he camouflages himself and his own destructive works.

So many people are blaming God for the terrible things the devil has been doing all along. They have been duped into believing God has been bringing all the adversity and difficulties into their lives. They begin to blame God.

Yet, the Bible tells us explicitly that when we are experiencing a temptation, test, or trial, we should not say, "'I am being tempted by God'; for God cannot be tempted by evil, and He Himself does not tempt anyone."[39] It is not God who is bringing evil and adversity into our lives. As Job was admonished by Elihu, "Far be it from God to do wickedness, and from the Almighty do wrong....Surely God will not act wickedly, and the Almighty will not pervert justice."[40]

"God is light, and in Him there is no darkness at all,"[41] which means there is absolutely no evil in God. Therefore, it would be impossible for

Him to use evil toward us. Since, as James said, "God cannot be tempted by evil," it would be a gross perversion of His Divine Righteousness for Him to bring such things upon anyone else, but rather, as the passage explicitly says, "He Himself does not tempt anyone."

Why Do Affliction and Persecution Come?

Besides the reasons already discussed, Jesus said the reason affliction and persecutions come is "because of the word."[42] It is no coincidence that while the Word is being sown into the hearts of these hearers of the Word, Satan is bringing external affliction and persecutions into their lives.

Contrary to the pious-sounding preaching of some, God in no wise intends for believers to be foolishly ignorant of the schemes of the devil. That would only give the enemy an overwhelming advantage. God explicitly warns against that: "in order that no advantage be taken of us by Satan; for we are not ignorant of his schemes."[43] The word translated "schemes" here, and in the passage, "Put on the full armor of God, that you may be able to stand firm against the *schemes* of the devil,"[44] actually connotes "strategic battle plans" in the original language. It speaks of military generals gathered around a battlefield map, carefully plotting out strategic battle plans.

This is precisely what the Holy Spirit is revealing about our enemy, the devil—that he meticulously and skillfully contrives strategic battle plans to launch against believers. His tactics are well-conceived and are by no means happenstance. He has a strategic battle plan tailor-made for each individual believer. He looks for chinks in the believer's armor he can exploit, which is precisely the reason it is so essential that every believer "put on the full armor of God, that you may be able to stand firm against the schemes of the devil."[45]

Any war-wise, battle-tested soldier will tell you that the stupidest and potentially most fatal mistake a soldier can make is to not be apprised concerning the "modus operandi" of the enemy. If you are informed concerning the enemy's usual methods, then you have a distinct advantage over him, rather than vice-versa. One of the most vital and extensive parts of a soldier's pre-battle training is instruction on the means and methods of the enemy; in other words—his strategic battle plans. Anyone who does not give attention to that block of instruction is not only foolish, but more often than not will not survive the battle. Likewise, it is stupid and oftentimes deadly for a believer not to be apprised concerning the strategic battle plans of his adversary, the devil. That only gives him a decided and unnecessary advantage. God does not intend for believers to be uninformed or ignorant concerning Satan's schemes and devices. Rather, He wants us to be informed concerning them, in order that we "may be able to stand firm against" them.

The next most essential element of a soldier's battle training is instruction on his own weapon. He must become thoroughly familiarized with every aspect of proper usage and maintenance of that weapon. His survival depends on it. He must learn how to become a skilled marksman with his weapon, and how to ensure that it continuously remains in proper working order. Similarly, believers are in an all-out, life or death, battle. It is a *spiritual* battle, fought in the *spiritual* realm, against *spiritual* foes.[46] Thus, we must use *spiritual* weapons, for fleshly weapons are utterly useless and powerless in this *spiritual* battle: "For the weapons of our warfare are not of the flesh, but divinely powerful for the destruction of fortresses."[47]

The chief offensive weapon in the believer's arsenal is "the word of the Spirit, which is the word of God."[48] The Word of God can be used to successfully resist the enemy every time. The spiritual foes against whom we battle are utterly defeated on every battle front when the all-powerful Sword of God's Spirit is wielded. Every believer must become thoroughly acquainted with his weapon, and through continuous practice become a skilled marksman with it. "All Scripture" is the believer's weapon, with which he/she is more than adequately equipped for defeat of every foe.[49]

You see, the fulness of God's power is contained in His Word! Every Word God has ever spoken is "the word of His power."[50] That means that all of God's omnipotence is released and executed by His spoken (Rhema) Word, which is the exact means by which He created the entire Creation, according to Moses' account. Jesus Himself is the Creator,[51] and the Word of God Embodied,[52] and thus He Himself is "the power of God."[53] When God's Word is spoken in accordance with His Ways to effect His Will, all the same might that conquered death and created the entire Creation is unleashed.

Moreover, in cases of inspired application, God's Word will accomplish yet today all it has ever accomplished as it is spoken by a believer into the atmosphere of the Creation. God says He personally watches over His Word to execute it.[54] He promises it will accomplish exactly what it says: "It shall not return to Me empty, without accomplishing what I desire, and without succeeding in the matter for which I sent it."[55]

Now Satan knows the truth of all this more than most people, including most believers. He is quite aware of the omnipotent might of God's Word. And he knows that all of God's omnipotence is unleashed through His Word. He is experientially cognizant that God's Word has more than ample might to "destroy the works of the devil."[56] He knows the destruction wreaked against his evil works through the discharge of the "weapons of our warfare."[57]

Satan has experienced firsthand the awesome power unleashed against him by "doers of the Word." He knows the validity of Jesus' Words: "Behold, I have given you authority to tread upon serpents and scorpions, and over all the power of the enemy, and nothing shall injure you."[58] He knows that he will have to flee in terror from the believer who is submitted to God and who offensively, proactively resists the devil with the spiritual weapons of spiritual warfare. He knows the believer who puts on the whole armor of God and boldly wields the Sword of the Spirit cannot be overcome by the greatest of his strategic battle plans.

So, it is because of all these truths concerning God's Word that Satan brings affliction and persecution against believers—"because of the word"—"the word of His power." Inundating with a barrage of affliction and persecution is his strategic battle plan against especially new as well as immature believers, in an attempt to steal the Word from their heart before it can take root and begin to produce some fruit.

Jesus said people are like rocky ground, "when affliction and persecution arises because of the word, immediately they fall away."[59] That is the ultimate goal Satan is aiming for—to cause everyone who has made a commitment to serve the Lord to fall away. In order to do that, he attempts to get the new and spiritually undeveloped believers to doubt the validity of the Word of God, and the ability of God to perform it in their own lives by inundating them with a flood of affliction and persecution. Then, as they become doubtful, discouraged, and disheartened, their faith in the Word begins to wane, and they cease to boldly utilize their arsenal of spiritual weapons. They also fail to put on the whole armor of God to defend themselves against the attack of the enemy.

Eventually, the believer who has ceased to resist the enemy offensively and defensively will be overcome by his strategic battle plans. Or, as Jesus said it, they will soon "fall away," i.e., from faith in God and His Word. This is the plight of this category of hearers mentioned in the Parable of the Sower—when afflictions and persecutions come into their lives because of the Word, they fall away, because they are only *temporary* believers.

This matter of whether or not a believer can fall away has been a topic of great controversy and debate in many ecclesiastical factions for centuries. To be sure, it is a subject many ministers avoid and evade whenever possible. However, I devoted an entire chapter in *Mystery of the Kingdom* to this very important issue of believers falling away as Jesus said in the Parable of the Sower these "rocky grounders" did. Much of that chapter and more is included in Chapter Seventeen of this book.

A Real Life Example of Fiery Trials Producing Repentance

Years ago, I was sitting in a cafeteria that was in a mall, eating dinner with my wife and another Christian brother who was part of our ministry. Though the cafeteria was entirely inside the mall, it had several windows to the mall corridor leading to the outside exit/entrance to the mall. As I was eating and talking, the Spirit had me focus on a couple in their late forties who were standing out in the mall corridor by the exit, as if they were waiting on someone. I had never seen them in my life, but they were all dressed up in formal attire as if they were going to a special banquet or something. Suddenly the Spirit said to me, "That couple are both believers, but they are in sin right now. He is a well-known piano player, but he is married to someone else, and has children, who have not heard from him in months. This woman is an adulteress who has seduced him into leaving his wife and family and they have been living together here in (the town I was living in at the time). They are both being influenced by deceiving spirits. They are not supposed to be together. The woman has visions of grandeur of a life married to this man because of his musical talents. Tell those with you what I just told you." I said to the Lord in my spirit, "Well, that's pretty fantastical. How am I supposed to know if what I believe you just told me is so?" He replied, "I will confirm it to you."

I felt led to tell my wife and the brother what I just experienced. I showed them the couple, and told them what the Lord told me about them. Of course, they were stunned, and almost in unison asked, "Well, what did the Lord tell you to do?" To which I replied, "Nothing; he didn't tell me to do anything. Hallelujah!" We all laughed rather awkwardly but were pretty shaken in our spirits by the event.

I tried to just forget about the situation, for fear the Lord would put me to the test and tell me to go talk to the couple and tell them what the Lord showed me. I was hugely relieved when we left the cafeteria to discover that the couple were no longer standing where I had seen them. So, I said to my wife, "Let's walk around a bit to walk off this dinner." I thought I was just walking randomly through the mall, but the first turn we made was in the direction of a piano and organ store that was in the mall. As we approached closer to the store, I suddenly began to hear someone absolutely "tearing up" some ivories, and I thought, "Wow, they've got a salesperson in that store that can really play the piano...WELL!" Which usually is not the case. But then as I walked closer, I realized it was Gospel music that was being played, and with that unmistakable Gospel music style, with grace notes and all. Whoever was playing was really GOOD!

Then, it dawned on me....no, that can't be...not that guy the Lord spoke to me about. Sure enough, when I gingerly peered into the store to see who was playing, it WAS THE GUY! Oh My God! Now what? What the Lord said is really true...He DID just confirm what He told me. Quickly I grabbed my wife's hand and turned her around and said, "We have to get away from here," and started walking in the other direction. We eventually left the mall and returned home, and I tried to just forget about the incident.

That was on Sunday night. On Wednesday of that week, I was scheduled to take part in a television telethon at a Christian station I had been helping with for a number of years. I was one of the first singers/speakers during the first part of the telethon as it went on air. While I was on camera singing my first song, the studio doors opened and in walked....yep, you guessed it...*that couple*...while I was singing my song. I almost messed up the next few lines of the song I was singing as I watched them walk into the studio and stand in the back of the standing room only crowd. When I finished the song, I made a beeline to the opposite side of the studio and propped myself up against a wall.

Out of the corner of my eye, I saw this guy motion to the woman to stay there where she was and watched as he began walking in my direction. "Oh no! Surely, he's not coming to talk to *me*, is he?" Sure enough, he came right over to me, and whispered, "Sir, I heard you singing that song when I was out in the lobby; there was such a powerful anointing that hit when you first started singing that I just had to come in to see who was singing." I thanked him in a whisper. Then he said, "I am here tonight to play the piano and sing with my wife, also, but God just told me that I need to speak to you, and you are going to minister to me." I gulped and almost choked, but gathered myself to respond in the calmest and most pleasant manner I could muster up, "Oh, okay, we can talk later then."

Of course, he had just lied in identifying the woman who was his singing partner as his wife. The whole rest of the segment of the telethon I was scheduled for I was trying to figure out what the Lord wanted me to do and/or say. After it was over the guy came back over to talk to me again, and said, "Please forgive me for being so forward, but I believe the Lord told me that I am suppose to ask you if we can come to your house and have dinner with you and your wife Friday night." "Oh," I replied as cheerfully as I could sound, "then, I guess I'll see you Friday night; ya'll like spaghetti?" We both laughed; he said yes; and I gave him directions to our house.

When they came that Friday night, after some small talk, and while we were eating, he began to tell me the story of his life, and what brought him to the town we were in. He had been somewhat of a child prodigy musically as a pianist and began playing professionally as a teenager for a number of well-known gospel music groups, first as a fill-in, then later full-time with various groups over the years. Over the current and previous week, he was away on a furlough from traveling with a famous Pentecostal evangelist as his pianist, though the evangelist fronted his own meetings singing and playing the piano as well in a self-taught Gospel-style. This man was the background piano player who "carried" the piano instrumentation while the evangelist picked out riffs and fills. He was supposed to return to the tour the following week.

After telling his story, he then began asking me about my ministry, because he said he had discerned that I had some special anointing in some areas that he was not knowledgeable in and that was very different than all the ministries he had worked with over decades in traveling music ministry, as well as the churches he attended. I tried to explain as best I could about my prophetic and deliverance anointing and ministry. What made it even more difficult to explain was that this was back in the early 1980s when these types of ministries were virtually unheard of in most church circles, and anyone who did speak about them were considered heretics or lunatics or both. But I was shocked when he started zeroing in on the deliverance part in particular and asking me question after question. And all during the meal, the woman kept kicking the guy under the table, trying to get him to stop talking about this deliverance stuff and to finish eating so they could leave. She was extremely nervous and uncomfortable.

One of the poignant moments in the conversation was when he told me that just before he left the tour, he asked the evangelist for some time to talk to him. During that conversation, he shared with the evangelist some personal battles he was having and actually had struggled with his entire life, though he had been saved when he was a very young teenager. He told the evangelist that he felt God had been revealing to him recently that it was demons that were driving him to the compulsions he was experiencing and seemed to have little control over, even though he had confessed and repented over and over again, and was greatly convicted about and remorseful for his behavior. The evangelist replied in anger and told him there was no way a Christian could possibly have a demon, and that if he had these problems, he would just have to either get help and get rid of the problem, or the evangelist would have to fire him. The evangelist told him to take a couple weeks off, and return to the tour, if he had dealt with the problem and essentially "fixed" it.

After we ate and retreated to the living room to talk a little more, he stayed on the subject, asking questions, until finally the woman said, "Well, honey, we need to be going, because we have to get up early in the morning." Finally, he acquiesced, and they excused themselves politely, and left.

Over the next month, I received a number of phone calls from this man on my answering machine, but every time he called, I wasn't there to receive the call, and he would never leave a number for me to call back (this was before caller ID and cellphones). Then, one day, I was in prayer in my study in my home, when I thought I heard a car pull into the driveway, and then heard a car-door shut. Then, my doorbell rang. When I opened the door, this man was standing on the doorstep with his baggage, and I saw a taxicab driving off. He said, Pastor Steven, I just got fired last night, and God told me to fly here today, and stay here until I am delivered. You are the only person I know who can help me. Will you?" Of course, I said I would and invited him in.

After putting his things away in a guest room, we began talking. I told him the story of when I first saw him in the mall through the cafeteria window, and he verified that he was there that day and playing the piano in the store. Then I proceeded to tell his "real" story and what God had showed me about him, past, present, and future, and that God only reveals in order to heal, and that the only way he could be healed was through deliverance. The long and the short of it is that the guy stayed with us for the next two weeks while God miraculously and dramatically delivered him from the demons that were controlling him.

Two weeks later, on Saturday morning, the first thing he said to me when I saw him in the morning was, "I have to call my wife and kids, and tell them where I am, where I've been, and hope that they still want me, so that God can restore our family." I told him, now I knew he was totally delivered. He called that morning, and that family was powerfully reunited! I've seen him a number of times since over the years on various television programs...along with his wife. Praise the Lord! God is good!

There's even another layer to this story that is really remarkable! About a year ago, I was invited by another minister friend to join him and some other ministers on a weekly Zoom meeting that was primarily for fellowship and encouragement between fellow ministers. A few months into that meeting, low and behold, who comes onto the call in response to an invitation by my friend? Yep! Incredibly this same man who I had ministered deliverance to some thirty years before. He even shared several times during the meeting how that had it not been for that two weeks of ministry he does not know what would have happened to him and his ministry, much less his relationship with his wife and children, that likely it would have all ended right then and there! But, by the grace of God, he and his wife and children were dramatically and powerfully reunited back then when he made that call and at 80 plus years old now, he has enjoyed the incredible fruits of that restoration all these years since! What an incredible story of redemption and I am so overjoyed that God allowed me to have a small part in it all happening! Praise God forever!

But my point in telling this story is that the man who camped out on my doorstep and repented, and cried out to God for deliverance, God delivered. But the famous evangelist who was enraged by his piano player's belief that God had showed him there were demons at work in his life, and fired him, was himself publicly exposed in a very publicized sin scandal as being demonized by the same kinds of demons the piano player was troubled with and controlled by the SAME kind of sin. I've heard that evangelist's theology regarding demons and Christian's being troubled by them has since drastically changed, indeed, reversed. I believe this public exposure happened because the evangelist did not treat the trespasser with a spirit of meekness, looking also to himself in self-examination, and that gave the evil spirits he had also been troubled with since childhood legal right to ramp up their activity in the evangelist's life until his sin could no longer be concealed. Sadly, the evangelist's ministry was never quite the same, though powerful restoration has certainly transpired over the years. I venture to say that few people, if any, know the real cause of his precipitous and unfortunate fall from grace. But, thank God for restoration!

Self-examination, godly sorrow, repentance of revealed sinful attitudes, and graciousness toward our human accusers is the only right response to accusations of wrongdoing that have some basis of truth to them at some level, whatever that level may be. On a personal basis, as long as we are trying to resist the accusations of the accuser of the brethren by defending ourselves and declaring our goodness, he has the legal right to continue to accuse, prosecute, and judge us. Jesus admonished, "Agree with thine adversary quickly, whiles thou art in the way with him; lest at any time the adversary deliver thee to the judge, and the judge deliver thee to the officer, and thou be cast into prison."[60] Peter made it clear our ultimate adversary is the devil, Satan.[61] As long as we are denying the charges Satan makes against us, we are in a prison of one sort or another. If we agree with the charges of the adversary QUICKLY, confess our sins, seek forgiveness, and repent, then we will receive the full pardon Christ provided through His sacrifice and be released from the virtual prison cell in which we've been confined.

"If we confess our sins, He is faithful and righteous to forgive us our sins and to cleanse us from all unrighteousness."⁶² The only kind of sin or wrongdoing that can be forgiven and pardoned is CONFESSED sin or wrongdoing. I would urge every minister and ministry in the days of Spirit-compelled circumspection that are now upon us, in which God is purifying the sons of Levi [church leaders]⁶³ and testing the building materials of every ministry,⁶⁴ not to be so quick to resist and deny the accusations of the enemy out-of-hand without sincere self-examination to determine if there is any semblance of truth in the spirit realm to the prosecuting attorney's charges. If there is, consider it a merciful and gracious purging by the Spirit. If not, no harm, no foul.

> Let a man regard us in this manner, as servants of Christ and stewards of the mysteries of God. In this case, moreover, it is required of stewards that one be found trustworthy. But to me it is a very small thing that I may be examined by you, or by any human court; in fact, I do not even examine myself. For I am conscious of nothing against myself, yet I am not by this acquitted; but the one who examines me is the Lord. Therefore do not go on passing judgment before the time, but wait until the Lord comes who will both bring to light the things hidden in the darkness and disclose the motives of men's hearts; and then each man's praise will come to him from God.⁶⁵

The Remnant Church Jesus is Building

The bottom line on all this is that though God is not the one who authors affliction and persecution in the lives of believers, He certainly allows or permits it to occur. The overriding reason He allows it to occur is not a *negative* thing, but rather a *positive* thing. In so doing He is testing, verifying, proving the quality of our faith. Again, as I indicated at the beginning of this chapter, the testing of our faith produces endurance and a "perfect result" that we "may be perfect and complete, lacking in nothing":

> Consider it all joy, my brethren, when you encounter various trials, *knowing that the testing of your faith produces* **endurance**. And let endurance have its perfect result, so that you may be perfect and complete, lacking in nothing. Blessed is the man who perseveres under trial; for once he has been approved *(or, passed the test, margin)*, he will receive the crown of life, which the Lord has promised to those who love Him. ⁶⁶

But there's more. I believe, and a substantial number of other Present Truth Fivefold Ministers believe as well, in a "Remnant Church" and that it is the Church that Jesus is building[67]—a Purified One-third Remnant Church to be more specific, that shall coincide with the prophecy of Zechariah:

> "Awake, O sword, against My Shepherd, And against the man, My Associate," Declares the LORD of hosts. "Strike the Shepherd that the sheep may be scattered; And I will turn My hand against the little ones. "It will come about in all the land," Declares the LORD, "That *two parts* in it will be cut off and perish; But *the third* will be left in it. "And I will bring *the third part* through the fire, Refine them as silver is refined, And test them as gold is tested. They will call on My name, And I will answer them; I will say, 'They are My people,' And they will say, 'The LORD is my God.'"[68]

This is the Church that will survive the cleaving that I believe has already taken place in the Spirit. The only way anyone can be a part of this One-Third Remnant Church is by remaining FAITHFUL when God brings him/her through the refining and purifying fire to "REFINE them as silver is refined, And TEST (PURIFY) them as gold is tested!"

In order for there to even be "a glorious church, not having spot, or wrinkle, or any such thing; but...holy and without blemish"[69] there must come a cleansing, a purification, of the Spirit, by the Spirit, unto the Spirit. To accomplish that there must come a second fulfillment of Malachi's prophecy, which I believe will transpire in the last days prior to the return of Christ to claim His Church as His Glorious Bride:

> Behold, I will send my messenger, and he shall prepare the way before me: and the Lord, whom ye seek, shall suddenly come to his temple, even the messenger of the covenant, whom ye delight in: behold, he shall come, saith the LORD of hosts. But who may abide the day of his coming? and who shall stand when he appeareth? for he is like a refiner's fire, and like fullers' soap: And he shall sit as a refiner and purifier of silver: and he shall purify the sons of Levi, and purge them as gold and silver, that they may offer unto the LORD an offering in righteousness.[70]

The first fulfillment of this prophecy, as Jesus revealed, was the coming of John the Baptist in his day.[71] However, in order to effect the purification of the last days Ekklesia Jesus is building, the Lord will come to His Temple, which now in its corporate form is the Church, in the form of a company of Judgment Prophets "to sit as a refiner and purifier of silver: and he shall **purify the sons of Levi, and purge them as gold and silver**, that they may offer unto the LORD an offering in righteousness." The sons of Levi are the Levites, and the Levites are the Old Testament counterpart to the New Testament Fivefold Ministers, who comprise the leadership of the Church Jesus is building. Judgment begins with the Household of God," and because the anointing flows down upon the head or leadership "like the precious ointment upon the head, that ran down upon the beard, even Aaron's beard: that went down to the skirts of his garments,"[72] judgment must begin with the leadership of the House of God. As goes the head, or leadership, so goes the body. And the "offering in righteousness" that the New Testament Levites will offer unto the Lord is the righteous saints who have endured all and remained faithful "to the end."[73]

As this all indicates, this purification must begin with the leadership of the Household of God. Every local Church reflects its leadership in terms of its spiritual condition, and no local church can grow spiritually past its leaders. Leaders are either the *gateway* through which spiritual beneficence flows or it is a *bottleneck* blocking it. God must purge, refine, and purify the leaders of the Church He is building. There is no other way, and no way around it. It is coming! For those who have volunteered to go first and to cooperate with the dealings of the Spirit, no matter what the personal cost, many of them have already gone through it. They will be the people the Lord, the Head of the Church, will elevate to lead, shepherd, and minister to the other leaders who have yet to go through the Refiner's Fire. Others will abandon their post and resign their commission when the fiery trials come—and they will indeed come[74]—and thereby purge themselves from the ranks of the New Testament Levites.

God spoke a prophetic word to me in 2006 that commencing that year purification was a byword for the Church and would continue to be a byword until He returns! Though, in typical fashion, the vast majority of believers, leaders included, knew nothing about it, God began to bring forth a new emphasis in the Spirit realm on purification of the Body of Christ, individually and corporately. And purification entails deliverance.

There will yet come a time when deliverance—the casting out of demons—will be thrust to the forefront in the Church Jesus is delivering. The purification that is coming will be effected in great measure through *deliverance*. Deliverance is part and parcel of sanctification. Demons are impure or unclean spirits. They defile those in whom they are operating and have influence, whether it be in the case of possession of unbelievers or oppression or obsession with believers. *Demonization* is the word in the New Testament original language describing people who are influenced by demons.

The word the Lord spoke to me in 2006 is that 2006 was an important year for the Pentecostal/Neo-Pentecostal Church in the Spirit realm. It marked the 100th Anniversary of the so-called Azusa Street Revival, and the Pentecostal Awakening that God brought forth at the turn of the 20th Century. The Winds of the Spirit blew repeatedly during that one-hundred-year period bringing forth the Pentecostal, Healing, Charismatic, Prophetic, and Apostolic Movements, in that order. But, what the Church has failed to recognize is that none of these refreshings, renewals, or revivals, whatever you want to call them, were an end in themselves, but rather just a part of the continuum of restoration God has been bringing forth in the Church Jesus is building since October 31st, 1517, when an obscure Augustinian priest by the name of Martin Luther nailed 95 Thesis of Protest against the Roman Catholic Church to the door of Castle Church in Wittenberg, Germany, thereby sparking the Protestant Reformation.[75]

Each of the aforementioned emphases that transpired since 1906 were vital elements in the restoration that God has been taking the Lamb's Wife through in order to prepare her for the return of Christ to claim her as His Eternal Bride. The Pentecostal movement initiated a renewed awareness regarding the imperativeness of the Baptism in the Holy Spirit. Yet, that Truth was not and is not an end in itself, nor a panacea by any means. Rather, it was one piece of the spiritual puzzle, so to speak.

The Pentecostal Movement spawned the Charismatic Movement, which brought a renewed emphasis and revelation concerning the Gifts of the Spirit, which inure from the Baptism in the Holy Spirit. But the Gifts of the Spirit are likewise no end or cure-all in themselves.

Out of the Charismatic Movement came the Prophetic Movement of the 1980s, restoring the function of the prophet and bringing attention to the prophetic gifts whose preeminent role is to edify the Church and speak edification, exhortation, and comfort into believers' lives.[76] Yet, the raising up and establishing of prophets and prophetic gifts was not the ultimate purpose and goal of the Prophetic Movement.

The company of prophets God raised up during the last two decades of the previous millennium disclosed, declared, and decreed things in the Spirit required for the most recent movement, wherein the Apostolic Dimension is arising in the Spirit realm, to be birthed. The apostolic function has been reestablished in the Spirit realm, and a new Apostolic Ambience is gradually manifesting. But the pertinences of the apostolic emphasis likewise are neither an end in themselves nor self-completing.

Rather, all these emphases, and the "special effects," so to speak, that have arisen from them, are vital elements of the Master Plan of purification of the Bride of Christ God has been effecting from before the foundations of the Earth. From the beginning of time God has been doing one thing overall—preparing for Himself a people, redeemed humanity. From before the foundations of the Earth, the Lamb was slain,[77] in order to redeem and purify a people who were "qualified" by grace through faith to live in eternal communion or relationship with God.

Not all professing to be Christians will have a part in the final chapter of that Master Plan. There will be a separating—the sheep from the goats, the wheat from the tares—before Jesus returns to claim the Church He is building as His Eternal Bride. Again, in the end, the Church Jesus claims as His Bride will be a One-Third Remnant Church, comprised of only one-third of all those claiming to be "Christians" and part of churches or groups of churches, per the prophecy of Zechariah the Prophet cited earlier.

In sum, the overall substance of this chapter is the required testing of every believer's faith that will ultimately result in him/her having a part in the End-Times One-Third Remnant Church Jesus is currently in the process of building, and without which no one can have a part in that Ekklesia.

Endnotes

1. Jas. 1:2-4,12
2. 1 Pet. 5:8
3. I Pet. 4:12-14
4. 1 Pet. 1:3-9
5. John 3:6; bracketed explanation added
6. C.f., Jas. 1:21
7. 1 John 4:4
8. Zec. 13:9
9. Psa. 12:6
10. 1 Cor. 16:13
11. Rom. 4:20
12. Luke 22:31
13. 1 Cor. 7:11
14. Luke 22:32
15. Gal. 6:1-5
16. John 10:10
17. 2 Pet. 1:3
18. John 16:33
19. Acts 14:22
20. Eph. 5:39
21. 2 Cor. 1:5
22. 2 Tim. 3:1
23. 2 Tim. 3:10-12
24. Rom. 8:29
25. Rom. 12:2
26. Eph. 2:2
27. Rom. 3:4
28. Isa. 53:4,5; 1 Pet. 2:24
29. Mat. 8:17, italics added by author

30 1 Pet. 5:8
31 Psa. 115:16
32 2 Cor. 4:4
33 John 14:30
34 Rom. 8:21
35 Luke 10:19
36 1 John 3:9
37 Psa. 56:9
38 Jas. 1:17
39 Jas. 1:13
40 Job 34:10-12
41 1 John 1:5
42 Mark 4:17
43 2 Cor. 2:11
44 Eph. 6:11
45 Eph. 6:11
46 Eph. 6:12
47 2 Cor. 10:4
48 Eph. 6:17
49 2 Tim. 3:16-17
50 Heb. 1:3
51 Col. 1:16
52 John 1:10
53 1 Cor. 1:24
54 Jer. 1:12
55 Isa. 55:11
56 1 John 3:8
57 2 Cor. 10:4
58 Luke 10:19
59 Mark 4:17

60 Mat. 5:25
61 1 Pet. 5:8
62 1 John 1:9
63 Mal. 3:1-3
64 1 Cor. 3:10-15
65 1 Cor. 4:1-5
66 Jas. 1:2-4,12
67 Mat. 16:18
68 Zec. 13:7-9
69 Eph. 5:27
70 Mal. 3:1-3
71 Mark 9:13
72 Psa. 133:2
73 Mark 13:13
74 1 Cor. 3:13-15
75 Acts 3:19-21
76 1 Cor. 14:3-4
77 Rev. 13:8

Chapter Thirteen

HINDRANCES TO GENUINE FAITH

It is fairly obvious that there would be various hindrances to obtaining and walking in faith. As a practical matter, most people are naturally aware hindrances to faith exist and exist, more particularly, in their own lives, which they must avoid and overcome. The Word of God describes believers as overcomers or conquerors.[1] One passage indicates that it is through *our faith* that believers overcome the world:

> **For WHATEVER is born of God overcomes the world**; and this is the victory that has overcome the world—**our faith.** Who is the one who overcomes the world, but **he who believes** that **Jesus is the Son of God?**[2]

Born Again believers are the "whatever" that are born of God!

In Revelation it goes so far as to say that believers overcame the accuser of the brethren (Satan), who had been thrown down to the Earth from his former estate in Heaven and who accuses them before God day and night because of the shed blood of the Lamb of God, who took away, remitted, abolished, our sin, and because of the word of their testimony, loving not their own life, even when faced with a real prospect of the death of martyrdom:

> Then I heard a loud voice in heaven, saying, "Now the salvation, and the power, and the kingdom of our God and the authority of His Christ have come, for the accuser of our brethren has been thrown down, he who accuses them before our God day and night. And they *overcame* him because of **the blood of the Lamb** and because of **the word of their testimony**, and they did not love their life even when faced with death.[3]

Also, in Revelation, the Ascended and Glorified Christ declared that He would grant that individual believers who overcome as He overcame to sit down with Him on His throne as He sat down with His Father on His throne:

> 'He who *overcomes*, I will grant to him to sit down with Me on My throne, as I also *overcame* and sat down with My Father on His throne.'[4]

The Apostle Paul by the inspiration of the Spirit wrote that believers overwhelmingly conquer adversities of life common to us all through Him (Christ Jesus) who loved us: "But in all these things we overwhelmingly *conquer* through Him who loved us."[5] The term "overwhelmingly conquer" is another way of saying overcoming and being overcomers. In the Greek, what it actually says is more akin to being super- or uber-conquerors! The point of all these scriptures is that believers have the ability through the indwelling Holy Spirit to overcome all the adversity that "our adversary, the devil,"[6] can conjure up and throw at us!

Deceiving Spirits and Doctrines of Demons

The Dark Ages (313—1517 A.D.) was the period of The Great Apostasy for the collective Church, an occurrence prophesied by the Apostle Paul:

> But the Spirit explicitly says that in *later times* some will fall away from the faith, paying attention to **deceitful spirits and doctrines of demons**, by means of the hypocrisy of liars seared in their own conscience as with a branding iron,[7]

During this twelve-hundred-year-long age of spiritual darkness, the Truth, as elucidated in the Word of God, was subverted by humanistic ideologies and vain philosophies of men[8]—the *"doctrines of demons"* of which Paul forewarned. Eventually, nearly every remnant of Divine Truth—the foundational teachings upon which the Church had been originally established—was distorted, debauched, diluted, degraded, abrogated, and abandoned.

While the collective church experienced what theologians and church historians have identified as this massive corporate Falling Away or Apostasy during "The Dark Ages," the Word of God, nonetheless, categorically identifies a GREAT FALLING AWAY or GREAT

APOSTASY that will transpire in the very last days just prior to the "catching up" or "rapture" of the genuine Church Jesus is building, which event shall be followed immediately by the revelation and activation, if you will, of the ultimate antichrist, who will be the devil incarnate, and who will orchestrate apocalyptic destructions upon the earth, and "who opposes and exalts himself above every so-called god or object of worship," seats himself in the temple of God (the rebuilt Solomon's Temple), displaying himself as—i.e., claiming to be—God:

> Let no one in any way deceive you, for it (*the day of the Lord*) will not come unless *the apostasy* comes first, and the man of lawlessness is revealed, the son of destruction, who opposes and exalts himself above every so-called god or object of worship, so that he takes his seat in the temple of God, displaying himself as being God.[9]

Demonization—Various Evil Spirits

Any type of demonization (obsession, oppression, possession) will severely hinder the ability for a person to appropriate and operate genuine faith in his/her life.

There is only one word used in the original language of the New Testament (Greek) to describe demonic influence and habitation—"daimonizomai"—which simply means "demonized." In terms of casting out devils, it serves no purpose to quibble or split hairs over semantics. If a person is being influenced by a demon, he/she needs to be set free from that influence and the demon needs to be cast out, regardless of what part of his being (spirit, soul, or body) it is affecting or inhabiting.

However, for the sake of identification, demonization is commonly classified into three categories: oppression, obsession, and possession. **Oppression** is solely *external* influence by demons affecting or seeking to affect either a person's body or his mind and emotions but without usurpation of his/her will.

Obsession is a more advanced stage of demonic incursion of the *human soul or body* than oppression, distinguished primarily by the fact that with obsession the demonized person has gradually given more and more place to the evil spirits, resulting in progressive usurpation of the demonized person's will and progressively diminishing self-control.

Possession is the most advanced stage of demonization and occurs when the *human spirit* has been invaded and inhabited by one or more demons, resulting in total captivation and control of the person. Relatively few people are actually demon-possessed, but those who are, are socially dysfunctional to some degree and require some form of psychological treatment or institutionalization. The vast majority of the demonized are either oppressed or obsessed, and in many cases, both, being merely oppressed by some spirits and obsessed by others.

Can a genuine Born Again believer be demon-possessed, is a frequently asked question? No! Actual demon-possession is when a demon or demons have entered and gained control of a person's *spirit*. As long as the Spirit of Christ (the Holy Spirit) is occupying a human spirit, it cannot be invaded by an evil spirit. However, a true Born Again Christian can fall away from the Lord, lose his salvation, and be subject to eventual demon-possession through persistent rebellious behavior. But the premise of this volume and the LOOSED! book I wrote is that true Born Again, even Spirit-baptized Christians, most definitely can be "demonized," i.e., influenced, troubled, vexed, tempted, and attacked by demons.

Some evil spirits are especially hindering to faith. The following are a few of those at the top of the list.

1. Spirit of Unbelief
2. Religious Spirits
3. Seducing Spirits
4. Spirit of Apostasy
5. Jezebel Spirit
6. Spirit of Fear (Timidity, Passivity)

Space will not allow me to address each of these here in this book, but I do address them thoroughly in my book, ***LOOSED!*** *Deliverance From Demonic Powers!* which will be published soon and available on the Real Truth Publications website. The original version, which is a small booklet designed to be only a primer on deliverance, is available now on the website, however.

Despising and Rejecting Authority

> then the Lord knows how to rescue the godly from temptation, and to keep the unrighteous under punishment for the day of judgment, and especially those who indulge the flesh in its cor-

rupt desires and *despise authority*. Daring, self-willed, they do not tremble when they revile angelic majesties,[10]

Yet in the same way these men, also by dreaming, defile the flesh, and *reject authority*, and revile angelic majesties.[11]

God is the ultimate authority. He is sovereign, omnipotent, and almighty in authority. So, people who despise and reject authority are ultimately despising and rejecting *God*!

All of fallen, unredeemed Mankind is rebellious against and disobedient of God, to be sure, but there are some people, a whole lot of people on this planet, who absolutely loathe and detest any and every semblance of authority from any source exercised in any circumstance. Some people loathe and detest it so much that they are driven by that hatred to become murderers! Such people have no ability to control their rage against all authority no matter who is exercising it! They are compelled to retaliate against it in every way they can get away with it!

Societies around the world are filled with this kind of uber authority-haters! And every single one of them are so because, like the man at Gadara, they are filled with demons who despise God! Their animosity against God is beyond human description and comprehension.

Demons are under eternal judgment, their fate is unalterably fixed, they know where they will ultimately be consigned and forever confined, and they can do absolutely nothing about any of it! Hell was specifically made by God for them![12] They are completely powerless to exact even an ounce of revenge against God Himself, so they unleash all their dastardly schemes aimed at stealing, killing, and destroying against the next best target available to them—the apple of God's eye, the Redeemed! When in Heaven they joined with their leader, Lucifer, in abject rebellion against God, they forever forfeited their formerly enjoyed fellowship with God and their right to fellowship with God, a right that only the Redeemed enjoy and have as their future hope!

Thank God, all of these things existing in this sin-corrupted world system believers overwhelmingly conquer through Him who loved us, because of His shed blood and by the word of our overcoming testimony! Praise God! Hallelujah!

Iniquity

> For my life is spent with sorrow And my years with sighing; *My strength* has failed *because of my* **iniquity**, And my body has wasted away.[13]

This passage is certainly not describing the life of a genuinely Born Again believer who is resisting the devil's attacks in his/her life,[14] but rather one who has not been born again or regenerated. It is pointing out that failure of physical strength through either sickness, disease, or inordinate aging effects can be, though not always, a result of years of unrepented iniquity. Iniquity is distinguished from other sin in that it refers in the original language to "twistedness" or what is better known as *perversion*. There are many kinds of perversion that can transpire in the lives of the unsaved, those who are not born again, in particular. However, even after a person is born again, unless those spirits of iniquity are specifically dealt with in deliverance, they will remain in that part of the person's being in which they have been dwelling (soul or body, in the case of a Born Again believer).

Operating in a Form of Godliness That Denies the Power

> But realize this, that in the last days difficult times will come. For men will be lovers of self, lovers of money, boastful, arrogant, revilers, disobedient to parents, ungrateful, unholy, unloving, irreconcilable, malicious gossips, without self-control, brutal, haters of good, treacherous, reckless, conceited, lovers of pleasure rather than lovers of God, **holding to a form of godliness, although they have denied its power**; Avoid such men as these.[15]

A "form of godliness" is religion, which is the polar opposite of righteousness. Satan is the master-religionist and author of it. It is the form of godliness he promotes and very successfully draws multitudes of people into. His faux righteousness is solely an outward simulation or imitation of holiness, or godlikeness, or piety, derived through self-works of humanistic religiosity.

Fallen Mankind is entirely incapable of achieving genuine righteousness on their own, for "we are all as an unclean thing, and all our righteousnesses are as filthy rags" in the sight of God![16] Genuine righteousness is not something humans can produce on their own by any means or works of their own, for genuine righteousness is something that is bestowed upon Born Again believers by God purely as a result of not our own works but rather the substitutionary works of Christ Jesus. It is the greatest of all exchanges, wherein unrighteous sinners exchange their "filthy rags" for the righteousness of God as a result of the Lamb of God taking upon Himself the accumulative sins of all Mankind, from the sins of Adam and Eve in the Garden of Eden to those of every human ever to live: "He made *Him* who knew no sin to be sin on our behalf, so that *we* might become **the righteousness of God** in Him."[17] Words totally fail in any attempt to properly exult the magnitude and magnificence of this Great Exchange!

The Third Chapter of Zechariah portrays an awesome prophetic prefigurement of what transpired following Jesus' resurrection on Resurrection Morning (commonly but incorrectly called, "Easter") when He was seen by Mary and some of the other disciples and He forbad Mary from embracing Him after finally recognizing Him after initially assuming Him to be the grave-keeper:

> Jesus saith unto her, **Touch me not; for I am <u>not yet</u> ascended to my Father**: but go to my brethren, and say unto them, **I ascend unto my Father, and your Father; and to my God, and your God.**[18]

Subsequently, He vanished from their sight as He reentered the Spirit realm and ascended into Heaven to present Himself as the *actual, real* Lamb of God, upon whom the sins of all Mankind had been laid as represented by the centuries of ceremonial offerings every year of the sacrificial lamb upon whom the High Priest laid the sins of the Israelites while all of Israel were made to watch as the wounded and bleeding out lamb slowly meandered over the horizon after being loosed until it finally disappeared from their sight, representing the "taking away" or abolishment of the nation's and each Israelite's sin! Therewith the disappearance of that wounded and dying lamb—went their sin! And the whole ceremony was a poignant picture of what the actual, real Lamb of God would do when He would come all those years later! Albeit the vast majority of the Jewish people over the centuries, sadly, were and are prevented from seeing the significance of the ceremony due to the spiritual blindness produced by the veil covering their spiritual eyes that is only removed in Christ.[19]

Failure to Study the Word of God to Draw Near to God

Study to shew thyself approved unto God, a workman that needeth not to be ashamed, rightly dividing the word of truth.[20]

It is imperative and vital that every believer not just casually and infrequently read a few passages of Scripture now and then whenever it strikes his/her fancy! Such is *not* studying! One dictionary defines the verb study as: "to apply oneself to the acquisition of knowledge, as by reading, investigation, or practice."[21] The primary reason for studying the Word of God is *not* to gain intellectual, academic, or "head" knowledge *about* the Word of God, but rather to actually come to know the God of the Word and to assimilate His Words to us as much as possible into our very being (spirit, soul, and body), allowing it to draw us nearer to God in real personal relationship with the three persons of the Godhead!

Draw near to God and He will draw near to you. Cleanse your hands, you sinners; and purify your hearts, you double-minded.[22]

God has promised to draw near to us when we initiate this process of drawing near to Him! He will not violate anyone's free will, but if we initiate this drawing near effort, He will reciprocate by drawing nearer to us in very real and tangible ways, not merely in some rhetorical, metaphorical, mystical, philosophical, symbolic, or ethereal sense.

Though it is often difficult for many people to comprehend and really accept it, God wants to draw near to Born Again believers in very real moment-by-moment relationship of constant interaction effected by the indwelling Holy Spirit. The very reason God created the Earth and Mankind was to satisfy His need for fellowship, relationship, with living beings other than Himself, i.e., the Trinity: Father, Son, and Holy Spirit, all of whom were/are divine; meaning they each, separately and together, are God! Fellowship limited to the Members of the Godhead, which intrinsically would be thoroughly narcissistic, was not enough for God; He has a desire and need to have fellowship some other living being, thus, He created the Earth and then created Mankind and placed Mankind on the Earth He created!

Unfortunately, Adam and Eve destroyed that fellowship in and by the Spirit God had with the first humans when they sinned against God and ate of the fruit of the Tree of the Knowledge of Good and Evil that God had expressly and specifically forbad them from consuming. The horrible result of Adam and Eve's disobedience was that they personally fell into utter perdition, and as the progenitors of humanity, they thereby took their entire progeny, meaning all of humanity, with them! Mankind was now a fallen creature, permeated with the sin nature, resulting in the necessity for every human being born after them to be Born Again by the regenerative working of the Spirit in their spiritually dead human spirit.[23]

In addition to the James passage cited at the beginning of this section, there are others in the New Testament that also speak of this concept of drawing near to God:

> Therefore let us *draw near* with confidence to the throne of grace, so that we may receive mercy and find grace to help in time of need.[24]

> (for the Law made nothing perfect), and on the other hand there is a bringing in of a better hope, through which we *draw near* to God.[25]

> Therefore He is able also to save forever those who *draw near* to God through Him, since He always lives to make intercession for them.[26]

> For the Law, since it has only a shadow of the good things to come and not the very form of things, can never, by the same sacrifices which they offer continually year by year, make perfect those who *draw near*.[27]

> let us *draw near* with a sincere heart in full assurance of faith, having our hearts sprinkled clean from an evil conscience and our bodies washed with pure water.[28]

These passages combine to make it irrefutable and unequivocal that God desires for humans to draw near to Him in intimate personal relationship. Indeed, eternal fellowship, i.e., Everlasting Life in communion with God, is the ultimate purpose and outcome of being Born Again. In the context of the topic of this book, regeneration unto redemption and resultant eternal life in communion with God is also the ultimate result and reward of genuine faith.[29]

Rebellion, Stubbornness, Disobedience, Willful Sin

> "If you will not listen to the voice of the LORD, but *rebel* against the command of the LORD, then the hand of the LORD will be against you, as it was against your fathers.[30]

> If ye be willing and obedient, ye shall eat the good of the land: But if ye refuse and *rebel*, ye shall be devoured with the sword: for the mouth of the LORD hath spoken it.[31]

> They are of those that *rebel* against the light; they know not the ways thereof, nor abide in the paths thereof.[32]

> For *rebellion* is as the sin of witchcraft, and *stubbornness* is as iniquity and idolatry.[33]

> An evil man seeketh only *rebellion*: therefore a cruel messenger shall be sent against him.[34]

To most Bible-believing believers this matter is manifestly obvious. But to the substantial number of purporting believers today who embrace the recent inundation of hyper-grace teachings it is not so obvious. Obedience is a volitional choice; meaning it is a matter of one's will. God has embedded into the soul of every human being a will—i.e., personal autonomy. This personal autonomy is inviolable. Under no circumstances will God ever violate a person's will. He does not force *anyone* to do *anything*. Believers often are ignorant of or forget this in praying for others, especially for unbelievers to become believers. For this reason, they are often disappointed or disillusioned with God when their prayers are not answered the way they prayed.

Illustrating the sanctity and absolute inviolability of the human free-will is the fact that, though He certainly is sovereign over all, God Himself will *never* usurp or in any way forcibly infringe upon the free will of any human being, even when our actions and their consequences are not in our own best interest. Albeit, when we have willingly subjected ourselves unto His Lordship and Fatherhood, as a part of His great Fatherly love for us, He will indeed chasten and discipline us.[35] Nevertheless, though He invites *"whosoever will"* affirmatively respond to be adopted into the Heavenly Family, and though He loves us ever so immensely, and deeply desires that all be saved, He will not *force* Himself, His Sovereignty, nor His Fatherhood, upon *any* individual, to the point that He will allow us to choose the abyss and agonies of hell over the bliss and blessings of Heaven!

One can only have autonomy with respect to his/her own life; not anyone else's. When a person attempts to impose his/her will on the life of another person, by definition, that is witchcraft or sorcery. I wrote extensively about this matter of witchcraft or sorcery in both my book, *Charismatic Captivation*, as well as *Charismatic Control*, available at: https://www.charismatic-captivation.com.

A definition of witchcraft or sorcery I provided in those volumes is:

Simply stated, the true Spiritual definition and application of "sorcery" or "witchcraft" is using any form of persuasion, influence, intrigue, or inducement, delusion, predomination, or outright coercion, whether of natural (human; psychological) or spiritual (i.e., evil spirits) origin, to unduly and improperly influence, manipulate, dominate, or control someone else, in order to gain ascendancy or advantage for self-aggrandizement. To put it in even simpler terms, sorcery or witchcraft is endeavoring to get someone else to do what *you* want them to do. It is prevailing upon others in order to get them to yield their will to your will. It is volition (will) captivation. It is self-imposition and usurpation. It is being an interloper. It is dominating and controlling others.

God revealed through the prophet Samuel's rebuke of the disobedient King of Israel, Saul, that witchcraft or sorcery is essentially synonymous with "rebellion," and that "disobedience" (which, in essence, is rebellion) is synonymous with "iniquity" (acts of specific trespass and offense against God) and "idolatry" (the imposition of false gods in God's place): *"For* REBELLION *is as the sin of* WITCHCRAFT, *and* STUBBORNNESS (disobedience) is as INIQUITY and IDOLATRY" (1 Sam. 15:23). What this means, in other words, is that witchcraft IS rebellion, and rebellion IS witchcraft; moreover, disobedience (stubbornness) is defiance, disregard, and displacement of God.

Of course, Satan is the ultimate though unseen source behind every kind and genre of sorcery and witchcraft, and there exits an innumerable company of his diabolical cohorts, evil spirits, whose sole function it is to perpetrate and propagate witchcraft all throughout the world and among all human beings. However, Satan and his imps can only intervene and invoke their devices in human affairs where and when they are given opportunity, license, and agency by cooperative human-beings. Since God has given authority on the Earth unto the sons of men,[36] Satan is powerless to implement his devices except through human cooperatives.

Sorcery originated with Satan. He is the original source, or author of it. The spirit of disobedience—"the *spirit* that is now working in the sons of disobedience"[37]—is a part of his nature. Through the Prophet Isaiah, God revealed by the Spirit what took place in Heaven when Lucifer fell into apostasy and perdition. His account delineates Lucifer's precise rebellious ruminations precipitating his abrupt descent into unrighteousness and spiritual ruin. Clearly, the source of his rebellion is *self-will*, evidenced by the fact that he says to himself five times, "I WILL":

> "But you said in your heart, 'I WILL ascend to heaven; I WILL raise my throne above the stars of God, and I WILL sit on the mount of assembly in the recesses of the north. 'I WILL ascend above the heights of the clouds; I WILL make myself like the Most High.'"[38]

This passage makes it clear that rebellion against God (sin) is predicated on self-will, or self-imposition. In essence, rebellion is self-imposition, following after one's own will instead of God's. Consequently, it is not hard to understand the meaning of the Spirit's statement: "Rebellion is as the sin of witchcraft." In fact, in a broad sense, witchcraft is following after the rebellious nature of Satan, "the spirit...of disobedience."[39] At bottom, witchcraft is Satan's most basic operandi that he manifests on earth through the "principalities," "powers," "rulers of the darkness of this world," and "spiritual wickedness in high places"[40] that are part and parcel to his kingdom of spiritual darkness, as the primary means of turning the hearts of human beings toward venerating himself as God rather than the true Almighty God. But, Praise God, it is these very "rulers and authorities" of darkness that Christ Jesus disarmed, spoiled, depowered through the Cross of Calvary, "making a public display of...having triumphed over them."[41]

While witchcraft or sorcery indeed did originate with Lucifer (now called, Satan), it is vital to understand also that regardless of how unpalatable to the average believer, the truth is that the nature of the devil, *the spirit of disobedience*, with all its attributes of rebellion and evil, is the carnal nature that pervades the soul of every human being ever born. Which means that within us all is the propensity to rebellion, including operating in sorcery and witchcraft. This Truth is corroborated by the Holy Spirit's Words conveyed through the Apostle Paul in his letter to the Galatians, wherein he included *"sorcery"* or *"witchcraft"* (depending on which Bible translation you read) among the attributes of the carnal nature:

> Now the deeds of the flesh *(carnal nature)* are evident, which are: immorality, impurity, sensuality, idolatry, SORCERY, enmities, strife, jealousy, outbursts of anger, disputes, dissensions, factions, envying, drunkenness, carousing, and things like these, of which I forewarn you just as I have forewarned you that those who practice such things shall not inherit the kingdom of God.[42]

Thus, sorcery, from the spiritual perspective, is an attribute of the carnal nature common to us all. To put it another way, sorcery is a natural tendency lurking within the unredeemed soul of every human being that we all are quite capable of operating on our own without any assistance from evil spirits.

Within every one of us mere mortals is the raw desire to in some way and degree predominate and impose our will upon others for our own self-aggrandizing and self-exalting purposes. This propensity is just as much a part of the inherent carnal nature (the source of our temptation to sin) as is immorality, enmity, strife, jealousy, anger, or a plethora of other, just as damning, iniquitous attitudes and actions with which we all, saved or unsaved, Born Again or not, are constantly tempted. (In the case of many people, the urge to control *others* is stronger than their urge to control *themselves*, as demonstrated by their undisciplined behavior.) The *proclivity*, or in some people, *passion*, to control others is a basic urge of "the roaring lion within" that must be resisted and mastered in the same way as any other evil temptation, else it will surely master and eventually utterly destroy *you*.

The paramount point in regard to this hindrance to faith is that *any* form of rebellion, disobedience, stubbornness, and self-will will always, at the minimum, *hinder* faith and at the maximum, *negate* genuine faith and prevent it from being effectually operational in one's life.

These kinds of behaviors and the attitudes behind them reflect self-reliance as opposed to God-reliance. We'll take up that matter further in the next section.

Pride, Arrogance, Egotism, Narcissism

Someone, somewhere, sometime ago, poignantly pointed out that, tellingly, the middle letter of the English word "sin" is the letter "I". Indeed, the epicenter or seat of sin is the "I" or ego in every human being.

A dictionary definition of the singular vowel, "I", states it is a nominative singular pronoun, used in referring to oneself, the person speaking, writing, or otherwise communicating. It is the word representing the ego or the conscious self of a person.

Dictionary.com provides a cultural definition of the ego:

The "I" or self of any person (*ego* is Latin for "I"). In psychological terms, the ego is the part of the psyche that experiences the outside world and reacts to it, coming between the primitive drives of the id and the demands of the social environment, represented by the superego.

Simply stated, sin is personal rebellion against God. The original enactment of sin, ironically and incredibly, occurred in *Heaven*! And, despite the theories propounded by theologians regarding "original sin," it was *not* Adam, the first human, who first sinned, but rather it was the Archangel, Lucifer, "star of the morning," who committed the very first act of outright, overt rebellion against God! An *angel*—a class of spiritual being created by God to give constant and continuous praise and worship of God—was the original perpetrator of sin! Unimaginable!

And the punitive consequence of that "original sin" or rebellion against God was as grave as grave can be—a spiritual grave: *spiritual death*, i.e., utter, total, and irreversible eternal separation from God! A class of being who was created to live eternally in the very presence of God was now instantaneously, by his own actions, removed, disconnected, detached, disenfranchised, separated from the presence of God! This is the very definition of "the grave"—utterly separated from the presence of God to forever live in a state of Godlessness! Due to the narcissistic attitude of the Archangel, whose name, Lucifer, means, Light Reflector, had now become not a *reflector* of God's light but rather a *refractor* of it. He instantly became the embodiment of darkness, completely devoid of light!

Rebellion against God or disobedience of God, i.e., sin, originated with Satan. Rebellion and disobedience permeates Satan's heart and is a permanent part of his nature—the spirit of disobedience, *"the spirit that is now working in the sons of disobedience."*[43] This *spirit* is the "sin nature." Through the Prophet Isaiah, God revealed by the Spirit what took place when Lucifer fell into apostasy and perdition. His account delineates the precise rebellious ruminations of Lucifer that precipitated his abrupt descent into unrighteousness and spiritual ruin. Clearly, the source of Satan's rebellion is *self-will*, evidenced by the fact that he says to himself five times *"I WILL"*:

> "But you said in your heart, '**I WILL** ascend to heaven; **I WILL** raise my throne above the stars of God, and **I WILL** sit on the mount of assembly in the recesses of the north. '**I WILL** ascend above the heights of the clouds; **I WILL** make myself like the Most High.'"[44]

In other words, Lucifer is engaging in self-deification, that is, posing and interposing as God, which was precisely what made Lucifer fall into perdition and disenfranchisement from God. Ever since that day when unrighteousness was found in the heart of Lucifer, he has been totally consumed with trying to take Jesus' place as *Lord*. He is the ultimate usurper and interloper. He is literally **dying to be god**. When you put all this together, it becomes clear that Satan's nature is the *Antichrist Spirit*, because it is opposed and antithetical to the Lordship of Christ.

Consequential to Lucifer's abject rebellion against God, this creature could no longer live in the presence and habitation of God, Heaven, but *had* to be evicted. So, Scripture informs us there was "war in heaven":

> And there was war in heaven, Michael and his angels waging war with the dragon. The dragon and his angels waged war, and they were not strong enough, and there was no longer a place found for them in heaven. And the great dragon was thrown down, the serpent of old who is called the devil and Satan, who deceives the whole world; he was thrown down to the earth, and his angels were thrown down with him.[45]

Worthy of note is the fact that God Himself did not directly engage in warfare against Satan to mete out his eternal punishment—banishment from Heaven—but rather He consigned the task to the Archangel Michael, who is the warring angel and the commander of the war angels, the military division of the angelic hosts. God could not engage in warfare against Lucifer Himself because that would have been an unjust and unfair act, due to the fact that the angels are subordinate in every way to Almighty God. So, He relegated the task to another of the angelic order to carry out the assignment of evicting Lucifer along with one-third of all the angels who sided with him.

In sum, what earned Lucifer this ultimate of fates was his innate and expressed pride, which he could not help but to express in that "out of the abundance of the heart, the mouth speaks!"[46] And, again, it is this "spirit of disobedience"—"the spirit that is now working in the sons of disobedience", which is "according to the prince of the power of the air"[47]—that is the "sin nature" that fills the heart of every person ever born! And this sin nature, it is imperative to understand, is absolutely replete with every type and form of evil and wickedness, so that therefore the spiritual state of all unredeemed Mankind is:

> as it is written, "THERE IS NONE RIGHTEOUS, NOT EVEN ONE; THERE IS NONE WHO UNDERSTANDS, THERE IS NONE WHO SEEKS FOR GOD; ALL HAVE TURNED ASIDE, TOGETHER THEY HAVE BECOME USELESS; THERE IS NONE WHO DOES GOOD, THERE IS NOT EVEN ONE." "THEIR THROAT IS AN OPEN GRAVE, WITH THEIR TONGUES THEY KEEP DECEIVING," "THE POISON OF ASPS IS UNDER THEIR LIPS"; "WHOSE MOUTH IS FULL OF CURSING AND BITTERNESS"; "THEIR FEET ARE SWIFT TO SHED BLOOD, DESTRUCTION AND MISERY ARE IN THEIR PATHS, AND THE PATH OF PEACE THEY HAVE NOT KNOWN." "THERE IS NO FEAR OF GOD BEFORE THEIR EYES."[48]

Pride, arrogance, egotism, narcissism is the core or center of the sin nature and therefore are the attitudes of the heart God despises the most. Numerous Proverbs speak about the spiritual as well as natural negative fruit of these self-exalting, self-deifying attitudes. Indeed, in Proverbs 6:16, David summed up the heart of God regarding them, by placing them at the very apex of a list of seven things God *hates*, indicating that as much as God despises these other six things, He hates pride and its variants even more:

> There are six things which the LORD *hates*, Yes, seven which are an abomination to Him: *Haughty eyes*, a lying tongue, And hands that shed innocent blood, A heart that devises wicked plans, Feet that run rapidly to evil, A false witness who utters lies, And one who spreads strife among brothers.

This divine sentiment is echoed also in another proverb that defines the fear of the Lord:

> The fear of the LORD is to hate evil: pride, and arrogancy, and the evil way, and the froward mouth, do I hate.[49]

Another proverb instructs all who will heed its wisdom that the inevitable and invariable produce of pride is *shame*, juxtaposed to the wisdom that accompanies the lowly (humble):

> When pride cometh, then cometh *shame*: but with the lowly is wisdom.[50]

The sole source of all *contention*, wherever it manifests, another Proverb reveals, is *pride*, juxtaposing it to the *wisdom* inuring to the well-advised:

> Only by pride cometh contention: but with the well advised is wisdom.[51]

The "rod of pride" (the term "rod" refers to disciplinary or punitive results) is unavoidably in the mouth, or the speech, of the foolish, in contrast to the "life-preservers" in the speech of the wise:

> In the mouth of the foolish is a rod of pride: but the lips of the wise shall preserve them.[52]

Pride precedes and is the precursor to *destruction* and an *haughty* (proud, vain, vainglorious, arrogant, conceited, pompous, superior, egotistical, condescending) *spirit* precedes and is the precursor to a *fall*, i.e., a sudden, rapid, uncontrolled, descent (nosedive, plunge):

> Pride goeth before destruction, and an haughty spirit before a fall.[53]

A person's unabated pride shall ultimately and inevitably "bring him low," meaning, to a place of dishonor and shame, albeit, by contrast, the humility of those who are "humble in spirit" will undergird their life and legacy:

> A man's *pride* shall *bring him low*: but *honor* shall uphold the humble in spirit.[54]

Secret Societies

Secret societies—clandestine groups aiming to appropriate and exert strong influence in the various aspects of society in the nations of the world—have existed from time immemorial. European history, going back several centuries, in particular, is flush with such organizations. Undeniably, many of these entities made their way into the substructure of America from its founding and continue yet today to significantly affect multiple foundational facets of American society, including government, education, medical, military, media, entertainment, and religious.

Some of the hallmarks of secret societies are "secret," i.e., closed-to-the public, meetings, attendance of which commonly are safeguarded by verbal or signed passcodes, secret handshakes, hidden badges, or special coins, or in some cases a more elaborate, expensive token of membership. In earlier eras, announcements regarding times and places of meetings typically were published in coded messages in newspaper columns, niche circulars, or other obscure channels, as a means of keeping the business of the societies shrouded in secrecy, obscurity, and mystery as a means of engendering intrigue to attract the naïve and unsuspecting into the throes of their demonic grasp.

Five of the best known such secret societies that were infused to whatever degree into the subculture of America are: The Freemasons, the Knights Templar, the Illuminati, Skull and Bones, and Bilderberg. These, certainly, as well as numerous other less known, are believed by many to have an ongoing latent influence in the steerage of the nation at the highest levels of dominant aspects of American society.

The Freemasons, one of the oldest extant so-called, "secret societies," significantly impacted the founding and formation of the United States of America. Many of the founding fathers were members or associates of the fraternity, also referred to by alternative monikers such as "The Lodge, "The Brotherhood," and "Masons." Thirteen of the thirty-nine signatories of the U.S. constitution were masons, including George Washington, Benjamin Franklin, John Hancock, Eldridge Gerry, William Hooper, and Richard Stockton. Among the prominent figures during the revolt against the British, who counted themselves as Masons, were Paul Revere, James Monroe, and Thomas Jefferson.

Freemasonry involvement and influence in the founding and formation of America is evident in various elements embedded in the nation's foundational institutions and infrastructure. One of the most iconic and revealing examples of that is the appearance on our currency of the Eye of Providence, aka, All-Seeing Eye positioned atop an unfinished thirteen-step pyramid featured on the reverse side of The Great Seal of the United States that was adopted by the Continental Congress in 1782, said to represent the thirteen then existing colonies with the unfinished aspect symbolizing hopefulness regarding the future of the newly founded nation. Inscribed in Roman numerals at the base of the pyramid is 1776, citing the year of the U.S. Declaration of Independence. The Seal contains three Latin phrases: *E Pluribus Unum* ("Out of many, one") on the obverse (front) side, and *Annuit cœptis* ("Providence has favored our undertakings") and *Novus ordo seclorum* ("New order of the ages") on the verso (reverse) side. Since 1935 a depiction of both sides of the Seal have been printed on every dollar bill issued by the U.S. Treasury. Irrefutably, each of these elements depicted on the Seal are also ancient high occult symbols.

A widely-believed theory holds that the appearance of the Eye of Providence on U.S. currency demonstrates the involvement of Freemasonry in the founding of America, in that it is a principal part of the iconography of the organization, though detractors of such theories point out that the symbol initially appeared in a Freemason publication in 1797, fourteen years *after* the adoption of the Great Seal, and the organization has steadfastly denied any correlation of its use of the All-Seeing Eye to America's founding, claiming it represents to them the altruism that humanity's thoughts and deeds are always observed by God, indicating their belief that the eye depicted is the eye of *God*. Albeit, Freemasonry critics contend the eye is the eye of Freemasonry, that is, the eye of Lucifer, the archangel who first rebelled against God and was thus evicted from Heaven and cast down to the Earth, whom Freemasonry official literature expressly states the organization venerates as the ultimate "god" over a pantheon of other "gods" worshipped by the various extant false religions of the world.

The original layout of America's capital city, Washington, DC, according to Freemasonry symbology is well-documented as well, backed up by the actual original architectural blueprints for the highly-complex street system, which were designed by Freemason architects, that are safeguarded under the auspices of the strictest security restrictions in the vaults of the Smithsonian Institute.

While these types of fraternal organizations are by definition "secret societies," in that membership requires secret initiation oaths, that secret passwords and coded lexicon are employed, that rituals and rites are rife with ancient occultic pagan symbols and symbology, and that members pledge (in many cases by "blood oaths") to do everything within their power to assist one another preferentially, in fact they are anything *but* "secret" in terms of their proliferation, recruitment, and stratagems for systemic ascendency—locally, translocally, and globally. In fact, their continuing existence and successful achievement of their objectives *depend* upon them *not* being secret. Indeed, the most enduring, entrenched, and effective of these supposedly societally beneficent unions are the supreme impetus of the centuries-long (really age-old, going back to Nimrod and Babylon), march toward the god of this world's ultimate design of a "one-world order."

A comprehensive compendium of detailed information is now available on the Internet concerning these secret societies, and through a plethora of published books, and so I will not consume space and time in this volume providing information about their histories, inner workings, and widespread impact on so many segments of American society and the world.

What I do want to provide here is the overreaching reason these satanically driven organizations are so spiritually destructive and "successful" in the attainment of their objectives. In reality, the secrecy and obscurity these fraternities are shrouded and rooted in is *darkness*—**Satan's domain.** Darkness best describes, from a spiritual perspective, the clandestine structure and modus operandi of these organizations because they are literally a product of the demonic realm of darkness. Satan, the arch-ruler of the fallen angelic hordes, who is a master at appearing as an "angel of light" (his name, before his fall, given to him by God, was "Lucifer," which means "light-bearer") *himself* is the ultimate power behind and architect of these so-called secret societies.

Darkness, it is little understood, is a powerful force that ruled over the Earth, rendering it "formless and void," before the Spirit of God began "moving over the surface of the waters."⁵⁵ The Amplified Bible renders this phrase as "formless and void *or* a waste and emptiness." Darby Translation renders it: "waste and empty." The Good News Bible renders it: "formless and desolate." The fact that the planet was in this ungodly, chaotic, and disordered state was the result of it being governed by *darkness*, which, again, is the domain of Satan, out of which believers have been translated and delivered from its power,⁵⁶ though, nevertheless, against which powers believers, the Church and the entire Creation continue to struggle.⁵⁷

When the Spirit of God began moving over the surface of the waters of the atmosphere over the Earth, God divided (separated) the Light from the darkness:

> God was pleased with what he saw. Then he separated the light from the darkness, and he named the light "Day" and the darkness "Night." Evening passed and morning came—that was the first day. Then God commanded, "Let there be a dome to divide the water and to keep it in two separate places"—and it was done. So God made a dome, and it separated the water under it from the water above it. He named the dome "Sky." Evening passed and morning came—that was the second day.⁵⁸

This verse in the Creation Story forms the foundation for the Biblical principle that God has always intended that the Light of His Kingdom be separated or divided from the darkness of Lucifer's, now Satan's, kingdom. This truth concerning separation from all that is darkness in the world is reinforced in such New Testament passages as:

> Do not try to work together as equals with *unbelievers*, for **it cannot be done**. How can *right* and *wrong* be *partners*? How can *light* and *darkness* live together? How can *Christ* and the *Devil* agree? What does a *believer* have in common with an *unbeliever*? How can *God's temple* come to terms with *pagan idols*? For *we* are the *temple of the living God*! As God himself has said, "I will make my *home* with *my people* and live among *them*; I will be *their* **God**, and *they* shall be *my* **people**." And so the Lord says, "**You must leave them and separate yourselves from them.** Have nothing to do with what is unclean, and I will accept you. I will be your father, and you shall be my sons and daughters, says the Lord Almighty."⁵⁹

> Do not be bound together with *unbelievers*; for what *partnership* have *righteousness* and *lawlessness*, or what *fellowship* has *light* with *darkness*? Or what *harmony* has *Christ* with *Belial*, or what has a *believer* in common with an *unbeliever*? Or what *agreement* has the *temple of God* with *idols*? For *we* are the *temple of the living God*; just as God said, "I WILL DWELL IN THEM AND WALK AMONG THEM; AND I WILL BE THEIR GOD, AND THEY SHALL BE MY PEOPLE. "Therefore, COME OUT FROM THEIR MIDST AND *BE SEPARATE*," says the Lord. "AND DO NOT *TOUCH* WHAT IS *UNCLEAN*; And I will welcome you. "And I will be a father to you, And you shall be sons and daughters to Me," Says the Lord Almighty.[60]

> The *night* is almost gone, and the *day* is near. Therefore let us lay aside the *deeds of darkness* and put on the *armor of light*. Let us behave properly as in the *day*, not in carousing and drunkenness, not in sexual promiscuity and sensuality, not in strife and jealousy. But put on the Lord Jesus Christ, and make no provision for the flesh in regard to its lusts.[61]

Scripture reveals some poignant and telling truths about the demonic domain of darkness and its operations in the world system. The following are a few self-explanatory instances:

> Jesus answered him, "I have spoken *openly* to the *world*; I always taught in synagogues and in the temple, where all the Jews come together; and **I spoke nothing in** *secret*.[62]

> But you, brethren, are not in *darkness*, that the day would overtake you like a thief; for you are all sons of *light* and sons of *day*. We are *not* of *night* nor of *darkness*; so then let us not sleep as others do, but let us be alert and sober. For those who sleep do their sleeping at night, and those who get drunk get drunk at night.[63]

> Therefore do not be partakers with them; for you were formerly *darkness*, but now you are *Light* in the Lord; walk as children of *Light* (for the fruit of the Light consists in all goodness and righteousness and truth), trying to learn what is pleasing to the Lord. Do not participate in the unfruitful deeds of *darkness*, but instead even expose them; for it is disgraceful even to speak of the things which are done by them in *secret*. But all things be-

come visible when they are exposed by the *light*, for everything that becomes visible is *light*.⁶⁴

Therefore do not be partakers with them; for you were formerly *darkness*, but now you are *Light in the Lord*; walk as *children of Light* (for the *fruit of the Light* consists in all goodness and righteousness and truth), trying to learn what is pleasing to the Lord. Do not participate in the *unfruitful deeds of darkness*, but instead even expose them; for it is disgraceful even to speak of the things which are done by them in *secret*. But all things become visible when they are exposed by the *light*, for *everything that becomes visible is light*. For this reason it says, "Awake, sleeper, And arise from the dead, And *Christ* will *shine* on you." Therefore be careful how you walk, not as unwise men but as wise,⁶⁵

For He *rescued* us from the *domain of darkness*, and *transferred* us to the *kingdom of His beloved Son* (Light, by contrast), in whom we have redemption, the forgiveness of sins.⁶⁶

But you are A CHOSEN RACE, A royal PRIESTHOOD, A HOLY NATION, A PEOPLE FOR God's OWN POSSESSION, so that you may proclaim the excellencies of Him who has called you out of *darkness* into His marvelous *light*; for you once were NOT A PEOPLE, but now you are THE PEOPLE OF GOD; you had NOT RECEIVED MERCY, but now you have RECEIVED MERCY.⁶⁷

My extensive deliverance experience in setting captives free from demonic influences over the better part of five decades at the time of this writing proved over and over that multigenerational strongholds ("the sins of the fathers") associated with involvement in these secret societies certainly exist and form some of the most deeply-seated strongholds in people's lives, including self-purporting "Christians." Often the demons associated with these secret societies are some of the most "difficult" to, first of all, identify (because they lie and deny as much and as long as they can), and dislodge and drive out of deliverees. I say, "difficult," not with respect to the dunamis-power of God to drive them out under the anointing during deliverance, but rather with respect to how the demons will do everything they possibly can in an attempt to remain hidden and avoid exposure, i.e., specifically identified, in their utterly mistaken belief that they can somehow by that tactic avoid having to leave their human host. In other words, these demons are extremely obstinate! Indeed, *obstinance* and *stubbornness* is one of the characteristics manifest in people who have these demons operating in their life, making those characteristics the tell-tale sign that they are in there!

Indeed, this is one of the tactics that shows that demons often "outsmart" themselves, so to speak, during deliverance sessions. Many times, when identified by name, they will actually reply, "We're not in here!" The seriousness of the scenario of bondage and its destructive effects on its victims is the only thing that keeps such outbursts from demons from being downright fall-down comical! I often said I could write a book on just the many comical and nonsensical things demons have said during deliverance sessions in attempt to elude eviction!

After so many years of dealing with the many kinds of demons one encounters in ministering deliverance to captives, I have come to understand that the reason the demons associated with secret societies are so "strong" compared to others is that these secret societies are rooted in abject idolatry, blasphemy, and the Antichrist spirit. All this is evident in the history of these societies and their members over the centuries, particularly prominent politicians and elected and appointed office-holders in every branch of government in the United States, as well as the nation's massive bureaucracy that serviced those branches.

Regardless, once they are identified and confronted with the dunamis-power of God operating through a Spirit-baptized Born-Again believer commanding them to "come out!" of a willing, cooperative deliveree, demons have no choice but to go, no matter their number or nature! That's the bottom line!

One other thing I will mention with respect to deliverance of this category of evil spirits is that they are terrified of any mention of the "blood of Jesus!" That is because the denial of the efficacy of the blood of Jesus is invariably a part of rituals and liturgy of these demonic societal cults. When the phrase, "the blood of Jesus rebukes you!" is invoked these demons invariably FLEE, because they literally cannot tolerate the mention of the shed blood of Christ Jesus, which was the very thing that sealed their eternal fate, granted believers unfettered entry into the holy place,[68] and cleansed believers of all sin,[69] making every believer the abject nemesis and conqueror of every demon!

Homosexuality and Other Sexual Deviance

These practices and behavior are all outward manifestations of iniquity of the unregenerate heart (spirit). God's word condemns all forms of homosexuality and other sexual deviance, declaring it to be abominable to God, detestable, degrading, indecent, not proper, and unrighteous:

> You shall not lie with a male as one lies with a female; it is an *abomination*.[70]

> If there is a man who lies with a male as those who lie with a woman, both of them have committed a *detestable act*; they shall surely be put to death. Their bloodguiltiness is upon them.[71]

> For this reason God gave them over to *degrading passions*; for their women exchanged the natural function for that which is *unnatural*, and in the same way also the men abandoned the natural function of the woman and burned in their desire toward one another, men with men committing *indecent acts* and receiving in their own persons the due penalty of their error. And just as they did not see fit to acknowledge God any longer, God gave them over to a depraved mind, to do those things which are *not proper*, being filled with all unrighteousness, wickedness...and although they know the ordinance of God, that those who practice such things are worthy of death, they not only do the same, but also give hearty approval to those who practice them.[72]

Those who practice homosexuality will not inherit the Kingdom of God, meaning, they are excluded from the Kingdom of God and fellowship with Him:

> Or do you not know that the unrighteous will *not* inherit the kingdom of God? Do not be deceived; neither fornicators, nor idolaters, nor adulterers, nor effeminate, nor *homosexuals*... shall inherit the kingdom of God.[73]

> But we know that the Law is good, if one uses it lawfully, realizing the fact that law is not made for a righteous person, but

for those who are lawless and rebellious, for the ungodly and sinners, for the unholy and profane, for those who kill their fathers or mothers, for murderers and immoral men and homosexuals and kidnappers and liars and perjurers, and whatever else is contrary to sound teaching, according to the glorious gospel of the blessed God, with which I have been entrusted.[74]

But for the cowardly and unbelieving and abominable and murderers and *immoral persons* and sorcerers and idolaters and all liars, their part will be in the lake that burns with fire and brimstone, which is the second death.[75]

Blessed are those who wash their robes, so that they may have the right to the tree of life, and may enter by the gates into the city (Heaven). *Outside* are the dogs and the sorcerers and the *immoral persons* and the murderers and the idolaters, and everyone who loves and practices lying.[76]

Moreover, as sad and unfortunate as it is, millions of those practicing homosexuality and other sexual deviance have/are receiving in their own physical bodies the just penalty for their ungodly, vile, and demonic behavior, just as God warned they would:

For this reason God gave them over to degrading passions; for their women exchanged the natural function for that which is unnatural, and in the same way also the men abandoned the natural function of the woman and burned in their desire toward one another, men with men committing indecent acts and *receiving in their own persons the due penalty of their error.*[77]

Today our television and device screens are inundated with commercial after commercial advertising medicines manufactured by the gargantuan multibillion dollar pharmaceutical corporations claiming to, in one way or another, "treat" the plethora of illnesses and medical conditions produced and propagated solely by such heinous sexual deviance. These diabolical pharmaceutical manufacturers portray themselves as the heroes rescuing the multitudinous poor and to-be-pitied victims of these awful diseases and the products they manufacture as the remedy for the debilitating and deadly conditions their sinful behavior has produced, when their only real motive is *money*—immense amounts of it!

Be gracious to me, O LORD, for I am in distress; My eye is wasted away from grief, my soul and my body also. For my life is spent with sorrow And my years with sighing; My strength has failed because of my **iniquity**, And my body has wasted away.[78]

This passage clearly describes the devastating results of Aids/HIV and some STDs that are endemic to practicing homosexuals and other sexual deviants. This iniquitous behavior, decades of medical science confirms, wreaks havoc on the human body and mind![79] The evil spirits behind these physical conditions are sent by the thief (Satan) for the trifold purpose of stealing, killing, and destroying its victims.[80] Sadly, the ravages of these diseases on the human body and psyche make it next to impossible to appropriate genuine faith—the God-Kind of Faith.[81] Such behavior is entirely incompatible with genuine faith! The ever-increasing number of homosexuals and other sexual deviants who claim to be "Christians," unfortunately are being deceived by "deceiving spirits and doctrines of demons"[82] that are most definitely *religious* demons. They are in no way genuine, biblical Christians, and certainly are not Born Again!

All the scriptures condemning homosexuality and other sexual deviance make it unequivocally clear that regeneration is impossible for those who continue in their sin and refuse to repent. Such people are operating in a "form of godliness" that appears to the untrained, ignorant, and undiscerning as religiousness, but it is really vain, life destroying, and eternal life denying religiosity!

> For if we go on sinning willfully after receiving the knowledge of the truth, there no longer remains a sacrifice for sins, but a terrifying expectation of judgment and THE FURY OF A FIRE WHICH WILL CONSUME THE ADVERSARIES.[83]

Worldliness—Love of the World

> Love not the world, neither the things that are in the world. If any man love the world, **the love of the Father is not in him**.[84]

Love of the world negates the love of God in a person's heart and life. The two are incompatible, antithetical, and complete enmity against one another.

One of the greatest problems with professing believers today is *worldliness*. There is nothing that will stunt a believer's spiritual growth and choke the Word of God in his or her life more than worldliness.[85] Jesus spoke extensively about this in the Parable of the Sower, which

He indicated was the most important of all His parables, in that in it He reveals the keys to revelation of the Kingdom and how to enter into it. My book, *Mystery of the Kingdom*, is devoted to explaining these keys and how to operate them in your life. Learn more about the book on the Real Truth Publications website at: https://realtruthpublications.com/catalog-store/mystery-of-the-kingdom/.

The Word of God renders a heavy indictment regarding those who are friends of the world and practitioners of its ways. James declared it was spiritual adultery:

> You adulteresses, do you not know that friendship with the world is hostility toward God? Therefore whoever wishes to be a friend of the world makes himself an enemy of God.[86]

He bluntly states if you are a friend of the world, you are "an enemy of God," plain and simple. One person whose enemy I do not want to be is God.

The Apostle John also gave some strong, straightforward warning against worldliness, saying that anyone who loves the world simply does not love God:

> Do not love the world, nor the things in the world. If anyone loves the world, the love of the Father is not in him. For all that is in the world, the lust of the flesh and the lust of the eyes and the boastful pride of life is not from the Father, but is from the world. And the world is passing away and also its lusts; but the one who does the will of God abides forever.[87]

The Apostle Paul informed us that the only way we can experientially prove the will of God in our own lives is to refrain from conformity to the world and to be "transformed" instead of being "conformed" by the renewing of our minds:

> And do not be *conformed* to this world, but be *transformed* by the renewing of your mind, that you may prove what the will of God is, that which is good and acceptable and perfect.[88]

You see, this world is traveling a certain course, a carnal, ungodly course, leading to Hell. In Ephesians 2:2, the Apostle Paul called it "the course of this world." He said it was devised by Satan, "the prince of the power of the air," and motivated by "the spirit that is now working in the sons of disobedience." As indicated previously, that "spirit" is the rebellious carnal nature of Satan himself, into which all of Mankind is born in the natural birth. It is the "spirit of disobedience."

Following this ungodly course, traveled by the mainstream of the people of this world, is what "worldliness" is. Conformity with the world is worldliness. Espousing the ideals and philosophies of the world is worldliness.

No one can follow after and be conformed to the course of this world, and at the same time have fellowship with God. As James said in the previously quoted passage, "friendship with the world is *hostility toward God.*" Godliness and worldliness are like oil and water—you can stir them up forever, but they will never mix.

Jesus said it was intrinsically impossible for anyone to serve two masters at the same time. A person's "master" is the one he serves and obeys.[89] Only two spiritual masters exist: Jesus and Satan. God is Master of those who will obey and serve Him. Satan is automatically god of the people of this world.[90]

Jesus said, "you cannot serve God and mammon."[91] "Mammon," by the way, does not just mean money, but all the trappings of this world. It really is "the things in the world" which John alluded to in the passage quoted earlier.[92] Jesus said a person simply cannot serve both the things of the world and God, "for either he will hate the one, and love the other, or else he will hold to one, and despise the other."[93]

This was the downfall of the third category of hearers in the Parable of the Sower.[94] They tried to serve both God *and* the world. They wanted to serve God, ostensibly, but they didn't want to detach themselves from the world to do it. They did not heed John's warning, and they still loved the things of the world. Thus, as Jesus warned, they ended up "hating" God in comparison to their love for the world. They tried to serve God and still "hold to" the world. Instead, in God's view, they "despised" Him.

Worldliness took its spiritual toll on these believers, who Jesus said had the "thorns" of worldliness growing in their lives: "the worries of the world, the deceitfulness of riches, and the desire for other things."[95] These spiritual thorns remained in their life after being saved, because they failed to extirpate them from their lives, producing the spiritually deadly result of rendering them spiritually sterile, non-productive. Thus, faith was not able to grow in their lives and produce the results faith naturally produces in obedient believers' lives.

> "Jesus answered, "My *kingdom* is not of this *world*...but as it is, My *kingdom* is not of this *realm*."[96]

This one statement by Jesus in response to Pilate's question as to whether He was a king renders the vast majority of the endeavors earthly entities that identify themselves as "churches" and "ministries," as well as ecclesiastical denominations, are engaged in "not of God" and contrary to His will! Why? Because the vast majority of what they are engaged in is endeavors to develop programs and purposes that intrinsically are not only *in* this world and natural realm, but *of* this world and natural realm. Jesus taught that believers are intrinsically and unavoidably, by virtue of occupying earthly bodies, *in* the world,[97] nevertheless we are not *of* the world;[98] meaning, how we live, what we do, and how we do it, should not be worldly means, methodologies, and mechanisms, but rather means, methodologies, and mechanisms *of* the Spirit *by* the Spirit and performed *in* the spirit realm, though manifest in the natural realm.

Oh, how revolutionary, and what a sea-change it would be if ecclesial entities and individual believers would begin to understand and implement this revelation in their lives and the agenda of the church! It would speedily advance us light-years closer to *BE-coming* the Church instead of constantly harping at spiritually disillusioned, disappointed, depressed, and downtrodden believers about *coming* to church. If churches would *BE-come* the Church that Jesus is building,[99] comporting with the blueprint laid out in the Word of God, more prospective attendees would be more likely to want to come to *that* church! For the Church that Jesus is building is a "glorious Church," i.e., filled with God's Glory, which, by definition, is the tangible manifestation of the Presence of God!

If local churches had the Glory of God manifesting in their services as they could and should have, there would be no need for carnal enticements of coffee and donuts, "pot luck" dinners, seniors' social events, and various imaginative youth events. People want to see a church that is being and doing what the Bible describes churches should be and doing! They want to see the supernatural signs and wonders that are the church bells ringing out the wooing invitation, "Come and see what the King of kings and Lord of lords is doing in our midst!"

They're sick of seeing people manifesting the vanities of religion. They want to see and connect with GOD!

Last Days believers who obtain and operate in the various kinds, levels, and degrees of faith enumerated in this book will see these things happen in their own personal lives as well as in the churches they attend! Conversely, the reason so many church programs and promotions fail to produce the results hoped for is that they are not predicated on biblical faith and are not in accordance with the will of God,[100] but rather only the will of those who are concocting and implementing them.

Failure to Resist the Devil By Conducting Spiritual Warfare

> Submit therefore to God. **Resist** the devil and he will flee from you.[101]

I do not remember hearing anyone teaching on this verse emphasizing its first clause: "Submit therefore to God!" In order to be empowered to defeat the devil in our lives, the first requisite is that we **submit to God**! Then, when we submit to God, in the next clause God commands believers to **resist** the devil. For some strange reason that I have never understood, some people reading this passage think it means run away from the devil or retreat! Running away is not resisting! The word "resist" is an *offensive* term, not defensive. We are commanded to offensively resist the devil! And to do that God has equipped us with spiritual weapons that are not of the flesh realm but of *His* realm, the **Divine** realm! They are not intellectual mechanisms or machinations we use to *outsmart* the adversary. Satan is a fallen angel. In this age, angels are of a higher order than humans. You're not going to outsmart the devil with your intellect no matter how high your IQ is! Rather, God has equipped believers with spiritual weapons that are actually *divine*! *We* are not divine, but the weapons God has equipped His army of believers with *are* divine! That is an important and important to remember fact!

> For though we *walk* in the flesh, we do not *war* according to the flesh, for **the weapons of our warfare** are not of the flesh, but **divinely** powerful for the destruction of fortresses.[102]

There is a warfare that believers are to conduct against our common adversary, the devil, and all the adversity that he sends our way, "for we are not ignorant"—or God does not want us to be—"of his schemes" (i.e., strategic battle plans, Gr.).[103] Further corroboration of the fact that believers are intended to be spiritual warriors conducting spiritual warfare against the enemy is found in the command to "Put on the full armor of God, so that you will be able to stand firm against the schemes of the devil.[104] Again in this verse this term "schemes" is evoked, which in the original language is the word for "strategic battle plans" of a military adversary. Soldiers put on armor to protect themselves against the attacks from the enemy.

Believers are in an all-out **war** against our adversary, Satan, whether they like it or not! That's just the facts! Living in denial about this reality or pretending it's not so will not make it go away for *any* believer! Passivity will only ensure Satan's triumph over the believer, making him/her a *victim* rather than the overwhelming *victor* God intends and has already equipped us to be.[105] Genuine believers are not passive, rather they are ferocious spiritual warriors who engage the weapons of our warfare that are not carnal or of the flesh, but are **mighty** through God for the pulling down or overthrowing of strongholds of the enemy!

What is a stronghold? It's simply a strong hold! But once it is engaged with the weaponry God supplies us by the Spirit operating in and through us those strong holds are broken, rent asunder, and brought down by the dunamis-power (dynamite) of God!

Believers must engage in spiritual warfare against all the devil's strategic battle plans he unleashes against us! We have no choice! It's either defeat *him* and his attacks against us or be defeated. It's that simple! So, we must learn what "the weapons of our warfare" as well as the elements of the "armor of God" are so that we can use them to our advantage in our warfare against the devil. The weapons of our warfare are *offensive* implements of war, and the armor of God is *defensive* implements of war. Space will not permit here a detailed exposition of what each of these sets of warfare implements are and how to effectively use them, but suffice it to say, we need *both* to be in operation in order to emerge victorious in our battles![106]

Fainting in the Day of Trial

If thou *faint* in the day of adversity, thy strength is small.[107]

If you are slack (careless) in the day of distress, Your strength is limited.[108]

If you are slack in the day of distress, Your strength is limited.[109]

If you are weak in a crisis, you are weak indeed.[110]

"The day of adversity" is a particular period of time when Satan attacks you with adversity. The Hebrew word rendered adversity is *tsârâh*. According to *Strong's Concordance*, the word means adversity, affliction, anguish, distress, tribulation, trouble. The word rendered "strength" is *kôach*; and it refers to ability, might, power, strength, substance, constitution. The word rendered "small" is *tsar*, meaning narrow or tiny as with a pebble. While it is Satan and not God who authors adversity in our lives, nonetheless, God permits it (else it couldn't occur) in order to test, or assay, the quality and quantity of our faith. James tells us that we are to consider it all joy when we encounter the various trials with which believers are commonly beset:

> Consider it all joy, my brethren, when you encounter various trials, *knowing that **the testing of your faith** produces endurance.* And let endurance have its perfect result, so that you may be perfect and complete, lacking in nothing. Blessed is the man who perseveres under trial; for once he has been approved *(or, passed the test, margin)*, he will receive the crown of life, which the Lord has promised to those who love Him.[111]

God is saying here that believers are to *know* that there will be a testing of our faith that will come in the form of adversity for the purpose of testing or assaying the quality and quantity of our faith. The passage goes on to say that the testing of our faith by way of adversity, if we do not faint in the day of adversity, will produce endurance, and if we apply the element of endurance in the face of adversity to our lives it will eventually and ultimately produce its perfect result, which is that we will be spiritually perfect (i.e., mature) and complete. I don't propose to know what spiritually perfect and complete means in its totality, but I do know *one* thing: you can't improve upon perfect, and you can't get more complete than complete. Perfect means perfect, and complete means complete! Hallelujah!

Not only all that, which relates firstly with *this* life, but it continues on to speak of what "persever(ing) under trial" will produce in the life to come—"the crown of life!" This crown of life is mentioned in only one other place in Scripture, which is in Jesus's promise to award it to those in the church of Smyrna who remained faithful unto death in the testing Satan would soon bring upon them:

> 'I know your tribulation and your poverty (but you are rich), and the blasphemy by those who say they are Jews and are not, but are a synagogue of Satan. 'Do not fear what you are about to suffer. Behold, **the devil** is about to cast some of you into prison, so that you will be **tested**, and you will have tribulation for ten days. Be faithful until death, and I will give you the **crown of life**. 'He who has an ear, let him hear what the Spirit says to the churches. He who overcomes will not be hurt by the second death.'[112]

It is in the face of adversity, trials, troubles, and tribulation, particularly at the outset, when a temptation unto fainting or a sapping of our strength comes upon us. That is common. The magnitude of the attack can oftentimes seem overwhelming when it first strikes. This is a tactic of the enemy—to hit us with shock and awe in an attempt to strike fear in us! It is in those times that we must not faint with regards to our faith. Being knowledgeable about it before it happens is to our advantage: "so that no *advantage* would be taken of us by Satan, for we are not ignorant of his *schemes*."[113]

"Fight the good fight of faith...."[114] There is only one fight or battle the Word of God commands believers to engage in, and actually identifies it as a *good* fight, that is, "**the good fight of FAITH!**" It is when we encounter sudden and stunning attacks of adversity that come in crisis or catastrophe that we must engage in the *fight* of our life and not *faint*, not in our own strength but in the strength of Lord's might that is appropriated by faith, and we appropriate that faith by **fighting** the good fight of faith in those times in the very face of the adversity when the adversary mocks and scorns us! How do we overcome in those times? Firstly, we must revert to the source of our strength, which is not by *our* own might, not by *our* own power but by *My* Spirit sayeth the Lord!"[115]

Jesus spoke to His disciples and followers about the necessity and reward of perseverance in a parable about the actions of an *unjust* judge to illustrate by comparison what He, the Just Judge, will do on our behalf when we persevere in our faith in times of adversity:

> And he spake a parable unto them to this end, that men ought always to pray, and not to faint; Saying, There was in a city a

judge, which feared not God, neither regarded man: And there was a widow in that city; and she came unto him, saying, Avenge me of mine adversary. And he would not for a while: but afterward he said within himself, Though I fear not God, nor regard man; Yet because this widow troubleth me, I will avenge her, lest by her continual coming she weary me. And the Lord said, Hear what the *unjust judge* saith. And shall not God avenge his own elect, which cry day and night unto him, though he bear long with them? I tell you that he will avenge them speedily. Nevertheless, when the Son of man cometh, shall he find faith on the earth?[116]

In the 22nd Chapter of 2nd Samuel, David authors a fierce screed against the cumulative of his many enemies he had to war against as the king of Israel, giving credit and glory to God for supplying him all the wherewithal to defeat every foe who ever rose up against him and Israel. But what is remarkable and poignant about the attitude and tone underlying his rant is that, despite all the fierce battles and ferocious warfare he has personally engaged in over many years, he is in no way conciliatory or appeasing regarding his enemies, but *defiant*. He describes how he pursued his enemies and utterly destroyed them, never turning away from his vicious pursuit of them until he had consumed or annihilated them. He speaks of how he mercilessly continued to wound them until they were fallen under his feet and could not rise again to fight. He exalts God for girding him with the inordinate strength needed to do battle against them and subdue them to the extent of placing his foot on the necks of those who hated him as a sign of complete defeat:

> I have *pursued* mine enemies, and *destroyed* them; and turned not again until I had *consumed* them. And I have *consumed* them, and *wounded* them, that they could not arise: yea, they are fallen under my feet. For thou hast girded me with strength to battle: them that rose up against me hast thou *subdued* under me. Thou hast also given me the necks of mine enemies, that I might *destroy* them that hate me.[117]

It sounds to the carnal mind that David is gloating in his exploits and victories as a warrior. But that is really not it at all! What he is doing, under the inspiration of the Holy Spirit, is exalting and crediting God for having worked through him as the chief military leader of

Israel to defeat the multitudes of enemies who have risen up against Israel driven by their demonically-inspired extreme enmity against the nation, all because its people were the chosen people of God!

The extreme hatred held by the peoples of the idolatrous heathen nations of Canaan, who were illegal trespassers and unauthorized occupiers of the land that God had designated for and consigned to Israel, came ultimately from Satan, by whose hordes of evil spirits these peoples were possessed. These devil-worshipping nations, beginning with the leadership of Joshua following the death of Moses, God charged Israel with defeating and dispossessing from the land they occupied.

> Now it came about after the death of Moses the servant of the LORD, that the LORD spoke to Joshua the son of Nun, Moses' servant, saying, "Moses My servant is dead; now therefore arise, cross this Jordan, you and all this people, to the land which I am giving to them, to the sons of Israel. "Every place on which the sole of your foot treads, I have given it to you, just as I spoke to Moses. "From the wilderness and this Lebanon, even as far as the great river, the river Euphrates, all the land of the Hittites, and as far as the Great Sea toward the setting of the sun will be your territory. "No man will be able to stand before you all the days of your life. Just as I have been with Moses, I will be with you; I will not fail you or forsake you. "Be strong and courageous, for you shall give this people possession of the land which I swore to their fathers to give them. "Only be strong and very courageous; be careful to do according to all the law which Moses My servant commanded you; do not turn from it to the right or to the left, so that you may have success wherever you go. "This book of the law shall not depart from your mouth, but you shall meditate on it day and night, so that you may be careful to do according to all that is written in it; for then you will make your way prosperous, and then you will have success. "Have I not commanded you? Be strong and courageous! Do not tremble or be dismayed, for the LORD your God is with you wherever you go."[118]

As indicated previously in this volume, all of this history concerning the Israelites, or *HIS-story*, were types and shadows that served as examples, illustrations, to *instruct* individual believers living in the end-times and the collective end-times Church Jesus is building regarding the end-times purposes and plans of God and how God intends for this end-times Ecclesia Jesus is constructing to fulfill and implement them:

> Now these things happened to them as an example, and they were written for *our instruction*, upon whom the ends of the ages have come.[119]

> For whatever was written in earlier times was written for *our instruction*, so that through perseverance and the encouragement of the Scriptures we might have hope.[120]

Spiritual Slumber & Lack of Vigilance

> But you, brethren, are not in darkness, that the day would overtake you like a thief; for you are all sons of light and sons of day. We are not of night nor of darkness; *so then let us not sleep as others do, but let us be alert and sober.*[121]

In this passage, the Lord is cautioning believers regarding spiritual slumber and lack of vigilance. "Let us not *sleep* as others do," He says. It's amazing how that often at the most vulnerable or perilous times, people tend to slumber and sleep. Law enforcement interrogating criminals are often confronted with what has come to be called in law enforcement circles, "the guilt sleep," wherein the perpetrators of crimes seem not to be able to help themselves but will fall asleep either sitting in a chair or will lay down on the bare floor of the interrogation room, where they know cameras are showing their every move, and will fall dead asleep to the extent that it is difficult to rouse them out of their slumber.

Those of us experienced in dealing with demons are also very familiar with this unnatural uncontrollable slumber and know demons are behind it. It often occurs also when dealing with demonized people in deliverance sessions. I've had people fall dead asleep while I'm talking to them, fall out of their chair onto the floor, and keep sleeping as if they are only semi-conscious! I call it the "demon sleep."

This is the same thing that people often talk about happens to them when they try to read the Bible or pray. It's demons behind that as well. When demons are being revealed by the Spirit, often through the operation of the Manifestation Gift of the Spirit, "discerning of spirits"[122] one of their common tactics is to cause their human host to fall into a deep sleep in attempt to hide or discourage the deliverance minister from casting them out. It's a dead giveaway to the experienced deliverance minister! It's essentially the same thing as the "guilty slumber" with criminals, because it's the same evil spirits behind both. Evil spirits do not always do the smartest things they could do. Actually, they are not "the sharpest knife in the drawer," as the saying goes. Another example of that is when in deliverance sessions I have called out certain evil spirits by name and on rare occasions have queried a certain spirit, "Are you in there?" Believe it or not, it is not uncommon for them to respond, "NO! I'm not in here!" I'm serious! In those cases, of course, my response after having a good laugh is to command that evil spirit to come out of the person, and they always do!

In other cases during the worship portion of my meetings, particularly in more intimate settings such as in my home or some other home I was ministering, I have opened my eyes during worship times wherein the anointing was especially strong, to see people who were dead asleep on the floor, and in some cases hiding under coffee tables or other furniture that made you wonder how in the world they ever got there in that position. In every case, it was not that they were "slain in the Spirit" but rather it was a demonic slumber caused by demons, to such an extent that the person was almost catatonic or semi-conscious, and I had to cast the demons out of them for them to be able to wake up! This is what I came to call "hiding spirits"; they are hiding in the hope that they won't be discovered and identified by name and driven out of their human host, the comfortable "home" where they've been safely living for as long as they've been living there!

But, in my meetings, when I see this happening, it is the demons' Water Loo!" because I'm *going* to call them out by name and cast them out every time! Their manifestation causes a holy, righteous indignation to rise up in me, as it should *every* genuine believer, and drives me to drive the demon(s) out of that person in Jesus' name! *Every* believer should have a holy hatred for demons and what they do to people they inhabit! If you purport to be a "Christian" and do NOT have that holy hatred, you should be questioning the authenticity of your salvation! Satan is someone believers are allowed to hate! If you don't, something's wrong!

Christians must not mollycoddle, indulge, or have a se la vie or que sera sera attitude concerning demons and their habitation of people in any way or degree! Satan comes into people's lives in order to steal, kill, and destroy,[123] Jesus said. I cannot fathom how anyone could have a lackadaisical attitude about such dastardly and grave intents. Satan is constantly roaming all over the earth seeking someone who will give him tacit permission to destroy them,[124] and in the face of that someone can just nonchalantly say, "Oh well! Such is life!" WOW! That is incredible to me!

> And he cometh unto the disciples, and findeth them asleep, and saith unto Peter, What, could ye not watch with me one hour? *Watch and pray, that ye enter not into temptation*: the spirit indeed is willing, but the flesh is weak. He went away again the second time, and prayed, saying, O my Father, if this cup may not pass away from me, except I drink it, thy will be done. And he came and found them asleep again: for their eyes were heavy.[125]

This incredible event took place when Jesus went to the Garden of Gethsemane to pray the most critical prayer He ever prayed, or *anyone* ever prayed, for that matter. (Read more about what occurred during the Lord's agony in purchasing our salvation in Gethsemane in Chapter Ten.)

Perhaps the cause of their deep and apparently uncontrollable slumber was simply the physical exhaustion the apostles had experienced leading up to Gethsemane. That could very well be, certainly. But it could also be the demonic, devil-caused slumber discussed previously. Or it could also be a combination of the two, which is the cause I favor. Remember, in a matter of hours from Gethsemane all twelve of the Apostles of the Lamb will betray Jesus, separate themselves from Him, deny being His followers and even that they know Him! Judas Iscariot will betray Him to the High Priest and chief priests for thirty pieces of silver and subsequently hang himself!

Gethsemane was *before* Jesus' crucifixion, miraculous resurrection, glorious ascension. It was *before* Resurrection Evening when the Glorified Christ walked right through the locked door of the Upper Room and greeted the disciples gathered there with the one-word greeting, Shalom! Which meant peace, all is well, because He was just returning from appearing before God the Father as the real Lamb of God who took away, remitted, removed, abolished, obliterated the sins of the world![126] Moments later, Jesus breathed upon the disciples gathered and said, "Receive the Holy Spirit!" It was then that the disciples gathered in that tiny room became the first people in human history to be Born Again by the infusion of the Holy Spirit into their previously dead human spirits.[127]

> Let us not grow weary or become discouraged in doing good, for at the proper time we will reap, if we do not give in.[128]

Ignorance of the Word of God

> Therefore My people go into exile for *their lack of knowledge*; And their honorable men are famished, And their multitude is parched with thirst.[129]

> My people are destroyed for *lack of knowledge*. Because you have rejected knowledge, I also will reject you from being My priest. Since you have forgotten the law of your God, I also will forget your children.[130]

There is an old saying that ignorance is bliss. Assuredly, when it comes to spiritual knowledge and understanding, ignorance is anything but bliss. As the second passage quoted above indicates, spiritual ignorance will absolutely destroy you. Lack of spiritual understanding or knowledge gives Satan, the enemy of our souls, a wide open door to destroy us; to keep us reeling our entire lives in destruction of every sort and kind.

In particular, God certainly does not want us to be ignorant of the entire panoply of Satan's tricks and schemes, thereby giving him an advantage over us:

> so that no advantage would be taken of us by Satan, for we are not ignorant of his schemes.[131]

The Apostle Paul, whose revelations concerning the Truths of the Kingdom of God comprise two-thirds of the New Testament, stated categorically as a prophetic warning to the end-times church of which we believers who are living right now in the 21st Century are a part:

> "But the Spirit explicitly says that in later times some will FALL AWAY FROM THE FAITH, paying attention to deceitful spirits and doctrines of demons, by means of the hypocrisy of liars seared in their own conscience as with a branding iron."[132]

Less than 300 years following the birth of the Church and the inception of the Church Age, the Church had devolved into a period of spiritual darkness known as the Dark Ages that spanned 1,200 long years, fulfilling the Apostle Paul's prophecy concerning a corporate Great Apostasy.

This was what theologians and church historians refer to as, "The Great Apostasy," for the *corporate* Church, concerning which the Apostle Paul prophesied. During this age of spiritual darkness, the Truth was subverted by humanistic ideologies and vain philosophies of men[133]—the doctrines of demons of which Paul forewarned. Many of the foundational doctrines of the Church were distorted, perverted, diluted, invalidated, or totally abandoned. Moreover, the Fivefold Ministry Offices, as well as the apostolic-prophetic governmental foundation of the Church, upon which it was originally established[134] were abrogated and replaced with an ecclesiastical hierarchy, as elite professional clergymen began to be driven more and more by what Augustine called (in Latin), "libido dominandi," lust for rule or dominion. Indeed, the greatest single factor contributing to the spiritual debacle of the Dark Ages was the drift, following the death of the original Apostles of the Lamb, from the apostolic-prophetic moorings upon which the Church was founded.

In Acts 2:42-43, Luke wrote of the early church:

They were continually devoting themselves to the *apostles' teaching* and to fellowship, to the breaking of bread and to prayer. Everyone kept feeling a sense of awe; and many wonders and signs were taking place through the apostles.

That is what the Lord Jesus Christ, the Head of the Church, had intended to take place in the "ekklesia" or Church that He said in Matthew 16:18, HE was building, against which the gates or power of Hell, i.e., Satan's Kingdom, would not be able to prevail. And thank God that that is the ultimate outcome we can rest our faith and hope upon concerning the true, genuine Church that Jesus is building—the power of Hell shall not be able to overcome it, ultimately.

But, by the Third Century, the church had devolved into a spiritually dead, man-controlled semblance of the Spirit-animated lively entity it was from its birth in power on the Day of Pentecost! Now it had gone from being a living organism, alive with the Zoe-Life of God, to a lifeless humanistic religious organization.

How did this happen so quickly? The Apostle Paul said it was because over time the early disciples gradually began "paying attention to deceitful spirits and doctrines of demons, by means of the hypocrisy of liars seared in their own conscience as with a branding iron."[135]

I've often said, the problem with deception, or delusion, is that the person who is deceived is deceived about being deceived. His deception prevents him from knowing he is deceived. Such became the case with the early church disciples. False teachers came along indoctrinating the church with false teaching, false doctrine, and that will always have a deadly result.

Today, the prevalence of Bible-illiteracy in the Body of Christ is a major problem. Despite the ever-growing number of "churches"—existing and startups—national surveys demonstrate the wholesale abject ignorance of the most basic matters related to the components of the Bible itself and understanding of the most rudimentary doctrines and spiritual principles delineated in it by purporting "Christians." Relatively few self-identifying Christians know how many books are in the Bible and the number comprising the Old Testament and New Testament respectively. An even fewer number of people claiming to be Born Again Christians possess even a cursory understanding of such basic doctrinal tenets as salvation, sanctification, grace, redemption, righteousness, the substitutionary sacrifice of Christ, and how one attains unto those benefits of the Zoe-life. The advent of the Internet, Social Media, and AI (artificial intelligence) has made this widespread lack of spiritual knowledge exponentially more problematic—in some cases proliferating misinformation and disinformation concerning vital matters relative to the life and death realities of Kingdom of God and Eternal Life. The sheer quantity of unbiblical and antibiblical raw data constituting the unquantifiable cornucopia of "information" proliferated in the ether realm exceeds by lightyears the Truth contained in the Sixty-Six books of Holy God-breathed canon. In other words, deception abounds, while Truth is fallen in the street ("The Information Highway"):

> And judgment is turned away backward, and justice standeth afar off: *for truth is fallen in the street*, and equity cannot enter.[136]

Conclusion

We examined in this chapter some of the top hindrances to genuine faith. By no means is this an exhaustive list of hindrances, however; there are many more. But these are some that most frequently manifest in the lives of believers to deter them from obtaining and walking in genuine faith. By being informed about, watchful for, and resistant to them, believers can avoid the faith failures that can otherwise occur during their personal journey in the "faith walk," which is the topic of the next chapter.

Endnotes

1 Rom. 8:37
2 1 John 5:4-5
3 Rev. 12:10-11
4 Rev. 3:21
5 Rom. 8:37
6 1 Pet. 5:8
7 1 Tim. 4:1-2
8 Col. 2:8
9 2 Thes. 2:3-4; parenthetic explanation added by author
10 2 Pet. 2:9-10
11 Jude 1:8
12 Mat. 25:41
13 Psa. 31:10
14 Jas. 4:7
15 2 Tim. 3:1-5
16 Isa. 64.6
17 2 Cor. 5:21
18 John 20:17
19 2 Cor. 3:14
20 2 Tim. 2:15
21 Dictionary.com: https://www.dictionary.com/browse/study
22 Jas. 4:8
23 Eph. 2:1-10
24 Heb. 4:16
25 Heb. 7:19
26 Heb. 7:25
27 Heb. 10:1
28 Heb. 10:22
29 Heb. 11:6

30 1 Sam. 12:15
31 Isa. 1:19-20
32 Job 24:13
33 1 Sam. 15:23a
34 Pro. 17:11
35 Heb. 12:5-11
36 Psa. 115:16
37 Eph. 2:2
38 Isa. 14:13,14
39 Eph. 2:2
40 Eph. 6:12
41 Col. 2:15
42 Gal. 5:19-21
43 Eph. 2:2
44 Isa. 14:13,14
45 Rev. 12:7-9
46 Mat. 12:34; Luke 6:45
47 Eph. 2:2
48 Rom. 3:10-18 (Caps, indigenous to translation)
49 Pro. 8:13
50 Pro. 11:2
51 Pro. 13:10
52 Pro. 14:3
53 Pro. 16:18
54 Pro. 29:23
55 Gen. 1:2
56 Col. 1:13
57 Eph. 6:12
58 Gen. 1:4-8; GNB
59 2 Cor. 6:14-18; GNB

60 Ibid; NASB
61 Rom. 13:12-14
62 John 18:20
63 1 Thes. 5:4-7
64 Eph. 5:7-13
65 Eph. 5:7-15
66 Col. 1:13-14; parenthesis added
67 1 Pet. 2:9-10
68 Heb. 10:19
69 1 John 1:7
70 Lev. 18:22
71 Lev. 20:13 (In the New Covenant era, "death" means spiritual death)
72 Rom. 1:26-32
73 1 Cor. 6:9
74 1 Tim. 1:8-11
75 Rev. 21:8
76 Rev. 22:14,15
77 Rom. 1:26-27
78 Psa. 31:9-10
79 The Diagnostic and Statistical Manual of Mental Disorders (DSM) for many decades prior to the nascent pervasive acceptance and normalization of homosexuality in its many variants listed homosexuality and related behaviors as mental disorders.
80 John 10:10
81 Mark 11:22-24
82 1 Tim. 4:1
83 Heb. 10:26-27
84 1 John 2:15 KJV
85 Mark 4:19
86 Jas. 4:4

87   1 John 2:15-17
88   Rom. 12:2; emphasis added
89   Rom. 6:16
90   2 Cor. 4:4
91   Luke 16:13
92   1 John 2:15
93   Luke 16:13
94   Mark 4:1-20
95   Mark 4:19
96   John 18:33-40
97   John 16:33; 17:11
98   John 17:14,15,16
99   Mat. 16:18
100 C.f., Jas. 5:14,15
101 Jas. 4:7
102 2 Cor. 10:3-4
103 2 Cor. 2:11
104 Eph 6:11
105 Rom. 8:37

106 Extensive teaching by other authors on these topics is readily available in the form of books available from Amazon and other book distributors.

107 Pro. 24:10; KJV
108 Ibid.; AMP
109 Ibid.; NASB
110 Ibid.; GNB
111 Jas. 1:2-4,12
112 Rev. 2:9-11
113 2 Cor. 2:11
114 1 Tim. 6:12; NASB

115 Zec. 4:6

116 Luke 18:1-8; KJV

117 2 Sam. 22:38-41; KJV

118 Jos. 1:1-9

119 1 Cor. 10:11

120 Rom. 15:4

121 1 Thes. 5:4-6

122 1 Cor. 12:10

123 John 10:10

124 1 Pet. 5:8; KJV uses the word "may," which is a term of permission.

125 Mat. 26:40-43; KJV

126 Ezk. 3 This chapter chronicles what transpired in Heaven when Jesus appeared as Joshua (Jesus, in Greek) as the real, actual, High Priest, before God the Father, presenting Himself as the real, actual, Lamb of God who was slain as the substitutionary sacrifice required to redeem Mankind!

127 Eph. 2:1-2

128 Gal. 6:9; AMP

129 Isa. 5:13

130 Hos. 4:6

131 2 Cor. 2:11

132 1 Tim. 4:1

133 Col. 2:8

134 Eph. 2:20

135 1 Tim. 4:1

136 Isa. 59:14

Chapter Fourteen

WALKING BY FAITH

For we know that if the earthly tent which is our house is torn down, we have a building from God, a house not made with hands, eternal in the heavens. For indeed in this house we groan, longing to be clothed with our dwelling from heaven, inasmuch as we, having put it on, will not be found naked. For indeed while we are in this tent, we groan, being burdened, because we do not want to be unclothed but to be clothed, so that what is mortal will be swallowed up by life. Now He who prepared us for this very purpose is God, who gave to us the Spirit as a pledge. Therefore, being always of good courage, and knowing that while we are at home in the body we are absent from the Lord—**for we walk by FAITH, not by sight**—we are of good courage, I say, and prefer rather to be absent from the body and to be at home with the Lord. Therefore we also have as our ambition, whether at home or absent, to be pleasing to Him. For we must all appear before the judgment seat of Christ, so that each one may be recompensed for his deeds in the body, according to what he has done, whether good or bad.[1]

Once a person has obtained faith, beginning with "the measure of faith,"[2] it is incumbent for that believer in Christ then to begin to *walk* by that measure of faith he/she has obtained by the Spirit. Walking by faith essentially means putting our faith into action; i.e., converting the *noun* of faith into the *verb* of faith. A verb is an action term. In other words, the believer must put his/her faith into action by living his/her life—the various aspects and actions that comprise his/her life—based on what he/she *believes* in his/her heart ("with the *heart* a person believes, resulting in righteousness"[3]) instead of based on what he/she *sees* with his/her physical eyes, or have experienced with his/her natural senses, which is the usual premise by which humans live their life.

This sort of "walking by sight" is what Thomas (Didymus), one of the original Apostles of the Lamb, was reflecting in his now rather infamous statement of unbelief:

> But Thomas, one of the twelve, called Didymus, was not with them when Jesus came. So the other disciples were saying to him, "We have seen the Lord!" But he said to them, "Unless I **see** in His hands the imprint of the nails, and put my finger into the place of the nails, and put my hand into His side, *I will **not** believe*."[4]

Without "the measure of faith" God gives to those who come to Him, acknowledging that He **IS**, that He EXISTS—"he who comes to God must believe that He IS"[5]—no one can *believe* in Him. This dilemma of the carnal mind is exactly what Thomas was expressing: that unless/until he actually **saw** with his eyes the nail imprints in Jesus' hand, put his finger into the nail holes and his hand into Jesus' side where He was pierced by the Roman soldier's spear, he would *not* believe the Lord had risen from the dead (though He testified He would) and was alive. With all the trauma Jesus' followers had experienced as they traced Jesus' footsteps during the last days and hours of His physical life on Earth—personally identifying, to a much lesser degree, with His sufferings—coupled with all the wild religious speculation, the events that transpired in that time-frame understandably became confusing and bewildering to the disciples, making it nearly impossible for them to know just *what* to believe! Thomas had made up his mind that he wasn't going to believe anything else about all this about Jesus and who He was and so forth until/unless he SAW it with His own eyes! No more religious gobbledygook! No more spiritualizing and unprovable imaginations! Henceforth, it would be "JUST THE FACTS" for Thomas!

Thank God, He is not offended or deterred in His determination to connect and commune with Mankind by our lack of faith! He knows faith was essentially denuded, or abrogated, as a result of the abject rebellion of the very first man and woman in the Garden of Eden—when they refused God's admonition not to eat of the fruit of the tree of the knowledge of good and evil, thereby, unwittingly, rejecting HIM!

Believing Without Seeing

Eight days after Thomas made this statement of unbelief, Jesus physically appeared to the disciples in the Upper Room, and the first person He addressed individually after a general greeting was Thomas:

> After eight days His disciples were again inside, and Thomas with them. Jesus came, the doors having been shut, and stood in their midst and said, "Peace be with you." Then He said to Thomas, "Reach here with your finger, and see My hands; and reach here your hand and put it into My side; and do not be unbelieving, but believing." Thomas answered and said to Him, "My Lord and my God!" Jesus said to him, "Because you have *seen* Me, have you believed? Blessed are they who did not *see*, and yet believed."

"Blessed are they who did not *see*, and yet **believed**"—that statement captures the essence of the entire concept of faith! Faith is believing what you do not see or "know" with your physical senses and mind (intellect). Or, it could rightly be said that faith is believing with your *spirit* what your *soul*—mind, will, and emotions—does not believe or accept as true. It's vital to understand here in this context the understanding I addressed or alluded to elsewhere in this book: that while the human *spirit* is saved, renewed, redeemed at the new birth, the *soul* is not! Rather, James made it clear that when a person receives the Word of God as a seed (*sperma*, in the Greek), the Word he/she receives is **able** to save his/her soul, but that receiving—as seeds are planted in the good soil of a receptive heart—does not in itself and of itself instantaneously save or sanctify (sozo, in the Greek, i.e., sanctify, save, redeem, renew, recreate) the soul in the manner as the spirit is instantaneously saved, sanctified, redeemed at the moment of the new birth. In other words, sanctification of the soul (mind, will, emotions) is not an *event* or *occurrence*, but rather a *process*, a lifelong process, that is predicated on repentance, and repentance requires knowledge and understanding of the offense in order to be able to repent from it, and that is why it is a lifelong process and not an event.

At bottom, believing is accepting as true or so. When you believe something, you accept it as being true, or real, or reality, or so. It is the Biblical "Amen," which means, yes, or it is so. "For as many as are the promises of God, in Him they are *yes*; therefore also through Him is our *Amen* to the glory of God through us."[6] In all this, God is saying that He wants us to live our lives based, not on what we see or perceive with our soul (mind [thoughts], will [desires], emotions [feelings]), but on what we *believe* with our heart, for faith resides in the heart, or spirit, the "tabernacle" or "temple" where God dwells in the Born Again believer! So, it's sort of: believing with and living by your "believer" (spirit) instead of your mind, will, and emotions (soul).

Let Peace Arbitrate

Another passage adds to this concept the precept of allowing the peace of Christ—the peace that inures from the Prince of Peace residing in the Born Again believer's heart—to *rule*, or *govern*, or the original word (brabeuō, Gr.) means to *arbitrate* or *act as an umpire* in your spirit: "Let the peace of Christ **rule** in your hearts...."[7] Arbitration is the process of considering, analyzing, judging a scenario in order to make a determination or ruling about it.

Applying this precept holistically to how Born Again believers should live their life, this passage is telling us we should govern our lives from or out of our spirit (the seat of the Holy Spirit), the inner man, rather than from our soul as the unsaved, unredeemed, non-Born-Again live their lives. To arbitrate or act as an umpire in the governing of your life would mean to consciously make the multiplicity of decisions and choices with which life presents us from the wellspring of our spirit man, i.e., what the Holy Spirit is instructing, guiding, leading us to do from within His dwelling place in our human spirit.

Concisely put: look/listen within your Born Again spirit for your guidance. What the Holy Spirit is communicating to you in your spirit is utterly reliable; what your soul (mind, will, emotions) communicates to you is not! Emotions, contaminated as they are by the flesh, are unreliable. Personal desires, rooted as they are in self-interest and narcissism, are unreliable. The human intellect (thinking), corrupted as it is with sin, is unreliable. The Holy Spirit, perfect and pure as He is, is reliable! He will *never* deceive or mislead you! He has been sent by God as our indwelling "Helper" to help us!

"I will ask the Father, and He will give you another *Helper*, that He may be with you forever;[8]

"But the *Helper*, the Holy Spirit, whom the Father will send in My name, He will teach you all things, and bring to your remembrance all that I said to you.[9]

"When the *Helper* comes, whom I will send to you from the Father, that is the Spirit of truth who proceeds from the Father, He will testify about Me,[10]

"But I tell you the truth, it is to your advantage that I go away; for if I do not go away, the *Helper* will not come to you; but if I go, I will send Him to you.[11]

As a former baseball umpire, I understand this matter of arbitrating based on the peace of the Spirit within to mean in practical terms knowing whether something you are considering or is being presented to you from whatever source as an option is either "*inside* the boundaries of the strike zone" (a strike) or "*outside* the boundaries of the strike zone" (a ball). A batted ball either lands *inside* the fair/foul boundary lines (a *fair* ball) or it lands *outside* the fair/foul boundary lines (a *foul* ball). A runner is *safe* if he is not put *out* when attempting to reach/return to a base by a ball thrown by a fielder and caught by a baseman with any part of his body making contact with the base prior to the runner making contact with the base in the case of first base or a force-out (and maintaining contact with the base in the case of a non-force-out).

Homeplate umpires do not think strike or ball on each pitch; they think **strike** if it is not a ball! Base umpires do not think safe or out on a play to a base; they think **safe** if not *out*! Umpires do not think fair or foul regarding a ball batted down the left or right field line; they think **fair** if not *foul*. This is how believers should rule or govern their lives: something they are contemplating is either a *strike* or *safe* (good, acceptable, allowable) or it's a *ball* or an *out* (bad, unacceptable, unallowable). For the believer, the Word of God, the Bible, is the "rule book," and our judgment is predicated on whether or not we have the peace of the Holy Spirit regarding a matter, and the first determination we must make is whether or not the matter is afoul of the written Word of God, the Bible. If it is afoul, we will not have the peace of the Spirit, for the Word and the Spirit always agree, and if we don't have the peace of the Spirit, obviously we should not proceed. If we have peace, we can proceed forward with confidence that the Lord is "in it" or it is His will. If we do not have peace about the matter, we should not proceed forward, at least at that particular time. I sometimes shorten the axiom to: "No peace, no pass!" Most matters, I have found, can be thought of the way an umpire thinks: *strike* if not a ball; *safe* if not out; *fair* if not foul.

Navigating by the Unseen

The term "walking," as it is used in the Bible, is not merely pedestrian travel, it is a metaphor for navigating or traversing or moving, and for the manner in which one lives his/her life. In a larger sense, walking is a metaphor for navigating through life. Walking *by faith*, thus, means to navigate, traverse, move through life based not on what is seen or perceived with one's physical senses and faculties, but by what one perceives or knows, or believes, about God. The faith that is referenced is faith in *God*! Though the Bible talks about confidence, which literally means, "faith within," and that believers should not "throw away" or discard, or discount, their confidence,[12] i.e., faith in themselves, the believer's faith is founded upon trust, reliance, dependence on God, ultimately! It is not a narcissistic faith. We need to maintain confidence in ourselves, but that confidence, for the believer, is formed by and founded upon knowing who God is in us and who we are in God!

The true foundation of genuine faith is who God is, His nature! It is who He is, His perfect and inimitable integrity and rectitude, that makes Him perfectly reliable and trustworthy *in* all things, *for* all things, and *to* whoever will place his/her complete trust in Him! He is Almighty God, the Perfect One! It is impossible for Him to ever fail anyone! Though it is true that "with Him nothing is impossible,"[13] it is nevertheless not a contradiction to say that with Him failure and faithlessness are impossibilities! He is utterly reliable and trustworthy to the nth degree! Thus, the term, "not by sight." We can literally shut our eyes and leap to Him or take His Hand and let Him lead us with the utmost trust that He will never fail us! He will never lead us down a wrong path or betray our trust! NEVER! That's just not possible with Him! God is *faithful*! The following scriptures tell us this is so.

> "Know therefore that the LORD your God, He is God, the *faithful* God, who keeps His covenant and His lovingkindness to a thousandth generation with those who love Him and keep His commandments."[14]

> Thus says the LORD, the Redeemer of Israel and its Holy One, To the despised One, To the One abhorred by the nation, To the Servant of rulers, "Kings will see and arise, Princes will also bow down, Because of the LORD who is *faithful*, the Holy One of Israel who has chosen You."[15]

Ephraim surrounds Me with lies And the house of Israel with deceit; Judah is also unruly against God, Even against the Holy One who is *faithful*.[16]

God is *faithful*, through whom you were called into fellowship with His Son, Jesus Christ our Lord.[17]

No temptation has overtaken you but such as is common to man; and God is *faithful*, who will not allow you to be tempted beyond what you are able, but with the temptation will provide the way of escape also, so that you will be able to endure it.[18]

But as God is *faithful*, our word to you is not yes and no.[19]

Faithful is He who calls you, and He also will bring it to pass.[20]

But the Lord is *faithful*, and He will strengthen and protect you from the evil one.[21]

If we are faithless, He remains *faithful*, for He cannot deny Himself.[22]

but Christ was *faithful* as a Son over His house—whose house we are, if we hold fast our confidence and the boast of our hope firm until the end.[23]

By faith even Sarah herself received ability to conceive, even beyond the proper time of life, since she considered Him *faithful* who had promised.[24]

Therefore, those also who suffer according to the will of God shall entrust their souls to a *faithful* Creator in doing what is right.[25]

If we confess our sins, He is *faithful* and righteous to forgive us our sins and to cleanse us from all unrighteousness.[26]

and from Jesus Christ, the *faithful* witness, the firstborn of the dead, and the ruler of the kings of the earth. To Him who loves us and released us from our sins by His blood—[27]

Because He is *faithful*, His word and commandments are faithful:

All Your commandments are *faithful*; They have persecuted me with a lie; help me![28]

holding fast the *faithful* word which is in accordance with the teaching, so that he will be able both to exhort in sound doctrine and to refute those who contradict.[29]

Because God and His Word are so utterly faithful, we can utterly trust Him with our lives and everything in them! This is the reason we can "walk by *faith* and **not** by *sight*!"

Walking By the Spirit

> But I say, *walk* by the Spirit, and you will not carry out the desire of the flesh. For the flesh sets its desire against the Spirit, and the Spirit against the flesh; for these are in opposition to one another, so that you may not do the things that you please. But if you are led by the Spirit, you are not under the Law.[30]

The term "walking" is a metaphor for navigating or traversing or moving, as well as for one's behavioral deportment, i.e., the morality or standards according to which one conducts his/her life. As previously stated, *walking* is a metaphor for living life. From the very first step to the very last step a person takes in the course of his/her life, the exercise of walking is essentially a balancing act. Each step is an exercise of maintaining equilibrium. One step begs the next.

Life is a balancing act and an exercise of maintaining equilibrium. Narrow is the line between sanity and insanity, according to psychologists, and history is replete with examples of human life that corroborate that reality. From a Biblical perspective, though profound the difference, narrow is the line between the flesh and the spirit, demonization and liberty of the Spirit, walking by the spirit and walking by the flesh. Living on the sane, holy, and spiritual side of the line is the challenge and choice for every human-being.

The Apostle Paul explains in the above-cited passage from his letter to the Galatians that resisting walking by the flesh, the carnal nature, is simply a matter of walking in the Spirit, the result of which will be: "you will not carry out the desire of the flesh." So many approach the matter of resisting the devil and his temptations as a face-to-face, all-out war, against the fleshly desires themselves, which can be wearying, when what Paul is saying here is that it is not a matter of trying to find a way to eliminate the temptations, or even fighting and resisting them, per se, but rather "walking by the Spirit" instead. Walking by the Spirit will automatically cancel out walking by the flesh and carrying out the deeds of the flesh. That's the solution!

To help us further, Paul even lists a litany of "deeds of the flesh," though he indicates the list he enumerates is not exhaustive, in that there are also "things like these," and contrasts them to the nine fruit of the Spirit that are, by their nature, opposing forces of the deeds of the flesh, or the carnal, sin nature, that keep believers from doing "the things that you please." Paul's letter is written to believers, and he is saying that even for Born Again believers, doing what they really, in their heart, *want* to do is a struggle against the "opposition" the deeds of the flesh inherent in the carnal nature pose against their inner desires of right-doing or righteousness.

> Now the deeds of the flesh are evident, which are: immorality, impurity, sensuality, idolatry, sorcery, enmities, strife, jealousy, outbursts of anger, disputes, dissensions, factions, envying, drunkenness, carousing, and things like these, of which I forewarn you, just as I have forewarned you, that those who practice such things will not inherit the kingdom of God. But the fruit of the Spirit is love, joy, peace, patience, kindness, goodness, faithfulness, gentleness, self-control; against such things there is no law. Now those who belong to Christ Jesus have crucified the flesh with its passions and desires.[31]

What do the deeds of the flesh and the fruit of the Spirit have to do with faith? Everything! Faith is a gift from God and thus a matter of the Kingdom of God, which is a realm of the Spirit that exists and is real, though unseen or unperceived by the natural senses. It's like what Jesus said about the work of the Holy Spirit, one cannot see with his physical eyes the Spirit Himself, but the workings of the Spirit when He moves are perceivable in the same way the wind blowing in trees is perceivable by the sound it makes and its movement of the trees' branches and their leaves:

> "That which is born of the flesh is flesh, and that which is born of the Spirit is spirit. "Do not be amazed that I said to you, 'You must be born again.' "The wind blows where it wishes and you hear the sound of it, but do not know where it comes from and where it is going; so is everyone who is born of the Spirit."[32]

Walking in the Spirit rather than walking in the flesh is the impetus of the Spirit that makes faith genuine and effectual. Contrastingly, faith does not work, is not effectual, when one is walking in the flesh or carrying out the desires of the flesh. Faith works through love,[33] and love is the first fruit of the Spirit from which the others emanate and manifest, for God is love[34]:

> But the fruit of the Spirit is *love*, joy, peace, patience, kindness, goodness, faithfulness, gentleness, self-control; against such things there is no law.[35]

So, in the broader spiritual panorama, the fruit of the Spirit are what undergirds the Kingdom of God, and therefore makes faith in God effectual in the life of the believer. Thus, in the aspects of our lives in which we are not walking by the Spirit, but rather walking by the flesh, faith will be ineffectual and inoperative, or at the very minimum, hampered or diminished. We can pray and petition, as we are instructed to do,[36] but our prayers will be answered commensurate to the degree to which we are walking by the Spirit because we are required to pray in "believing" faith in order for our prayers to be answered according to what we have asked:

> And all things, whatsoever ye shall ask in prayer, *believing*, ye shall *receive*.[37]

> And Jesus answering saith unto them, **Have faith in God**. For verily I say unto you, That whosoever shall say unto this mountain, Be thou removed, and be thou cast into the sea; and shall not doubt in his heart, but shall *believe* that those things which he saith shall come to pass; he shall have whatsoever he saith. Therefore I say unto you, What things soever ye desire, when ye pray, *believe* that ye *receive* them, and ye shall have them.[38]

Walking Worthy

What I am attempting to identify and insert here is the precept of walking worthy according to the calling with which God has called believers, which precept is corroborated by the following scriptures:

> Therefore I, the prisoner of the Lord, implore you to *walk in a manner worthy* of the calling with which you have been called,[39]

> so that you will *walk in a manner worthy* of the Lord, to please Him in all respects, bearing fruit in every good work and increasing in the knowledge of God;[40]

> so that you would *walk in a manner worthy* of the God who calls you into His own kingdom and glory.[41]

> 'But you have a few people in Sardis who have not soiled their

garments; and they will *walk with Me in white*, for they are worthy.'[42]

The essence of what God appears to be wanting to communicate to us in such passages is that things go better in life when you are walking or living your life in the Spirit! Perhaps even more importantly, He appears also to be instructing us that our faith will be more effectual in bringing into being the things we hope for when we live our lives in accordance with the principles and precepts He has delineated in His Word. Such godly living produces in our lives a powerful proactive faith-in-God-consciousness that counters the sin-consciousness with which Satan constantly attempts to bombard our minds via his non-stop condemnatory accusations against us "before our God day and night"[43] and allows us to truly believe that what we say in prayer believing "is going to happen" or come to pass in our lives[44] because we are walking in rightstanding with God. The result of such faith activated in the course of prayer, Jesus informed us is a granting and receiving of "all things for which you pray and ask":

> Therefore I say to you, ALL things for which you pray and ask, believe that you have received them, and *they will be granted you.*[45]

Enoch Walked With God

These four words form one of the most poignant and mysterious passages in the Bible concerning one of the most mysterious characters mentioned in the Bible!

Enoch walked with God; and he was not, for God took him.[46]

What does it mean that Enoch *walked* with God?

Well, to begin with, again, "walking," as it is used in the Bible, is a metaphor for life and for the manner in which one lives. So, what this verse is saying is that Enoch lived his life in step with God. Now, since he could not have been Born Again or sanctified in spirit and soul or body—because Christ Jesus had not yet been slain as the Lamb of God who purchased salvation for us—he could not have possibly been perfect! No one, other than Jesus, is or was! In fact, the passage does not say Enoch was perfect, but just that he walked with God. Though the mind of man longs for heroes and super-humans, and therefore wants to make perfect people out of Bible characters, nevertheless, that was not so of any of the mere mortals mentioned therein.

This mysterious man, Enoch, about whose existence on the Earth we are told little within canonized scripture, was not perfect, but Moses and God Himself testified concerning him that he "walked with God." That alone is about as strong of a testimony as one could have!

What we *do* know about Enoch is that he was the firstborn son of Cain, the firstborn son of Adam; and that the city that Cain built for his family to inhabit in the land of Nod, east of Eden, after he fled Eden as a fugitive of justice to save his life, he named after his son, Enoch.[47] Additionally, we know that Enoch lived 65 years before producing his first son, Methuselah; that he walked with God 300 years after he begat Methuselah and begat other sons and daughters during that time;[48] and we are told that "all the days of Enoch were three hundred and sixty-five years."[49] Then, the writer of Hebrews references Enoch's unusual death, saying:

> By faith Enoch was taken up so that he would not see death; AND HE WAS NOT FOUND BECAUSE GOD TOOK HIM UP; for he obtained the witness that before his being taken up he was pleasing to God.[50]

So, again, what does it mean? Well, for one thing, it tells us that Enoch's relationship with God was not a sprint—he did not *run* with God; he *walked* with God in what was an enduring marathon of persistency and consistency. You don't even get the idea that it was a "power-walk," but rather a normally paced *striding* with God.

The preposition "with" speaks something as well: that his life was largely "synced up" to God. He lived his life synchronized with the footsteps of God, not rushing out ahead of Him or lagging behind Him, but in stride with Him. The pacesetter was God, not Enoch. He didn't live his life *independent* of God, but *dependent* upon Him. Doubtless, this brief reference to Enoch in Moses' writings about all things beginning-related appears so as to pass along principles of the Spirit to everyone desirous of having the testimony that he/she "walked with God."

Of course, Enoch was one of only two people who ever lived who escaped death prior to being "raptured" or "taken up" into the presence of God. The other was the prophet, Elijah. These two extraordinary men will be the "two witnesses"—"the two olive trees and the two lampstands that stand before the Lord of the earth"—who will be raised from the dead at the beginning of the Great Tribulation to perform extraordinary miracles in the witness of the entire world for a period of three-and-a-half years, and who at the mid-point mark of the Great Tribulation will be martyred by execution ordered by the Antichrist, and who will, after their dead bodies are displayed in the streets of Jerusalem for three-and-a-half days, via the rolling cameras of all the news agencies of the entire world recording the events, be suddenly raised from the dead when "the breath of life from God" comes into them, and at the command of God heard by the world, "Come up here!" will be visibly transported, raptured, back up into Heaven!

> Then there was given me a measuring rod like a staff; and someone said, "Get up and measure the temple of God and the altar, and those who worship in it. "Leave out the court which is outside the temple and do not measure it, for it has been given to the nations; and they will tread under foot the holy city for forty-two months. "And I will grant authority to my two witnesses, and they will prophesy for twelve hundred and sixty days, clothed in sackcloth." These are the two olive trees and the two lampstands that stand before the Lord of the earth. And if anyone wants to harm them, fire flows out of their mouth and devours their enemies; so if anyone wants to harm them, he must be killed in this way. These have the power to shut up the sky, so that rain will not fall during the days of their prophesying; and they have power over the waters to turn them into blood, and to strike the earth with every plague, as often as they desire. When they have finished their testimony, the beast that comes up out of the abyss will make war with them, and overcome them and kill them. And their dead bodies will lie in the street of the great city which mystically is called Sodom and Egypt, where also their Lord was crucified. Those from the peoples and tribes and tongues and nations will look at their dead bodies for three and a half days, and will not permit their dead bodies to be laid in a tomb. And those who dwell on the earth will rejoice over them and celebrate; and they will send gifts to one another, because these two prophets tormented those who dwell on the earth. But after the three and a half days, the breath of life from God came into them, and they stood on their feet; and great fear fell upon those who were watching them. And they heard a loud voice from heaven

saying to them, "Come up here." Then they went up into heaven in the cloud, and their enemies watched them. And in that hour there was a great earthquake, and a tenth of the city fell; seven thousand people were killed in the earthquake, and the rest were terrified and gave glory to the God of heaven. The second woe is past; behold, the third woe is coming quickly.[51]

It is *appointed* unto every human *once to die*:

And inasmuch as it is *appointed* for men to *die once* and after this comes judgment,[52]

Concerning this topic, I wrote and published an article as well as a podcast online, which I entitled, "The Appointment That No One Will Miss!" I highly recommend readers and listeners access both. The URL for the article on SLM Online website is: https://www.slm.org/the-appointment-no-one-will-miss/, and the podcast on Spreaker can be found at: https://www.spreaker.com/episode/47045408.

Every human born *must* die; i.e., undergo physical death. Some people, because of their fear of death, get upset when the matter of dying is spoken of in such stark terms. Nevertheless, death is a stark reality! Death is a part of life! Dying is a part of living! Like it or not, these are just the plain, unadorned *facts*!

Despite this, there are two people who, according to Scripture, did not die physical death before being taken up into Heaven: Enoch and Elijah:

> Enoch walked with God; AND HE WAS NOT, FOR GOD TOOK HIM.[53]

> As they were going along and talking, behold, there appeared a chariot of fire and horses of fire which separated the two of them. And ELIJAH WENT UP BY A WHIRLWIND TO HEAVEN.[54]

Thus, these two men *must* come back to Earth as humans, living in human bodies, in order to die physically, bodily, otherwise they cannot inherit the Kingdom of God:

> Now I say this, brethren, that FLESH AND BLOOD CANNOT INHERIT THE KINGDOM OF GOD; nor does the perishable inherit the imperishable.[55]

Without any doubt or equivocation, the two witnesses of Revelation Eleven are Enoch and Elijah! Without experiencing bodily death, they both "slipped the surly bonds of earth" to "touch the face of God."[56]

Other than what we've already seen, the only other thing we know about Enoch from the biblical record is a reference that Jude made in his brief letter regarding him:

> It was also about these men that Enoch, in the seventh generation from Adam, prophesied, saying, "Behold, the Lord came with many thousands of His holy ones, to execute judgment upon all, and to convict all the ungodly of all their ungodly deeds which they have done in an ungodly way, and of all the harsh things which ungodly sinners have spoken against Him."[57]

It appears, then, that the primary message God is conveying in His Word concerning Enoch is that he faithfully and indefatigably lived his long life of 365 years walking step-by-step with God, and that by doing so he gained God's approval and acceptance (i.e., rightstanding),[58] and that he will be used by God, along with Elisha, to demonstrate the boundless miraculous power of God during the ends of the ages when they both are suddenly raised from the dead and given authority from God to perform extraordinary miracles bearing witness to the eyes of the world as the prophesied "Two Witnesses" of the End-Time.

Moreover, "through the encouragement of the Scriptures,"[59] God is also, in the account of the Two Witnesses and how they became so, encouraging all believers with the great hope that one day, when we each appear before God at the Bema-Seat of final judgment, we too shall similarly receive our rewards of recompense based on our deeds in the body while living on the Earth:

> For we *must* **all** appear before the judgment seat of Christ, so that each one may be recompensed for his deeds in the body, according to what he has done, whether good or bad.[60]

It is Jesus Himself, the Door, who will honor us with those rewards for our faithfulness and grant us entrance into the everlasting joy of eternal fellowship with Him:

> "His master said to him, 'Well done, good and faithful slave. You were faithful with a *few* things, I will put you in charge of *many* things; enter into the joy of your master.'"[61]

Endnotes

1 2 Cor. 5:1-10
2 Rom. 12:3
3 Rom. 10:10
4 John 20:24-25
5 Heb. 11:6
6 2 Cor. 1:20
7 Col. 3:15
8 John 14:16
9 John 14:26
10 John 15:26
11 John 16:7
12 Heb. 10:35
13 Luke 1:37
14 Deu. 7:9
15 Isa. 49:7
16 Hos. 11:12
17 1 Cor. 1:9
18 1 Cor. 10:13
19 2 Cor. 1:18
20 1 Thes. 5:24
21 2 Thes. 3:3
22 2 Tim. 2:13
23 Heb. 3:6
24 Heb. 11:11
25 1 Pet. 4:19
26 1 John 1:9
27 Rev. 1:5
28 Psa. 119:86
29 Tit. 1:9

30 Gal. 5:16-18
31 Gal. 5:19-24
32 John 3:6-8
33 Gal. 5:6
34 1 John 4:8,16
35 Gal. 5:22-23
36 Eph. 6:18
37 Mat. 21:22
38 Mark 11:22-24
39 Eph. 4:1
40 Col. 1:10
41 1 Thes. 2:12
42 Rev. 3:4
43 Rev. 12:10
44 Mark 11:23
45 Mark 11:24
46 Gen. 5:24
47 Gen. 4:16-17
48 Gen. 5:22
49 Gen. 5:23
50 Heb. 11:5
51 Rev. 11:1-14
52 Heb. 9:27
53 Gen. 5:24
54 2 Kgs. 2:11
55 1 Cor. 15:50
56 Excerpt from President Ronald Reagan's Speech honoring the Challenger astronauts lost in its explosion minutes following lift off January 28, 1986.
57 Jude 1:14-15

58 Heb. 11:2, 39
59 Rom. 15:4
60 2 Cor. 5:10
61 Mat. 25:21

Chapter Fifteen
FAITH WITHOUT WORKS

But someone may well say, "You have faith and I have *works*; show me your faith *without* the works, and I will show you my faith *by* my works."[1]

But someone may say, "You [claim to] have faith and I have [good] works; show me your [alleged] faith without the works [if you can], and I will show you my faith by my works [that is, by what I do]."[2]

But someone will say, "One person has *faith*, another has *actions*." My answer is, "Show me how anyone can have *faith* WITHOUT actions. I will show you my *faith* BY my *actions*."[3]

But are you willing to recognize, you foolish fellow, that *faith without works* is useless?[4]

But are you willing to recognize, you foolish [spiritually shallow] person, that faith without [good] works is useless?[5]

You fool! Do you want to be shown that faith without actions is useless?[6]

For just as the *body* without the *spirit* is dead, so also *faith* without works is *dead*.[7]

For just as the [human] body without the spirit is dead, so faith without works [of obedience] is also dead.[8]

So then, as the *body* without the spirit is *dead*, also *faith* without *actions* is *dead*.[9]

Faith **must** be accompanied by "works" or "actions" to be genuine and Biblical faith. These three verses in the three different versions quoted above unequivocally prove that. Genuine, Biblical faith is not ethereal or without substance. Indeed, the primary passage regarding faith, from which the title of this book is derived, in part states categorically: "Faith is the *substance* of things hoped for...."[10] Faith is not just a concept. Real faith is real; it exists and has substance in the spirit realm. It bears spiritual weight. It is that weight that makes real faith work. Thus, this book's subtitle: "Faith That Works!" It works because it has spiritual substance. It works because it provides God what He needs from us, that only we can supply, to cause those things that we hope for or have a desire for to manifest in our lives. Indeed, this spiritual substance of faith that we provide God as something to work with is the very kind of "good works" the above passages are talking about. I like to call them: "Godly works!" They are Godly works because they consist of trust, reliance, faith in *God*, as opposed to trust, reliance, faith in *ourselves* or in some other idolatrous entity elevated to deity status in human thinking.

This kind of Godly works can be likened unto or regarded as the seven loaves of bread and two fish garnered from the crowd and given to Jesus that He then blessed and used to feed the five-thousand men plus women and children.[11] We—those who are trusting in Him—must give Him something of ours, something we own, to work with, which makes it "Godly works." Kingdom principles of financial blessing are based on this precept of Godly works. The tithe belongs to the Lord in the first place,[12] so in obedience, believers worship God with their tithes, for starters, and their offerings, which is the portion that we give out of what we own, because we do not own the first ten percent of our income because it belongs to God; meaning, God owns it. It came into our lives (income), but it came into our lives in order to give it back to God as worship and honoring of Him, Jehovah Jireh, the God who abundantly supplies all our needs! So, even though the returning/giving of this tithe unto the Lord is credited to us and our account with God, yet God is the source of it, He provided it! From the remaining ninety percent we make freewill offerings of our choosing, and it is that portion that we give that God promises to bless and multiply, "thirty, sixty, and a hundredfold."[13]

This precept is also known as the Law of Reciprocity, or Law of Sowing and Reaping, one of the foundational laws of the Kingdom of God. It's the simple law of seed-sowing: plant a seed, and it returns a multiplied harvest, more bountiful than the seed itself. Each seed is sacrificed in order to plant rather than to eat it. Planting in faith perpetuates the harvest process. In the Kingdom, as long as you sacrifice some of your seed by not consuming it and plant it in faith in the good soil of an obedient and worshipful heart, you will always be guaranteed a bountiful harvest. You will always reap what you sow![14]

Seeing faith in this vein provides a picture of how the faith process works. We give God something from ourselves, something we own, something from our storehouse, our treasury, so to speak, and when we give it in sincere faith and honor and worship of Him, He receives what we have released from our hands and have put into His as a faith-seed, and honors our faith by returning to us an abundant harvest many times more in quantity than what we sowed. That is who God is! That's His nature! He's not el-cheapo, but El Shaddai, the God who is more than enough! He always does "exceeding abundantly above all that we ask or think, according to the power (dunamis, Gr.) that worketh in us!"[15]

Faith Is Personal and Individualistic

Faith is personal and individualistic. It is not a group-think thing! Multiple individuals may share the same faith regarding a particular and specific thing hoped for, i.e., agree together about it, but the faith being applied is nevertheless personal and individualistic for each person in agreement. Each person sharing faith about the matter must exercise everything required to be exercised for his/her faith to be real, effective, and productive. This is important in this day when socialistic philosophies are being proliferated by the political powers of this world as agitprop in every segment of every society of the world. The goal of all that socialistic propagandizing ultimately is the One-World/One-Religion World that will be the master goal of the Antichrist and allow him for a short time to seize political control of the nations of the world under the auspices of the One-World Government called "the beast" in the book of Revelation.[16] While the Ekklesia (Church) that Jesus is building is an aggregation of all the saints (believers) throughout eternity, nevertheless, each of those saints are a part of the Remnant Church due to their individual faith and belief in the only Messiah of the world, Christ Jesus! Again, faith is personal and individualistic. No one can rely on anyone else's faith to save them or to produce the results in their life that genuine faith produces. Your faith only produces in *your* life what faith produces, *not* in anyone else's. Agreement in faith between individuals produces,[17] yes, but it is effective and produces because it is shared by each individual in agreement. This is the reason that "two are better than one"[18] because the return on their faith is doubled or more.

The reason God has made faith personal and individualistic is that faith is the primary ingredient in our relationship with God: "...for he who comes to God must believe that He is and that He is a rewarder of those who seek Him."[19] Genuine faith is not a *religious* matter, but a *relationship* matter. We put our trust in Him because He is the ultimate in trustworthiness! We put our trust in Him because He is the ultimate in faithfulness! We put our trust in Him because He is Almighty God! We put our trust in Him because He, and He alone, is worthy to be trusted, honored, and worshiped as God!

Faith is Like an Appliance—It Must Be Applied

In describing faith, I've often used the metaphor of electrical kitchen appliances. They can be the most perfectly and exquisitely made appliance, but they are worthless just sitting atop the kitchen counter until they are made operable by plugging them into an electrical socket, the source of electricity. Likewise, faith becomes operable and effective when it is plugged into the electrical flow of the Spirit—the dunamis-power of God. As in the case of household electricity once the house is built, properly wired, and connected to the source, that power of the Spirit is always flowing from its Source—God. It is up to the individual believer to plug his/her "believer" (the appliance of the heart; "for with the heart a person believes"[20]) into the continually flowing dunamis-power of God! Once the believer's believer is plugged in, the dunamis-power makes the appliance operable, and it continues to operate until the thing hoped for is manifest in the natural realm, as long as it remains plugged in. If at any point subsequently the believer's "believer" is disconnected from the spiritual electrical flow via unbelief, disrupting the flow of spiritual power, the manifestation process is discontinued until the "believer" is reconnected to the source. Thus, a disconnection of belief or faith—caused by unbelief—is not permanent but can always be overcome by reconnecting at any subsequent juncture, resulting in a restoration of power to the manifestation process until it is either interrupted again or it is completed with the result of the manifestation of the thing hoped for or desired.

Hallelujah! God's dynamo of electricity continues to flow faithfully and reliably regardless of any faltering or faith failures on the believer's part! God is faithful![21]

In this technological world we live in today, "apps" (short for appliances) are ubiquitous on our computers and smart devices. There seems to be an app for just about everything now. The Lord gave me a message for one congregation to which He sent me some years ago based on that concept of apps. The message, entitled, "Faith App," essentially laid out how that faith is an app in the Spirit realm that we can download from Heaven and use in our everyday lives to produce the things that we hope for or desire. The message began with me quoting someone I would otherwise not quote, but whose quotation I found on the Internet that was quite fitting for the message the Lord was giving me. The quote stated: *"Faith is the 'App' that turns on and causes your Spirit to operate!"*[22] Based on that quote, I titled my message, "Faith App."

As a longtime radio broadcaster and now podcaster, I have often evoked the analogy of radio signals in the air to explain how faith (and other spiritual principles) works. Radio signals are sent into the air by the transmitter to a tower that has some sort of an antenna mechanism that "broadcasts" the signal (sound waves) into the air. A radio set essentially is a receiving device that due to the workings of its components is able to "pick up" or receive those radio sound waves that are broadcast by the broadcasting "station" and translate them into audio waves that can be heard with the human ear. These signals travel at the speed of sound for a limited, gradually decreasing, distance. A chain of "translators" can be used to "boost" the strength and length of the signal, and this is all regulated by the Federal Communications Commission, in order to bring order to the otherwise total chaos that would result without regulation. Faith, in a manner of speaking, functions similarly to radio signals. God has issued "the measure of faith" into the air or atmosphere on the Earth—some particular situations that faith can be stronger or more powerful than in others—and it is up to individual believers to plug their "believer" (the device or app) into the power source and "tune" it to the frequency of faith that is being broadcast by the Spirit, receive the message, believe the message, and add Godly works (action) to the message (a la the radio receiver) along with a real expectation that what is being transmitted is from and of

God and received. Jesus said, as reiterated in this book, if we receive what we believe in the receiver of our heart (spirit) and retransmit, or say, or verbalize precisely what we believe, it will manifest or come to pass in our lives, so that we "have" or own them as our personal present possession:

> And on the morrow, when they were come from Bethany, he was hungry: And seeing a fig tree afar off having leaves, he came, if haply he might find any thing thereon: and when he came to it, he found nothing but leaves; for the time of figs was not yet. And Jesus answered and **said** unto it, No man eat fruit of thee hereafter for ever. And his disciples heard it.
>
> And in the morning, as they passed by, they saw the fig tree dried up from the roots. And Peter calling to remembrance saith unto him, Master, behold, the fig tree which thou cursedst is withered away. And Jesus answering saith unto them, Have FAITH in God. For verily I say unto you, That whosoever shall **say** unto this mountain, Be thou removed, and be thou cast into the sea; *and shall not **doubt** in his heart*, but shall **believe** that those things which **he saith** shall come to pass; he shall **have** whatsoever he **saith**. Therefore I say unto you, What things soever ye desire, *when ye pray*, **believe** that ye **receive** them, and ye shall **have** them.²³

Again, to express the concept again: faith is the app (device) we download and utilize to bring into being those things we desire that are according to the will of God to be manifest in our lives. We must apply faith into every situation and circumstance of our lives in which we need the supernatural intervention of God. Faith waves are constantly being broadcast through the Rhema (spoken, verbalized) Word of God, and it is up to believers to "capture" or "tune into" those audio waves, retransmit them through our mouths, and believe (expect) the what we say is going to happen or manifest, and we shall have them manifested in our lives.

The Hall of Faith

Heb. 11:1-40

(1) Now faith is the assurance of things hoped for, the conviction of things not seen.
(2) For by it the men of old gained approval.

(3) By faith we understand that the worlds were prepared by the word of God, so that what is seen was not made out of things which are visible.
(4) By faith Abel offered to God a better sacrifice than Cain, through which he obtained the testimony that he was righteous, God testifying about his gifts, and through faith, though he is dead, he still speaks.
(5) By faith Enoch was taken up so that he would not see death; AND HE WAS NOT FOUND BECAUSE GOD TOOK HIM UP; for he obtained the witness that before his being taken up he was pleasing to God.
(6) And without faith it is impossible to please Him, for he who comes to God must believe that He is and that He is a rewarder of those who seek Him.
(7) By faith Noah, being warned by God about things not yet seen, in reverence prepared an ark for the salvation of his household, by which he condemned the world, and became an heir of the righteousness which is according to faith.
(8) By faith Abraham, when he was called, obeyed by going out to a place which he was to receive for an inheritance; and he went out, not knowing where he was going.
(9) By faith he lived as an alien in the land of promise, as in a foreign land, dwelling in tents with Isaac and Jacob, fellow heirs of the same promise;
(10) for he was looking for the city which has foundations, whose architect and builder is God.
(11) By faith even Sarah herself received ability to conceive, even beyond the proper time of life, since she considered Him faithful who had promised.
(12) Therefore there was born even of one man, and him as good as dead at that, as many descendants AS THE STARS OF HEAVEN IN NUMBER, AND INNUMERABLE AS THE SAND WHICH IS BY THE SEASHORE.
(13) All these died in faith, without receiving the promises, but having seen them and having welcomed them from a distance, and having confessed that they were strangers and exiles on the earth.
(14) For those who say such things make it clear that they are seeking a country of their own.
(15) And indeed if they had been thinking of that country from

which they went out, they would have had opportunity to return. (16) But as it is, they desire a better country, that is, a heavenly one. Therefore God is not ashamed to be called their God; for He has prepared a city for them.
(17) By faith Abraham, when he was tested, offered up Isaac, and he who had received the promises was offering up his only begotten son;
(18) it was he to whom it was said, "IN ISAAC YOUR DESCENDANTS SHALL BE CALLED."
(19) He considered that God is able to raise people even from the dead, from which he also received him back as a type.
(20) By faith Isaac blessed Jacob and Esau, even regarding things to come.
(21) By faith Jacob, as he was dying, blessed each of the sons of Joseph, and worshiped, leaning on the top of his staff.
(22) By faith Joseph, when he was dying, made mention of the exodus of the sons of Israel, and gave orders concerning his bones.
(23) By faith Moses, when he was born, was hidden for three months by his parents, because they saw he was a beautiful child; and they were not afraid of the king's edict.
(24) By faith Moses, when he had grown up, refused to be called the son of Pharaoh's daughter,
(25) choosing rather to endure ill-treatment with the people of God than to enjoy the passing pleasures of sin,
(26) considering the reproach of Christ greater riches than the treasures of Egypt; for he was looking to the reward.
(27) By faith he left Egypt, not fearing the wrath of the king; for he endured, as seeing Him who is unseen.
(28) By faith he kept the Passover and the sprinkling of the blood, so that he who destroyed the firstborn would not touch them.
(29) By faith they passed through the Red Sea as though they were passing through dry land; and the Egyptians, when they attempted it, were drowned.
(30) By faith the walls of Jericho fell down after they had been encircled for seven days.
(31) By faith Rahab the harlot did not perish along with those who were disobedient, after she had welcomed the spies in peace.
(32) And what more shall I say? For time will fail me if I tell of Gideon, Barak, Samson, Jephthah, of David and Samuel and the

prophets,
(33) who by faith conquered kingdoms, performed acts of righteousness, obtained promises, shut the mouths of lions,
(34) quenched the power of fire, escaped the edge of the sword, from weakness were made strong, became mighty in war, put foreign armies to flight.
(35) Women received back their dead by resurrection; and others were tortured, not accepting their release, so that they might obtain a better resurrection;
(36) and others experienced mockings and scourgings, yes, also chains and imprisonment.
(37) They were stoned, they were sawn in two, they were tempted, they were put to death with the sword; they went about in sheepskins, in goatskins, being destitute, afflicted, ill-treated
(38) (men of whom the world was not worthy), wandering in deserts and mountains and caves and holes in the ground.
(39) And all these, having gained approval through their faith, did not receive what was promised,
(40) because God had provided something better for us, so that apart from us they would not be made perfect.

Delineated in the above passage is what could be called, "The Hall of Faith." It is the most comprehensive listing and enshrinement in Scripture of various great possessors and employers of uncommon faith! The individuals referenced therein, some by name and some anonymously, each accomplished great exploits in their lifetime on behalf of God and the Kingdom of God by exercising and applying extraordinary and very real faith! This Hall of Faith memorializes for all eternity in a single multiverse passage examples of what ordinary people applying extraordinary faith can accomplish as human agents of God! Each and every person cited fought horrendous battles, endured hardships, pressed through multiple obstacles and catastrophic circumstances, and refused the temptation to defer to defeat.

Some of the mighty acts those of the Hall of Fame performed by faith, we are told, included:

- conquering kingdoms;
- performing acts of righteousness;
- obtaining promises;
- shutting the mouths of lions;

- quenching the power of fire;
- escaping the edge of the sword;
- from weakness being made strong;
- becoming mighty in war, putting foreign armies to flight;
- passing through the Red Sea as though they were passing through dry land, while their mortal enemies and captors drowned when they attempted same (the Israelites led by Moses).

Among the afflictions and trials they suffered through by faith were:

- Moses refused the prestige and privilege of being called the son of Pharaoh's daughter, choosing rather to endure ill-treatment with the people of God than to enjoy the passing pleasures of sin, considering the reproach of Christ greater riches than the treasures of Egypt, for he was looking to the reward, leaving Egypt, not fearing the wrath of the king, for he endured, as seeing Him who is unseen;
- Israelites kept the Passover and the sprinkling of the blood, so that he who destroyed the firstborn would not touch them (Israelites under the leadership of Moses, Aaron, and the Levites);
- women received back their dead by resurrection;
- being tortured, yet they did not accept their release from incarceration but rather yielded to unjust execution, so that they might obtain a better resurrection;
- experienced mockings and scourgings, and other inhumane indignities of captivity via chains and imprisonment;
- some were stoned to death;
- some were sawn in two;
- they were sorely tempted to give up their faith in Jehovah;
- some were put to death with the sword;
- going about in sheepskins, in goatskins, being destitute, afflicted, ill-treated (men of whom the world was not worthy);
- wandered as vagabonds in deserts and mountains and caves and holes in the ground, without secure lodging and living accommodations.

Through all of these severe sufferings and extreme adversities these individuals remained indefatigable and indomitable, doggedly persevering in unswerving devotion and worship of Jehovah God, refusing to revert to the comparatively less deprivations captivity afforded. But what they suffered, as the Apostle Paul said, is in no way "worthy to be compared with the glory that is to be revealed to us,"[24] which they also were promised but did not receive during their lifetimes on Earth "because God had provided something better for *us*, so that apart from us *they* would not be made perfect," all of which, however, ultimately resulted in "all these having gained approval (of God) *through their* FAITH!"[25]

The Faith Giants mentioned by name in this passage in chronological order of their first mention in the Bible are: Abel, Enoch, Noah (twice), Abraham (twice), Sarah, Isaac, Jacob, Moses, Rahab, Gideon, Barak, Samson, Jephthah, David, Samuel, and the Old Testament prophets. The extraordinary faith of others is described anonymously.

Among the results that these individuals' faith produced, according to the passage, are:

- men of old gained approval;
- we (believers) understand that the worlds[26] were prepared by the word of God, so that what is seen was not made out of things which are visible;
  This verse completely refutes and disproves the inane "Evolution" theory that falsely hypothesizes that the world self-created itself ("Big Bang Theory") and all living creatures (animal and plant species) "evolved" and continue to "evolve," perfecting itself, over time from itself. The Greek word in this verse translated "framed" in the KJV and "prepared" in the NASB is: katartizō, which Strong's Expository Dictionary of New Testament Words defines as: to complete thoroughly, that is, repair (literally or figuratively) or adjust: - fit, frame, mend, (make) perfect (-ly join together), prepare, restore.
  Thus, the import of the verse is that God made the universe through the Rhema, i.e., verbalized Word of God, which is the Son of God, who was MAN-ifested on Earth in human bodily form as Jesus Christ—"And the Word became flesh, and dwelt among us, and we saw His glory, glory as of the only begotten from the Father, full of grace and truth,"[27] and

that the universe the Word formed was formed of things which do NOT appear or are NOT visible in the Creation, i.e., the natural realm.

In other words, the Creation was created by God speaking it into existence rather than it "evolving" out of itself, and He created it out of nothing that existed in the Creation but rather existed only in His infinitely vast intelligence, wisdom, and understanding. GOD created the Creation! The Creation could not and did not create itself, because it did not exist, nor was it animated with Life to enable it to do anything until God created it by speaking it into existence, and because all things comprising the Creation are subjected to the Creator under his feet, and "He left nothing that is not subject to Him!"[28]

How do we know or understand this about the how the Creation was created? BY FAITH in God and His Word (vis-à-vis, science), which "cometh by hearing, and hearing by the word of God."[29] Bottom line is believers simply *believe* God's own testimony expressed in the very first verse of the Bible: "In the beginning GOD created the heavens and the earth."[30]

- Abel offered to God a *better* sacrifice than Cain—better because it was a living entity (lamb) with blood flowing through it, for "the life of the flesh is in the blood"[31]—through which better sacrifice he obtained the testimony that he was righteous, God testifying about his gifts, and through faith, though he is dead (physically), he still speaks (spiritually);

- Enoch was taken up so that he would not see death; and he was not found because God took him up (the original "rapture"); for he obtained the witness that before his being taken up he was pleasing to God; (this illustrates to believers that) without faith it is impossible to please God, for he who comes to God must believe that He IS and that He is a rewarder of those who seek Him;

- Noah, being warned by God about things not yet seen, in reverence prepared an ark for the salvation of his household, by which he condemned the world, and became an heir of the righteousness which is according to faith;

- Abraham, when he was called, obeyed by going out to a place which he was to receive for an inheritance; and he went out, not knowing where he was going; he lived as an alien in the land of promise, as in a foreign land, dwelling in tents with Isaac and Jacob (Abraham's sons), fellow heirs of the same promise, for he was looking for the city which has foundations, whose architect and builder is God; moreover, even Sarah (Abraham's wife) herself received ability to conceive, even beyond the proper time of life, since she considered Him faithful who had promised, and therefore there was born even of one man, and him as good as dead at that, as many descendants as the stars of heaven in number, and innumerable as the sand which is by the seashore (the Jewish people); when he was tested, offered up Isaac, and he who had received the promises was offering up his only begotten son; it was he (Abraham) to whom it was said, "In Isaac your descendants shall be called;" he considered that God is able to raise people even from the dead, from which he also received him (Isaac, his son) back as a type (typologically foretelling what God would experience with the sacrifice of His only begotten Son through whom He redeemed Mankind);
- Isaac blessed Jacob and Esau, even regarding things to come (the perpetuation of the Jews, from whom the Messiah would descend);
- Jacob, as he was dying, blessed each of the sons of Joseph, and worshiped, leaning on the top of his staff;
- Joseph, when he was dying, made mention of the exodus of the sons of Israel, and gave orders concerning his bones;
- Moses, when he had grown up, refused to be called the son of Pharaoh's daughter, choosing rather to endure ill-treatment with the people of God than to enjoy the passing pleasures of sin, considering the reproach of Christ greater riches than the treasures of Egypt; for he was looking to the reward; he left Egypt, not fearing the wrath of the king; for he endured, as seeing Him who is unseen; he kept the Passover and the sprinkling of the blood, so that he who destroyed the firstborn (Satan, the destroying angel) would not touch them (the Israelites);

- Israelites passed through the Red Sea as though they were passing through dry land; and the Egyptians, when they attempted it, were drowned; caused the walls of Jericho to fall down after they encircled them for seven days, shouting forth victory on the seventh day;
- Rahab the harlot did not perish along with those who were disobedient, after (and because) she had welcomed the spies in peace (God reckoned her acts of faith and favor toward the Jews as righteousness);
- Gideon, Barak, Samson, Jephthah, of David and Samuel and the prophets, who by acts of faith of conquered kingdoms, performed acts of righteousness, obtained promises, shut the mouths of lions, quenched the power of fire, escaped the edge of the sword, from weakness were made strong, became mighty in war, put foreign armies to flight;
- women (anonymous) received back their dead by resurrection; and others were tortured, not accepting their release, so that they might obtain a better resurrection.

The reward all these Faith Giants, who "died in faith, without receiving the promises, but having seen them and having welcomed them from a distance, and having confessed that they were strangers and exiles on the earth received," God testifies that: "all these, having gained approval through their faith, did *not* receive what was promised (while living in mortal bodies on Earth), because God had provided something better for us, so that apart from us they would not be made perfect."

The Holy Spirit inspired the author of the Book of Hebrews to delineate and allude to the specific faith acts of these Old Testament individuals as a testament to all New Testament believers of all ages since that God promises to so reward us with the same rewards inuring from eternal fellowship and communion with God those Old Testament believers received. This is the reason God through the author of Hebrews took so much time and words to explain this matter to us, in order to encourage and motivate us to apply our faith with intentional faith acts, and they assure us that everything we do in the course of our life on Earth by and with faith, God will reckon it unto us as righteousness, thus qualifying us for the eternal rewards of same.

Conclusion

So, I reiterate here the contextual foundations of this chapter to re-center our thinking about its contents. Faith *without* works is dead, or spiritually ineffectual and unproductive. Faith **must** be accompanied by "works" or "actions" to be genuine and Biblical faith. Genuine, Biblical faith is not ethereal or without substance. Faith is not just an ethereal concept. Real faith is real; it exists and has substance in the spirit realm. It bears spiritual weight. It is that weight that makes real faith work. It works because it has spiritual substance. It works because it provides God the requisite "good works," or "Godly works" consisting of trust, reliance, faith in *God*, as opposed to trust, reliance, faith in *ourselves* or in some other idolatrous entity elevated to deity status in human thinking that only we can supply Him, to cause those things that we hope or have a desire for to manifest in our lives.

All this is "Faith That Works!" And faith that works certainly is what we want to be operating in our lives! Remember also that faith is always *now*, or it's *never*! When you pray and ask God for whatever you are asking from Him, in accordance with His written Word, believe that what you have asked for is yours, for "this is the confidence that we have in him, that, if we ask any thing according to his will, he heareth us: And if we know that he hear us, whatsoever we ask, we know that we have the petitions that we desired of him."[32] Faith is expectation, a knowing in your spirit, that you have received now what you have asked God for and that what you say will ultimately manifest! When you pray, believe that you received, and it shall be so! Amen and Amen!

Endnotes

1   Jas. 2:18; italics added
2   Jas. 2:18; AMP
3   Jas. 2:18; GNB; emphases added
4   Jas. 2:20; italics added
5   Jas. 2:20; AMP

6 Jas. 2:20; GNB

7 Jas. 2:26; italics added

8 Jas. 2:26; AMP

9 Jas. 2:26; GNB; italics added

10 Heb. 11:1

11 Mat. 14:15-21

12 Lev. 27:30

13 Mark 4:8, 20; c.f., Mat. 13:8, 23

14 Gal. 6:7; 1 Cor. 9:11; 2 Cor. 9:6

15 Eph. 3:20

16 Rev. 11:7; 13:2,3,4,14,15,17,18; 14:9,11; 15:2; 16:2,10,13; 17:7,8,11-13,16,17; 19:19,20; 20:4,10

17 Mat. 18:19

18 Ecc. 4:9

19 Heb 11:6

20 Rom. 10:10

21 1 Cor. 1:9; 10:13; 2 Cor. 1:18; 1Pet. 4:19

22 Robert H. Schuller; Sermon preached at Crystal Cathedral entitled, "The Shoe Can't Tell The Foot How Big To Grow;" c. 2010

23 Mark 11:12-14; 20-24; KJV; emphases added

24 Rom. 8:18

25 Heb. 11:39

26 αἰών; aiōn; (Gr.); properly an age; by extension perpetuity (also past); by implication the world; Strong's Expository Dictionary of New Testament Words

27 John 1:14

28 Heb. 2:8

29 Rom. 10:17

30 Gen. 1:1

31 Lev. 17:11

32 1 John 5:14-15; KJV

Chapter Sixteen

CONTENDING FOR THE FAITH

Beloved, while I was making every effort to write you about our common salvation, I felt the necessity to write to you appealing that you *contend earnestly for the faith* which was once for all handed down to the saints. For certain persons have crept in unnoticed, those who were long beforehand marked out for this condemnation, ungodly persons who turn the grace of our God into licentiousness and deny our only Master and Lord, Jesus Christ. Now I desire to remind you, though you know all things once for all, that the Lord, after saving a people out of the land of Egypt, subsequently destroyed those who did not believe. And angels who did not keep their own domain, but abandoned their proper abode, He has kept in eternal bonds under darkness for the judgment of the great day, just as Sodom and Gomorrah and the cities around them, since they in the same way as these indulged in gross immorality and went after strange flesh, are exhibited as an example in undergoing the punishment of eternal fire. Yet in the same way these men, also by dreaming, defile the flesh, and reject authority, and revile angelic majesties. But Michael the archangel, when he disputed with the devil and argued about the body of Moses, did not dare pronounce against him a railing judgment, but said, "The Lord rebuke you!" But these men revile the things which they do not understand; and the things which they know by instinct, like unreasoning animals, by these things they are destroyed. Woe to them! For they have gone the way of Cain, and for pay they have rushed headlong into the error of Balaam, and perished in the rebellion of Korah. These are the men who are hidden reefs in your love feasts when they feast with you without fear, caring for themselves; clouds without water, carried along by winds; autumn trees without fruit, doubly dead, uprooted; wild waves of the sea, casting up their own shame like foam; wandering stars, for whom the black darkness has been reserved forever. It was also about these men that Enoch, in the seventh generation from Adam, prophesied, saying, "Behold, the Lord came with many thousands of His holy ones, to execute judgment upon all, and to convict all the ungodly of all their ungodly deeds which they have done in an ungodly way, and of all the harsh things which ungodly sinners have spoken against Him." These are grumblers, finding fault, following after their own lusts; they speak arrogantly, flattering people for the sake of gaining an advantage. But you, beloved, ought to remember the words that were spoken beforehand by the apostles of our Lord Jesus Christ, that they were saying to you, "In the last time there will be mockers, following after their own ungodly lusts." These are the ones who cause divisions, worldly-minded, devoid of the Spirit. But you, beloved, building yourselves up on your most holy faith, praying in the Holy Spirit, keep yourselves in the love of God, waiting anxiously for the mercy of our Lord Jesus Christ to eternal life. And have mercy on some, who are doubting; save others, snatching them out of the fire; and on some have mercy with fear, hating even the garment polluted by the flesh.[1]

"*Contending* for the faith" is a different matter regarding faith than has been addressed elsewhere in this volume. The key word here is "the". It is a specifier pointing to the matter of the Christian or Biblical Faith with respect to its inherent doctrinal dogmas as distinguished from all other satanically-inspired, man-made religious systems. Yes, though many eschew the term, there is such a thing as doctrinal dogmas. Essentially this refers to the particular principles or tenets of faith delineated in the Bible, the sixty-six books of canonized Scripture.

Dictionary.com defines dogma this way:

1. an official system of principles or tenets concerning faith, morals, behavior, etc., as of a church.
2. a specific tenet or doctrine authoritatively laid down, as by a church: *the dogma of the Assumption; the recently defined*

dogma of papal infallibility.
3. prescribed doctrine proclaimed as unquestionably true by a particular group: *the difficulty of resisting political dogma.*
4. a settled or established opinion, belief, or principle: *the classic dogma of objectivity in scientific observation.*[2]

Some Christians do not like the word "dogma," but it is a legitimate concept in orthodox theology, nonetheless. It basically identifies generally accepted doctrine predicated on and proven by canonized Scripture. Sometimes people will invoke the phrase: "I don't want to sound dogmatic...," ostensibly in an attempt to not sound too polemic or unyielding or adamant in stating their beliefs. But really being dogmatic about doctrine is perfectly legitimate and warrants no apologies. The Word of God IS dogmatic; it IS polemic; it IS unyielding; it IS adamant! We don't need to apologize for the way the Word of God is written or what it says! Apologizing for any of that is essentially apologizing for or about God! It's not warranted or needed in any way! If you are merely quoting or citing scripture, you are not responsible for what or how it says it! **GOD** is! It's not *your* word, but *God's*!

The concept of **contending** for *the* faith refers to the personal responsibility of every believer to fight to ferret out and keep the faith "which was **once for all** handed down to the saints," as the above passage denotes. The "once for all" phrase in this verse alludes to the eternality of God's Word, meaning that it does not change over time and is not subject to external influences such as "culture" or sectarian or private/personal interpretation[3] or as some today erroneously allege it is. *Strong's Hebrew and Greek Dictionaries* defines the Greek word rendered "contend" (epagōnizomai) as to "struggle," as if to discover and maintain. Inferred in the word "contend" is also to carry out, walk out, or to obey these doctrines that are delineated and elucidated in the Word of God.

Though it is fairly obvious, it nevertheless needs to be stated that to "walk by faith," the subject of the previous chapter, one must individually and personally discover or learn what these biblical precepts are in order to walk in them. One cannot walk in something of which he/she has no awareness or knowledge. This is where the command to "*Study* to shew thyself approved unto God, a workman that needeth not to be ashamed, rightly dividing the word of truth"[4] comes into play. Every genuinely Born Again believer should have an innate desire to study the Word of God, otherwise the genuineness of their spiritual regeneration is suspect. That desire comes with salvation in a similar way as does the tongue of a shoe—you don't have to buy a set of tongues separately when you buy a pair of shoes, the tongue comes with the shoe. Hebrews 6:9 speaks of "things that accompany salvation"—the desire to study the Word of God is one of those "things". It should be natural to every believer.

The Essentials of the Christian faith

Theologians talk about "the essentials of the faith":
1. The deity of Christ;
2. salvation by grace through faith in Christ Jesus alone and not by works;
3. the death, burial, and resurrection of Christ;
4. the Gospel of Christ (as delineated in 1 Cor. 15:1-8);
5. Monotheism;
6. the Holy Trinity;

My view about those particulars is that while they are a good start and would certainly be included in biblical doctrine, nevertheless, there's far more doctrines or dogmas that are essential to the faith than just those.

What Has Contending for the Faith Have to Do With It?

You may be thinking at this point: What does contending for correct or sound doctrine have to do with the faith I need to fight the battles I am fighting daily as a believer in Christ? That is a completely legitimate question worthy of being asked and answered.

The answer starts with how faith comes, which, as indicated repeatedly in this book, is by hearing and hearing by the Word of Christ (Rhema, Gr.).[5] It must be understood that "the Word of Christ" is what comprises the entire Bible (the Old *and* New Testaments). Jesus was/is the Word of God *man*ifest as a Man! The Word became flesh and dwelt among us![6] So when we talk about the Word of Christ or God, we are talking about Jesus, the Man, and Jesus the Son of God, and Jesus God the Son. There is no separation between them. Thus, Jesus IS correct or sound doctrine as well, because it is comprised of dogmas or doctrines delineated in the Word of God, the Bible.

The Dangerous Path of Doctrinal Deviation

In 2016, I published a Kindle Article entitled, *The Dangerous Path of Doctrinal Deviation*, warning that doctrinal deviation, degeneration, and denigration is a perilous path leading not to genuine unity of the Spirit, as posited by its propagators, but rather *disunity* with the Spirit, apostasy, perdition, and ultimately hell itself! I encourage you to obtain your copy of that important message. I believe it is from God and that it is something that the modern churches desperately need to hear and heed! It is available on Amazon at: https://amzn.to/3Ph37DV.

I will do my best to refrain from republishing the whole article here in this book, but I will provide some select excerpts from that article to establish why contending for the faith is so vital to every believer.

I say frequently that a common problem to us all is that we are all full of something. As believers what we need to do is divest ourselves of what we are full of that is *not* of God in order to make room for receiving into our spirits and souls what *is* of God! Applying that axiom to the matter of contending for the faith, we need to ensure that we empty ourselves of false teaching and doctrine in order to make room, so to speak, for Truth, i.e., biblical teaching and doctrine. It's a matter of out with the bad and in with the good!

Doctrinal deviation, degeneration, and denigration is a perilous path leading not to genuine "unity of the Spirit,"[7] as posited by its propagators, but rather *disunity* with the Spirit, apostasy, perdition, and ultimately hell itself!

Right now, at this very moment, as I write/speak, multiplied millions of people around the world are caught up in what Jesus Himself, along with the New Testament writers, prophesied and predicted would be a great falling away or apostasy. The collective church and myriad individual purporting "Christians" desperately need to be shaken out of its/their spiritual lethargy and slumber to the reality that we are right now, in the 21st Century, in the very midst of the greatest time of apostasy and falling away in human history from the genuine faith elucidated in the Bible.

While the collective church experienced what theologians and church historians have identified as a massive corporate Falling Away or Apostasy during what is known as "The Dark Ages"—and that certainly was true—nevertheless, the Word of God categorically identifies a GREAT FALLING AWAY or GREAT APOSTASY that will transpire in the very last days just prior to the "catching up" or "rapture" of the genuine Church Jesus is building.

The Apostle Paul prophesied of this great falling away or apostasy in his prophetic delineation of the last days events, wherein referring to the "Day of the Lord," which is the day of the Judgment of Christ upon the unbelieving world, he stated:

> Let no one in any way deceive you, for IT (i.e., the Day of the Lord) will not come unless (or until) THE APOSTASY (NASB) [falling away; KJV] comes first, and the man of lawlessness is revealed, the son of destruction (meaning the antichrist).[8]

So, he is saying that the great apostasy will precede the revelation of the ultimate antichrist, who has not yet, in this hour in which we are living, been revealed as the antichrist, though the man who will one day assume that role as the devil himself comes to possess him, is almost certainly alive at this very moment here as I write/speak.

Millions of those claiming to be "Christians" in America and other nations around the world are really nothing but what could be called, "CINOs"—Christians in name only—as they blithely go about their apostate lives in acute contradiction to what the Word of God proclaims to be Biblical Christianity! They claim to be worshipers and followers of Jesus, but the "Jesus" they are worshiping and following is NOT the Jesus of the Bible—the genuine Jesus Christ—who is the Son of God and God the Son, the Second though coequal Member of the Godhead—but rather a counterfeit savior, lord, and master, a religious idol, that is in reality a demon named "Jesus," masquerading as the genuine Jesus!

In First Corinthians 8:4, the Apostle Paul said, "we know that there is no such thing as an idol in the world," but rather what is behind idols or false objects of worship and veneration is really *demons*. There is a demonic power, and perhaps a principality, that is being worshiped by multitudes today throughout the world that is not the REAL Jesus Christ, who was the Word of God made flesh, God incarnate, born of the Virgin Mary, who cast aside His deity and voluntarily departed the portals of Glory in order to come to earth and take on the "appearance of a man," as the Apostle Paul wrote in Philippians 2:8, and humbled Himself even unto the point of death, even death on a cross, who miraculously arose from the dead, and who ascended into Heaven on the Day of the Ascension from the Mount of Ascension, which moment Luke described thusly: "And when he had spoken these things, while they beheld, he was taken up; and a cloud received him out of their sight"[9]—and subsequently SAT DOWN at the right hand of God, reclaiming His throne of dominion and sovereignty!

Trifling with the Truth is a grave and even dangerous thing. Personally, I am always wary of individuals who in any way devalue the importance of pursuing the Truth and being established in sound doctrine. And I emphasize that when I speak of "sound doctrine," I am not referring to academic, abstract, intellectual theological superfluities, but rather foundational, pragmatic teaching from the Word of God by which one patterns his thinking and conduct in practical God-centered living. Believers not only should not be demeaning or denigrating the Truth, but to the contrary, we should have a genuine love for the Truth, a love that compels us to have a reverent respect for and desire to pursue and preserve the Truth.

There is a very true axiom that those things that we properly respect and cherish have a way of gravitating toward us, and those things which we do not, seem invariably to gravitate away from us. The matter of Truth is no exception. It has been my studied observation over the years that those who are the most established in the Word of Truth are those who have an intense love, respect, and desire for the Truth. Truth is a Person—His name is Jesus! The more we draw near to Him by earnestly loving, honoring, and desiring Him, the more He draws near to us.[10]

As I said at the outset of this section, trifling with the Truth is a grave and even dangerous thing, and I am always wary of individuals who devalue and demean the importance of pursuing and living by sound teaching or doctrine. This is far from being merely a personal opinion or judgmental attitude, rather it is predicated on the opinion and attitude of God as expressed in His Word, wherein He testifies that He Himself sends "strong delusion" upon those who demonstrate a persistent lack of "love of the Truth" which will cause them to "believe what is false":

> And then that lawless one [the Antichrist] will be revealed...; that is, the one whose coming is in accord with the activity of

Satan, with all power and signs and false wonders, and with all the deception of wickedness for those who perish, because they did not receive the love of the truth so as to be saved. And for this reason GOD will send upon them A DELUDING INFLUENCE {STRONG DELUSION (KJV)} so that they might believe what is false, in order that they all may be judged who did not believe THE TRUTH, but took pleasure in wickedness.[11]

This passage reveals a number of things. One, it indicates in no uncertain terms that without proper respect and regard for the truth, what is termed here as "the love of the Truth," a person simply cannot be "saved" (remember, the root Greek word for "saved" is "sozo," which means saved, sanctified, i.e., made holy, made whole, restored, etc.). A person who denigrates and demeans doctrine just cannot be wholly "saved" or "sanctified," spirit, soul, and body[12]—something has to be unrenewed in one of those parts of his being. If he is genuinely "saved" in his spirit, then the sanctification of his soul (mind, will, and emotions) definitely has to be incomplete.

The second thing we see in unmistakable terms in this passage is that denigrating or degrading the Truth will eventually end in delusion, for God Himself will send "a deluding influence" or "strong delusion" upon those who trifle with the Truth. This will not be the work of the devil, but rather, this passage clearly says that it will be God Himself who will send the deceiving or deluding influence.

It almost sounds evil and cruel that God would do such a thing, but we know that God has no part in evil.[13] It is the same in this case as it is with all judgment that comes to people—it is not God who has brought it on them, but rather they bring it on themselves by violating His order and ordinances. If a person foolishly jumps off the top of a building, it is not God's fault if he hurts or kills himself; he brought the result on himself.

God will not strive with people forever. There will come a time when God sends upon people a superabundance of the very thing they have been ceaselessly dealing in—in this case it is deception. If you do not eventually "receive the love of the Truth" so as to be sanctified by it, spirit, soul, and body, God will send upon you a deluding influence that will cause you to be hopelessly and helplessly seared over in deception "in (your) own conscience as with a branding iron."[14] You will wholeheartedly believe you are pursuing and believing the Truth, but it is in actuality the lies of the devil, "doctrines of devils" propagated by "deceitful spirits"[15] that you are so earnestly and adamantly believing.

Sadly, though this passage speaks of the final great apostasy that will occur during the Great Tribulation when the antichrist has been revealed, I am convinced this is not something that will happen only then, but that God has already given some people over to **"reveling in their deceptions."**[16] I have personally seen many people, both in and out of the church to whom this has happened. Certainly, the veracity of this should not be a question to us since Paul, Peter, and Jude all spoke in their writings of such people to whom this had already occurred back in their day in the Early Church history.

As I've often said, the problem with deception, or delusion, is that the person who is deceived is deceived about being deceived. His deception prevents him from knowing he is deceived. Such will be the case with this deluding influence that God will send—once it has come upon people, they will be forever deceived. Their relentless lack of affinity for the Truth of God will be regarded and rewarded as an affinity for the lies of the devil. They will finally receive their just desserts.

Indeed, the very hypothesis that the power of God can somehow be stifled by sound doctrine is itself ludicrous delusion of the highest order. Scripture declares the Word of God IS the power of God: "For the WORD (rhema) of the Cross...is the POWER (dunamis) of God."[17]

The same import is expressed in Hebrews 1:3, which invokes the phrase "the Word (rhema) of His power (dunamis)." Now it is important to note two things about this phrase. First, the term translated "Word" is "rhema," which is God's vivified/spoken Word, as opposed to the "graphe," the written/non-verbalized Word, which in itself, in that form, is inanimate and has no efficacy, or power. The Word must be spoken, i.e., verbalized, in order for its power to be operating, which is the reason, for example, people can have a huge Family Bible displayed prominently on their living room table, yet have none of its power effectual in their lives.

The second important thing about this passage is that it does not say "the power of His Word," though that would be a truism as well, for God's Word certainly does have power. Rather, the actual phrasing is evoking an even stronger import—that all of God's power is inherent in His Rhema-Word, that is, His active/living/verbalized Word. How true and consistent that is with the rest of Scripture. In the Creation, we see that God literally SPOKE the world into existence. God's creative dunamis-power was unleashed and activated when He vocalized His Word; it did not return unto Him void, but accomplished His desire, the purpose for which it was sent.[18] After the creation of Man, over and over again throughout Scripture we see God putting His Word/Will into the mouths of human surrogate spokesmen and compelling them to vocalize it in order to effect His purposes. God always speaks whatever He desires (wills) to transpire.

The Word of God and the power of God certainly are not counterposing or contradictory forces. Anything that is a true operation of the Spirit and power of God will always be in complete agreement and harmony with the Word of God. Thus, the unequivocal fact that all of God's dunamis-power is contained in and effectuated through His spoken-Word, and that these two forces concur and work together in tandem, renders absurd and impossible the notion that the Word of Truth, or "rightly dividing" it to formulate and prove sound doctrine, could somehow hinder or negate the effectuality or operation of the power or Spirit of God. If anything, the obverse of this notion is true: the more congruously with the Word of God we are living and operating, the more of the power of God will be available for us to operate.[19]

Dunamis-power is effectuated and activated by means of the Rhema, alive/spoken, Word of God. The true Gospel does not come "in word (logos) only, but also in power (dunamis) and in the Holy Spirit and with full conviction."[20] The true Gospel is a "full Gospel"—a Gospel full of the Spirit and power of God, because "the kingdom of God does not consist in words (logos) only, but in power (dunamis)."

The Inextricable Link of Jesus and Sound Doctrine

Jesus is the Word of God...the word made flesh.[21] Jesus **IS** "the Teaching." He is the "foundation-rock" upon which the Church is built.[22] To denigrate, demean, or devalue the Truth, the Teaching (doctrine), or the Word, is to denigrate, demean, and devalue Jesus Himself, and therefore also the very spiritual foundation upon which every spiritual house (i.e., an individual believer's life or a church) is founded. To in any way so "corrupt the Word of God,"[23] as the Apostle Paul said many do, is utter blasphemy against Jesus and the Holy Spirit, who inspired the writing of the written Word, and who reveals Christ to us through the Word.

Jesus proclaimed that whoever annuls, that is to say, negates or sets aside, any of even the "least" of the precepts concerning the Kingdom of God and so teaches others shall himself be called "least" in the Kingdom of Heaven, but whoever himself keeps (practices) and teaches them to others shall be called "great" in the Kingdom of Heaven:

> "Whoever then annuls one of the least of these commandments, and teaches others to do the same, shall be called least in the kingdom of heaven; but whoever keeps and teaches them, he shall be called great in the kingdom of heaven."[24]

The Apostle Paul urged believers to grow up (mature) in every aspect of the Life of Christ and that "we henceforth be no more children, tossed to and fro, and carried about with every wind of doctrine, by the sleight of men, and cunning craftiness, whereby they lie in wait to deceive."[25] This speaks of deliberate deception through the means of doctrinal degradation for selfish gain.

Biblical Warnings Against Doctrinal Deviation

The New Testament is replete with warnings that such corruption of the Word of God would take place especially in the last days in which we now live. One of the foremost such passages is the Apostle Paul's admonition in his letter to his young protégé, Timothy:

> "But the Spirit explicitly says that in the later times some will fall away from the faith, paying attention to deceitful spirits and doctrines of demons, by means of the hypocrisy of liars, seared in their own consciences as with a branding iron...."[26]

The irony within this text is that it indicates *bona fide* believers will fall into apostasy because they are paying attention to deceiving evil spirits and false doctrines concocted and promulgated by demons in this day in which degradation and devaluation of doctrine is rampant. The Apostle Paul even urged his "son" in the Lord, whom he had personally mentored, Timothy, to remain on in Ephesus following his own departure for Macedonia, specifically,

> in order that (he) may instruct certain men not to **teach strange doctrines**, nor pay attention to myths [i.e., non-Biblical teachings]..., because some men, straying from these things, have

turned aside to fruitless discussions, wanting to be teachers of the Law, even though they do not understand either what they are saying or the matters about which they make confident assertions.[27]

The writer of Hebrews trumpets forth a similar admonition against being caught up in and enticed by unbiblical teachings, or "strange doctrines": "do not be carried away by VARIED AND STRANGE TEACHINGS [doctrines, KJV]."[28] Teaching is what doctrine is. Doctrine is teaching. Doctrine is simply made up of the teachings of the Word of God.

Just as Paul urged Timothy to stay in Ephesus for the expressed purpose of instructing "certain men not to **teach strange doctrines** nor pay attention to" Scripturally unfounded teaching, so also did the apostle charge Titus to remain on the Isle of Crete to "set in order" what remained by, in every Cretan city in which a work had begun, appointing as overseeing elders men who were:

> holding fast the faithful word which is in accordance with THE TEACHING [doctrine], that he may be able both to exhort in SOUND DOCTRINE and to REFUTE THOSE WHO CONTRADICT (the sound doctrine, that is).

Indeed, the full text of Paul's charge to Titus is rich with reference to the imperativeness that ministering elders establish believers in sound doctrine both by teaching correct doctrine and by correcting contradictory doctrines as well.

> For this reason I left you in Crete, that you might **set in order what remains**, and appoint ELDERS in every city as I directed you, namely, if any man be...**holding fast the faithful word which is in accordance with THE TEACHING**, that he may be able both to **exhort in SOUND DOCTRINE** and to **refute those who contradict**. For there are many rebellious men, empty talkers and deceivers, especially those of the circumcision, who must be silenced because they are upsetting whole families, **TEACHING things they should not TEACH**, for the sake of sordid gain....For this cause **REPROVE** [correct] **THEM severely** that they may be **SOUND in the faith**, not paying attention to **Jewish myths and commandments of men** who **turn away from THE TRUTH**. To the pure, all things are pure; but

to those who are defiled and unbelieving, nothing is pure, but both their mind and their conscience are defiled. They profess to know God, but by their deeds they deny Him, being detestable and disobedient, and worthless for any good deed. But as for you [Titus, and by extension, all ministers], **speak the things which are fitting for SOUND DOCTRINE.**[29]

The Mandate to Correct False Doctrine

Paul said he had a reason for leaving Titus in Crete, "that you might set in order what remains," by appointing elders in every city as Paul had previously directed Titus, pursuant to the qualification for eldership was "holding fast the faithful word which is in accordance with *THE* TEACHING." The Bible talks about "*THE* TEACHING," it talks about "the teaching of the apostles," "THE TEACHING...." Additionally, not only must an elder candidate hold fast to the teaching, but also "...that he may be able both to exhort in SOUND DOCTRINE and to refute those who contradict." He's talking about instruction with regard to appointing elders and that the elders that Titus appoints must be first of all men—elders are to be *men* (males)—who hold fast to the faithful Word of God which is in accordance with THE TEACHING, that he may be able to exhort in sound doctrine and that he might be able to refute those who contradict sound doctrine. THAT is the role and the calling of God of every true elder in the Church that Jesus is building.

And the reason Paul said that Titus must do this, is (it goes on to say) "for there are many rebellious men, empty talkers and deceivers, especially those of the circumcision who must be silenced because they are upsetting whole families, teaching things they should not teach for the sake of sordid gain." So, Paul is identifying a number of important matters here. One, that the people who teach these kinds of *strange* doctrines that are not *sound* doctrine, not in accordance with the Word of God, Paul the Apostle says that they are "rebellious men," they are "empty talkers," and that they are "deceivers," and "they are teaching things they should not teach," and that when they teach these things that they should not teach they are "upsetting whole families"—and for these reasons, Paul said these false teachers needed to be "silenced."

The same thing is happening today; in fact false teaching is rampant in supposed "Christian" streams. There are many people that are teaching things they should not teach. Paul said they were doing it for sordid gain. We have the same thing today, they do it for their own self-aggrandizement, their own selfish reasons—for sordid gain. Paul said they need to be *silenced*! "For this cause" *reprove* them, the imminent apostle said! Reprove, reprove, reprove, correct—that is the calling from God, especially for true genuine elders. And let me say, in sum, that true elders are those who have a Fivefold Ministry calling upon their life, Fivefold Ministry anointing upon their life. They are called by God, and they have an anointing from God. He says that such people who are promulgating false teaching must be reproved. If they must be reproved, *somebody* has to reprove them.

Indeed, the appearance in Scripture of these instructions to these two younger ministers (Timothy and Titus) has much more significance and purpose than to merely provide the historical record. It also conveys the solemn charge by God unto every Fivefold minister and elder in the Church to "**STUDY to show thyself APPROVED unto God, a workman that needeth not to be ashamed, [a workman who is] rightly dividing THE WORD OF TRUTH,**"[30] as well as the necessity to counter "strange doctrine," or "myths," by teaching sound doctrine:

> I solemnly charge you in the presence of God, and of Christ Jesus, who is to judge the living and the dead, and by His appearing and His kingdom: preach the word; be ready in season and out of season; reprove, rebuke, exhort, with great patience and instruction (detailed teaching). For the time will come when they will not endure **SOUND DOCTRINE**; but wanting to have their ears tickled, they will accumulate for themselves **teachers in accordance to their own desires**; and will **turn their ears from THE TRUTH**, and will **turn aside to MYTHS**. But you, be sober in all things, endure hardship, do the work of an evangelist, fulfill your ministry.[31]

Indeed, virtually every epistle in the New Testament was written at least partly in order to counter and correct false teaching (doctrine) that was being taught and espoused in the churches to whom the letters were sent. The Apostle Peter indicated it was inevitable that false teachers, sent by the enemy and motivated by selfish ambition and personal gain, would come and infiltrate the churches, "secretly" (subtly) introducing damnable occult (hidden) heresies, or false teachings, that are a product of corruption, i.e., perversion or mutilation, of Scripture, by which they would entice many followers, but whose final end would be spiritual destruction and eternal damnation:

> But false prophets also arose among the people, just as there WILL also be false teachers among you, who will **secretly introduce destructive {damnable; KJV} HERESIES**, even denying the Master who bought them, bringing swift destruction upon themselves. And many will follow their sensuality {pernicious [i.e., deadly, destructive ways]}, and because of them **the way of THE TRUTH will be maligned**; and in their greed {covetousness} they will exploit you with **FALSE WORDS** (teaching); their judgment from long ago is not idle, and their destruction {damnation} is not asleep.... But these, like unreasoning animals, born as creatures of instinct to be captured and killed {destroyed}, **reviling where they have no knowledge**, will in the destruction of those creatures also be destroyed, suffering wrong as the wages of doing wrong. They count it a pleasure to revel in the daytime. They are stains and blemishes, reveling in their deceptions, as they carouse with you, having eyes full of adultery and that never {cannot} cease from sin, enticing unstable souls, having a heart trained in greed {an heart they have exercised with covetous practices}, accursed children; forsaking the right way they have gone astray, having followed the way of Balaam....These are springs without water, and mists driven by a storm, for whom the black darkness has been reserved. For **speaking out ARROGANT WORDS of vanity** they entice by fleshly desires, by sensuality, those who barely escape from the ones who live in error, promising them freedom while they themselves are slaves of corruption; for by what a man is overcome, by this he is enslaved {brought into bondage}.[32]

The Apostle Paul chided the Galatian church, whom he said had been "bewitched" by false teaching of false teachers who they allowed to teach them, for "deserting" Christ "for a different Gospel," which he said was "really not another" gospel but rather a distortion or perversion of the Gospel of Christ, and told them that anyone who preached such "a gospel contrary," or counterfeit gospel, was "anathema," or "accursed":

> I am amazed that you are so quickly deserting Him who called you by the grace of Christ; for a **different gospel**; which is really not another; only there are some who are disturbing you, and want to distort {pervert} the GOSPEL OF CHRIST. But even though we, or an angel from heaven, should preach to you **a gospel contrary** to that which you have received, let him be accursed. As we have said before, so I say again now, if any man is preaching to you **a gospel contrary** to that which you received, let him be accursed.[33]

In his letter to the Romans, concerning those who promulgate teachings contrary to "THE teaching," the Apostle Paul admonished to "avoid them":

> Now I beseech you, brethren, mark them which cause divisions and offences CONTRARY TO THE DOCTRINE which ye have learned; and avoid them. For they that are such serve not our Lord Jesus Christ, but their own belly; and by good words [skillful oratory] and fair speeches [flattery] DECEIVE the hearts of the simple [untaught].[34]

In his closing remarks in his letter to Timothy, Paul enjoined: **"Teach and preach these principles"**—the principles he delineated within the letter. He followed that charge with these revealing comments concerning those who "advocate a different doctrine," that is, teaching contrary to the teaching he taught in this and his other letters, as well as in all the other aspects of his ministry:

> If anyone advocates **a different DOCTRINE**, and does not agree with **SOUND WORDS, those of our Lord Jesus Christ**, and with the **DOCTRINE conforming to godliness**, he is conceited and understands nothing; but he has a morbid interest in controversial questions and disputes about words, out of which arise envy, strife, abusive language, evil suspicions, and constant friction between men of depraved mind and deprived of the truth, who suppose that godliness is a means of gain.[35]

Heretics and Heretical Teaching

The apostle is saying here that people who corrupt the Truth of the Word of God and concoct contrary teachings, or who, in other words, denigrate doctrine, do so because their minds are void of the Truth and have become corrupted, or depraved, by perverse thoughts of self-gratification and selfish gain.

In his letter to Titus, the Apostle Paul was a little more terse and direct concerning the ulterior motivation of "an heretick," as it reads in the King James Version, and how such a person is to be dealt with: "**REJECT a factious man {an heretick}** after a first and second warning; knowing that such a man is **perverted** and is **sinning**, being self-condemned."[36] The Greek word translated "an heretick" in the King James Version, and "a factious man" in the New American Standard Version, literally means "a self-opinionated man," meaning a person who lives by and constantly asserts his own self-willed opinions, rather than living and advocating the will and thoughts of God as revealed by the Word of God. We are straightforwardly told to "reject" such a person, "KNOWING"—not merely speculating, suspecting, or improperly judging, but "KNOWING"—that such a person is "perverted and is sinning," and knowing also that it is not we who are condemning him, but rather that he is "*self*-condemned," that is, condemning himself by his own stubborn, self-willed perversion of the Word of God and outright sinful actions and attitudes against others.

Now a word of caution in this regard. One must be very careful not to condemn or categorize as "a heretic" a person who adamantly and unrepentantly advocates the Truth of the Word of God. Adamancy and intransigence when it comes to standing on and speaking the Truth is not only not wrong, but it should be the unrelenting and dogged pursuit of every believer. Yet, it is quite common for less developed, less mature, less knowledgeable, and less zealous, professing believers to disparage and label "radical" those who are more arduous in their walk, more scripturally-knowledgeable, more Spirit-trained, and, frankly, more mature than they. A person who is attempting to fashion his every thought and deed after the Word of God is certainly anything but a heretic, or *self*-opinionated, rather he is **God**-opinionated.

In fact, Jesus indicated that being self-willed juxtaposed to God-willed is the litmus test of the veracity of the teaching a person advocates. Read carefully the following passage recounting an occasion on which the Jewish religious leaders were questioning Jesus' qualifications, and by extension the validity of His teaching:

> But when it was now the midst of the feast Jesus went up into the temple, and began to TEACH. The Jews therefore were

marveling, saying, "How has this man become learned, having never been educated?" Jesus therefore answered them, and said, "My teaching is not Mine, but His who sent Me. If any man is willing to do His will, he shall know of the teaching, whether it is of God, or whether I speak from Myself. He who speaks from himself seeks his own glory; but He who is seeking the glory of the one who sent Him, He is true, and there is no unrighteousness in Him."[37]

Now as a quick aside, in a scant few words, Jesus settles, at least for me, unequivocally, the long-debated question regarding the requisite method of a minister's training, whether or not it must be formal and academic, or if God also employs other means of equipping those whom He appoints. There is little doubt that the persons speaking were "ordained" rabbis who had been trained in the traditional and authorized rabbinical schools, which tradition continues yet today for the training of Jewish rabbis. These rabbis categorically stated that Jesus, though regarded as a "teacher" or "rabbi" by the people, had not been "educated" in their rabbinical schools. Yet, after having listened with a critical ear to His teaching, these very erudite academicians unabashedly admitted, though doubtless reluctantly, that Jesus was indeed "learned." *That* they could not deny, but rather it was concerning the "how," or method, by which He had become so learned which they questioned.

Those yet today who adamantly contend that a minister must be "educated" by means of formal education and academic curricula in their seminaries under the tutelage of intellectual professional theologians are similarly bewildered by the undeniable "learnedness" of those who have been trained not by mere human instructors in the abstractness of reality-removed ivory-tower classrooms but by the Preeminent Professor, the Holy Spirit, in reality-related desert dens, the classrooms of the School of the Holy Ghost in the Desert. The truth of the matter is made clear in a passage that teaches us that one does not need to be "educated" by men in order to be certifiably "learned" in "the things of the Spirit of God"[38] which are "taught by the Spirit."[39] Of such things, the ultimate Teacher is the Spirit of God.[40] Of these things, "they shall all be taught of *God*."[41]

But beyond the matter of the method by which Jesus obtained His knowledge and wisdom, lay the deeper issue which was really the heart of these religious leaders' question: the veracity or legitimacy of the teaching. Resisting the temptation to defend and verify Himself by responding to the method matter, Jesus cut instead to the ulterior, ultimate issue. He indicated essentially that the litmus test of the veracity or legitimacy of a person's teaching is inherent in its origination and its objective. As to origination: whether it originated from God, making it God-authored, or from one's own reasonings, making it self-authored. As to objective: whether it is God-glorifying or self-glorifying, for Jesus said: "He who speaks from himself SEEKS HIS OWN GLORY; but He who is SEEKING THE GLORY OF THE ONE WHO SENT HIM, HE IS TRUE, and there is no unrighteousness in Him." Jesus' response regarding the teaching He taught was that it originated with God: "My teaching is not MINE, but HIS who sent Me," and that any person who "is willing to do HIS will" will know with certainty that it originated with and was authored by God.

Deceitful Spirits and Doctrines of Demons

Less than 300 years following the birth of the Church and the inception of the Church Age, the Church had devolved into a period of spiritual darkness known as the Dark Ages that spanned 1,200 long years, fulfilling the Apostle Paul's prophecy concerning a corporate Great Apostasy:

> But the Spirit explicitly says that in later times some will **fall away from the faith**, paying attention to *deceitful spirits and doctrines of demons*, by means of the hypocrisy of liars seared in their own conscience as with a branding iron,[42]

According to the Apostle Peter's message he spoke to the doubting and mocking Jews on the Day of Pentecost, in which he emphatically declared that "this is that" of which the prophet Joel prophesied, the "last days" began that day and that period of time continues to the present hour! Those who are alive right now as I speak are part of the Last Days generation, which can also be called the End-Times Generation. This, of necessity, *has* to be true because the "end" and all that will entail per eschatological scriptures has not yet occurred. The next eschatological event we await is the appearance of the Lord Jesus Christ in the clouds in the air, where and when, "every eye shall see Him,"[43] at which event and time He will initiate the "catching up" or "rapture" of the Betrothed of Christ, the Ekklesia, or Church, He has been building since the Day of Ascension when from the Mount of Ascension (i.e., Mount Olivet) He "ascended on high"[44] in the sight of those who were physically there.[45] It is to that very spot from which He ascended that He will return as the Commander of the Angelic Hosts to engage the unbelieving nations of the world in the final battle, Armageddon, *after* the rapture of the Church, and *after* the completion of the seven-year tribulation period on earth ("For God has not destined us for wrath, but for obtaining salvation through our Lord Jesus Christ"[46]), to claim His Church as His Eternal Bride.

> but this is what was spoken of through the prophet Joel: 'AND IT SHALL BE IN **THE LAST DAYS**,' God says, 'THAT I WILL POUR FORTH OF MY SPIRIT ON ALL MANKIND; AND YOUR SONS AND YOUR DAUGHTERS SHALL PROPHESY, AND YOUR YOUNG MEN SHALL SEE VISIONS, AND YOUR OLD MEN SHALL DREAM DREAMS; EVEN ON MY BONDSLAVES, BOTH MEN AND WOMEN, I WILL IN THOSE DAYS POUR FORTH OF MY SPIRIT And they shall prophesy. 'AND I WILL GRANT WONDERS IN THE SKY ABOVE AND SIGNS ON THE EARTH BELOW, BLOOD, AND FIRE, AND VAPOR OF SMOKE. 'THE SUN WILL BE TURNED INTO DARKNESS AND THE MOON INTO BLOOD, BEFORE THE GREAT AND GLORIOUS DAY OF THE LORD SHALL COME. 'AND IT SHALL BE THAT EVERYONE WHO CALLS ON THE NAME OF THE LORD WILL BE SAVED.'[47]

We continue to live in that period of the "last days" that Joel and Peter prophesied will be characterized by a globally pervasive falling away from the authentic, biblical, "faith which was once for all handed down to the saints."[48] We await a prophesied "period of restoration" that will enable Christ Jesus to be released from Heaven and return.

None Says Restore!

Listen to what the prophet Isaiah said:

> But this is a people plundered and despoiled; All of them are trapped in caves, Or are hidden away in prisons; They have become a prey with none to deliver them, And a spoil, with none to say, "Give them back!" ("None says restore"—KJV)[49]

On October 31st, 1517, an obscure Augustinian Priest by the name of Martin Luther, began to say "restore," as he nailed his "95 Theses" of remonstration against the unbiblical teachings of the Roman Catholic Church to the door of Castle Church in Wittenberg, Germany, sparking what became known as the Protestant Reformation.

In Acts 3:21, the Apostle Peter prophesied concerning that "period of restoration," saying that "Heaven must (retain; lit, Gr.) the Christ until the period of restoration of all things about which God spoke by the mouth of His holy prophets from ancient time" has been completed and fulfilled. The Protestant Reformation was the beginning of that restorational period that continues yet today more than 500 years later.

Less than 300 years following the birth of the Church and the inception of the Church Age, the Church had devolved into a period of spiritual darkness known as the Dark Ages that spanned 1,200 long years, fulfilling the Apostle Paul's prophecy concerning a corporate Great Apostasy quoted previously:

"But the Spirit explicitly says that in later times some will FALL AWAY FROM THE FAITH, paying attention to deceitful spirits and doctrines of demons, by means of the hypocrisy of liars seared in their own conscience as with a branding iron."

This was what theologians and church historians refer to as, "The Great Apostasy," for the *corporate* Church, concerning which the Apostle Paul prophesied. During this age of spiritual darkness, the Truth was subverted by humanistic ideologies and vain philosophies of men[50]—the doctrines of demons of which Paul forewarned. Many of the foundational doctrines of the Church were distorted, perverted, diluted, invalidated, or totally abandoned. Moreover, the Fivefold Ministry Offices, as well as the apostolic-prophetic governmental foundation of the Church, upon which it was originally established[51] were abrogated and replaced with an ecclesiastical hierarchy, as elite professional clergymen began to be driven more and more by what Augustine called (in Latin), "libido dominandi," lust for rule or dominion. Indeed, the greatest single factor contributing to the spiritual debacle of the Dark Ages was the drift, following the death of the original Apostles of the Lamb, from the apostolic-prophetic moorings upon which the Church was founded.

In Acts 2:42-43, Luke wrote of the early church:

They were continually devoting themselves to the apostles'

teaching and to fellowship, to the breaking of bread and to prayer. Everyone kept feeling a sense of awe; and many wonders and signs were taking place through the apostles.

That is what the Lord Jesus Christ, the Head of the Church, had intended to take place in the "ekklesia" or Church that He said HE was building, against which the gates or power of Hell, i.e., Satan's Kingdom, would not be able to prevail.[52] And thank God that that is the ultimate outcome we can rest our faith and hope upon concerning the true, genuine Church that Jesus is building—the power of Hell shall not be able to overcome it, ultimately.

Moreover, it is that Church—the End-times One-Third Remnant Ekklesia—that we believers living in these last days have the unfathomable and inexpressible honor of being the living participants, i.e., the human agents, through whom God Almighty is working to build that spiritual entity that will ultimately rule and reign with Christ over the entire Cosmos! Hallelujah! Glory to God!

This is the day which the LORD has made; Let us rejoice and be glad in it.[53]

"Behold, it is coming and it shall be done," declares the Lord GOD. "*That* is the day of which I have spoken."[54]

Endnotes

1. Jude 1:3-23
2. https://www.dictionary.com/browse/dogma; biblical Christians reject #2.
3. 2 Pet. 1:20
4. 2 Timothy 2:15; KJV
5. Rom. 10:17
6. John 1:1-14; 1 John 1:1-3
7. Eph. 4:3
8. 2 Thes. 2:3
9. Acts 1:9; KJV
10. Jas. 4:8
11. 2 Thes. 2:8-12
12. 1 Thes. 5:23
13. Jas. 1:13
14. 1 Tim. 4:2
15. Ibid, v. 1
16. 1 Pet. 2:13
17. 1 Cor. 1:18; cf., Rom. 1:16
18. Isa. 55:11
19. c.f., Rev. 3:8
20. 1 Thes. 1:5
21. John 1:14; 1 John 1:1-2
22. Mat. 16:13-18; 1 Cor. 3:11
23. 2 Cor. 2:17; KJV
24. Mat. 5:19
25. Eph. 4:14; KJV
26. 1 Tim. 4:1-2
27. 1 Tim. 1:3-7
28. Heb. 13:9

29 Tit. 1:5-14
30 2 Tim. 2:15; KJV; parenthesis added by author
31 2 Tim. 4:1-5
32 2 Pet. 2:1-19 {bracketed italicized portions from the KJV}
33 Gal. 1:6-9, {bracketed portion from KJV}
34 Rom. 16:17-18; KJV [brackets added]
35 1 Tim. 6:2-5
36 Tit. 3:10, {bracketed portion from KJV}
37 John 7:14-18
38 1 Cor. 2:12
39 1 Cor. 2:13
40 1 John 2:27
41 John 6:45
42 1 Tim. 4:1-2
43 Rev. 1:7
44 Eph. 4:8
45 Acts 1:9
46 1 Thes. 5:9
47 Acts 2:16-21
48 Jude 1:3
49 Isa. 42:22
50 Col. 2:8
51 Eph. 2:20
52 Mat. 16:18
53 Psa. 118:24
54 Ezk. 39:8

Chapter Seventeen

Falling Away From The Faith

Jesus specifically said that in the case of this second category of hearers in the Parable of the Sower, Those Like Rocky Ground: "when affliction and persecution arises because of the word, immediately they fall away."[1] According to Jesus, the result when they met with adversity after having believed is that "immediately they fall away." According to the doctrine of a number of Christian denominations today, this just cannot be so. Nevertheless, according to Jesus and God's Word, it is immutably so.

Before going any further, some readers may note that the King James Version says they were "offended," rather than that they fell away. However, this Elizabethan English usage does not accurately convey the intention of the original language. In the Greek, that word actually means to cause someone to stumble with the end result of falling. It is always used metaphorically to connote a falling away. Most translations other than the King James Version do indicate a falling away in this passage and others where the same Greek word is used.

There are a number of Christian denominations today who espouse what is commonly known as "the doctrine of eternal security." Simply stated, this belief purports that once a person has made a verbal confession of Jesus Christ as his Savior, there is virtually no way he can ever lose his salvation or fall away, but that somehow, someway, God guarantees his eventual salvation; hence, that person's salvation is "eternally secure."

While I must say such an ideology would be extremely convenient, it is nonetheless quite unscriptural. Many people have used the auspices of this doctrine for license to continue in their sin and licentiousness under this false sense of "eternal security," by which they are duped into believing they shall escape divine judgment for their deeds.

Now this is not at all to say that salvation for true, obedient believers is not eternally secure. On the contrary, the salvation and redemption that Jesus purchased with His own blood is most sure and forever secure. The obedient believer can be utterly assured of his salvation, and know with total certainty that he has Eternal Life: "These things I have written to you who believe in the name of the Son of God, in order that you may know that you have eternal life."[2]

God certainly does not want any believer to be in a quandary concerning his salvation and eternal destiny. Yet, at the same time, He has published innumerable warnings and exhortations in His Word concerning the fact that it is quite possible for someone who confesses Jesus Christ as Lord and Savior to fall away from following Him and consequently lose his salvation.

Scriptures regarding believers falling away of which I have personal knowledge number at nearly one-hundred. Space simply will not permit an exhaustive study of them all, but the inevitable, unbiased conclusion is that a believer can indeed fall away from the faith, and that the wrath and eternal judgment of God awaits all those who refuse to repent of their sin and rebellious deeds. All the weight of Divine Writ bears forth the Truth that no one, believer or unbeliever, can elude accountability for his deeds:

> Or do you think lightly of the riches of His kindness and forbearance and patience, not knowing that the kindness of God leads you to *repentance*? But because of your stubbornness and unrepentant heart you are storing up wrath for yourself in the day of wrath and revelation of the righteous judgment of God, who will render to every man according to his deeds: to those who by perseverance in doing good seek for glory and honor and immortality, eternal life: but to those who are selfishly ambitious and do not obey the truth, but obey unrighteousness, wrath and indignation. There will be tribulation and distress for every soul of man who does evil...but glory and honor and peace to every man who does *good*...For there is no partiality with God.[3]

"But God Is Love!"

Inevitably, when you start talking about matters of judgment and believers falling away, proponents of eternal security will begin to cite scriptures concerning God's love, kindness, mercy, and patience. Of course, all these qualities are an inherent part of God's nature in boundless measure. Yet, scriptures proclaiming those Divine Attributes can never be used as a counterclaim against the validity of other scriptures concerning Divine Judgment. Scripture never contradicts itself. No passage of Scripture refutes or nullifies another.

What is difficult for the finite, humanistic mind to comprehend is that God's wrath and eternal judgment are not contradictory to His Divine Nature of Love, but an inherent part of it. Righteous indignation and wrath are an inherent part of the Righteousness of God. They are a part of Divine Love. As the last scripture quoted, Romans 2:4-11, indicates, the rich kindness and forbearance and patience of God is intended to lead people to repentance, not to give license to their continuance in sin. But those who refuse to repent from their sin because of their "stubbornness and unrepentant heart" are only "storing up wrath" for themselves for "the day of wrath and revelation of the righteous judgment of God." And, on that Day of Wrath and Judgment, God will "render to every man according to his deeds." Those who have done good will inherit Eternal Life. Those whose deeds were evil will inherit wrath and righteous indignation.

"But We're Saved by Grace!"

Another counterclaim often levied by proponents of the eternal security doctrine is that we are saved by grace. They misuse such scriptures as, "For by grace you have been saved through faith...not as a result of works, that no one should boast"[4] for support of their ideology, and to counter scriptures concerning the judgment of apostate believers.

Of course everyone is saved by grace through faith, but we must never misconstrue the grace of God for license to sin, something which the Apostle Jude warned that "ungodly persons" do:

> For certain persons have crept in unnoticed, those who were long beforehand marked out for this condemnation, *ungodly persons* who turn the grace of our God into licentiousness and deny our only Master and Lord, Jesus Christ.[5]

God's grace is that "while we were still helpless, at the right time Christ died for the ungodly."⁶ We all were the "ungodly" for whom Christ died, though we in no wise deserved or merited it. That is God's grace.

God's grace is not a license to sin. Because God has through Jesus' shed blood justified us with Himself, does that mean He did it so that we could be permitted to continue in sin? Never! "Shall we sin because we are not under law but under grace? May it never be!"⁷ Or, "Are we to continue in sin that grace might increase? May it never be! How shall we who died to sin still live in it?"⁸

It is true that we are saved by grace through faith. But once we are saved we should "bring forth fruit in keeping with repentance."⁹ Our deeds should give proof of our salvation. As James said, "faith without works (*deeds*) is dead."¹⁰ The Amplified Bible translates that passage this way: "So also faith if it does not have works (*deeds and actions of obedience to back it up*), by itself is destitute of power—inoperative, dead" (italics added).

In other words, if we have truly been "saved by grace through faith," then our lives will be living testimony of that faith. Again, The Amplified Bible says it well:

> What is the use (*profit*), my brethren, for any one to profess to have faith if he has no (*good*) works (*to show for it*)? Can (*such*) faith save (*his soul*)?¹¹

Of course, the understood answer to that question is that such a "faith" is not the real faith through which one is saved. Such a "faith" that is void of corresponding good works cannot save anyone.

Second Corinthians 5:17 says, "Therefore if any man is in Christ, he is a new creature; the old things passed away; behold, new things have come." For a person to be "in Christ" means that he has surrendered his life unto the Lord, and has been saved by grace through faith. That person is "a new creature" because "the old things," the sinful deeds of the carnal nature, are passing away through repentance, and are being replaced with the "new things," the godly deeds and behavior of the Born Again nature.

Are we saved by grace through faith? Of course we are! But the grace of God is not a license to sin. The substitutionary sacrifice of Jesus Christ does not in any wise extend to justify the sin of those who "go on sinning willfully after receiving the knowledge of the truth."[12]

No one, professing believer or unbeliever, who continues to practice willful sin will ever enter into Heaven, for:

> nothing unclean and no one who practices abomination and lying, shall ever come into it.[13]

> But for the cowardly and unbelieving and abominable and murders and immoral persons and sorcerers and idolaters and all liars, their part will be in the lake that burns with fire and brimstone, which is the second death.[14]

Last Days Apostasy

There are multitudes of people today who are in this second category of hearers of the Word of God, who because of insufficient repentance are like "rocky ground." When adversity arises against them, because they are only "temporary" believers, they fall away. And adversity of many sorts is exactly what many believers are experiencing today.

In its own way, these last days in which we live are very difficult times, including for Christians. As the Living Bible says it, "in the last days it is going to be very difficult to be a Christian."[15] Sin has run its course in perverting the entire Creation of God, from the condition of humanity itself, to the air Man breathes, to the Earth he inhabits. Thus, every element of the world in which we live has been corrupted down to the very foundation. The consequence is the effects of sin—adversity and tribulation.

However, the fire of testing is bringing purification to individual true believers and to the collective Body of Christ. The true wheat is being separated from the chaff; the *temporary* believers are being separated from the *eternal* believers. Purification is the result when true believers go through adversity, which is the reason God does not eradicate it entirely from their lives. Temporary believers, on the other hand, fall away as a result of afflictions and persecutions. The Lord Himself has testified concerning this, saying, "Behold, I have refined you, but not as silver; I have tested you in the furnace of affliction."[16]

In the same last days in which God is pouring out His Spirit upon all mankind,[17] and multitudes are coming into the Kingdom of God, at the same time, many temporary believers are falling away from the faith. Many of them continue to attend church services, however, masquerading behind a facade of piety while their personal lives and behavior is as apostate as can be. As Jude said of such false brethren: "These men are those who are hidden reefs in your love feasts (*worship services*) when they feast with you without fear."[18]

Yet, this last day apostasy has not come upon us unawares. Jesus Himself prophesied it would happen, saying, "And at that time *many* will fall away."[19] The Apostle Paul also echoed that prophesy through the same Spirit, and even added some insight as to what and who will motivate people to fall away in these last days: "But the Spirit explicitly says that in later times some will fall away from the faith, paying attention to deceitful spirits and doctrines of demons."[20]

In the past, some theologians have surmised that this last day's apostasy would occur in some sort of a prevailing "a-religious" climate. However, the Apostle Paul indicated in the passage just quoted that those who would fall away in the last days would do so not because of being "a-religious" or antireligious, but because they were indeed "paying attention," only to the wrong spirit. Instead of paying attention to the Holy Spirit, they would be paying attention to deceiving religious spirits of Satan, and to religious doctrines concocted and propagated by demons.

Thus, while church people look for some great, contemporaneous, concerted mass defection from Christianity, multitudes of ultra-religious and pious-appearing church-goers are being surreptitiously led astray from the Truth as they pay attention to the deceitful religious spirits and erroneous doctrines of demons. And it's all happening right under the noses of those church people and clergymen.

Israelite Example

As mentioned earlier, there are quite a number of scripture references and examples of people falling away. One prime example is the case of the Israelites. Their supernatural deliverance from the bondage of Egypt and subsequent supernatural sustenance during their forty year trek through the wilderness toward the Promise Land was all supernaturally orchestrated and accomplished by the Lord Himself. Yet, they repeatedly defected from their pledge of faith in the Lord during those forty years. They often wanted to return to the bondage of Egypt instead of espousing the freedom of serving the Lord, and even fashioned and worshiped false gods which they could see.

Finally, their persistent apostasy provoked God to anger. He swore they would never enter into the Promise Land because of their disobedience and disbelief. In His righteous wrath and judgment, God allowed that entire generation to be destroyed in the wilderness without ever entering in to the Promise Land, all except the only two men of an estimated million plus who believed God, Joshua and Caleb.

The Apostle Paul said this whole case of the Israelites was "written for our instruction." He repeatedly referred to it as his prime example of the falling away of people who had been saved by God. Here are some key passages of some of those references:

> Now these things happened to them as an example, and they were written for our instruction, upon whom the ends of the ages have come. Therefore, let him who thinks he stands take heed lest he *fall*.[21]

> Take care, brethren, lest there should be in any one of you an evil, unbelieving heart, in *falling away* from the living God.[22]

> Therefore, let us fear lest, while a promise remains of entering His rest, any one of you should seem to have come short of it. (11) Let us therefore be diligent to enter that rest, lest anyone *fall* through following the same example of disobedience.[23]

The Apostle Jude also alluded to the example of the Israelite apostasy and its consequences in his short but powerful letter. At the outset, Jude says that while it was his intention to write about "our common salvation," he was rather compelled to write instead "appealing that you contend earnestly for the faith." His exhortation closely paralleled that of the Apostle Paul in the same regard: "Fight the good fight of faith."[24] Certainly, if Christians could not lose faith, neither of these eminent apostles would have written what would then be irrelevant exhortations, aside from the fact that God would certainly not have included it in His Word, of which nothing is superfluous.

Jude explained that the reason he was diverted by the Spirit to address this other topic was that there were "certain persons" who had:

> crept in (*to the fellowship of the saints*) unnoticed, those who were long beforehand marked out for this condemnation, un-

godly persons who turn the grace of our God into licentiousness and deny our only Master and Lord, Jesus Christ.[25]

Jude forthrightly declared such ungodly, licentious people "were long beforehand marked out for this condemnation." He asserts that such people are indeed "condemned," and then he goes on to describe "**this** condemnation" as comparable to that of the Israelites:

> Now I desire to remind you, though you know all things once for all, that the Lord, *after* saving a people out of the land of Egypt, *subsequently* destroyed those who did not believe.[26]

Notice that Jude was reminding the saints that it was "**after**" God had "saved" the Israelites out of the land of Egypt that he "**subsequently** destroyed those who did not believe." As the Apostle Paul said, "these things happened to them as an example" to US, and the whole thing was recorded for posterity "for OUR instruction."[27] The typological instruction given to us through the Israelite example is that Christians, those who have been saved out of the world (Egypt), subsequently, can be spiritually destroyed, and lose their rightstanding and fellowship with God (The Promise Land), if they fall away from faith in Christ Jesus.

The Angelic Example

But Jude did not stop with the Israelite example. He strengthened his case even further by alluding to the fact that even a third of the angels fell away into utter apostasy with the high treason of Lucifer:

> And **angels** who did not keep their own domain, but abandoned their proper abode, He has kept in eternal bonds under darkness for the judgment of the great day.[28]

The Example of Sodom and Gomorrah

Jude even went on to associate the fate of these ungodly, licentious pseudo-Christians with that of the people of Sodom and Gomorrah:

> Just as *Sodom and Gomorrah* and the cities around them, since they in the same way as these indulged in gross immorality and went after strange flesh, are exhibited as an example, in undergoing the **punishment of eternal fire**.[29]

Legalism: Galatian Type of Apostasy

In his letter to the Galatian church, the Apostle Paul rebuked and reproved them for reverting back to Judaistic legalism. He asserted that when people fall back under religious legalism after receiving salvation based on grace through faith in Jesus Christ, they actually sever their relationship with Christ and forfeit salvation by grace: "you have been **severed** from Christ, you who are seeking to be justified by law; you have *fallen from grace.*"[30]

The Galatian church made the grave mistake of reverting back to trusting in adherence to Jewish Laws in order to gain rightstanding with God, *after* they had been saved on the basis of undeserved favor which came through faith in Jesus Christ. Judaizers had infiltrated the Galatian church, propagating the false doctrine that once you are saved, you still must obey all the Jewish Laws and customs. (Unfortunately, some so-called "New Testament" Judaism sects are deceiving people today also with such ridiculous claims and bondage.)

The Apostle Paul was incensed and dumbfounded as to how the Galatian church which had understood "the meaning of Jesus Christ's death as clearly as though I had waved a placard before you with a picture on it of Christ dying on the cross,"[31] could possibly become so deceived. They had actually cut themselves off from God through this legalistic form of apostasy. Paul's entire motivation in this letter was to rebuke, reprove, and to restore those who would repent back into fellowship with God. The following passages from that letter are key elements of the case he presented. The Living Bible rendition is quite good and understandable:

> ...some so-called "Christians" there — false ones, really — who came to spy on us and see what freedom we enjoyed in Christ Jesus, as to whether we obeyed the Jewish laws or not. They tried to get us all tied up in their rules, like slaves in chains. But we did not listen to them for a single moment, for we did not want to confuse you into thinking that salvation can be earned by being circumcised and by obeying Jewish laws.[32]

> ...we Jewish Christians know very well that we cannot become right with God by obeying our Jewish laws, but only by *faith* in Jesus Christ to take away our sins. And so we, too, have trusted Jesus Christ, that we might be accepted by God because of *faith*

— and not because we have obeyed the Jewish laws. *For no one will ever be saved by obeying them.*[33]

Rather, we are sinners if we start rebuilding the old systems I have been destroying, of trying to be saved by keeping Jewish laws, for it was through reading the Scripture that I came to realize that I could never find God's favor by trying — and failing — to obey the laws. I came to realize that acceptance with God comes by believing in Christ.[34]

I am not one of those who treats Christ's death as meaningless. For if we could be saved by keeping Jewish laws, then there was no need for Christ to die.[35]

Did you receive the Holy Spirit by trying to keep the Jewish Laws? Of course not....if trying to obey the Jewish laws never gave you spiritual life in the first place, why do you think that trying to obey them now will make you stronger Christians?[36]

...those who depend on the Jewish laws to save them are under God's **curse**....Consequently, it is clear that no one can ever win God's favor by trying to keep the Jewish laws, because God has said that the only way we can be right in his sight is by **faith**.... How different from this way of **faith** is the way of law which says that a man is saved by obeying every law of God, without one slip. But Christ has brought us out from under the *doom of that impossible system* **by taking the curse for our wrongdoing upon himself.**[37]

So Christ has made us free. Now make sure that you stay free and don't get all tied up again in the chains of slavery to Jewish laws and ceremonies. Listen to me, for this is serious: if you are counting on circumcision and keeping the Jewish laws to make you right with God, **then Christ cannot save you**....Christ is useless to you if you are counting on clearing your debt to God by keeping those laws; you are **lost** from God's grace.[38]

In the same letter, the Apostle Paul also destroys the counterclaim to the possibility of a Christian falling away based on Jesus' promise to never leave or desert us. Without at all being contradictory, Paul asserted that it is quite possible for believers to desert Jesus with his assessment that the Galatians had done precisely that: "I am amazed you are so quickly deserting Him who called you by the grace of Christ."[39]

The subsequent verses also admonished against deserting Christ by following after a varied and distorted Gospel, like the one of legalism which deceived the Galatians, or like the one of "eternal security" by which so many are duped today:

> I am amazed that you are so quickly deserting Him who called you by the grace of Christ, for a different gospel; which is really not another; only there are some who are disturbing you, and want to distort the gospel of Christ. But even though we, or an angel from heaven, should preach to you a gospel contrary to that which we have preached to you, let him be accursed.[40]

Bona Fide Believers?

Some of those who espouse the eternal security doctrine, in view of such scriptures as the ones cited in this chapter, retort that these are references to people who so-called "fall away" because they really are not true believers in the first place. They contend that these people only feigned their initial commitment. Thus, they had not actually fallen away.

However, that theory simply does not hold water. It is most definite that *someone* is falling away, because the Word of God says so. Besides, it is quite elementary that one must actually be "in" something to even be able to "fall away" from it.

Yet, even beyond all that, there is at least one particular scripture that completely explodes this theory. The following passage proves beyond the slightest doubt that a person can be truly saved and a partaker of all the fruits of redemption, and yet *then* fall away. This one is a real clincher. Eternal security proponents are never able to conjure up even a slightly reasonable counterclaim against this scripture.

> **Hebrews 6:4-8**
> 4 For in the case of those who have once been enlightened and have tasted of the heavenly gift and have been made partakers of the Holy Spirit,
> 5 and have tasted the good word of God and the powers of the age to come,
> 6 and then have fallen away, it is impossible to renew them again to repentance, since they again crucify to themselves the Son of God, and put Him to open shame.
> 7 For ground that drinks the rain which often falls upon it and

brings forth vegetation useful to those for whose sake it is also tilled, receives a blessing from God;
8 but if it yields thorns and thistles, it is worthless and close to being cursed, and it ends up being burned.

It is astounding to see in this passage just how extensive a person's Christian experience can be, how many wonderful blessings and benefits they can receive, and then still fall away from their relationship with the Lord Jesus Christ. In verses four and five, Paul lists all the fruits of redemption of which these people had partaken. In a nutshell, they "got all there was to get."

In verse four, Paul says they were first of all, "enlightened," which meant they had consciously perceived the revelation of the Gospel of Jesus Christ, something which can only be effected through the illumination of the Holy Spirit. That in itself testifies of the validity of these peoples' experience, because the Holy Spirit does not enlighten false believers, and He cannot be fooled as to who is true and who is false.

Next, Paul reveals these people "have tasted of the heavenly gift and have been made partakers of the Holy Spirit." This is incontrovertible proof-positive that these people were indeed saved. "The heavenly gift," of which they had tasted is true salvation, for the Word of God says, "the gift of God is eternal life."[41] Plus, the fact that they were "partakers of the Holy Spirit" really seals it, because the Holy Spirit only avails Himself to true, repentant believers. Unbelievers simply cannot be partakers of the Holy Spirit:

> that is the Spirit of truth, *whom the world cannot receive*, because it does not behold Him or know Him, but you know Him because He abides with you, and will be in you."[42]

Not only were these people "partakers of the Holy Spirit" in regards to the regenerative work and indwelling of the Holy Spirit, but they had also received the "baptism in the Holy Spirit," through which they experienced "the powers of the age to come" mentioned in the next verse. That experience, separate from the regenerative work of the Holy Spirit, is also available exclusively to bona fide believers. Bogus believers simply cannot receive the baptism in the Holy Spirit. Only true, Born Again believers can receive it.

In verse five, Paul says these people also had "tasted the good word of God." Like those in all four categories of hearers in Jesus' Parable of the Sower, these people had definitely heard the Word of God, and were by no means ignorant concerning it. Indeed, Paul says they were indeed "enlightened" to the Word. Moreover, they had to have heard and understood it in order to have been saved.

Then, the Apostle Paul says in the same verse that these people had also tasted even of "the powers of the age to come." This is a reference to the power which Jesus said Born Again believers would receive when the Holy Spirit came *upon* (not "in," but "*upon*") them when they received the Baptism in the Holy Spirit: "but you shall receive power when the Holy Spirit has come UPON you."[43] Through this experience adjunctive to salvation, believers are empowered to operate the nine supernatural gifts of supernatural power of the Holy Spirit[44] via the unction of the Spirit. This power which is available to all believers is indeed "the powers of the age to come" which can be "tasted" of now in this age.

Still, incredibly, after partaking of all those magnificent benefits of redemption, these people subsequently fell away, according to verse six. They had been saved, were given Eternal Life, received the Indwelling and Baptism of the Holy Spirit, heard the Word of God, and had received an activation of the supernatural power of God. Yet, they still fell away.

The primary reason they fell away is precisely the point of this part of Jesus' parable as well as this book, which is that such people fall away because they are like "rocky ground" still full of the rocks of sin. They have not fully repented. Thus, they are still carrying out the deeds of the old nature. In this passage, God says by their sinful and apostate lives "they again crucify to themselves the Son of God, and put Him to open shame." This is God's view of what a person does when he has been saved by God and subsequently returns to a life of sin.

Another clue to these individuals' downfall is found in the word used twice in this passage—"tasted." Perhaps that was their shortcoming: they should have "feasted" on instead of having merely "tasted" of all these spiritual provisions from God.

Renewal Impossible

In verse six of the same text, God explicitly says that in the case of these people who have fallen away, "it is impossible to renew them again to repentance." It is not a matter of God not wanting to receive them back into fellowship with Himself, but that they can never again come to the point of true repentance in deed, which is a mandatory requirement for obtaining fellowship with God. On His own part, God is not desirous that anyone be banned from fellowship with Him and perish. However, all must come to repentance in order to obtain fellowship with Him. It is impossible for Him to have fellowship with those who unabatedly continue to participate in the unrighteous deeds of darkness, for "what partnership have righteousness and lawlessness, or what fellowship has light with darkness?"[45] The incontrovertible and immutable fact is that genuine fellowship and communion with God is contingent upon genuine repentance.

It is so very sad as well as hard-sounding to say, but the people described in these passages have passed the point of no return and entered a kind of spiritual "twilight zone" in that they can never again get themselves to repent, and thereby loose themselves from the throes of sin, and return to God. God would certainly receive them if they could, but they simply can't, though, like Esau, they seek for repentance in deed with tears of remorse.[46]

Now let it be clear: we are not talking about backsliding here—there is a difference between backsliding and falling away. Though it need not be that way, *many* sincere believers have come to the harsh realization some time in their lives that instead of growing and maturing, they had actually backslidden. In varying degrees, they had somewhat "left their first love," and had allowed their love for the Lord to "wax cold." Some are neither hot nor cold, but just "lukewarm," the kind of person Jesus said He will vomit out of His mouth.[47] If a backslidden person will but repent, and "remember therefore from where (he has) fallen"[48] and confess his sin, God will forgive him or her.

These hearers mentioned in the Parable of the Sower are not mere backsliders, however. No, these people have completely and totally fallen away, and therewith have "again crucif(ied) to themselves the Son of God, and put Him to open shame." They have denied, rejected, and spiritually "crucified" Jesus by reneging on their previous acceptance of Him as their Lord and Savior and their commitment to serve and obey Him.

As in the case of the first three categories of hearers in the Parable of the Sower, though these apostate believers "have tasted the good word of God," they nonetheless do not bring forth any godly fruit from the Word in their own lives. The consequences of that is tragic and terrifying. Using again the simile of "ground" for believers, God says, ground that drinks the rain of spiritual blessings which God showers upon it "and brings forth vegetation useful to those for whose sake it is also tilled," will receive a blessing from God.[49] However, if it only yields spiritual "thorns and thistles, it is worthless and close to being cursed, and it ends up being burned,"[50] which means their final judgment will be to be cast into the everlasting fires of Hell.

Personal Experience

The most unfortunate part of cases such as those described in this passage in Hebrews is that there really are people like that. It has been my unfortunate experience to personally know, know of, and to have ministered to many people who have gone precisely this way. They have passed the point of no return. Like Esau, they have sold their birthright, who "afterwards, when he desired to inherit the blessing, he was rejected, for he found no place for repentance, though he sought for it with tears."[51]

I have personally witnessed the cases of people who knew they would be "rejected" from Eternal Life and Heaven if they did not turn away from their sin, but who could not come to the place of actual repentance in deed, though they sought for it with tears of remorse. They rejected Jesus' offerings after once having had fellowship with Him, and publicly shamed Him by their lives of apostasy and sin. By and by, the bonds of sin tightened its grip on them, and their minds eventually became depraved, preventing them from being able to come to the place of actual repentance though they sought for it with rivers of tears of remorse.

The Apostle Peter knew well of these gone-astray former believers. He said they had become "accursed children; forsaking the right way they have gone astray, having followed the way of Balaam, the son of Beor, who loved the wages of unrighteousness."[52]

In saying they had become "accursed children, forsaking the right way," he was indicating they were formerly children of God who had become accursed, "anathema," because they subsequently forsook the "right way." It is self-evident that in order to forsake it, they must have formerly been following the right way. He also said "they have gone astray," which intrinsically means they must have once been true sheep in the Flock of God in order to go astray from it.

Then, Peter goes on in his dissertation to make some comments concerning these fallen away believers that very aptly describes their plight:

> For if after they have escaped the defilements of the world by the knowledge of the Lord and Savior Jesus Christ, they are again entangled in them and are overcome, the last state has become worse for them than the first. For it would be better for them not to have known the way of righteousness, than having known it, to turn away from the holy commandment delivered to them. It has happened to them according to the true proverb, "a dog returns to its own vomit," and, "A sow, after washing, returns to wallowing in the mire."[53]

A Final Example From Jesus

Jesus Himself gave us some enlightenment into this matter of the possibility of Christians falling away. One primary example is contained in a section of Scripture from which we have already quoted often. It begins with Jesus exhorting everyone to "Enter by the narrow gate; for the gate is wide, and the way is broad that leads to destruction, and many are those who find it."[54] In the next verse, He gives us an indication of the exactitude of the true Christian walk in terms quite dissimilar to the "easy-gospel" preached by many today: "For the gate is small, and the way is narrow that leads to (Eternal) life, and few are those who find it."

In the subsequent six verses, Jesus talks about false believers, and how to recognize them by their fruit. And then, He gets to the real bottom line of this section:

> **Matthew 7:21-23**
> 21 Not everyone who says to Me, "Lord, Lord" will enter the kingdom of heaven; but he who does the will of My Father who is in heaven.
> 22 Many will say to Me on that day, "Lord, Lord, did we not prophesy in Your name, and in Your name cast out demons, and in Your name perform many miracles?"
> 23 And then I will declare to them, "I never knew you; depart from Me, you who practice lawlessness."

Some misguided people contend that if a person merely professes Jesus as Lord they are saved and are assured of going to Heaven. They go around so-called "witnessing," buttonholing people based on the idea that if they can badger them into repeating a prayer and merely saying Jesus is their Lord, then those people are "saved," and no matter what happens, they are going to Heaven, "because they confessed Jesus as Lord." But that is NOT the way it is!

Indeed, the very point of Jesus' admonition in this passage is that that most certainly is not the way it is. In verse twenty-one, He specifically warns, not everyone who merely calls Him "Lord, Lord," will enter into Heaven. Mere verbal profession of Christ is not the criteria upon which fellowship with God and entrance into Heaven is granted. Rather, it is obedient performance of the "will of My Father who is in Heaven" (v. 21). Talk is cheap. It is the "doers of the Word" who are justified before God.[55]

Yet, according to verse twenty-two, these people described in this passage, are not people who just made some by-rote or mindless confession. These people were definitely saved at one point. We can know that with absolute certainty because they had received the "dunamis" power[56] of God to prophesy, cast out demons, and to perform *many* miracles, which are all manifestations of the supernatural power of God that are operable only by means of the unction of the Holy Spirit. This enablement is only given to Born Again believers through the gift of the Baptism in the Holy Spirit.

Parenthetically, it is important to note here that these people did legitimately perform these supernatural feats. But, it was not through the "power of the devil" as some people ignorantly and blasphemously contend. Evidence of that is found in these people's words to Jesus in which they rightly say they did these things "In YOUR Name." It was not done in the name or through the power of the devil, but in the name of Jesus. Moreover, Jesus did not refute either that they performed these deeds or that they were done in His name and behalf.

Permit me, if you will, to make one more point regarding another parenthetic issue here. Some people become quite disturbed and do not understand how people like these can continue to be channels of supernatural power from God if they are indeed fallen away in their personal conduct. In answer to that, let me point out that the Word of

God forthrightly declares, "the gifts and callings of God are irrevocable."[57] Once God gives a person supernatural gifts, and anoints and appoints someone into set-apart ministry, He does not subsequently revoke those gifts when they go astray spiritually. Besides, as evidenced by the case of the prophet Balaam being rebuked by his donkey, God reserves the Sovereign right to use any vessel He chooses.

However, Eternal Life and rightstanding with God is not predicated or dependent on one's gifts and accomplishments. The manifestation of God's power through these people was certainly a good thing, especially to its intended recipients. God is most desirous that people be beneficiaries of His supernatural power, and His usual modus operandi is to channel it through believers who make themselves available to Him. However, operation of these works of power had no bearing whatsoever on these people being qualified or disqualified from Eternal Life and entrance into Heaven.

In verse twenty-three, Jesus revealed the reason these people were rejected was because they practiced "lawlessness." They disobeyed God's Laws. They did not fully repent, or we could say they subsequently repented from their repentance after repenting. They did not just "slip up a little" or experience a momentary lapse as all of us have, rather they actually "practiced" lawlessness. They persistently practiced ungodliness. They willfully rejected godliness and holiness. So, God rejected them and banned them from Heaven and Eternal Life.

Instead of receiving the approval and commendation Jesus will give every faithful believer on that day, in which He will say, "well done, thou good and faithful servant," these people will receive Jesus' terrifying command of eternal judgment: "Depart from Me, you who practice lawlessness."

Summary

The message of this portion of Jesus' parable, which focuses on the second category of hearers, those who are like "rocky ground," is to exhort believers to make a complete repentance, to renew their mind according to the Word of God, and allow the Lord to restore their soul through the sanctifying power of the Holy Spirit. Otherwise, those who refuse, foolishly toy with the possibility of falling away, and ending up in an apostate condition, unfit for and disqualified from the Kingdom of God, having become a "castaway." As the Word says, "Take care,

Brethren, lest there should be in any one of **you** an evil, unbelieving heart, in falling away from the living God."

However, at the same time, if a believer will successfully complete this second step to bringing forth the fruit of Eternal Life, surrendering his entire life unto obedience of God and His will, he shall secure for himself Eternal Life by grace through faith in Jesus Christ. The believer who does these things need never concern himself about his salvation, for he is eternally secure, indeed:

> ...for as long as you practice these things, you will never stumble (*lit., fall away*); for in this way the entrance into the eternal kingdom of our Lord and Savior Jesus Christ will be abundantly supplied to you.[58]

All this is also the essence of the message of this chapter of this book. Born Again believers must be diligent to walk and work out their salvation to the end of the journey, which is the moment they breathe their last breath, trusting in a faithful Savior to be faithful in saving them as He promised He would, knowing it is impossible for Him to do anything other than what He has promised!

Endnotes

1. Mark 4:17
2. 1 John 5:13
3. Rom. 2:4-11
4. Eph. 2:8,9
5. Jude 4
6. Rom. 5:6
7. Rom. 6:15
8. Rom. 6:1,2
9. Mat. 3:8
10. Jas. 2:17
11. Jas. 2:14; parentheses and italics added by author
12. Heb. 10:26
13. Rev. 21:27
14. Rev. 21:8
15. 2 Tim. 3:1
16. Isa. 48:10
17. Joel 2:28
18. Jude 12, parenthesis and italics added
19. Mat. 24:10, italics added
20. 1 Tim. 4:10
21. 1 Cor. 10;11,12
22. Heb. 3:12
23. Heb. 4:1,11
24. 1 Tim. 6:12
25. Jude 4; parenthesis and italics added
26. Jude 5
27. 1 Cor. 10:11
28. Jude 6
29. Jude 7

30 Gal. 5:40
31 Gal. 3:1; L.B.
32 Gal. 2:4,5
33 Gal. 2:16
34 Gal. 2:18,19
35 Gal. 2:21
36 Gal. 3:2,3
37 Gal. 3:10-13
38 Gal. 5:1-4
39 Gal. 1:6
40 Gal. 1:6-9
41 Rom. 6:23
42 John 14:17
43 Acts 1:8
44 1 Cor. 12:8-10
45 2 Cor. 6:14
46 C.f., Heb. 12:17
47 Rev. 3:16
48 Rev. 2:5
49 Heb. 6:7
50 Heb. 6:8
51 Heb. 12:17
52 2 Pet. 2:14,15
53 2 Pet. 2:20-22
54 Mat. 7:13
55 Rom. 2:13
56 Acts 1:8
57 Rom. 11:29
58 2 Pet. 1:10,11, parenthesis and italics added

Chapter Eighteen

The Shield of Faith

in addition to all, taking up *the shield of faith* with which you will be able to extinguish all the flaming arrows of the evil one.[1]

Here, the Apostle Paul, who himself experienced during his ministry career as much or perhaps more persecution than any other believer in the first church, includes in his delineation of the various parts of "the armor of God," "the shield of faith," urging believers to take it up, therewith to extinguish all the flaming arrows of persecution flung at believers by "the evil one," Satan. Scripture makes it clear in a plethora of passages that Satan indeed is the ultimate author of all persecution.

Paul made mention of his extreme "persecutions and sufferings" several times in his letters to the churches that are now part of the twenty-seven canonized chapters comprising the New Testament. One such mention is in his writings to the young minister Timothy, who had learned greatly under the tutelage of Paul, not only from his extraordinary revelation knowledge, but also from his exemplary life, which was replete with afflictions and persecutions:

> But you followed my teaching, conduct, purpose, faith, patience, love, perseverance, *persecutions and sufferings*, such as happened to me at Antioch, at Iconium and at Lystra; what *persecutions* I endured, and out of them all the Lord delivered me! And indeed, **all** who desire to live godly in Christ Jesus will be *persecuted.*[2]

Under the inspiration of the Holy Spirit, Paul declared that *everyone* who sincerely *desires* to live godly in Christ Jesus in this world will indeed be persecuted. Believers, the Born Again children of God, are the only ones who are "in Christ Jesus." Paul said all believers "who desire to live godly" **will be** persecuted. He didn't say they "*might be*." He said they "will be" persecuted. It is not even required that a believer be entirely perfected in godly living in order to be persecuted, necessarily, but just have the "desire" to live godly in Christ Jesus.

The more conformed into the Image of Jesus[3] and less conformed to the world[4] a believer becomes, the more persecution he/she will experience in this world through those who are *not* conformed into His Image, who walk "according to the course of this world, according to the prince of the power of the air."[5]

"Yes, but we should not 'believe' for persecution," some say today, "because if we do, then we will be sure to get it."

My friend, my Bible says if you desire to live godly in Christ Jesus, you "**will be** persecuted," whether you are "believing" for it or not. Jesus foretold His death, burial, and resurrection many times. He told the apostles that He would be mocked, spit upon, beaten, and brutalized in unimaginable ways. Were all those things fulfilled because He made a "bad confession" and was "believing" for it?

Jesus forewarned the apostles *they* would be mistreated, persecuted, and even killed for the sake of the Gospel, which they were. Were those prophesied sufferings, including the eventual martyrdom of those great men, fulfilled because they were "believing" for it?

Did the great Apostle Paul experience all the afflictions and persecutions he experienced, which he enumerates seemingly endlessly in Second Corinthians 11:23-28, because he was "believing" for them? How absurd!

It is when someone who purports to be a believer is *not* being persecuted and afflicted with adversity that I begin to seriously wonder why not! Indeed, that is a legitimate concern because God's Word says, "**all** who desire to live godly in Christ Jesus **will be** persecuted." I say let God be true and every man a liar.[6] Anyone who is *not* being persecuted to some degree, had better do some serious self-testing and -examination[7] to see how he/she is doing in the godly living department.

No Promise of a Rose Garden

What I write about the matter of persecution in Chapter Twelve in the context of the testing of our faith, bears repeating here in the context of this chapter.

Mark 4:6,17
6 And after the sun had risen, it was scorched; and because it had no root, it withered away.
17 and they have no firm root in themselves, but are only temporary; then, when *affliction and persecution* arises because of the word, immediately they fall away.

Nowhere has God promised believers a rose garden. Some people have a confused understanding of what Jesus meant when He said, "I came that they might have *life*, and might have it abundantly."[8] The Greek word translated "life" is not a reference to physical existence on Earth, per se. That word "zoe," is actually the word God uses in Scripture for spiritual life; that is, "the Eternal Life."[9] Jesus *did* come to bring us *that* Life in overflowing abundance! In the same regard, the Apostle Peter even said, "His divine power has granted to us everything pertaining to life (*zoe*) and godliness."[10]

The Abundant Life Jesus came to give every true believer is the Eternal Life, His Life, which indwells every true, Born Again (there is no other kind) believer, in the person of the Holy Spirit. God spares nothing in giving believers that Life. He pours His Life into us in abounding superfluity, which is what the Greek word Jesus used that is translated "abundantly" means. It means that Jesus came to give us His Life in overflowing measure. It means we have exceedingly more than we will ever need to utilize in any circumstance.

That is the Abundant Life Jesus was talking about. He was not referring to our span of physical existence in this present world. He was not saying that our existence in this world would be so "abundant" so as to be absolutely free of any negative or adverse circumstances. No, such a euphoric state of utopia will *never* exist on planet Earth in the present age. Much to the contrary, Jesus forthrightly declared, "*In this world* you will have tribulation."[11] The Apostle Paul said, "Through *many* tribulations we must enter the kingdom of God,"[12] Life in this present world is *full* of tribulations.

The Abundant Life of Jesus is abundant with nothing but "goodness and righteousness and truth."[13] Nevertheless, our physical existence in this present world is inevitably abundant with "the sufferings of Christ": "The sufferings of Christ are ours in abundance."[14] Especially in these last days in which we live are our lives full of tribulations and difficulties, something which the Spirit of God predicted: "But realize this, that in the last days difficult times will come."[15]

Now all these admonitions concerning tribulation are directed to *believers*, indicating that believers are *not* impervious to tribulations. *No one* who lives in this present world on planet Earth is impervious to tribulation! It comes with the territory, as they say. In fact, the real truth is that believers may be the target of *more* adversity than unbelievers. More about affliction and persecution in the lives of believers—what they are, who authors them, why they come, and more—is in Chapter Twelve of this book, if you did not read that chapter yet, as well as in my book, *The Mystery of the Kingdom* (for more information on that book, see the promo page in back of this book).

What I will restate here in the context of this chapter, however, is a definition of persecution. "Persecution," in Biblical context, usually refers to adversity brought against a person or group of persons by another person or group of persons. Persecution can range from subtle contrariety to repression to oppression to physical harm and abuse, and all the way to outright murder on the extreme end of the spectrum.

Affliction and persecution would also be included in what the Bible terms "tribulation." Again, in Chapter Twelve of this book, we examined several Scriptures concerning the fact that our lives, as believers, in this world will be intrinsically laden with tribulations. Many people, however, may not be able to readily identify with the term "tribulations," until it is rendered as its literal meaning—i.e., "pressures." Most people *can* readily identify with having "pressures" in their lives. Understanding that "tribulation" is "pressure" makes it easier to understand what Jesus meant when He said that "in this world" we would have "tribulations."[16] He meant that during the course of our lives we would often experience a variety of "pressures." Nearly every day of our lives, especially in this hectic, fast-paced modern era, we are inundated with pressures of various types and degrees, just as Jesus predicted. However, Jesus also added, "but take courage; I have overcome the world!"

As indicated in the opening scripture citing of this chapter, it is against persecution, in particular, that God, through the Apostle Paul, instructs and urges believers to take up the shield of faith, in order to by it extinguish all the flaming arrows (NASB, et al.) (fiery darts, KJV) of the evil one, the devil. This is the weapon in the believers' arsenal of weapons of warfare God has provided to every believer by which to negate the intended effects of persecution.

Believers must be ever mindful of the irrefutable fact that we are constantly in the midst of spiritual warfare in which spiritual battle is being waged all around and against us every hour of every day we live. We, thus, leave ourselves vulnerable to every kind of spiritual assault, from our common adversary, the devil, whenever we fail to don every element of our spiritual armor!

What Is the Shield of Faith

The concept of a shield conjures varying thoughts in terms of shape, dimensions, constitution, and function to each person, depending on what he/she personally relates it to. Paul's allegorical mention of the shield of faith in this Ephesian passage, undoubtedly, was predicated on the imagery of the type of shields carried by Roman soldiers, in that he lived his entire life during the reign of the Roman Empire. Their shields, forged from the strongest medal, offered protection for the Roman soldier from their shoulders to their lower extremities during certain battle postures and formations, which meant effectively all their vital organs and internal systems. Similarly, the shield of faith protects against the "fiery darts," or "flaming arrows," aimed at believers' internal spiritual organs in their allegorical anatomical counterparts (lungs, heart, stomach, liver, kidneys, et al.).

What Are Flaming Arrows

What those fiery darts or flaming arrows consist of is *words*—words of the enemy of our souls uttered by human enemies and "frienemies!" Words formulate thoughts. Thoughts, thinking, are formulated from and consist of words. Part of the process of extinguishing negative thoughts formulated from devil-inspired thoughts and thinking is "taking every thought captive to the obedience of Christ,"[17] by which believers "(destroy) speculations and every lofty thing raised up against the knowledge of God!" Every thought planted in the human mind or thinking by the devil is a speculative process, in that, the thoughts and thinking Satan, "the father of all lies,"[18] communicates, is really not the Truth, for Jesus Himself is the Truth,[19] but rather is mere sophistry ("every lofty thing raised up against the knowledge of God")! Sophistry is defined as: 1) a subtle, tricky, superficially plausible, but generally fallacious method of reasoning; 2) a false argument; sophism.[20] In other words, sophistry, is deceptive mumbo-jumbo purporting to be sophisticated and superior wisdom or knowledge. Satan is the master of sophistry. What he speaks or communicates is really complete deception that sounds like truth. Satan is the master-deceiver. Jesus called him a "liar" and said that "whenever he speaks a lie, he speaks from his own *nature*."[21] He believes his thinking and thoughts are truth, but he is deceived about being deceived and his own deceptive thoughts. If his lips are moving, so to speak, as the saying goes, he is lying! He cannot do anything but lie; that is his nature! He is thoroughly incapable of speaking truth, but can only speak lies, because out of the abundance of the heart, the mouth speaks, and his heart is thoroughly corrupted with nothing but deception and falsehood. He "does not stand in the truth because there is no truth *in him*,"[22] Jesus declared!

Lucifer's (now Satan) "fall from grace" resulted in utter deception, falseness, and deceit, and as the "ruler of this world" and "the prince of the power of the air" he has corrupted the very air and atmosphere that permeates the present Earth, which is the very reason that God must create and activate "a new heaven and a new earth!"[23] The creation and activation of this new heaven and a new earth is the only remedy for the deception that now permeates the nascent Heavens and Earth!

Knowing Your Enemy and His Tactics

As repeatedly stated in this book, the Holy Spirit made it abundantly clear who our adversary is, "Be of sober spirit, be on the alert. YOUR ADVERSARY, *the devil*, prowls about like a roaring lion, seeking someone to devour."[24] He is the one who wages the war of words against believers and unbelievers alike on the battlefield of the mind. Assaulting believers with vile and dastardly thoughts is a major part of his continual tactics of warfare against believers in particular. In fact, one verse tells us he wages this mind-warfare "day and night" against believers, accusing them of all kinds of things to keep them reeling in condemnation, which is an extremely effective faith-killer: "for the accuser of our brethren…which accused them before our God day and night."[25]

As I said in Chapter Ten, the King James Version of this Petrine passage says Satan walks around on the Earth "seeking whom he MAY devour." The word "may" is a term of permission. So, this scripture is saying that Satan is looking for those who will give him permission to devour them, whether tacitly, ignorantly, or passively, instead of offensively resisting him, as James tells us we must do in order to make him flee from us.[26]

Satan attacks believers and non-believers in their minds, their thinking. Why? God tells us the answer to that question in Psalms 23:7 saying that as a person *thinks* in his *heart*, so **is** he. In other words, at any given moment in the lives of humans, their entire life, whatever it consists of, is the sum-total of the accumulative of all their thinking or thoughts. What I just said is a mouthful! You may want to read it again…and again…and again…and even memorize it. According to this passage, whatever your life is today, it is what it is because your thinking has produced what it is! Notice what that passage says, "as a person *thinks* in his *heart*, so **is** he." Most people don't know that the human heart or spirit (the words *heart* and *spirit* are interchangeable in Bible parlance) thinks or formulates thoughts! It's true! While intellectual thought transpires in the brain or mind, spiritual thought transpires in a person's heart, their spirit, what is also referred to in the New Testament as "the inner man."[27]

Now this being the case, there is a "good" side to it and there is also a "bad" side to it. The good side is that when a person is Born Again, he/she becomes a "new creation" or "new creature" in Christ Jesus.[28] Meaning, at the moment of the rebirth, an entirely new human entity comes into existence that did not exist before, having no past and no future. No past because it has been thrown into the "sea of forgetfulness,"[29] never to be remembered again, and no future because as of that moment no actions or acts have been committed for which this new creature is responsible and answerable to God. It's better than "turning over a new leaf;" it's a brand new life without blemish, free of sin!"[30] Praise God forever!

The bad side is that as a result of Adam and Eve's sin and apostasy against God in the Garden of Eden, which they brought about by partaking of the fruit of the tree of the knowledge of good and evil, in direct disobedience to God's explicit commandment not to, their human spirit instantly died, because the Holy Spirit, the third member of the Godhead, instantly departed from their human spirit in which He had resided, with the result that their entire progeny—the human race—from then on is born spiritually dead.

God spoke to Adam and Eve and told them not to eat of the tree of the knowledge of good and evil, for He said that in the day that they ate of it, they would surely die. Yet, we see that they lived for over 900 years *after* they disobeyed God's explicit commandment and ate anyway. However, they *did* indeed die when they partook of the fruit of the tree of the knowledge of good and evil, which was the *carnal nature*, the *sin nature*, but it was not *physical* death that transpired, but rather *spiritual* death, in that their human spirit died. Every human being that has ever been born since the fall of Man has been born with a human spirit that exists, but is *dead* spiritually.

That is what Ephesians 2:1 is speaking about when it says:

And you *were* **dead** in your trespasses and sins, in which you formerly walked according to the course of this world, according to the prince of the power of the air, of *the* **spirit** *that is now working in the sons of disobedience.*

The "*spirit* that is now working in the sons of disobedience," is the spirit of Satan, the carnal nature, the sin nature. The Holy Spirit cannot abide with sin. He cannot occupy the same place where sin is present, for He is holy! When unholiness is added to holiness, the mixture is unholiness. This is the reason Adam and Eve immediately died when they disobeyed God's explicit commandment not to eat of the fruit of the tree of the knowledge of good and evil. This fruit was the "sin nature," the nature of Satan, which is "according to the course of this world, according to the prince of the power of the air,"—who is Satan. Satan is the "prince of the power of the air." It is his spirit—"the spirit that is now working in the sons of disobedience"—that permeates and pervades the atmosphere on Earth and the heavens or firmament above the Earth, which is the prime cause of all evil and wickedness upon the Earth. That evil and wickedness not only fills the atmosphere on the Earth and its firmament, but it also fills, permeates the hearts (spirits), of all the inhabitants of the Earth at any given moment in time. This is the cause and source of all that is evil and wicked that happens on the Earth—it comes from people! People—people living in unfettered cooperation with Satan, who is the ultimate author and source of evil—are the agents of evil and wickedness! The billions of unredeemed humans dotting the globe are Satan's co-ops! Evil spirits (fallen angels, devils) are powerless to act upon the Earth on their own as spirits; they must occupy human bodies in order to operate on the Earth. "The *heavens* are the heavens of the LORD, But the *earth* He has given to *the sons of men* (lit. Adam)."[31] One must possess and be enshrouded by an "earth suit" (physical human body) in order to function on the Earth. Spirits cannot function on Earth as spirits; they must occupy a human body to function here. This is why evil spirits are so obsessed with occupying people, in their spirits, souls, and bodies. This is why—

> "When the unclean spirit goes out of a man, it passes through waterless places seeking rest, and not finding any, it says, 'I will return to *my house* from which I came.' "And when it comes, it finds it swept and put in order. "Then it goes and takes along seven other spirits more evil than itself, and they go in and live there; and the last state of that man becomes worse than the first."[32]

Alive But Dead

So, how is it that humans can be alive and living, but yet dead at the same time? That's a very good and important question, the answer to which is fundamental to the Gospel. The Bible makes it clear that humans are tripartite beings, that is, consisting of three parts. As God is Triune, consisting of *three* Persons—Father, Son, and Holy Spirit—yet being *one* Divinity, or Godhead, so also we, having been made in the Image of God,[33] were made in three parts—spirit, soul, and body[34]— and thus are tripartite beings. We **are** essentially a s*pirit*. God is Spirit,[35] and being made by Him and in His image, we are also essentially *spirit*. Moreover, in the original Creation, God also formed Man a physical body out of the dirt of the ground and breathed or infused the "breath of Life," i.e., God's very breath or Spirit (both the Hebrew and Greek word for *spirit* is the same word for *breath*), and Man thereby became a "living *soul*": "And the LORD God formed man of the dust of the ground, and breathed into his nostrils the breath of life; and man became a living *soul*."[36]

So, the result is that humans are first and foremost a *spirit*, who **have** a *soul*, which is made up of our mind, will and emotions, and, then the spirit and soul is contained or enshrouded **in** a physical human *body*. So, we have three parts, making us tripartite beings.

But, in the Garden of Eden, when Adam and Eve sinned against God by partaking of the fruit of the tree of the knowledge of good and evil, in direct disobedience to God's explicit command not to, their human spirit died. Moreover, everyone who has ever been born, every human being that has ever been born since then, has been born with a human spirit that exists, but is *dead* spiritually. It is spiritually dead. That is what Ephesians 2:1 is speaking about when it says, "And you were *dead* in your trespasses and sins." The entire progeny of Adam and Eve—all humanity—are born into this world spiritually *dead. That* is the reason we all "must be born again."[37]

Spiritual Resurrection

When Jesus comes to live in our spiritually dead human spirit, it becomes *alive*, as it is infused with the *regenerative* power of the Holy Spirit. By that infusion of the Spirit into our dead human spirit we are literally raised from the dead, resurrected, just as Jesus was raised from the dead or resurrected, only spiritually rather than physically.[38]

That—what I was just talking about—is the *initial* working of the Holy Spirit in our lives—what takes place when we are born again. But, again, that is the *regenerative* working of the Holy Spirit, when the Holy Spirit comes to live in our spiritual hearts or human spirits. When we ask Jesus to come and live in our hearts, He *regenerates* our human spirit. He gives *Life* to our spirit at that moment of the rebirth. But that experience and working of the Holy Spirit in *regeneration,* or the New Birth, is separate and distinct from the working of the Holy Spirit that takes place through the *Baptism* in the Holy Spirit.

In verse six of the text cited at the beginning of this chapter, Jesus said, "That which is born of the flesh is flesh," referring to the natural birth. Then, He said, "and that which is born of the Spirit is spirit." And, what He was describing there is when we are born again, when Jesus comes to live in our spirit, our human spirit, in the form of the Holy Spirit, it is at that moment that the *regenerative* working of the Holy Spirit begins to *regenerate* our human spirit, which *was* dead in our trespasses and sins, according to Ephesians 2:1, as a result of the spiritual death that took place when Adam and Eve fell into perdition in the Garden of Eden.

The difference is that believers have the capability to extinguish these flaming words by taking *every* thought captive unto the obedience of Christ. Notice this verse isolates and individualizes each and every thought that seeks entrance into our minds. A common phrase with people is: "I've got a thousand things on my mind." Well, you may *think* you do, but every thought, according to this passage, comes to the door of your mind, individually, one thought at a time!

There is some very significant revelation—life-changing revelation—right there in that verse! It is telling us that we can isolate every single thought that comes wistfully to the frontals of our minds and literally take it captive—seize it—analyze it according to Scripture, and then decide whether or not it is a thought that is of God, meaning Scriptural, and if not, we can choose to disallow it and discard it from our thought process! Powerful! As someone has said metaphorically, "You can't keep the birds from flying over your head, but you can sure keep them from building a nest in your hair!" If believers would practice doing this with respect to their thought-life, it would revolutionize their lives!

New believers and immature believers are often uninformed and thus timid and reticent with regard to exercising this Spirit-powered prerogative, despite reading it in the Word of God. Often this is due to their lifetime of conditioning and programming by the enemy to accept his thinking and thoughts about everything in life in general, but especially about *themselves*. Condemnation for their past life and living often factors heavily into that response, even though the Word of God states categorically that "Therefore there is **now** *no* (zero, nada, zilch, none) condemnation to those who are in Christ Jesus."[39] That's why I often speak about the absolute essentialness of believers knowing who *they* are in Christ **and** who *Christ* is in *them*! Both are vital to biblical living! In fact, I have made available without cost on several of my websites a listing of scriptures that speak of both sides of that win-win coin. Walking by faith and not by sight is dependent upon knowing and appropriating the truths of these scriptures. In fact, *everything* discussed in this book regarding faith and it being effective in a believer's life is dependent upon those truths and believers applying them to their daily walk with God!

The Renewing of Our Minds

This concept is reinforced by several New Testament passages, one of the most prominent of which is:

> Finally, brethren, whatsoever things are *true*, whatsoever things are *honest*, whatsoever things are *just*, whatsoever things are *pure*, whatsoever things are *lovely*, whatsoever things are

of *good report*; if there be any *virtue*, and if there be any *praise*, **think on THESE things.**[40]

When we think on "these things" with thoughts from above and not below, we are retraining or transforming our mindsets to comport with what God says—thoughts from above—as opposed to what Satan, the enemy of our souls, says or communicates to human beings—thoughts from below (in the sin-corrupted atmosphere of Earth)!

And do not be *conformed* to this world, but be *transformed* by the renewing of your mind, so that you may prove what the will of God is, that which is good and acceptable and perfect.[41]

Another New Testament passage reinforcing the concept of retraining or transforming one's thinking to comport to what God says about us is:

Be careful for nothing; but in every thing by prayer and supplication with thanksgiving let your requests be made known unto God. And the peace of God, which passeth all understanding, shall keep your hearts and minds through Christ Jesus.[42]

A common colloquialism when people are parting company is: "Take care!" A saying that believers should never use, because this passage is saying just the opposite: DON'T take care! Be careful for NOTHING! But instead of being filled with care about things, meaning worrying about them, many of which you can do nothing about, convert those concerns to prayer and supplication with thanksgiving, letting your requests be made known unto God, Who has the ability to do something about them, answering those faith-filled prayers favorably so that you do not have to be constantly worrying about them. Essentially, this is saying give your concerns to God, take them to the Lord in prayer, as the chorus of a standard hymn says, and leave it there!

Leave it there, leave it there,
Take your burden to the Lord and leave it there.
If you trust and never doubt, He will surely bring you out,
Take your burden to the Lord and leave it there.

For more on the matter of "the worries of the world," as Jesus termed them in the Parable of the Sower, read Chapter Eleven of my book, *Mystery of the Kingdom* (see promotional page at the back of this book), where I go into extensive detail concerning its negative effects in the believer's life, including how it "chokes the word" and thereby negates faith.

Extinguishing the Flaming Arrows of False Accusation

Anyone who has labored for any appreciable length of time in the ministry will have experienced the reality that the day you announce publicly that you have been called to the ministry by the Lord, you just painted an invisible but very real red target on your back! It's not crying in your beer; it's just the truth! From that day on, you and all your loved ones with you, will begin to experience some of the most bizarre and incredible events that often defy description and explanation. Flaming arrows, coming out of nowhere and everywhere all at the same time, it seems! At first, they will shock, shake, and sadden you, until you learn once and for all, that it really does just come with the territory, as the saying goes, the territory that you are taking for God, that is! Taking the territory—every place where your feet shall trod[43]—is indeed what draws the fire, the attacks, mostly unjustly, but almost always unexpectedly. And by people you would never in a million years suspect of launching such a vicious and uncalled for all-out, merciless attack of words and actions. Very often it is "friendly fire."

When the attacks first start coming, you'll be tempted to run for cover and jump into your foxhole mentally, never to reemerge! You will be so offended and taken off guard by the viciousness and acrimoniousness of the attacks that throws you into a tailspin trying to figure out what you actually said or did to warrant such bitter assaults. What did I do? What did I say that caused these people who claim to love or at least care about you to do what they are doing?

You've heard other older or more experienced ministers talk of these kinds of attacks, but you secretly thought that those things were happening to them because they are doing something wrong to trigger the attacks and that will never happen to you because you are better, wiser, and more likable than those other ministers. What in the world is this all about, you ask yourself and maybe your spouse, or family member, or someone close to you, not yet ready to actually ask God what it's all about, because deep down you fear there may be some truth to the accusations and you're not ready to talk to God about that yet. Slowly, surely, as you turn to the Scriptures for help in understanding and consolation, you begin to understand that what this actually is, is **persecution**! the ultimate author of which is the devil himself, who is influencing the assailants to launch these horrific, demonic, dastardly, unjust blindside onslaughts against you out of nowhere!

That's the good news! The bad news is that this is just the first of these types of experiences that you will experience over and over and over again, interminably, until Jesus comes, or you go to Him, as long as you are continuing to pursue fulfilling your calling to the ministry He called you to and anointed you for! The only thing that will bring an end to such unwanted and unwarranted adversity, evil persecution from human and demonic adversaries, is when you draw your last breath! You say you want to be a minister? Welcome, my friend, to the ministry! Praise the Lord and pass the ammunition!

Personal Experiences of Extinguishing the Flaming Arrows of the Evil One

What follows is a number of incidents in my history of personal experiences in which I had to extinguish the flaming arrows of the Evil One in order to be victorious over what the Adversary was attempting to do through them in my life and ministry. They do not appear in chronological order.

Do My Prophets No Harm

"Do not touch My anointed ones, And do My prophets no harm."[44]

Though this Divine command is too often abused and misused, God said it twice in His Word, which is special emphasis indicating He certainly meant it! Though, of course, God always says what He means and means what He says! Thus, I would say it would be a good idea for anyone to give heed to that warning. Anytime you think God is leading you to engage in an ad hominem attack of words and/or actions or some sort of an insurrection against a genuinely anointed and appointed man of God, another good idea is to remember the fate of the company of "Korah & Sons," who participated in a personal attack and insurrection against the man God had chosen and anointed to deliver Israel, Moses, and the principle of unintended consequences!

And Moses said, "By this you shall know that the LORD has sent me to do all these deeds; for this is not my doing. "If these men die the death of all men, or if they suffer the fate of all men, then the LORD has not sent me. "But if the LORD brings about an entirely new thing and the ground opens its mouth and swallows them up with all that is theirs, and they descend alive into Sheol, then you will understand that these men have spurned the LORD." Then it came about as he finished speaking all these words, that the ground that was under them split open; and the earth opened its mouth and swallowed them up, and their households, and all the men who belonged to Korah, with their possessions. So they and all that belonged to them went down alive to Sheol; and the earth closed over them, and they perished from the midst of the assembly. And all Israel who were around them fled at their outcry, for they said, "The earth may swallow us up!" Fire also came forth from the LORD and consumed the two hundred and fifty men who were offering the incense.[45]

Mall Madman

Let me share with you one of many illustrative stories taken from the vault of my own experiences in regard to mistreating or coming against a genuine God-anointed, God-appointed prophet—someone who walks in the Fivefold Ministry Office of a prophet.

Long ago, by the direction of the Lord, my late wife and I started a business that almost immediately became popular and well-known in the town we lived in at the time. God prospered it and us as we applied His principles of success and prosperity, including being generous in our giving to Him and to those in need.

One day, a few years later, a representative of a man who owned a mall in a town about thirty miles away, called to tell us about a new outside shopping mall the man was in the process of building next to the mall on a plot of previously undeveloped land he owned that they called, "The Hill," and that the owner was very familiar with our business (in fact his wife frequented it), and he was very interested in having us open a new location in the new mall that was nearing completion. Over the course of a couple of months, the rep called multiple times with the intention of persuading us to take up the offer. As we prayed, I myself was not as persuaded that it was a "God thing" than was my wife. I couldn't explain all the reasons why, because it truly seemed like a good opportunity and one God could use to increase our business and bless us further so that we could be a greater blessing to others.

As we continued to pray about and discuss the pros and cons of the matter, the rep continued to call to ask if we were any closer to making a decision. Each time I said, "Closer, but not there, yet."

Finally, I said to my wife, "Tell you what, to do this we would need such-and-so amount of money to purchase additional inventory to stock the store, as well as the owner would have to underwrite the build-out of the store; if that were to somehow materialize, I will see it as a sign that God wants us to do this."

That day, the rep called again. I candidly told him that we could handle everything required from us in terms of purchasing the equipment and furnishings for a new location, hiring/training personnel to attempt to duplicate ourselves in the operation of the new store, designing a layout for the contractor to work with for the build-out of the new store, etc., etc., but we could not finance the build-out and did not currently have the funding to purchase the initial stock of inventory we would need. Those two things, I said, would preclude us from accepting the offer. He asked if he could call me back in a few minutes. I agreed.

A few minutes later, he called back and asked if I could meet with the owner the next day at such-and-such time. Again, I agreed.

Next day I went into the owner's office at the appointed time. It was a huge, expansive office, that seemed much like a cave to me, hidden away in a subterranean level that was not even visible from the outside of the building at one end of the large mall in this North Central Florida town. It was decorated in a 19th Century-like, opulent Italian motif with huge, ornate (to me, gaudy), furnishings and appointments that I imagined how an early-20th-Century Caesar's or mega-wealthy global business magnate's office might look like.

The diminutive elderly Italian man stood from his desk and walked toward me with his hand outstretched as I entered his office, accompanied and introduced by the young man who was the rep I had talked to so many times. He invited me to sit down in one of the two throne-like armchairs affronting his massive dark wood desk. Speaking with a slight Italian accent, he got straight to the point, "Mr. Lambert, I want your business in my new shopping center. I think it would be an asset to our mix of businesses, as well as a good draw of customers to the mall. And I think it will be very successful for you here in this new center. What can I do to help make that happen?"

"Well," I said, "as I told your rep, the two things precluding the prospect right now is lack of funding for the build-out and inventory stock." Without the slightest hesitation, he immediately responded, "We'll do the build-out. How much do you think you need for the inventory?" I gave him the figure I felt the Lord had told me.

He rose from his chair, and said, "Would you allow me to buy your lunch where I eat most every day, accompanied by my assistant, and return here to my office when you're finished?" The restaurant was an Italian chain in the food court of the mall, and he said, "It's not on the menu, but tell them I said to make you the veal piccata they frequently make for me."

Since, veal piccata is my all-time favorite Italian meal, I felt the moving of the Spirit to graciously and unhesitatingly accept his offer. It was great too! After a zabaglione and double espresso for dessert, and small talk with the rep, we returned to the mall-owner's man-cave.

Again, wasting no time, he said to me, "Mr. Lambert, if you will go to the bank right here on the property," which he named, "and ask for the branch manager, he will give you a check in the amount you said you needed for inventory. Do we have a deal?"

"Uhhhh...ookkaayy, we have a deal," I replied, sounding like Hank on King of the Hill. We shook hands again, I left the office, went to the bank, asked for the manager, and sure enough, he handed me a check for the amount I said I needed.

Over the course of a couple of months, as the build-out was being completed according to the design I laid out myself, we did all we needed to do to acquire the furnishings, carpet, equipment, hiring/training new employees, etc., etc., for our second location. When we moved in, the store was beautiful, the inventory was great, the employees were well-trained, and we set out attempting to duplicate in that location what had been so successful in our home base location.

We had *some* success, but nothing near what we had experienced at the original location. There were a number of reasons for that, including that we underestimated the value of my wife and I's involvement;

we wrongly thought our contribution to the business was pretty much reproducible by anyone with certain qualifications, requisites, and the training we gave them. So, some of the miscalculations were on us. We learned valuable lessons from this excursion, many more than can be shared here. But, in addition to our own over-zealous estimations, so also were those of the owner and his rep, but more critical than that was that even after more than a year from when the deal was struck, they never did produce the things they promised with respect to securing well-known and established tenants that they projected would draw lots of foot-traffic and customers to the new shopping mall. None of what they had promised ever materialized, and by and by the public image of the center steadily deteriorated. Several businesses went out of business, vacating their units. There was less and less foot-traffic with each passing day.

Finally, at the close of our second year, my wife and I agreed that we needed to close the business because it had become too much of a drain on our resources, time, effort, and energy without sufficient return on our investment. When I called and informed the rep of our decision, he was very adamant and exercised in saying that we could not do that according to the lease and proceeded to tell me in very threatening words and tones that the owner had a long-standing reputation for using every means available to him, litigation and otherwise, for exacting every dollar of lease revenue from lessees of his properties. I thanked him for the information, and told him our decision was made and not negotiable, and we would be moving out and closing the store, which we did at the end of that year.

Over the ensuing several months, as advertised, the litigation was begun, along with repeated threatening phone calls from both the owner and his rep. I did my best to hold back my ever-increasing anger, and finally told them to do whatever they wanted, and stopped taking their phone calls. We were served with papers, and a court date was set. We prayed and prayed about what we should do, and if we needed to spend the money to hire an attorney.

About a month before the scheduled court date, the Lord woke me up at 3:00 A.M., the time he often chooses to awaken me when he has something prophetic to speak to me. He told me in very stern terms, "I want you to call this man tomorrow, and tell him this...." At the end of it, He said, "And, I'll be your defense attorney; you won't need another!" The sternness of His voice and the sharpness of the words He gave me to say to the man, shook me to my core, but I knew without a shadow of a doubt it was God speaking to me."

As He told me, I called the man the next day. I said exactly the words the Lord had given me to say:

"Sir, I know you don't know this, because I've never told you, and I also know you will not accept or believe one word I say, but God Almighty woke me up last night and told me to tell you that He is giving you one last opportunity to listen to what He's told you three times now, the last time being last night in your sleep, that if you do not drop this lawsuit there will be grave consequences for you, because this man who is speaking to you is not just an ordinary man, he's one of my prophets, and I said in My Word TWICE, 'Touch not My anointed ones, and do My prophets NO HARM!'"

Then, I said, "Sir, I believe God, and that these were the words He told me to speak to you; if I were you, I'd do what He says." And I hung up the phone.

About three weeks later, we had not heard a thing from the man, and I got a phone call from one of my former employees who lived in an apartment complex right behind "The Hill," which was also owned by the mall-owner. She said, "Dr. Lambert, you heard about it, right?"

I said, "Heard about what? No, I don't know what you're talking about."

She snapped back, "Well, it was on the news, thought sure you had seen it! You know all those torrential rains we've had over the last three weeks that they've been talking about on the weather and news?"

"Yes," I replied, wonderingly.

"Well, all that rain caused a huge sink-hole under 'The Hill'—the ground opened up and swallowed half the hill and the entire one semi-circle of building that your store was in! Your store and half of the shopping center is GONE! It's 50 to 100 feet down in the sink-hole! Can you believe it?!"

I paused a few moments to absorb what she had just said, then, finally, I responded in an even tone, "Well, to tell you the truth, and you will find this hard to believe, but, yes, I CAN believe it; we serve an AWESOME and MIGHTY God! Thank you for calling."

I hung up the phone, told my wife the news, and we had a shoutin', laughin', rejoicin', and dancin' hoedown for about two hours until we had no more strength and fell into bed exhausted that night!

We never heard from the man, his rep, or his attorneys again. I guess if you don't have a building anymore, it's pretty much, "CASE CLOSED," as far as any lawsuits are concerned!

"Do not touch My anointed ones, And do My prophets no harm!"[46] This story illustrated to me just how much God means what He says concerning not opposing and doing anything to come against one of God's chosen, anointed, and appointed prophets to harm them in any way. As I said, I know how abused and misused this scripture is by men, especially those trying to excuse or justify their wrongful actions and conduct. But we must always bear in mind that what man does with God's Word does not alter or detract from the fact that He means what He says and says what He means! And no matter how often a scripture is cited or overly-used, God's Word is never a meaningless cliché, for, "The grass withers, the flower fades, But the word of our God stands forever."[47]

It's just not wise to "tempt God," for as Korah and the entire several generations of his lineage along with 250 leaders of the congregation, "men of renown," found out when they engaged in a rebellion against Moses, whereby the ground opened up and swallowed Korah and his family, followed by fire of the Lord coming down and burning up the 250 leaders, doing so can result in some very unusual and harsh, unintended (by you) consequences, orchestrated by God Himself! Note that this wasn't the devil doing this to bring judgment against these rebels, it was GOD!

That's the moral of that story, as well as mine. But the other moral is that we serve an AWESOME and MIGHTY God, who takes care of His people, leaders and laymen alike! He is the defense attorney of those who will but put all their trust in Him to save and deliver them...from the guttermost to the uttermost! **Vengeance is Mine, sayeth the Lord!**

We *never* have to take up our own cause and enact a plan of vengeance against our enemies who fire their flaming missiles our way; God will always do a much better job of that than we could ever even conjure up! I know that's true from personal experience, and this one story I shared is just one of many wherein the Lord was my defender and justifier as I left the vengeance to Him and fought the good fight of faith!

Extinguishing Flaming Arrows of the IRS

Another experience of such outright persecution authored by the devil I experienced occurred back in the mid-1980s associated with that business I spoke about in the previous experience I related.

As I said, by the direction of the Lord, my late wife and I started a business that almost immediately became very popular and well-known in the town we lived in at the time. God prospered it and us as we applied His principles of success and prosperity, including being very generous in our giving to Him and to those in need. With my background in radio and television, I wrote and recorded in my own voice, many very unusual radio spots promoting our business, that aired on a prominent local radio station in an advertising campaign consisting of a package of ads encompassing and sponsoring Paul Harvey News and Commentary at Noon. It was probably the most valuable and effective advertising spot on the station or any station in that listening area, Monday through Friday. It was expensive, but good advertising always is, and absolutely vital to the success of any business. As I said, the scripts were very unusually written, for both a 30-second and 60-second spot in each daily package, airing as a "doughnut" around the program.

Just about every week someone would come into the store and hear me talking and would exclaim, "That's the voice!" or "I recognize that voice!" To which I would plead guilty and thank them for listening and patronizing our store. My wife, Sandy, was the unchallenged "celebrity" of our business, which was a women's fashion center predicated on the highly popular and trending "Color Analysis" principle that was becoming so well-known at the time. Many of the scripts I wrote were centered on this procedure many women had heard about and were anxious to put to work for themselves with respect to their outer appearance and image. The ads were bringing women into our store by the droves. Everything we had envisioned for our new business venture was all working and working in spades! We were grateful to God and thrilled at how God was working through all our efforts and bringing glory to Himself in the process.

At the start of fall in our third year in business, a reporter for a small local newspaper came into the store, asking to speak to the owners. Sandy first spoke to her, and then called me in my office and asked me to come out to speak to the lady. Her story was that she had recently repented from a long involvement in the occult and as a practicing psychic, and surrendered her life to the Lord Jesus, which was thrilling to hear! She then proceeded to explain that she had very recently been hired by the newspaper as the editor and writer for local human-interest stories and she had heard so many good things about our business that she wanted to do what turned out to be a six-part story about our business focusing specifically on the concept of God prospering believers in Christ who put their trust and belief in Him. Well, we could hardly turn down this God-provided golden opportunity to give glory to God for all that He was doing with and through our new business venture, along with the wonderful side-effect of more exposure for our business! We graciously agreed to her interviews and pledge to publish the articles in six special forthcoming issues highlighting our business! We were thrilled, honored, and humbled!

As promised, she conducted several interviews over the ensuing weeks, and wrote the articles based on our comments about how the business came about and what we believed God was doing through the agency of our lives and business. I explained that when we started the business, we had given our lives to the Lord some ten years previously, and all during that time, my primary work was various forms of ministry in which I was fully ensconced. Ironically (or perhaps not), the year we started our business I had just finished writing and publishing my very first book, which was the *Mystery of the Kingdom* book I've mentioned several times in this book, and which has a promotional page in the back of this book.

My wife adamantly and boldly declared often that one of the reasons she felt so strongly about launching out into the deep to start this business was so that God could use it as a source of funding for my writing/publishing ministry, which she just knew that God wanted to use long into the future. Sandy was without any doubt my strongest supporter for all the thirty years we were married. Bless her heart! She was always all-in when it came to my ministry. In her mind, I was the greatest minister who ever preached a message! God help the person who would dare to criticize or denigrate me and my ministry in her hearing! She would very nicely, calmly, but firmly "rip them to shreds" verbally!

Without any doubt whatsoever I know that Sandy's name is written in the Lamb's book of life, and that she is now enjoying her eternal rewards, dancing, rejoicing, and singing in her alto voice at the top of her lungs the high praises of God, just as she used to always accompany me in our worship ministry, singing many worship choruses with me playing rhythm 12-string guitar! Oh, how wonderful those days were! I miss them horribly! But I know that I know that I know that I will someday soon see Sandy again. I owe her so much, including that I surrendered my life to the Lord because she did it very publicly one Christmas Eve in a small church in the then tiny town of Longwood, Florida, in which she replied to a simple altar call and was heard by everyone in attendance weeping and wailing at the altar, begging God for the forgiveness of her sin and to be saved! Her actions that night totally embarrassed me in my unsaved state in which my ego reigned superior to all else. But beginning a few weeks later when I too surrendered my life to the Lord (that's another story altogether that I plan to write about someday), in a safety zone in a parking lot of the Altamonte Springs Mall with two other men obliviously praying with their eyes closed and hot wet tears flowing from their eyes while car after car drove all around them! Little did those patrons know that in those few minutes another soul was being snatched out of the cold, strong grip of the devil, and an international ministry was being inaugurated! No one but God could have known what was happening in that mall parking lot and all its ramifications! Glory be to God! Bottom line was God won and the devil lost big time! Hallelujah!

The good news of that newspaper series was that God used it to produce a significant increase in enthusiastic patrons that at times was too much for our small staff to handle! We had to add to our sales staff, who we had to hurriedly train, just to service the influx of patrons! That was the good news, but the other shoe, that we could not have possibly envisioned, was about to fall.

At the start of our third year in business we heard through our accountant, and it was later published in the local newspaper, that the IRS was opening some new offices in various parts of the country and especially in Florida, where we lived. Not only did that happen, but when the new office replete with some fifty new agents opened it was located in the same mall of converted offices our store was located in down on the ground floor! The IRS was on the hunt for businesses that were not paying their taxes, ostensibly based on reports and allegations by tipsters that there was a lot of tax-evasion going on in that town and its environs! As it turned out years later, most of those reports and allegations turned out to be just that—allegations and innuendo—that were never proved to the extent alleged. The new special IRS office was opened and staffed based on false information a few people were reporting in an effort to weaponize the IRS against business owners and businesses they opposed or were jealous of. The claim of a vast number of business owners who were evading paying taxes was a hoax and did not exist!

When I heard about this development, I thought great, I'm all in favor of Americans paying their taxes! I believe in that! I had no concerns whatsoever, because I knew how properly and legally our business was accounting for everything it did financially, because I was the one keeping the books! I had had some education and training in accounting before we started the business during my schooling days. Never did it even cross my mind that OUR business would be one of the businesses targeted by the IRS in their initial "witch-hunt" for businesses to prove they were paying their taxes as they should. But ours was one of the very first who received those letters the IRS sent out, indicating that we would be subject to a complete audit. After we got over the shock of that, we had another layer of shock and dismay to deal with in the matter, in that the agent assigned to our case had *never* conducted an audit before; ours was her very *first* one, she informed me on her initial visit! Wonderful! Uhhh...but it turned out it wasn't wonderful, but unimaginable in terms of what we would have to deal with over the next *five* years!

The first thing the agent did after examining our books, after I happily provided her copies of all requested documents and reports for the previous three years of our business history, was to formulate her version of a profit and loss statement, the likes of which I had never in my life seen, and which defied every generally accepted practice (GAP) ever devised in the history of modern accounting systems! When I showed it to my accountant, we both just sat there staring at it, wondering what in the world we were looking at. It appeared to both of our trained eyes as complete hieroglyphics, and this is the standard by which our audit would be conducted! We were both *stunned*, to say the least! When we talked to the newbie agent about it later, we went round and round with her, informing her that what she had presented was not a legitimate profit and loss statement by all generally accepted practices and we could not make heads or tails of it! She kept insisting it was right and it was we who were wrong!

For over five years I had to expend massive amounts of my time, energy, and money answering all the crazy and non-sensical questions and veiled accusations this woman was levying against us, as well as wrangle with her about her lack of knowledge about proper accounting processes. It was horrible! At times, unbearable! We agonized over it! It progressively became an all-out persecution by a government agency of our native nation which we loved, whose government we respected, and in whose Armed Forces I served honorably for the best part of five years! It was outrageous, but also disheartening. For five long years we endured the attacks, accusations, and falsehood waged against us, though we had always gladly paid every single dime of tax we rightfully owed the government, grateful that we had earned the money we had for which the tax was due!

Finally, after nearly five years of enduring this long, drawn out process, I received a notice to appear before a special magistrate who functions as the arbiter between auditees and the IRS in Orlando, Florida, approximately thirty days hence, to which I was to bring any supporting documents regarding the audit and the accounting procedures we employed relating ultimately to the paying of taxes due. It all seemed so ominous, and not at all something I was relishing. But it had to be done. So, I went to the hearing, having fought the good fight of faith during this whole long ordeal, believing with everything within me and prophesying that God would ultimately be my defense and thoroughly vindicate us of any and all accusations of wrongdoing!

What a complete and utter surprise it was when the magistrate commenced the hearing with just me and her in small room in an Orlando business district building from whence the cold, impersonal, imposing "business" of the IRS was conducted, and after swearing me in, began by saying, "Mr. Lambert, thank you for appearing here today. On behalf of the federal government, I offer you our sincerest apologies for all that you have endured during this lengthy audit process. My findings, after thoroughly investigating all matters pertinent to the audit, are that no irregularities or improper accounting practices were found, and that not only did you and your business pay all the taxes due during the last five business years, but it was discovered that there were additional tax deductions to which you were entitled under the IRS laws and rules you did not take that would result in additional refund of taxes paid. I have performed an administrative revision of your refund forms, and have issued a check from the U.S. Department of Treasury payable to your business, for the amount of refund to which your business is entitled." With that she stood up, reached out her right hand for a handshake and a check in her left hand, and asked that I accept her and the U.S. federal government's apology and refund check. Of course, I graciously and with all sincere humility accepted both and shook her hand. After asking if I had any questions, she adjourned the hearing, for the recorded record!

What a great phone call I was able to make to my wife who was tending the store while I attended the hearing! We both did a lot of shouting and thanking God for His mercy and grace and intervention in having this matter brought to its rightful and proper close.

In the end, what I kept saying throughout turned out to be exactly the case: that this was all the flaming arrows of false accusation from the evil one, who was attempting to do everything he could to impugn my personal integrity and desecrate the public image of our business that God had told us to start and He would use as a source to supply our personal financial needs and to bring glory and honor to His Name! He did all of that, just as He had promised us prophetically, proving that both Joshua and King David indicated, not one word of all His good promises in His Word have ever failed:

> "Now behold, today I am going the way of all the earth, and you know in all your hearts and in all your souls that *not one word of all the good* words which the LORD your God spoke concerning you *has failed*; all have been fulfilled for you, *not one of them has failed*."[48]

> "Blessed be the LORD, who has given rest to His people Israel, *according to all that He promised*; *not one word has failed of all His good promise*, which He promised through Moses His servant."[49]

We found out in the course of time that the false allegations made against us and our business were reported to the IRS by jealous and malicious "tipsters" who despised the whole "prosperity gospel" and what God had done in our lives based on His published promises to those who are "givers" to give unto them and return their giving to them in "good measure, pressed down, shaken together, and running over!"[50] The Lord did in our lives *exactly* what He promised to do in His Word! He prospered us, rewarding us in many ways for our faithful and diligent labors and faith in His promises by which we gained His favor and rightstanding![51] Praise the Lord!

> "Now it shall be, if you *diligently obey the LORD your God, being careful to do all His commandments which I command you today,* the LORD your God will *set you high above all the nations of the earth.* "*All these blessings* will come upon you and overtake you if you obey the LORD your God: "Blessed shall you be *in the city,* and blessed shall you be in *the country.* "Blessed shall be the *offspring of your body* and *the produce of your ground* and the *offspring of your beasts,* the *increase of your herd* and the *young of your flock.* "Blessed shall be your basket and your *kneading bowl.* "Blessed shall you be when you *come in,* and blessed shall you be when you *go out.* "The LORD shall cause your enemies who rise up against you to be *defeated before you*; they will come out against you one way and will *flee before you seven ways.* "The LORD will command the blessing upon you in your *barns* and in *all that you put your hand to,* and He will bless you in the *land* which the LORD your God gives you. "The LORD will *establish* you as a holy people to Himself, as He swore to you, *if you keep the commandments of the LORD your God and walk in His ways.* "So all the peoples of the earth will see that you are called by the name of the LORD, and they will be afraid of you. "The LORD will make you *abound in prosperity,* in the offspring of your body and in the offspring of your beast and in the produce of your ground, in the land which the LORD swore to your fathers to give you. "The LORD will open for you *His good storehouse,* the *heavens,* to give rain to your land in its season and to *bless all the work of your hand*; and you shall lend to many nations, but you shall not borrow. "The LORD will make you the *head and not the tail,* and you only will be *above,* and you will not be *underneath,* if you listen

to the commandments of the LORD your God, which I charge you today, to *observe them carefully*, and *do not turn aside* from any of the words which I command you today, to the right or to the left, to *go after other gods* to serve them.[52]

The Lord fulfilled all these good promises of prosperity and success, all because of our simple, child-like faith and obedience. We obeyed; He fulfilled!

Not only that did God do through this series of articles in that small hometown newspaper as a result of our faith and obedience, but He also used the exposure generated through those articles to ultimately propel me back into full-time ministry when the time for this period of our lives in which I had left the ministry to pursue this business venture was suddenly and abruptly brought to a screeching halt. It all happened during the stock market crash and mortgage rate crises set in motion by the Fed, and ensuing deflation-inflation that occurred in the nation that generated a monstrous financial fall beginning in 1986. It devastated the many horse farms on which the economy in the area where we lived was founded, never to return to its former state and status. As suddenly and unexpectedly God blessed the founding of our business, He also suddenly and unexpectedly brought it to an end! "The LORD gave and the LORD has taken away. Blessed be the name of the LORD."[53]

The Lord later told me in no uncertain terms that the time He had used our business as a source of supply was only a temporary allowance He had granted us because we had asked in faith believing for it, but that it was only intended to be a temporary allowance, not His *perfect* will, but His *permissive* will,[54] for a time. Now that time, He said, had ended, and it was time for me to return to the ministry to which He had called me! Now it was time for me to "endure hardship" and fulfill my ministry calling—the hardship fraught ministry of an apostolic-prophet, of which I had grown so weary before starting our business.

God had provided a temporary shelter for me for my discomfort about the ministry office He had appointed me to, much like Jonah and the plant God provided him for temporary shade from the physical heat of the summer as well as the "heat" of his ministry:

> But it greatly displeased Jonah and he became angry. He prayed to the LORD and said, "Please LORD, was not this what I said

while I was still in my own country? Therefore in order to forestall this I fled to Tarshish, for I knew that You are a gracious and compassionate God, slow to anger and abundant in lovingkindness, and one who relents concerning calamity. "Therefore now, O LORD, please take my life from me, for death is better to me than life." The LORD said, "Do you have good reason to be angry?" Then Jonah went out from the city and sat east of it. There he made a *shelter for himself and sat under it in the shade* until he could see what would happen in the city. *So the LORD God appointed a **plant** and it grew up over Jonah to be a **shade** over his head to deliver him from his **discomfort**. And Jonah was extremely happy about the plant. But God appointed a **worm** when dawn came the next day and it attacked the plant and it **withered**.* When the sun came up *God appointed a scorching east wind, and the sun beat down on Jonah's head so that he became **faint** and begged with all his soul to die,* saying, "Death is better to me than life." Then God said to Jonah, "Do you have good reason to be angry about the plant?" And he said, "I have good reason to be angry, even to death." Then the LORD said, "You had compassion on the plant for which you did not work and which you did not cause to grow, which came up overnight and perished overnight. "Should I not have compassion on Nineveh, the great city in which there are more than 120,000 persons who do not know the difference between their right and left hand, as well as many animals?"⁵⁵

As with so many trials, troubles, and tribulations I experienced in my career as an apostolic-prophet, this was another in which God ultimately caused all things to work together for the good to those who love Him and are called according to His purposes, in order to conform me more into the image of His Son, and make me more of a mature son of God myself:

And we know that *God causes **all things** to work together for good* to those who love God, to those who are called according to His purpose. For those whom He foreknew, He also *predestined to become conformed to the image of His Son*, so that He would be the firstborn (πρωτοτοκος, prototokos, Gr. [prototype, model]) among many brethren; and these whom He predestined, He also called; and these whom He called, He also justified; and these whom He justified, He also glorified.⁵⁶

For as many as are *led by the Spirit of God, they are the* (mature; υἱος, Gr.) *sons of God*.⁵⁷

For the anxious longing of the creation waits eagerly for the revealing of the *sons of God*.⁵⁸

That ye may be blameless and harmless, *the sons of God*, without rebuke, in the midst of a crooked and perverse nation, among whom ye shine as lights in the world;⁵⁹

Extinguishing Flaming Arrows of a Louisiana Lunatic

More than a decade ago now, I was contacted by a man from Louisiana, who had been receiving my emails and following my online teaching ministry in the form of the many articles I have published that are posted on several of our websites. In the beginnings of my online presence in the mid-1990s, I published articles primarily on my main ministry website, SLM.org in the form of a blog. In time, when blog hosting became available through various platforms, I created three different blogs to post my articles on. Later, the capacity to post articles to blogs made it more practical to take advantage of that methodology. Most of the articles I write, I write with the intention of one day incorporating the content into books I intend to write when I can on a larger topic as a part of a bigger picture.

This man from Louisiana had been reading my articles for several months, particularly the articles touching on the matter of Fivefold Ministry and the function of each of those offices as delineated in Scripture. Anyone who has investigated my ministry thoroughly enough to see the big picture of what I do in the Kingdom and for the advancement of the Kingdom of God, will at some point be confronted with one of the books for which I am best known by many, despite the fact that that is far from my intention. I speak of my book, **Charismatic Captivation**—*Authoritarian Abuse & Psychological Enslavement in Neo-Pentecostal Churches*, to which an entire website is devoted, Charismatic-Captivation.com. The book was originally published in 1996, after requiring more than three years to write. As the title and subtitle indicate, the primary subject of the book is the systematic hyper-authoritarianism that emerged and was widely propagated in the 1970s through the vehicle of what became known as the "Shepherding Movement" or "Discipleship Movement." For more information about the book, and the booklet I wrote and published as somewhat of a primer on the larger book, **Charismatic Control**, I refer you to the promotional pages at the back of this book.

Since the book was originally published, it has become somewhat of a classic, and perhaps the most recognized book on the subject of hyper-authoritarianism in Neo-Pentecostal church streams. A search of various topics pertinent to the Discipleship Movement or Shepherding Movement on Wikipedia will turn up various articles citing my book as an authority on the topic. As I state in the book:

> Extending a hand of deliverance and recovery to victims of *Charismatic Captivation* resulting from erroneous doctrines and practices is the sole motivation for the writing of this book. And, that hand is extended to every victim of this demonic perpetration, which, I believe includes...the other surviving original propagators of the Discipleship doctrines and practices, those who remain proponents and participants, as well as those who were unwittingly captivated in the throes of deception. Debunking and disproving these heretical doctrines is only a necessary precursor to this overriding objective of ministering to those who need ministry.
>
> People are not the problem. Nor are they the adversary, the devil is (1 Pet. 5:8). Without equivocation or qualm, I reiterate that this book is a spiritual counteroffensive, launched against the satanic powers that have been surreptitiously laboring virtually unimpeded and unknown for years within the Church through the propagation of this doctrine of demons. Every weapon of spiritual warfare is being deployed herewith, and precisely trained to score a direct hit against these demonic powers, in order to expose and totally decimate them. That is the sole objective and mission. In no way, is anything in this volume a personal attack on any person. That would serve no useful purpose.
>
> Many in the Church today fail to recognize that whatever God does, He does through willing members of His Body. Jesus is the Head, but **WE** are His Body. The supernatural intervention of God unto those needing His outstretched hand of ministry, of which I have spoken, will be manifest only through someone

with the fortitude and willingness to be used by the Lord to bring the needed attention and reproof to the matter, despite the personal cost. Thus, having circumspectly counted the cost, selected five smooth stones from the brook of the Spirit, and looked the adversary dead in the eye, I echo the words of David unto the Philistine champion, Goliath:

"You come to me with a sword, a spear, and a javelin, but I come to you in the name of the Lord of hosts, the God of the armies of Israel, whom you have taunted. This day the Lord will deliver you up into my hands and I will strike you down and remove your HEAD from you. And I will give the dead bodies of the army of the Philistines this day to the birds of the sky and the wild beasts of the earth, that all the earth may know that there is a God in Israel, and that all this assembly may know that the Lord does not deliver by sword or by spear; for the battle is the Lord's and He will give you into our hands." (1 Sam. 17:45-47)[60]

After the book was published, a somewhat strange phenomenon began to emerge, which in time I began to understand was really not "strange" at all, but is something that should be expected. The phenomenon I refer to is that people who are guilty of practicing the very thing a book such as this exposes—hyper-authoritarianism, in this case—are attracted to the book and discussion about the subject-matter! What I learned about this, as well as the same phenomenon involving other matters, is that the evil spirits that are behind such spiritual "problems" cause violators or perpetrators to be drawn to the writing on the subject like flies to ointment, as the saying goes. Write on the subject of exposing the Jezebel Spirit, as I have in many articles and portions of my books, for example, and people operating in the Jezebel Spirit are drawn to and somehow always find such writings when and where they are posted. Write on sexual perversion and deviancy, as another example, and sexual perverts and deviates somehow are supernaturally drawn to and find the articles, and either become critics of what you are teaching in the writings, or they RUN from your ministry and every vestige they find of it, so as to evade conviction on the matter, and the resultant "repentance that leads to life."[61]

A prime example is the matter of my website, DeliveranceNow.com, which is my deliverance counseling ministry website that I have operated online for more than twenty years now. Who is drawn to the website and the articles posted there on the subject of deliverance, i.e., casting out of demons? Well, demonized people, of course, who because they are demonized become "stirred up" inwardly by all the information on the site concerning the operation of demons in people's lives, including the lives of purporting "Christians," believers! But does the wealth of information concerning demonization and being delivered from same motivate those people to pursue freedom via deliverance? Oh no! The effect is the opposite: demonized readers are repelled by the site and *run* from it! So, in a way, such a site is a catch-22—you create and maintain it to minister to people who desperately need it, but the demons influencing them are what drives them away from the site. Demons are *petrified* of any mention of deliverance ministry, especially some who are genuinely anointed for deliverance ministry! Literally *petrified*! They know that all that needs to occur is someone command them to leave in Jesus Name, and they must obey and leave! They have no choice. The Name which is above every other name named on Earth is higher and exerts more authority than any other name on Earth, and every knee must bow to that Name!

> For it is written, As I live, saith the Lord, *every knee shall bow to me*, and every tongue shall confess to God.[62]

> That at the name of Jesus *every knee should bow*, of things in heaven, and things in earth, and things under the earth;[63]

Such was the case with this man, who I have come to call, "The Louisiana Lunatic!" Why? Because in the process of time he demonstrated that he literally was a demonized lunatic, deeply affected with demons of mental illness! When he first started contacting me by email, he was relating to articles about Fivefold Ministry, and the matter of "authority" related to same, in particular. In time, he revealed that he was a disciple of some of the founders and principals of the Latter Rain Movement that began in 1949 in Battleford, Saskatchewan, Canada. There were good things that emerged from that movement, such as some understanding about the matter of Fivefold Ministry and its continued function in the Church that Jesus is building. As I recall, I believe this man, who considered himself to be a pastor and Bible teacher, was 18 years or so older than me. He was drawn to many of the core matters and topics my ministry focused on over the years.

After some email exchanges, this man called me one day, and began to fill in more details about himself and his ministry. He said he was a retired mail carrier with the U.S. Postal Service with a thirty-year career in same. Because of his job, he was personally well-known in the city in the area in which he was born and lived his entire life. While that would normally be a good thing, in this case, not so much, because what I later learned was that he had developed a reputation in terms of his ministry as being a nut-case and whacko! Especially among the other ministers and church leaders of the many churches in the area. His obvious mental issues were common knowledge, though he had never been so officially diagnosed by a mental health professional. When he contacted me, he was in his fifth year of a new marriage to a woman who was herself formerly married to another preacher in the area, whom she justly divorced for various scriptural causes. This was his second marriage as well, as a result of the fact that his first wife divorced him after nearly 30 years of marriage, due to his increasing mental illness and the plethora of issues stemming from that, including a fiery, uncontrolled temper, and fits of rage against his wife and their children.

Of course, when I first started talking to the man, I knew none of this in the natural, but in the spirit, I was sensing and discerning things about him, right from the get-go. He was saying all the right things, especially about the spiritual matters our conversations encompassed, but still, my spirit was telling me, something's not quite right. In the process of time I learned a whole lot of somethings was not right about this man—his "ministry," and his personal life.

Eventually he invited me to come to minister at his church in Louisiana. When the Lord sends me out, it is generally in my capacity of an apostolic-prophet, though my medium of ministry is often that of a teacher. I teach more than I preach generally speaking. So, when I travel to churches, the Lord uses me to discern and define problem areas of the church, though many times the reason for my host's inviting me to minister is their desire for me to affirm and/or confirm *them* in their leadership of the church. Thus, the reason the host has invited me and their goals in that respect are often in direct conflict with the Lord's reasons for sending me there. My role and assignment from God is to speak on behalf of God what *He* wants to speak to the congregation and its leaders, not to speak on behalf of and as a proxy for the leaders. This is what genuine, God-anointed and God-appointed ministers do! Prophets are spokesman of *God*, not *men*. Therein lies the crux of the confrontation. Then when the apostolic aspect is added to the mix, invariably, the focus becomes the government and operandi of the church, because apostles and prophets, together with Christ Jesus as the Cornerstone, formulate the foundation of the church.[64] Again, it is almost invariably here where conflicts arise and create contention with the local church house leadership, who invariably wholeheartedly believe they are "owners" and therefore ultimate leaders of the church entity, while God holds that Christ Jesus is the legitimate and literal Head of the Church He is building,[65] which He purchased with His shed blood!

This was *certainly* the case in this case. God sent me to minister to the man as the leader of the local house, which in the end would filter down to ministry to the congregation. This was a classic case of the leader using the podium and platform as a bully-pulpit, as a means to browbeat the people, rather than lovingly educate, edify, and encourage them, which is what the ministry is all about. This man was verbally and emotionally abusive to his congregation and his family members, which now were his wife and her grown children from another marriage, because his own family members with his former wife had all left and were estranged from him, and wanted nothing to do with him, due to his lifetime of abusiveness towards them!

The gist of this prophet versus house-leader was: differing perspectives and roles of the two participants—me and him. Each side saw the mission and purpose of God's sending to the group from opposite perspectives. On the one hand, the local house leadership, who consisted of a few sycophants, yes-people, who were scared to death of the chief leader, thought they were remunerating the visiting minister in the form of any honorarium they would deign to give me over and above all travel expenses in exchange for affirmation and approval of them and their leadership before the rest of the congregation by me. On the other hand, *my* perspective was that I obeyed God who was sending me there as His agent, representative, proxy, working on *His* behalf to discern and detect problematic issues between the leadership and the congregants that require reproof and correction to resolve them. This was a congregation that obviously wanted to stay together to serve God, but were reeling under the heavy hand of hyper-authortarianistic abuse! I sensed in the Spirit that the situation was grievous to God, and therefore to me.

From the moment the leader picked me up at the airport, despite the surface cordiality, there was demonically-inspired tension between us I could literally feel, that continued for the entire three days I was there! It was not a pleasant experience. It was not until my plane was flying over the territory where I had just spent those three long days and nights that the cloud of darkness of the spirits operating in that situation finally left me. I was so glad to get out of there and be on my way home!

The weird thing was, when we parting company at the airport, the leader said he would be calling me in a few weeks, because he wanted me to return and speak to his small congregation more. When he said that, I was shocked, and thought to myself, "Yeah, that ain't happening! He's just trying to save face and put a good look on what we just experienced, he'll never call again, and if he does, I'm darn sure not going to go back!

I wish that was what happened, but it wasn't! What happened was: he did call and ask for me to come back, and told me he would again pay for all my travel expenses for another three days of ministry as well as an honorarium. And the worst part was when I prayed and prayed and prayed about it, the Lord kept telling me the same thing, that He wanted me, it was His will, that I accept the invitation and go back to what to me was a horrible, demon-charged, scenario, and He told me (actually showed me in a dream) exactly what and how He wanted me to minister.

The first night I arrived, he and his wife took me out to eat at one of their favorite restaurants with typical "Luzanna" fare! It was delicious food, but overshadowing the whole event was this dark, evil, demonic tension in the air, between them, and between them and me. Again, it was anything but pleasant. But the food sure was good! No matter what is going on when it's time to eat, I eat, and in those days, I was on a "see-food" diet, I ate all the food I saw! And when it's time to sleep, no matter what is going on, I sleep! Scripture says the God of Israel neither sleeps nor slumbers, so I always figure there's no sense in both of us staying awake, so I go to sleep! Hallelujah! So, I slept well that night, despite the dark pall hovering over my bed in my bedroom in the man's house he had himself designed!

One of the preacher's obsessions was wanting his local ministry to be known, not as a church, but a "teaching center." He was trying to establish the impression that the focus of the ministry was teaching, in particular, vis-à-vis being a local church. He had various reasons for that objective, some of which was related to his divorce and the common perception about the "qualifications" of an elder indicated in the New Testament Scripture, some of which are misconceptions.[66] He also did not want the ministry to be viewed as local churches typically are, which has legitimacy I agree with. I have implemented the same approach with my local endeavors in the past as well, though I am not currently leading or even attempting to develop a local ministry, per se, myself, despite maintaining a local church ministry administratively, chartered under the auspices of the network I oversee as the prefect and overseer, Ephesians Four Network of Churches & Ministers (ephesiansfour.net).

In this case, the problem was not with the teaching center model, but rather *was* his dogmatic teaching, which was reflective of the aberrant Latter Day Rain teachings; more particularly, the more radical, bizarre, unbiblical teachings of William Branham, who died prematurely in 1960 as a result of injuries suffered in a head-on automobile crash at that hands of a drunk driver who had suddenly swerved into the lane his car with trailer in tow travelling in the early morning hours on a lonesome stretch of highway in Texas on his way home to Missouri for Christmas holidays. The Lord was taking him out, unfortunately, due to some of these outlandish and heretical teachings. Branham's calling was not a Bible teacher, and got out of his lane in attempting to be one—a story that should serve as a profound lesson to anyone else who would launch out on his own to pursue a ministry to which he/she is not called. This preacher would have done well to have, as an avid Branham devotee, learned this lesson. Sadly, he did not.

I am convinced this preacher used the second visit as a means to discredit me before his followers because they had such a favorable reaction to my ministry and what occurred during the three nights of meetings and were clamoring for more. The meetings we had were powerful: many healings, deliverances, prophetic words, and release of anointing upon most everyone in attendance, a large percentage of which were people not of his small congregation but people who had heard about the meetings through radio spots which were running in advance of the meetings, some of whom attended other churches and some who did not. Every night ended up with most everyone in the building being "slain in the spirit" at least once, many multiple times. The feedback from attendees after the meetings were glowing, with many reports of healings, deliverances, and prophetic direction and counsel received as I ministered by the Spirit.

The odd thing was that in the days leading up to the meetings, both the first and the second trip, the Lord specifically told me: Don't *teach* on any particular topics; let me fill your mouth prophetically and extemporaneously"; which is what I did! Everything I uttered in each of the total of four meetings was prophetic! One of the things that made the man so angry that he couldn't see straight was how my ministering was touching his wife and her children—they were all slain in the spirit and received from the Lord, some several times. His jealousy absolutely enraged him and was like waving a red cape in front of a bull! He was infuriated in a very obvious manner! None of which made any sense, because, obviously, none of those things were me doing it, but *God* doing it! *God's* dunamis-power is what causes people to be slain in the spirit and experience inordinate supernatural experiences in His presence, not any that I have!

His next move was to wait until most of the attendees had left the building, and he called me back to his office, where he had assembled members of his "board." He had solicited each and every member to back him in his attempt to "dress me down" and levy his complaint against me, which, since there was such overwhelmingly favorable response to all the ministry, required him to come up with some lame, non-sensical, and certainly demonic criticism, which, essentially, was, "You never did teach! This is a teaching center! We brought you here to teach!"

My response the Lord filled my mouth with was: "Everything I did in all four of the meetings *was* teaching—that all the attendees desperately needed and were looking for! I just didn't deliver it through a teaching mode, but as a prophet!"

"That wasn't teaching, and it wasn't prophetic either; that was all horse _ _ _ _!" he fired back!

I heard the Lord say in my spirit, "Say no more!"

His reaction was so vehement and he was so enraged in his flesh that when we returned to his house after having a breakfast meal following the meeting, after getting out of the car and allowing his wife to enter the door from the garage to the house, he shoved me against the door jam and actually took a swing at me, which I easily sidestepped, and growled in a low-volume and -pitched voice, trying to keep his wife from hearing, "I'd like to kill you, you son-of-a-bitch!" I immediately recognized it was demons talking through him, though the man himself was obviously a biblically certified *murderer*, thereby disqualified from eternal life.[67] I knew he had multiple weapons in the house, some of which were displayed in a gun rack in the recreation room. Though my adrenaline was flowing, I wasn't at all shaken emotionally, but surprisingly calm. The man went to his bedroom and never came out. Later, I heard his wife making the rounds to close up the house and set the coffeemaker for the next morning.

That night, about two hours after I had laid down to sleep, around 1:30 AM, the Lord awakened me, and said to me in forceful words, "I want you to get up right now, get dressed, pack your bags, leave the house while the man is asleep, and call a taxi to pick you up and take you to the airport. Call Angela (my daughter)," who I had already told everything that had transpired, "while you are waiting to change your flight to a direct flight home to PBA," all of which I immediately did. The taxi met me several blocks down the street at the entrance of the development where this man's extravagant house was located (he claimed to have a lot of money). By noon that day, after a 45-minute limo trip, all at my own expense (the man also had not yet paid me any honorarium or remuneration for my travel expenses), I was home safe and sound, none the worse for the wear of the harrowing adventure.

I never talked to the man again! His wife was planning to divorce him, but before she could, a few years later, I learned he had suddenly died of a heart attack! Sadly, I don't believe this man made it to Heaven, but I'm certainly not the one who determines that.

Extinguishing Flaming Arrows of a Panama City Psycho

Sometime in 2006, the secretary of the chief leader of a church and ministerial network read some of my online writings on the prophetic and apostolic. She was particularly struck by the truths I wrote about "apostolic attributes," that mirrored some of what the leader she served had spoken over the years on the topic. Soon after, she emailed that the leader wanted to talk to me by phone, and an appointment for same was subsequently arranged.

In the ensuing phone conversation, after some pleasantries were exchanged, the man talked about who he was; his long history in apostolic leadership; how he had left the prominent Pentecostal denomination he had been a part of and had even served as the local presbyter over, some thirty years before over apostolic, prophetic, and other doctrinal differences. He then turned to the articles he had read that his secretary had given him links to. He commented about how closely what I wrote mirrored his own teachings over the years on the topics my articles addressed. Of course, that we agreed on so many aspects of same was both affirmational and encouraging. It's always good to know that there's at least someone out there in the world who agrees with what you have written about any matter. But I would soon learn there were also some glaring differences between his personal application to himself of some of the aspects of his extrapolations of the teachings from mine.

In many of his meetings, videos of which staff personnel had prepared and posted on the church's website, this now elderly, distinguished looking, eloquent leader frequently extolled the virtue of his departure in the years between 1969-1970 from that prominent Pentecostal denomination he had been a part of, as a masterful act for him and the beginning of a forty-plus year track as an apostle, though unaffirmed by his former denomination, or any other independent source, for that matter. Over time since, he became, in his own estimation, *"greater than* the Apostle Paul," he quipped frequently, in numerous ways, and based on those conclusions, had for decades been gradually gathering young and spiritually immature men and women to him as personal "sons and daughters" in order to grow his spiritual "family" over whom he had installed himself as their "Papa Apostle," he termed it, of the south Panhandle county in Florida from which he hailed. As he continued his campaign of drawing disciples unto himself,[68] he began commanding, essentially, his "sons and daughters" to give him honor and deference over the Lord, rebuking them when they failed to make a "draw" on *him* exclusively with questions about any and all spiritual matters. He frequently rebuked his followers when he learned that they were drawing from the ministry of any other legitimate ministers in the form of books, articles, and blogs on the now nascent World-Wide Web. He further spoke frequently about his "voice" being the primary "oracle" that God uses to impart wisdom and knowledge to his spiritual "children" and discouraged them even from studying the Bible and drawing upon the Lord over him. In the last few years, astoundingly, he expanded his maniacal vision, to include that one day he would conquer the world with *his voice*, thus becoming the "super apostle" of the universe to whom Jesus would impart special revelation and authority, *exclusively*.

Clearly, he saw himself as some sort of "super-hero" to the Body of Christ at-large, the international Church at-large, certainly to his own cult following, though relatively few in Christendom knew who he was, let alone his status as a *super apostle*, who was able to carry out actions and deeds greater than the Apostle Paul and reveal greater revelation than John the Revelator, the apostle whom Jesus loved![69]

From his bully-pulpit, which he had renamed when he withdrew the church-entity from the denomination it had been founded under, he pontificated frequently about his "voice" and the "Gospel" according to him, frequently perverting the Gospel and telling his congregants to cease studying the Bible on their own and instead exclusively listen to him as the proxy-interpreter sent to them by God, and to his "voice" as an oracle of God. He had progressively become a bona fide cult leader, instituting and indoctrinating his adherents with false doctrines promulgated during the Discipleship/Shepherding movement as well as extreme doctrines associated with The New Order of the Latter Rain movement, and all the well-documented, classic tenets of cults, throughout the churches under the auspices of his church-organization and likewise in the spiritual lives of his "sons and daughters."

His church's website documented that he had fathered twenty-three or more "spiritual sons" who "by choice" were now senior leaders of churches they had founded that were affiliated with him and the ministry network over which he presided, describing it was a free will covenant relationship he had with these spiritual "sons" though he also touted that this came in exchange for large sums of financial support they had received from his organization in order to plant churches and clone more "sons and daughters" after the likeness and image of the super-apostle. Each new church, the website touted, adopted the cult-brand, "The Rock of (whatever town or region they were headquartered in) for its name, growing the brand across the U.S. and other nations or protectorates, including the U.K. and another in Trinidad. All of these daughter-churches were required to tithe back to the mother-church, something which the super-apostle boasted about incessantly in his sermons, and that he was now a wealthy man due to the faithful giving of the congregants in the mother-church along with the tribute-tithes his "spiritual sons" paid him personally. Certainly, the spiritual law of tithing is from God and works as it promises to,[70] and every believer should be practicing it, but it is not meant to be abused by compulsion for the self-aggrandizing purposes of leaders who demand and require it.[71] The abuse is compounded when adherents are required and brow-beaten by the leadership into giving more than the ten percent tithe required by God on a regular and consistent basis even if it cuts into the money they need to pay their household expenditures and they are made to suffer consequences if they don't in terms of their "elevation" in the organization, and then on top of that they are forbidden to give to anyone other legitimate ministry of the Lord they may be receiving from. This compulsion and abuse of authority was a common denominator in all of the churches backed by this super-apostle. But it was just one of many abuses and common control devices he and his spiritual sons likewise employed to line their pockets with the blood, sweat, and tears of their congregants, with little thought of the financial hardship and debt their requirements were inflicting upon their adherents.

Moreover, though he certainly had an uncommon, expansive grasp of Scripture, he often used Scripture to wield authoritarian abuse upon members of his staff or affiliated leaders, publicly, in live meetings, many of which were on video that were posted online, though since his death, they have been taken down. There were many quotes I documented that demonstrated, in his own words, the heretical and demonic nature of many of his doctrines. While I myself never published anything about what I personally witnessed in this regard, there were a handful of other websites that did, including videos as irrefutable evidence. A short time before his death, there was one particularly censorial campaign he waged publicly and online regarding a young minister who had been one of his faithful acolytes and worship leaders for many years, who had recently left the church to launch out on his own to plant a church in the area. It was the most ungodly, demonically-motivated ad hominem attack I had personally ever witnessed in my decades of ministry! I felt so horrible for the super-apostle's vicious and malicious all-out assault on this young man! It made me weep several times when I watched the videos. It grieved me so, and so did it the Lord, I know. I even tried to reach out to the young man to console and encourage him, but he was too terrified of his human master to be able to receive it. I finally gave up. It still pains me to think about it, that any elderly spiritual leader could stoop so low as to inflict such a vehement malicious assault on *anyone*, much less a former faithful servant!

On my first visit to this man's church, the Lord had instructed me to talk to him not about apostolic and prophetic ministry matters, per se, but about his estranged relationships with his children, especially his son. He told me, however, to frame it in the context of the content of my book, *Charismatic Captivation*. On the way there, it was a little difficult for me to understand what exactly the Lord wanted me to say in this respect. However, He told me that when I was there sitting at a table, which He showed me, He would fill my mouth. And he did!

The Lord had told me to bring a copy of the book and present it to him as my gift to him. I did, and he asked me to sign it for him, which I did, with a personal inscription. He seemed genuinely grateful and certainly was gracious in receiving it. He had no idea what I had seen about him and his ministry before I arrived; I never told him. But, compared to how I knew he was capable of treating people, it was a bit of relief how graciously he responded to me. He complimented me on my writings about the apostolic and prophetic he had read, and said some of what I wrote was very similar to his teaching on the topic, and that he had never read anyone's writing that so eloquently and thoroughly captured the essence of the subject matter, and, he added, he had read a lot of books and articles, everything he could find, but none of it had the spiritual depth my teaching had. He was even kind enough to say that he even learned some things from my writings that were beyond his own personal depth. Those kinds of comments from leaders are a rarity, trust me, as someone who knows it well!

But the irony was, I knew I was there because God wanted me to be the placard waving in his face the whole time I was there, showing him that he was guilty of everything I had written in both *Charismatic Captivation*, and *Charismatic Control*. The man was the poster-child for what hyper-authoritarianism, particularly of the Pentecostal/Charismatic specie, looks like! Take the contents of those books together and you have a complete description of his entire ministry and the methods by which he operated his church and churches and his ministerial network. Each were a mirror of the other. I knew why I was there from God's perspective, but the man held an entirely different perspective of why I was there.

And, yes, I did say above, "On my first visit!" Again, like the Louisiana Lunatic, despite our tension-filled time on my first visit, and despite me knowing that things the Lord had me to say to him and several conversations he asked me to participate in with his subordinate leaders that were contrary to what his and their understanding was on a host of matters, for some reason I can never quite identify he and they, like others before, somehow "liked" me and even liked what I was saying, though I could often see in their eyes their anxiety about how the chief leader would ultimately react to all I was saying after I left, and their responses at the time were certainly tempered as they weighed out that unknown. They asked me questions about apostolic-prophetic leadership and particulars of the offices, and I answered every question as truthfully yet circumspectly as I could, giving special deliberation to answers I knew would be controversial among them because my answers ran contrary to the leader's teaching and positions on those matters.

Again, as I've said before in this book and others, I'm a spokesman of *God*, not any human. If you ask me a question about spiritual matters, I'm going to respond with what I believe to be what the Lord would say about the matter, based on my knowledge and understanding of the Word of God, which I've spent the better part of five decades studying as diligently as I was able, as opposed to my own or anyone else's personal opinion. That's what a prophet should do; even more so, an apostolic-prophet. When they speak, it's always going to be on the backdrop of biblical doctrine relative to the foundation of the Church Jesus is building, because both offices are intrinsically foundational.[72]

While I could clearly see the anxiety, and in some cases consternation, in the eyes of these men, I could also see that what I was saying was "clicking" in their minds, that they knew it lined up with the Word of God, and thus they were unable to refute what I said. Even the occasional reactive smile and chuckle they could not suppress surfaced, though they could literally feel and smell (he was a firm believer in the generous consumption of garlic supplements for his heart condition) the breath of the senior leader wafting around the table. (I truly feel he even used his halitosis as a means to control people.) They were obviously fearful and hungry for truth simultaneously, which made for a lot of obvious stress I could feel all around the table, even when we were meeting over breakfast at public restaurants. It was palpable.

I was amazed at how calm and straightforward the Spirit was helping me to be, even though the questions made for a situation "where angels fear to trod!" Here I am, totally by myself, it seemed for anyone looking in, like a lion in a den of Daniels, yet I felt the powerful presence of the Lord embracing and emboldening me, and not even a tinge of fear or intimidation. They even, I could sense by the Spirit, were afraid for me, as if they were thinking, if you only knew what it is like to be on the receiving end of the senior leader's wrath and how he can make you wilt when he targets you in front of others, there's no way you would be speaking your beliefs so boldly in his presence like you are! But, again, I had not done everything I needed to do to take this valuable time away from my other work to *go there* and be a wilting wallflower! No way! I was going to speak what the Lord told me to speak come hell or high water!

I always have a little bit of a chip on my shoulder when I travel, because I've had to the leave comfort and familiarity of my prophet-cave! I hate travelling with a passion! I'm by no means one of these people who love leaving my home and globetrotting all over the world; I despise it! Though once I'm away somewhere I always do my best to make the best of it and make it count for God! I was certainly getting my money's worth in this case, especially by the time the third day rolled around of being there, being chained, so to speak, to my host, following him around like a little lap dog, going where he took me and doing what he wanted to do, and yet I had not yet been given the opportunity to speak in even one meeting! He purposely was "muzzling the ox"[73] and not allowing me to speak to the congregation. I didn't come all this way to merely shadow this septuagenarian around for days on end. He knew he was frustrating me, and he was doing it on purpose, hoping to take the fire out of me and the wind out of my sails, eventually, so that he could pounce on me before I departed, either in front of some of his cronies, or alone. I knew it was coming and I wasn't going to get out of there without facing his wrath before I got to the airport where I would be home free! He didn't know it, but I could see clearly how it was building up in him, because I had been saying things that obviously was "hitting his way!" I was there because God wanted to speak some things to this man before he died, to give him an opportunity to repent, before time ran out, and I knew it well!

He had his own agenda, which the Lord had shown me exactly what it was. His whole reason in bringing me there was that he thought maybe he could "turn" me and use his "authority" which he felt he had, that always worked on other people, to "capture" them under his spell of what he believed was "apostolic authority," and make me one of his henchmen and place me in a position he would make for me to be his personal proxy and spokesman in the organization he had built. He was so puffed up about his "power" and what he could do for someone he put his cache and endorsement behind, as a "king-maker," that in his mind he thought once he rolled out the whole plan for me, I would *jump* headlong at the opportunity to be his Aaron. He had always wanted that person who filled that role to be his oldest son, but his son had been running from the God represented by his biological father his whole adult life and wanted nothing to do with Him. The iron fist of authoritarian abuse this man had spent fifty years exercising in trying to capture his son had taken a heavy toll on his son, who had become an alcoholic, suffered two divorces and estranged children, and had numerous run-ins with the law, even being in and out of jail, the latest incident of which was still ongoing when I came there. The man had no idea that the Lord had showed me everything he was thinking, and I knew from the start that there was no way I was ever going to succumb to this man's web of captivity! No way! He thought he had brought me there on his own dime to capture me, but he did not understand that God had me there to speak some things to *him*! The irony was not lost on me that the name of his oldest son was the same as mine. That was significant in this whole matter, since he was basically looking for a "replacement" for what he had thought his son's whole life *he* would be.

The second visit, which happened only about a month after the first, was basically a repeat of the first visit. By the time I left a midweek service and two Sunday services had occurred, and, of course, since he was my host, I had to attend all the services and endure all his shenanigans and performance in which he was pulling out all the stops trying to impress me with his place as king of his kingdom, in which everyone, his wife, his kids, his subordinates, and all the congregation feared him and were all psychological captives in his kingdom! By the time Sunday night came, I was so glad I had obeyed the Lord's leading to book my flight out that night after the Sunday night service, which he cut short, knowing he would be taking me to the airport so that he could give me his last spiel and pitch that he had been saving up and working toward the whole time. When he finally came out with it, explaining that he would like to "bring me on" and make me his "second in command" over his entire organization, I told him that after all the time we had spent together and everything I garnered during my thorough examination of everything he had going on, which is what he brought me there to do, that I would continue to pray about it, but that my thoughts and impression at that moment was that I didn't think that would work and I was not his man. With just the two of us in his car, he in the driver seat, me in the passenger seat, he seemed crestfallen and hurt by my response. I tried to be as gentle as I could be, speaking to him in a tone of respect and honor, and as if speaking to my grandfather, as I had the entire time on both trips. I told him how much I honored him and that he was worthy of all honor for all he had accomplished in his now eight decades of living, and how God had obviously prospered him along his life's journey. I was very respectful, as respectful as I could comfortably be, calling him, "Sir" or "Apostle" most of the time, only occasionally addressing him by the name he went by, to show him I knew he was human and not merely an officeholder, just as was I. What made it all more difficult was that with his white hair and height, he reminded me so much of my late father, who had passed only a couple years before, I couldn't stand it at times. Many times I would look at him and his face would morph into the face of my father. It was eerie.

So, here we were, saying goodbye before him dropping me off at the airport, and we both felt something we couldn't quite identify or communicate, yet I think we both knew we would never see each other again, and we didn't. It was only about two years later, that I learned he had passed. It saddened me, thinking what could have been if only things were different, though I knew that was an impossibility. Yet, I was grateful and exceedingly humbled that out of all the people in this world and all the prophets God has around the world, for whatever reasons, He chose me to go to speak on His behalf to this 80-year old man the things God had me to share with him. I have no idea if he ever really understood what I was saying and what the Lord was trying to communicate to him before he passed. All I *did* know was that I had obeyed God, and that's all I'm called to do, and I always must leave the results in *His* hands. One day, I'll know.

Extinguishing Flaming Missiles of a Denomination

Friendly fire of flaming missiles also came in the form of criticism from the denomination of my first church and its leadership. I wrote a letter to the interim pastor of the church, about criticism that had gotten back to me about my meetings, in which attendees of the church were saying that, behind the scenes, there was some attempts by the leadership to discourage members and attendees of the church from coming to my meetings. In his response to my letter the interim pastor, of course, denied it was happening. Apparently, he had forwarded the matter to officials at the Florida district of the denomination, including the overseer. They too denied, in writing and phone conversations, it was occurring.

I responded to their letters graciously and there was some back and forth discussion by letter and phone. At one point, even my dad got involved due to the fact that the interim pastor was now his direct leader with respect to the home fellowship group my father was conducting under the auspices of the church. I had one discussion with my father about the matter and then dropped it.

The brief flap ended with some people from the church not attending my meetings, but I continued my meetings undeterred, and others not involved with that church in any way we're coming to replace those who stopped coming. Though at some point, a couple years later, I discontinued meetings in the Central and South Florida areas, and limited my ministry to a home church I had started while living in Jupiter, Florida, were I lived for twenty years, my ministry continued more and more through my writings of articles I posted on my main ministry website (slm.org) blog as well as a new website I started called Spirit Life Magazine (spiritlifemag.com), as well as the writing and publishing of my books. I also launched a publishing house for Christian books and audiobooks, helping other ministers to get their books and audiobooks into print and audio. That ministry continues today, and I continue to write articles regarding various aspects of Fivefold Ministry and other matters, and post articles by other ministers as well. The articles I write about Fivefold Ministry I also post on the Ephesians Four Network website. While I have written and posted many articles about

Fivefold Ministry, one of the next books I will be publishing pertains to the Fivefold Ministry Model in particular. I also host The Real Truth Podcast and Radio on the Spreaker distribution platform, available for free at: https://www.spreaker.com/show/the-real-truth-podcast.

I've learned over the years to take such matters in stride and not let it deter me and the fulfillment of my calling from God in any way. Many new incidents of basically the same have come, but now I pay little if any attention to them at all, which is always the best thing to do because no-reaction strikes terror and panic in the heart of the enemy and all his demonic minions more than anything one can possibly do in terms of reaction. The devil absolutely bristles when believers ignore him.

I remember hearing a story about this involving Smith Wigglesworth. One night the devil himself appeared at the foot of The Apostle of Faith's bed in the middle of the night. When he opened his eyes and saw the devil, he simply and calmly said, "Oh, it's just *you*," and turned over and went back to sleep. That's how we need to respond to the devil and all his shenanigans trying to strike fear into our hearts.

> You are from God, little children, and have overcome them; because *greater* is *He* (the Holy Spirit) who is in you than *he* (the devil) who is in the world.[74]

Extinguishing Flaming Arrows of a Non-prophet Evangelist

Another incident of flaming missiles from the evil one came in the form of criticism concerning my ministry and meetings in the late 1980s and 1990s in the Central Florida region from another ecclesial source.

At some point after holding numerous monthly meetings in the Central Florida region and subsequently in the South Florida region, some in hotel meeting rooms, some in churches, and some in homes of people who asked me to hold them in their homes to minister to their friends or home fellowship group, I was contacted by a professional associate of a person who was best friends with and next-door neighbor of a prominent evangelist, who also lived in an exclusive community in the Orlando Metroplex. He explained on the phone that he and his wife had attended several of my meetings and how impressed they were with the nature and quality of the ministry, and how they had never experienced what they did in my meetings, especially the prophetic aspect. He then asked if I was willing to hold a meeting in his home a couple of months hence, explaining to me that he was an associate of this evangelist's best friend and next-door neighbor. I agreed. When my wife and I came to their house before the meeting, the hosts took us aside and told us who all he felt would probably be attending the meeting that evening and that they were expecting a good turnout. They also told us that they were hoping that the naturopath physician and his wife whose practice he was affiliated with would be coming. They had invited them, but had not gotten a firm commitment from them as to whether or not they would attend. They explained this couple was next-door neighbors and close friends of this well-known evangelist, who he had had on his television program several times talking about his naturopathic practice and various related products he sold.

By the time the meeting was suppose to commence, the house was filled to capacity, and over-capacity. I was told later somehow they had squeezed almost a hundred people into the house. The streets were lined with cars, and people were jammed into every room of the house, many of whom could not even see the foyer area they had reserved for me to minister from. When I saw how many people were there, I pared down my pre-ministry message to just a bare-minimum overview of what God was doing with respect to the nascent prophetic movement, and moved into ministering to people. Most everyone there had come hoping to receive a personal prophecy, as they had heard that that was what the Lord was doing in my meetings—speaking personal prophecy to everyone who wanted one, often until two or three o'clock in the morning. I knew also that this meeting could not go that long due to number of cars parked near their house and causing traffic flow problems, plus the fact that there were far more people in the house than the legal limit, and many there had arranged for babysitters for their children, besides the fact people had to get some sleep before rising for the next day's events. So, I knew, I couldn't prophesy over everyone, and would have to choose certain people as led by the Spirit.

A few minutes after I had started speaking, the doorbell rang, and when the people standing in front of the door opened it and waved the guests in, everyone around the door scrunching together to make room, in walked this young, well-dressed couple with their two young children in tow, each of them carrying one of them. At the time, I didn't pay much attention to them, except in the back of my mind, as I continued to speak what the Lord was having me to speak about the prophetic and what God was doing in that hour. After about twenty-minutes, I started explaining what would be happening next and what those who were not familiar with personal prophecy could expect.

When I told the people I would be calling a few people out to prophesy over as many as our limited time would allow, I reached out my arm and hand, swinging it a clockwise swoop of the people crowded into the front edge of the living room and foyer immediately in front of the door and then swung it back the other way, and, for whatever reasons landed on the couple that had come in late. I said, "I feel that the Lord wants me to start here with this couple that came in last." I began saying what the Lord put in my mouth, having no idea who the couple was, having never seen them in my life, and knowing nothing about them in the natural. The moment I picked them out, there was some sort of tangible rise from the people who immediately began whispering and muttering things I couldn't hear or understand, being so tuned into the Spirit. From the first words I uttered, which I don't remember now what they were, people began muttering things that I knew from experience were people's acknowledgments that what I was saying "fit" the couple perfectly, that it was all right. I do remember at one point focusing on what the couple did professionally and describing it and that they were becoming very well-known for what they did both locally and nationally and that they could expect to see even more of that notoriety as they continued to be faithful to what God had called them to. I then asked if he was a doctor. Many let out a shriek of amazement, and the man replied, that he was, and seemed to be a bit miffed by all this. Then, I asked if he had written a book, and he said, yes, he had. Then I asked the wife if she helped him in his practice and to write his book, and she replied in the affirmative with tears welling up in her eyes. Then, I said, "Oh, and I see you prophesy as well, right?" Again, she welled up, and said, "Yes!" with a note of amazement in her voice. Again, people all around were murmuring things related to the words I was speaking, as if they were astonished at the accuracy. I continued to prophesy over each of them separately, then as a couple and things about their present and future, and how God was going to use them.

Then, I said, "And you have a close friend in the ministry who is going to ask you about this meeting and how it went, in fact, he asked you to go ahead and check it out, and you can't wait to report to him how it went, and will talk to him about it yet tonight after you go home and put the kids to bed, is that right?" "Yes! Yes! Yes! That's right!" they both responded in unison enthusiastically. Everyone in the house, including the hosts and the couple seemed a bit blown away by the prophetic ministry over them and then the twenty or so others I picked out to prophesy over. Most everyone who received prophecy also were slain in the spirit afterward. People were literally holding people up who were "out" on their feet because they had nowhere to fall.

When I finished, I turned the meeting over to the hosts, and the couple who came in late asked the host if they could say something and then prophesy over me. He gave them permission. They both talked about how amazed they were about the prophecy they had received as well as the prophecy they witnessed other people had received. They said they knew some of those who had received ministry and knew how accurate those prophetic words were, and that they had never seen anyone minister to so many people in one meeting, and how that this must be a new anointing that God is releasing as I had been saying in my teaching. Obviously, they were blown away by what God had done that night in their firsthand witness.

I had no idea who they were talking about as being this minister friend they would be reporting to after the meeting. But I did, however, hear from our hosts later that they had gone over to this evangelist's house that night after the meeting and told him everything that had occurred, giving a glowing report of how accurate the prophetic words were that night and how there were so many who were prophesied to. When I inquired what the evangelist's response was, he told me that it was not good, he had boo-pooed what occurred, and said how he didn't believe that prophetic words can come that way with so many being prophesied over in one meeting. He even suggested that this might be demonically-inspired and that I was a false prophet and psychic.

Over the course of time and ministry, I have learned over and over that it is human nature for people in ministry to feel a need to "protect their territory." I've come to expect it, though it shouldn't be. New Testament scripture talks about where jealousy (competition) and selfish-ambition and strife exist there is disorder and every evil thing, and compares it to the wisdom that comes from above:

Who among you is wise and understanding? Let him show by his good behavior his deeds in the gentleness of wisdom. But if you have bitter jealousy and selfish ambition in your heart, do not be arrogant and so lie against the truth. This wisdom is not that which comes down from above, but is earthly, natural, demonic. *For where jealousy and selfish ambition exist, there is disorder and every evil thing.* But the wisdom from above is first pure, then *peaceable*, gentle, reasonable, full of mercy and good fruits, unwavering, without hypocrisy. And the seed whose fruit is righteousness is *sown in peace by those who make peace.*[75]

Now, after seeing this jealousy and competition and selfish-ambition occurring too often with those in the ministry, I simply take it in stride, knowing that "territory protection" comes with the territory of ministry. This is what occurred in this case—a clear case of territory protection. It also got back to me that the evangelist had also been speaking things against my ministry and me and the things I was teaching concerning the nascent prophetic and coming apostolic movements. This was certainly nothing new; I'd heard it all before, especially coming from the "old wineskin" Pentecostal denominations, who were notorious for resisting change. They certainly didn't like what I was saying about God passing these "old wineskin" denominations by with the movements He was instituting, because, as Jesus said,

> "And no one puts new wine into old wineskins; otherwise the new wine will burst the skins and it will be spilled out, and the skins will be ruined. "But new wine must be put into fresh wineskins. "And no one, after drinking old wine wishes for new; for he says, 'The old is good enough.'"[76]

I've learned to always forgive the perpetrators of this kind of censorial criticism quickly when I hear about it, and I have never allowed bitterness to enter in my heart against any of these people in any way! I've had plenty of opportunities to practice on. I remember one day I had just learned that a certain well-known prophet, who was regarded as "the papa-prophet" of a network of purporting prophets, had been speaking against me and denigrating my ministry as a prophet, and saying I was not "approved" by him and their network of prophets, I was feeling sorry for myself and wallowing in the muck and mire of self-pity, when I heard the Lord say, "What did I tell you to do "when men hate you, and ostracize you, and insult you, and scorn your name as evil, for the sake of the Son of Man?"

I thought for a moment, and thought I knew what scripture He was referring to, so I turned to it in my Bible, and began reading it out loud:

> "Blessed are you when men hate you, and ostracize you, and insult you, and scorn your name as evil, for the sake of the Son of Man. *Be glad in that day and **leap for joy**,* for behold, your reward is great in heaven. For in the same way their fathers used to treat the prophets.[77]

I saw what He was saying for me to do, but I responded, "But, Lord, I don't have any joy right now! To which He immediately replied, "That's why I said to leap for it—to get it!"

I replied, "I don't feel like leaping right now." To which He responded, "Well, if you want it, you've got to do what I said to do to get it!"

I said, "Leap for it?" "Yes! Leap for it!"

I said, "That seems so silly and inappropriate right now; this is so serious!" "That's why you need to change the atmosphere and replace your attitude with JOY!"

I said, "Okay; I'll try." I took one little crow-hop, and all of a sudden UTTER JOY UNSPEAKABLE AND FULL OF GLORY hit my feet and I started leaping around my living room like a kangaroo and laughing hilariously, which went on for about twenty minutes until I collapsed on the floor out of breath, but still laughing uncontrollably! "Oh, I cried out to the Lord, THAT'S what you meant: Leap for joy when we don't have any, in order to get it!" "Yes! Exactly, He said!" "Man this WORKS," I said. "Yep!" He said. I've never forgotten that incident, and I've never forgotten the passage He then quoted to me:

> Why are the nations in an uproar *And the peoples devising a vain thing*? The kings of the earth take their stand And the rulers take counsel together Against the LORD and against His Anointed, saying, "Let us tear their fetters apart And cast away their cords from us!" **He who sits in the heavens laughs, The Lord scoffs at them.** Then He will speak to them in His anger And terrify them in His fury, saying, "But as for Me, I have installed My King Upon Zion, My holy mountain." "I will surely tell of the decree of the LORD: He said to Me, 'You are My Son, Today I have begotten You. 'Ask of Me, and I will surely give the

nations as Your inheritance, And the very ends of the earth as Your possession. 'You shall break them with a rod of iron, You shall shatter them like earthenware.'" Now therefore, O kings, show discernment; Take warning, O judges of the earth. Worship the LORD with reverence And rejoice with trembling. Do homage to the Son, that He not become angry, and you perish in the way, For His wrath may soon be kindled. How blessed are all who take refuge in Him!"[78]

I was delivered that day from the pangs of the fiery darts of men's words launched against me. From that day forward I have always countered the critical works of denigration by mere men with laughter from the Spirit of the Lord, knowing that He Himself laughs and even scoffs at them, because He is the One who has anointed and appointed me, and He has always known what He is doing and has done, and that I "have *an anointing from the Holy One* and (I) know...!"[79] God has already anointed and appointed me to the calling He has called me to, and "the gifts and the calling of God are irrevocable."[80] So, there's nothing any critics or naysayers can do about any of it. What God thinks about me and has done with me far outweighs and trumps anything and everything any of these adversaries can think, say, or do. What they think, say, or do is meaningless in the face of what God thinks, says, and does! I learned many years ago, that what your enemies do against you have no effect at all—except what you allow it to have in your mind. Now, my attitude regarding my enemies and critics is: "Jimmy crack corn, and I don't care!"

That was how I came to view the criticisms of this evangelist, well-known, or not! It meant nothing to me. His assessments were completely wrong and wrong-headed, and his words carried no weight at all, and really just showed how shallow and wrong his thinking about the apostolic and prophetic was at the time, and how competitive, strife-filled, and frankly immature he was. And he was! I let it all run off my back like water off a duck's back. And I simply carried on with my ministry, allowing God to be the defense of my life.[81] Forgiving quickly and thoroughly, actually praying for him per Matthew 5:44 and Luke 6:28—it was the right thing to do in all aspects. This evangelist was the son-in-law of my pastor, having married his oldest daughter.

I saw him at the memorial service for my pastor held more than ten years ago now in the church facility he had helped to build. He ignored me, though he knew who I was sitting just a few seats from him, and I was pleased to know that I held no bitterness or unforgiveness against him, and actually felt genuine love for him in my spirit, and enjoyed what he had to say that day about his father-in-law.

Later, it became public knowledge that he was having an adulterous dalliance with a well-known female minister, who had recently divorced her husband for his unfaithfulness and drug abuse, also from the Orlando Metroplex, that did not last long, for which the evangelist's wife divorced him, though they later remarried.

One of the things so obvious to so many other ministers regarding this man was his blatant arrogance and sense of superiority that oozed out of him regarding other ministers who he considered inferior to him. This was something that certainly harmed his ministry and effectiveness. I believe God was dealing with him in that respect with all the negative publicity he generated by his own actions. That was all genuinely grievous to me, and I prayed for the couple and their children. I remember my pastor saying many times in his messages, "If you don't humble yourself, God will! It's better to humble yourself voluntarily than for God to humble you, because when He humbles you, He *humiliates* you!" And He does! And He did in the case of this evangelist! God has since done wonderful things, apparently, with regard to the restoration of all the affected relationships, and I think I see some semblance of humility has entered his life and heart; maybe not as much as I would like to see, but *some*. Praise the Lord! God is faithful!

Extinguishing Flaming Arrows of Friendly Fire

This story is about my experience of extinguishing flaming arrows of friendly fire from my original pastor. He was a tremendous communicator and Bible teacher. His father had been one of the original founders of their Pentecostal denomination's branch in England. Smith Wigglesworth had been a frequent dinner guest when he was young, and he even played accordion and led worship in some of The Apostle of Faith's meetings. He himself also became a prominent leader in the denomination as the pastor of one of the first so-called "megachurches" in the nation. When he assumed the pastorate of the church in Orlando area in 1970, there were 300 members on the rolls and about 50 attending Sunday morning services. When he resigned in 1980, there were more than 10,000 attending five services every Sunday. Under his leadership, what was spawned was not simply a church, but a movement in the metropolitan area. He was featured on several *Charisma Magazine* covers, as also was the minister of music, who was also well-known throughout churchdom in the nation, who I actually began working for when I helped him launch a new ministry that eventually ministered all throughout this nation and numerous other nations over a span of twenty years, Festival of Praise. *Charisma Magazine* was started with the financial help of that church. He and his wife were the in-laws of a well-known evangelist, who married their oldest daughter.

Forced to resign after ten years as the senior leader due to a series of indiscretions, he started a new church plant about eight years later, which I helped him with in various ways. One day he called me to ask to meet for lunch at a location about halfway between our respective hometowns, along with another elder/board member. I agreed.

During the lunch, he asked numerous questions about my views on Fivefold Ministry, the apostolic and prophetic aspects, in particular. I didn't fully understand at the time where he was coming from. In a non-confrontational conversational way, he shared his views on the subject, referring to some of what he apparently felt were ways my views exceeded his to some degree. He was gracious enough to say he was learning some things from my view as I explained them, but then again, he usually was a very gracious man. The differences focused mostly in regard to how I saw the foundation of apostles and prophets, particularly in the local church application, and my view regarding apostolic-prophetic foundation being the biblical model vis-à-vis the pastoral model. But, by the end of my responses, he said he was seeing it better and in a different light, though my views were a departure from his denomination's teaching and positions on the matter. Having read the denomination's position papers on the topic published in 1948 in response to the teachings of the Latter Rain teachings, I was very familiar with its position on this matter as well as others, such as Deliverance and whether or not a believer can be demonized. Their position was the polar opposite of mine.

After responding to each and every one of his questions in a good-natured, conversational manner, finally, I looked up from staring at my plate, looked him into the eyes, and said,

"Well, Pastor, I don't know why you're asking all these questions, I am happy to answer all of them, but I want you to know *one thing*. **Everything** I've ever known about Fivefold Ministry or anything else of a spiritual nature, I've learned sitting under *your* ministry, I learned it from **YOU**! I feel I've received the equivalent of a post-graduate level spiritual education directly from your teaching and tutelage! The first Sunday morning I came to your church, I had been saved only *six days*. In that service, when I experienced what I did, in a packed out building with people all around me enthusiastically singing, clapping, weeping, shouting, praising God, I decided in that very moment that I would never miss another service, and I didn't, for more than three years my wife and I attended every service we could when we were in town, and sang in the choir for every one of them, five services on Sunday plus the Wednesday night service. Whatever I ever become and my ministry ever becomes, I owe it all to *you* in terms of human leadership. You are my pastor, and I will always consider you my pastor, no matter what happens."

I saw his eyes quickly well up, and he looked down at his plate, and there was a long silence at the table; no one spoke. He never asked another question. Shortly after, he insisted on paying everyone's tab for the meal, we shook hands, hugged, and went our separate ways.

I really never understood the purpose and upshot of the discussions that day until years later, from the other elder, who just recently passed. Apparently, the board had been considering bringing me on to leadership of the church in some capacity. In a subtle and roundabout way, they had asked me if I would be interested in that, at the time, I didn't receive the question as being anything but a hypothetical. My response was, not as long as the pastor was the leader, because I didn't want to disrespect him in any way, or be seen as undermining his ministry in any way.

The final result of the meeting—what were subtle non-malicious flaming arrows that I rebuffed with the help of the Holy Spirit—He had told me in advance He would tell me what to say, and He did!

After that meeting, I arranged with the leadership of the church to hold a series of meetings I was conducting in the Central Florida region during the mid-to-late-1980s, in which I was teaching on and prophesying about the coming prophetic movement the Lord had shown me was coming, followed by an apostolic movement, both of which *did* come just as I prophesied. To my knowledge, our conversation never harmed or negatively impacted my relationship with that church and the leadership. Indeed, they were very supportive of my meetings, which packed out the facility. If I recall correctly, I believe we had three such meetings there over the next three months.

Unfortunately, however, the board again forced the pastor to resign, this time, they said, based on financial malfeasance. I never got involved with the matter, but when he was again without a church, it was very grievous to me. One day, I came to the church facility and everything in the building was being stripped out, including the chairs. The elder, who was also a somewhat well-known evangelist, told me that they were forced to ask the pastor for his resignation and the reasons why. He never pastored again.

My respect and honor for my pastor, despite his many faults and flat sides, continued until his passing more than ten years ago now. Some of my other minister-friends have told me they thought my insistent honoring of him, was a bit too much, more than he deserved, but I never paid any attention to that. I attended his memorial service held in the new building at the church, the plans for which were initiated under his administration. The new building, with an unheard of (at the time) seating capacity of 5,000, was completed some five years following his departure. I saw this building as being a testament to the quality and effectiveness of his ministry. Though the church honored him before his passing with a special service for that purpose, that church never, to this day, has returned to its former glory. The main reason, I believe is that my pastor was functioning in the office of an apostle, not just a pastor, whether he or the congregation understood that or not. He had an uncanny ability to draw followers, which is an attribute of genuine apostles. When people heard him speak in his still slightly evident British accent, they were always highly impressed. I still honor him today as my original pastor and friend in every conversation I have about him, especially as the greatest teacher I ever heard and sat under! Despite his flaws—Who among us does not have them?—he was a great man in the Kingdom of God! God used him mightily, and many people are in Heaven at this moment because of his and his wife's extraordinary ministry! And more will someday soon join them there! I loved him and his wife (she also passed away a few years ago), and have seen his surviving children in some special events held at the church facility since. I will always be grateful to God for that man and what his ministry did for me.

Extinguishing the Flaming Arrows of the Jezebel Principality

The JEZEBEL SPIRIT is an evil spirit obsessed with domination and control in realms of authority, that operates through witchcraft/sorcery to achieve its goals. The covert operations of the Jezebel Spirit remains to be one of the most prevalent and dastardly problems in all of Christendom—in families and businesses of believers, churches, ministries, and every other arena of interrelations of believers—as well as in every segment of secular society where human relationships exist.

In psychology, the effects produced by this demonic spirit are known as "narcissism," or Narcissistic Personality Disorder (NPD)[82] in clinical cases (see, DSM-IV). While as a deliverance counselor with Doctoral Diplomate Christian Counseling Board Certification, I personally believe effective therapeutic relief from the effects of NPD requires deliverance (casting out of demons). The Mayo Clinic has published an information-rich and enlightening article on NPD, which, due to unusual copyright restrictions I am constrained from quoting, that you can read by going to the link provided in the endnotes of this chapter.[83]

The references in the Bible to two different women with the name "Jezebel" are portrayed by the Spirit as being classic narcissists. For a partial list of the characteristics of narcissism follow the link provided in the endnote cited here.[84]

Jezebel is a decimating spirit, that if not discerned, uncovered, and resisted via the supernatural gifts of the Spirit and effectual spiritual warfare, often produces catastrophe and tragedy in the lives of those it targets. It is one of the most unrelenting and dogged spirits there is, that if unable to completely destroy, in the meanwhile will do all in its power to *neutralize* its human target through an almost endless array of dastardly, demonic wiles and schemes that defy common human prescience. Personally, I believe this is the evil spirit behind abortion. It certainly, without any doubt, is the demonic spirit behind extreme and aggressive feminism that has wreaked untold decimation in every aspect of American society, including ecclesiastical.

The Jezebel Spirit operates through an unholy alliance with one of the most powerful demon spirits there are: the Python Spirit (divination, sorcery, witchcraft). Undetected and unresisted these spirits will wrap themselves around the soul (mind, will, and emotions) of unsuspecting and unwary victims like a PYTHON snake, and do what a real python snake does to its victims in the natural—i.e., begin to squeeze their chest, lungs, and trachea, until they cannot breathe, as a means to a slow, agonizing death! Jezebel wants to KILL YOU! and will stop at nothing in an attempt to do so, unless it is countered through spiritual warfare employing spiritual weapons.

When you are under spiritual attack of this spirit, you will have episodes in which you literally cannot breathe, and feel like you are going to asphyxiate and DIE! It often manifests in the form of severe anxiety or PANIC ATTACKS! It will wrap itself around you and continue to squeeze you—mentally, emotionally, psychologically, and even physically!

MINISTERS—PROPHETS AND PROPHETIC PEOPLE, in particular—are its most desired target! Jezebel's number one enemy—the enemy that spirit fears the most—is the PROPHETIC ANOINTING!

Strong and effectual spiritual warfare employing all the "weapons of *our* warfare," which "are not CARNAL, but mighty through God to the pulling down of strongholds,"[85] is absolutely essential in defeating these *powerful* spirits!

If you are under attack by these spirits, don't try to battle alone. Rather, reach out for help from other Bible-believing, devil-chasing, Fire-Baptized believers, who know how and are experienced at spiritual warfare and casting out of demons; i.e., deliverance.

And He said to them, "I was watching Satan fall from heaven like *lightning*."[86]

In 2004, I learned in extremely dramatic fashion that the JEZEBEL SPIRIT is really not merely an earth-bound demon, but rather a PRINCIPALITY, when it literally physically appeared at the foot of my bed in the middle of the night as I was in a deep-sleep, declaring in the most eerie voice I've ever heard, "I'M GOING TO KILL YOU!" It appeared like a cloud-like specter in the room, and the voice came out of the cloud. I shouted out the name of Jesus, and...POOF!...it disappeared. The room temperature literally dropped down to below freezing instantly when the principality entered the room, which is what woke me up. I was shaking uncontrollably both from the cold and terror, and yelled out to the Lord, "WHAT WAS THAT?" He immediately answered, "IT WAS THE PRINCIPALITY JEZEBEL!" I queried Him, "Jezebel is a PRINCIPALITY?" He immediately responded, "YES, and it is obsessed with killing you, and has been trying to kill you since the day you were born, and you almost died that day when you were born (which was true), but for My COMMAND to Satan that he COULD NOT KILL YOU!"

HALLELUJAH! PRAISE GOD FOREVER!

Two weeks later, again a freakish, in the middle of the night event, transpired. I was startled awake out of a deep-sleep by an explosive "CRACK" that sounded like an exploding incoming mortar round! Somehow, I immediately knew what it was—a lightning strike! Seconds later I was smelling smoke, as I grabbed some shoes and pants and a flashlight and ran outside to see what I could see on the roof of the house. Some smoke billowed through the roof, and I saw only a quick flash of light showing through the boards of the roof, but it was just a flash, which my mind was not capable of processing at the time.

A call to 911, one trusts, alerts the nearest fire station, which in this case was only about two miles down the road. But, after a minute or two, I still had not heard any sirens, and something inside me told me something was wrong, so I jumped in the car and sped down the road as fast as the car would go to the fire station, and sure enough, what I was concerned about was indeed the case—both firetrucks were out on another call.

By now torrential rains from the flash storm the lightning flash was associated with were falling. I drove back to the house, calling 911 again on the way, and calling out to Jesus to protect the house and all my possessions inside. When I got back, the two big fire-engines were coming up the other end of the street and toward the house.

Fireman quickly entered the house, hauling in their huge fire-hoses, and doing what firemen do at a fire. I smelled smoke, but I saw no flames, and was hoping and praying for a miracle. After about only five minutes, the captain of the crew came out of the house with his helmet off, making a beeline for me, at a brisk pace. He shouted at me in a somewhat angry demeanor, "WHO PUT OUT THE FIRE?"

In the semi-dazed state I was in, I wasn't sure that what I thought he asked was really right, so I said, "Excuse me, Sir?" Again, he shouted at me fairly close to my face, like my old drill sergeant in Army boot camp, in the pitch darkness except for the lights of the fire trucks, "WHO PUT OUT THE FIRE?!" Again, I had to take a second to process what he was asking me, and I replied, "What do you mean, 'Who put out the fire?'"

He yelled back over the loud roar of the running fire-engines, "SOMEONE put that fire out up in the attic of that house! We can see where every board and rafter in that attic was flashed by fire, but it's as if a hurricane-force wind came into that attic and instantaneously blew that fire completely out! In my thirty-year career, I've NEVER seen anything even remotely like THAT! The roof of that house should be burning right now! WHO DID THAT?!"

With him yelling in my face, the only answer I could come up with is the one I shouted back, "JESUS! HALLELUJAH!" His response was, "Mister, I think you're right! I think we've just witnessed a real modern-day MIRACLE!" Then, *he* shouted, "HALLELUJAH! PRAISE GOD!"

There was some fire damage in the attic and more damage caused by the firemen and all they did to reach the attic and put hundreds of gallons of water on the interior of the attic and on their way to it, but the insurance claim took care of repairing all the damage, though it took about four months to get it repaired.

When the firemen were gone and I was doing my best to go back to sleep, the Lord told me the culprit was that Jezebel principality that had vowed to kill me. But, once again, God intervened, and kept me. My belief is that the Lord allowed that incident to transpire to prove to me in a very dramatic and unforgettable way that the principality called Jezebel is real, and really powerful, and if it wasn't that "greater is He that is in me than he that is in the world," the house could have burned down with all my possessions inside, and possibly even worse. "BUT GOD!" HALLELUJAH!

Jezebel is REAL, and Jezebel, like its supreme commander, Satan, wants to steal, kill, and destroy! **AND IT DESPISES AND DESPERATELY FEARS PROPHETS!**

Since the day my mother was giving birth to me, Jezebel has been doing all it can to attempt to KILL ME! BUT GOD! The Lord has kept me and has prevented that spirit from having its way over me scores and scores of times through the course of my now 75 years (at the time this book is being published)! Praise God!

Time and time again, I have battled Jezebel over the course of my nearly five decades of ministry. At times, it has seemed that I was swimming in and surrounded by Jezebels. Jezebels here; Jezebels there; everywhere I go, JEZEBELS! Somehow, wherever I go, they are there! They seek me out! They show up everywhere I go. They are drawn like moths to light to my meetings. I conduct a meeting, and it's guaranteed the Jezebels will show up! I minister at a church, and the Jezebels come out from the woodwork and slither out from their dens under the rocks! Over and over and over, circumstances have been devised by card-carrying, certified Jezebels, attempting to hinder or if they could, *stop* me and my ministry! But I guess I'm like a Timex watch, no matter what, I just keep on ticking! It must literally drive the devils crazy that they can't stop me and this God-ordained, God-anointed, God-appointed ministry that carries on through this "earthen vessel."

But, OH! How I know that the JEZEBEL SPIRIT is REAL! It exists! No one can tell me any different! Now, I can actually say I've seen it with my own eyes!

Friendly Fiery Arrows From the Panhandle Prophets

In the mid-1980s God began restoring the office of the prophet back into its rightful and proper place of function in the Church that Jesus is building. Today, thousands of churches and ministers accept and themselves advocate this premise.

My brief encounter with this organization began in 1985, when I received a letter from the organization, reaching out to me as a "prophetic person," explaining of the organization's relocation from Arizona to Florida, and that it was their desire to connect with "prophetic people," like myself in Florida. The letter asked that I send any writings (books or articles) I had written on the subject of the prophetic realm, and that in return, I would be sent the latest book by the leader on the subject of the eternal bride of Christ. I complied and in return received a signed book by the leader. Soon, I received another letter informing that the organization would be conducting a "Ya'll Come," meeting for prophetic people in September of the following year that I was invited to attend to become acquainted with the prophet leader, the other leaders of the organization, and fellowship with the other attendees.

In 1986 I attended what was billed as a "prophetic gathering" in a tiny Florida Panhandle town. What it was billed as is not what it was in reality. It really was a cleverly disguised recruitment rally for membership in a network of prophetic ministries that was a newly formed subsidiary of the hosting organization, which, in the words of the leader, who they called "papa-prophet," would soon be recognized as "the international prophetic clearinghouse." Over the years since, the principals of this organization have progressively added to their utter blasphemy and unabashed and shameless hubris by attributing to the chief leader the attribution of being "The Father of the Prophetic Movement" and making the preposterous claim that he is recognized as such around the world. He is neither. No man is the father of the prophetic movement; Jesus, the Head of the Church and Premier Prophet, is, and He initiated and orchestrated it through the administration of the Holy Spirit, not this man-made organization.

Indeed, that same year I sent this organization and its leadership a letter stating precisely that, and that their attempt to hijack the then nascent prophetic movement was seen by God as being akin to when David attempted to bring back the ark of the covenant on a man-made wooden, ox-drawn cart. Right idea; wrong order! And I also prophesied to them that their attempts to hijack the prophetic movement and to carry it on their man-made, wooden (symbolic of human works), ox-drawn cart—this organization—would eventually suffer the same fate as David's debacle. And it did and has.

Of course, I immediately became persona non-grata and was quickly black-balled by these self-appointed Mafiosi of the prophetic movement. Over the years, that organization, its stature and influence have gradually dwindled down to a place of relative insignificance, and I have yet to see any signs that it and its principals get that "the prophetic movement" never was and never has been their idea or something that God appointed them to be in charge of and take dominion over; rather it was and remains to be God's in every way, from its origins and initiation on Earth and its continued administration. Its Administrator is the Holy Spirit, and anyone else who claims ownership or authorship is a fraud and interloper!

As preposterous and arrogant as that sounds to rational minds, that is exactly what that organization was successful in convincing a fairly large percentage of the Neo-Pentecostal stream out of that initial conference. Aided by the approbation and endorsement of a number of other Neo-Pentecostal ministerial "networks" with whom they were in league, this organization—"The Panhandle Prophets"—essentially achieved their goal of duping the majority of Charismatica into accepting the premise that this single, man-made organization was chosen and appointed by God as the supreme sanctioning prophetic organization in the world.

To a large degree, depending on one's perspective, this organization under the auspices of its leader either successfully hijacked the emerging prophetic movement, or presided over a false "prophetic movement" that was a Satanic preemption of the emergence of a company of prophets that has yet to commence.

Over the past three and a half decades, the Panhandle Prophets have had somewhat of a lock, of sorts, on the prophetic, which they have jealously guarded because of the manifold self-aggrandizing benefits it has produced for them, not the least of which has been significant personal wealth accruing from their network of prophets and churches that requires membership dues and organization-set levels of tithing percentages from members commensurate to the level of recognition and status desired (their "pay-to-play" system).

The stranglehold of influence this organization has been able to exert over the prophetic movement since the mid-1980s, which has been extremely detrimental to the prophetic movement as well as the fulfillment of God's intended purposes for the prophetic within the true Church Jesus is building, is due to the fact that many carnally-minded Charismatic leaders simply accepted without appropriate investigation and prayerful consideration this self-promulgated and self-promoting proposition of this organization—i.e., that they are the premier and elite prophets in the world and their network of prophetic ministries is the supreme sanctioning organization for prophets.

The self-stated self-view of the leaders of this organization is that God has appointed them to recognize, approve, and authorize prophets, church-wide and worldwide. The level of hubris reflected in the self-view and attitudes of those associated with this organization, and

I personally know quite a number of them, is absolutely astounding, but the fact that so many church leaders have accepted their grossly arrogant, unChristlike assertions is absolutely mindboggling!

Absurd as it sounds to the sane, many Neo-Pentecostals leaders actually accepted the ludicrous sales pitch of this organization and would only allow their "authorized and approved" prophets to minister in their churches, or called them to see if a prophet who was contacting them to minister in their churches was authorized and approved by them. The upshot of the organization's methods, though they have always adamantly denied that that was their intent, was blatant de facto black-balling of prophets who were not a member of their organization, resulting in untold damage, not only to those prophets' ministries, and thus their lives, but also to the Body of Christ who were prevented from receiving the benefits of those prophets' ministries. To this day, I have never heard anyone affiliated with this organization express any sort or degree of concern about any of the harm they have perpetrated upon outside prophets or the prophetic movement itself.

At the "prophetic gathering" hosted by this organization that I attended back in 1986, there apparently arose a debate among the attendees who had come from all over the world under what turned out to be an erroneous assumption that what was being convened was an open forum for prophets and prophetic people to discuss what they sensed God was speaking and doing in the church, the nation, and across the globe. Obviously, this was never the real intention of the conveners. The "question," as the leader referred to it, was over the existence of "judgment prophets," and apparently there was sufficient cause for him to address it in one of the meetings. I remember his response was vague and equivocating. The essence of it was that while he could not entirely dismiss the existence and functioning of "judgment prophets" today, he also could not justify the concept with the requisite that prophecy should be unto edification, exhortation, and consolation.

While it's not my intent to be unkind, I have to confess my inward reaction to his response was, "This is the prophetic *pope*, and that's his answer to what may be one of the most crucial issues to the church as we await the return of Christ?"

Time and space will not permit a treatise on the Biblical evidence of judgment prophets here, and that is not the purpose of referencing it here, but the overwhelming answer to that question from the preponderance of Scripture is that judgment prophets do indeed exist today, have always existed, and will always exist, certainly through the end of the Church Age. Just one example based on the papa-prophet's response is that the main passage he is referring to, First Corinthians 14:3, is not even talking about "prophets," per se, that is, the *office* of the prophet, but rather the *gift* of prophecy, which is made clear by its prefatory phrase, "One who *prophesies.*"

There are vast differences between the *office* of the prophet and the *gift* of prophecy, and confusion resulting from convergence of the two has always caused a lot of problems in terms of the operation of each. To expand upon the differences very briefly, the Ministry Gift of prophet is given by *Jesus* as the Head of the Church only to "*some,*"[87] not "*all.*"[88] The Manifestation Gifts [charismata], on the other hand, are distributed by the *Holy Spirit* "to *each one* as He wills."[89] The simple Manifestation Gift of prophecy is indeed limited to edification, exhortation, and comfort; however, the Ministry Gift of the prophet has no such restrictions, but also includes the six facets of the prophetic office: to root or pluck up, break down, destroy, overthrow, build, and plant.[90]

There is no doubt or equivocation in my mind that there are judgment prophets and that they are beginning to emerge in significant numbers. I have also made my stance clear on the topic in numerous articles I posted online. In light of the multiplicity of problematic matters existing in the church at-large, including the deluge of deception that has been released from the pits of hell that is bringing to pass Jesus' prediction that even the elect shall be deceived in the last days, I personally pray that the day of the company of judgment prophets God will bring upon the scene comes quickly.

I hasten to say that none of what I say here is spoken with any malice, bitterness, anger, or any unforgiveness regarding this legitimate prophetic leader or anyone else ever associated with the leader or organization (many have since left the group and disassociated themselves from the leader). Despite some of the wrong positions they've held regarding the prophetic and apostolic realm, some claim that they have done a lot of good in terms of helping some prophetic people to "have a home" friendly to same. I don't doubt or disclaim that. I merely hold there have been errors along the way as well that have been harmful to a lot of people. I have personally heard the testimonies of a number of leaders whose ministries were seriously harmed, some even destroyed, by the bad side of this organization's dealings with ministers and ministries. I have personally told the chief leader of this organization that there were many errors and misdeeds made in this respect when they brought in a supposed "apostle," and put him in charge of building churches under the auspices of the organization in the 1990s, which I had warned them about and that it was not of God.

I am not the ultimate judge or the jury. I don't hand out the punishment for such things, but I am commanded by God to judge such things as to whether there has been wrongful conduct or not.[91] I have and I believe there has been. Judgment, temporal or eternal, is far beyond my pay-grade. I don't and haven't engaged in it.

Art Katz posits in an article I quoted from in the article I posted on this topic (the above) the proposition that God actually requires His true prophets to be spokesmen of His judgments as a prerequisite of the privilege of speaking genuine words of benevolence, a premise with which I fully agree. Inherent in the article is the concept I also wholeheartedly agree with that it's really not so much a matter of whether there are "*judgment* prophets" and prophets who, in juxtaposition, would be "*benevolence* prophets," but rather that prophets are prophets, and genuine prophets are called upon by God to pronounce words of judgment as well as announce words of blessing. His perceptions concerning the prophetic function are dead on target, and could only be articulated as they are by someone who has himself lived it. I can truthfully say I also have. I recommend you read the rest of this article online on the Spirit life Magazine website at: https://www.spiritlifemag.com/judgment-prophets-2/. I also highly recommend the book from which the excerpt is excerpted, The Apostolic Foundation, available on Amazon at: https://amzn.to/400AA8U. The Kindle version of this book is published by Real Truth Publications, through which the accompanying audiobook will soon be published as well.

Your Enemies Have No Power Over You

There have been so many more incidences of flaming arrows fired in my direction by our adversary the devil, trying to impede, or, if possible, cause me to abandon my calling, but space simply won't allow me to write about any more of them. Such is the ministry of a prophet! It's just the nature of it. But, in the process, what I've learned, and what I hope you take from this chapter, is that our enemies, of the flesh or of the spirit, cannot have any power over us except what we give to them. Ignore them, and they are powerless! Allow their flaming arrows to fly into your thinking, and you are doomed and will be defeated by them! Don't do it! IGNORE THEM! Or, at most, speak to the demonic forces trying to attack your mind, and tell them to leave and go back to whence they came, in the name of Jesus! This, I have found, is the most effective way to "resist the devil," which will always cause him and his minions to flee from you, post haste![92]

None of These Things Move Me

> *But none of these things move me*, neither count I my life dear unto myself, so that I might finish my course with joy, and the ministry, which I have received of the Lord Jesus, to testify the gospel of the grace of God.[93]

When the Apostle Paul called together the elders and overseers at Ephesus to give his farewell message to them, he told them that he was on his way to Jerusalem, not knowing what all awaited him there, but that it wasn't good in terms of what he would suffer, that bonds and afflictions awaited him, and that they would see his face no more:

> "And now, behold, bound by the Spirit, I am on my way to Jerusalem, *not knowing what will happen to me there*, except that the Holy Spirit solemnly testifies to me in every city, saying that *bonds and afflictions await me*. "But I do not consider my life of any account as dear to myself, so that I may finish my course and the ministry which I received from the Lord Jesus, to testify solemnly of the gospel of the grace of God. And now, behold, I know that all of you, among whom I went about preaching the kingdom, *will no longer see my face*.[94]

This is the attitude I have learned to adopt through all the trials, troubles, and tribulations I've experienced: "None of these things move me!" I can honestly say now, at seventy-five years old and nearly five decades of apostolic-prophetic ministry, that I am not at all moved by the criticism and naysaying of critics and naysayers! It just doesn't affect me at all. I know who I am in Christ and who Christ is in me! I know what my calling is! I am not moved by men's words! Flaming or otherwise! Now, when criticisms and push back on my ministry come, I simply thank the Lord for another opportunity to humble myself in the presence of the Lord,[95] and to love and pray *for* my enemies and persecutors.[96] I always remind myself that the words of these people can never rise to the level of the abuse my Lord willingly took upon Himself for *me*, being wounded for our transgressions, bruised for our iniquity![97] Compared to that, it's all nothing!

In closing this chapter, I want to say that I've learned over and over through the years that any perceived ineffectiveness of the ministry of a prophet lies not with the prophet or the Sender, but with the receivers, who invariably, due to their carnal thinking, only see the sent one as a mere man, and fail to receive the prophet as a prophet, thus precluding themselves from receiving the *reward* the prophet carries with him—the prophet's reward! As Jesus said,

> He that receiveth a *prophet in the name of a prophet* shall receive a prophet's **reward**; and he that receiveth a *righteous man* in the name of a *righteous man* shall receive a *righteous man's reward.*[98]

WOULDN'T TAKE NOTHING FOR MY JOURNEY NOW

> Well I wouldn't take nothing for my journey now
> Gotta make it to Heaven somehow
> Though the devil tempts me and he tries to turn me around
> He's offered everything that's got a name
> All the wealth I want and worldly fame
> If I could still I wouldn't take nothing for my journey now
>
> I started out traveling for the Lord many years ago
> I've had a lot of heartache and I've met a lot of grief and woe
> But when I would stumble then I would humble down
> And there I would say I wouldn't take nothing for my journey now
>
> Well I wouldn't take nothing for my journey now
> Gotta make it to Heaven somehow
> Though the devil tempts me, and he tries to turn me around
> He's offered everything that's got a name
> All the wealth I want and worldly fame
> But if I could still I wouldn't take nothing for my journey now
>
> There's nothing in this world that'll ever take the place of God's love

All the silver and gold wouldn't buy a touch from above
When my soul needs a healin' and I begin to feelin' His power
I can say Praise the Lord I wouldn't take nothing for my journey now

Well I wouldn't take nothing for my journey now
Gotta make it to Heaven somehow
Though the devil tempts me, and he tries to turn me around
He's offered everything that's got a name
All the wealth I want and worldly fame
But if I could still I wouldn't take nothing for my journey now

Yeah if I could still I wouldn't take nothing for my journey now[99]

Endnotes

1   Eph. 6:16
2   2 Tim. 3:10-12
3   Rom. 8:29
4   Rom. 12:2
5   Eph. 2:2
6   Rom. 3:4
7   2 Cor. 13:5
8   John 10:10
9   1 Tim. 6:12
10 2 Pet. 1:3
11 John 16:33
12 Acts 14:22
13 Eph. 5:39
14 2 Cor. 1:5
15 2 Tim. 3:1
16 John 16:33
17 2 Cor. 10:5

18 John 8:44
19 John 14:6
20 Dictionary.com
21 John 8:44
22 John 8:44
23 Rev. 21:1
24 1 Pet. 5:8
25 Rev. 12:10; KJV
26 Jas. 4:7
27 Eph. 3:6
28 2 Cor. 5:17
29 Cf., Mic. 7:19; Isa. 1:18; Psa. 103:12
30 Cf., Jer. 31:34
31 Psa. 115:16
32 Luke 11:24-26; see also, Mat. 12:43-45
33 Gen. 1:26,27
34 1 Thes. 5:23
35 John 4:24
36 Gen. 2:7
37 John 3:7
38 Cf., Rom. 8:10-11
39 Rom. 8:1
40 Plp 4:8; KJV
41 Rom. 12:2
42 Plp. 4:6-7 KJV
43 Jos. 1:3
44 1 Chr. 16:22; Psa. 105:15
45 Num. 16:28-35
46 1 Chr. 16:22; Psa. 105:15
47 Isa. 40:8

48 Jos. 23:14
49 1 Kgs. 8:56
50 Luke 6:38
51 Heb. 11:6
52 Deu. 28:1-14
53 Job 1:21b,c
54 Rom. 12:2
55 John 4:1-11
56 Rom. 8:28-30; parenthesis and brackets added
57 Rom. 8:14; KJV; parenthesis added
58 Rom. 8:19
59 Plp. 2:15
60 Charismatic Captivation, Steven Lambert, ThD, DMin; Real Truth Publications, 1996; pp. 39-40
61 Acts 11:18
62 Rom. 14:11
63 Plp. 2:10
64 Eph. 2:20
65 Mat. 16:18; Eph. 1:22; 5:23; Col. 1:18
66 Titus 1:5-9
67 1 Pet. 4:15; 1 John 3:15
68 Acts 20:30
69 John 13:23; 19:26; 20:2; 21:7,20
70 Mal. 3:6ff
71 1 Cor. 9:16; 2 Cor. 9:7; Phm. 1:14
72 Mat. 16:18; Eph. 2:20
73 1 Cor. 9:9; 1Tim. 5:18
74 1 John 4:4
75 Jas. 3:13-18
76 Luke 5:37-39

77   Luke 6:22-23

78   Psa. 2:1-12

79   1 John 2:20

80   Rom. 11:29

81   Psa. 27:1, et al.

82   http://en.wikipedia.org/wiki/Narcissistic_personality_disorder

83   http://www.mayoclinic.com/health/narcissistic-personality-disorder/DS00652

84   https://www.slm.org/wp-content/uploads/2013/05/Some-Characteristics-of-Narcissism.pdf

85   2 Cor. 10:4

86   Luke 10:18

87   Eph. 4:11

88   1 Cor. 12:28-30

89   1 Cor. 12:4-6

90   Jer. 1:10

91   2 Cor. 13:5,6; 1 John 4:1; Rev. 2:2; et al.

92   Jas. 4:7

93   Acts 20:24

94   Acts 20:22-25

95   Jas. 4:10; 1 Pet. 5:6

96   Mat. 5:44; Luke 6:27,35

97   Isa. 53:5

98   Mat. 10:41

99   Music video by Bill & Gloria Gaither, performing I Wouldn't Take Nothing for My Journey (feat. The Happy Goodmans) [Live]. (P) (C) 2012 Spring House Music Group. All rights reserved. Unauthorized reproduction is a violation of applicable laws. Manufactured by EMI Christian Music Group. Watch at: https://youtu.be/IKZ_hV1TyoU?si=5Kj5WoqvoNZHgdwI

Epilogue

In all earnestness, I hope this book has helped you to understand this critical and all-important matter of faith a little better. I have done my best to communicate in as simple terms as possible what I believe the Lord has shown me about the matter. If you have benefited in some way from this volume, please consider contacting me to let me know by writing me an email to: slambert@slm.org. Doing so would be very encouraging to me. Please check out my various websites as well. A good starting place is my main ministry website at: slm.org.

Health Update

In that I began this book in the Preface discussing information about my health situation and that the subject of this volume is faith, I feel it is fitting that I should provide a brief update on my health currently at the time when I am finishing up this book. My oncology doctors tell me that the cancer markers in my blood are now at a place they call, "stable," which from their standpoint they consider a win-win. The last scans showed the metastatic tumor in my abdomen had decreased in size significantly, though it is not yet totally gone. However, with the continuing chemotherapy treatments every two weeks I can physically see and feel that the tumor has shrunk even more since that last set of scans. Additional scans will be taken during the fall 2023, which I fully expect will show even more significant tumor shrinkage. I praise the Lord for all of this progress!

One thing I can honestly say during this entire battle is that I have always maintained a sense of expectancy for signs of recovery from this dastardly disease called "cancer." I repeat out loud most every day that the name of Jesus is higher than and rules over cancer and therefore cancer must bow its knee to complete and total physical healing. I believe it! He who has promised is well-able also to perform that which

He has promised!

Additionally, every day I profess out loud, "I BELIEVE! I am a believer, and believers believe!" I am fully expecting to one day soon receive the report from my oncologists that my body is completely free of cancer. I will not stop believing until those doctors speak those words! Throughout this ordeal I have strained with every ounce of spiritual strength within me to live out everything I have taught about genuine faith in this book! This I know!

Again, I want to thank everyone who has been agreeing with me for my healing! I am extremely grateful that you would devote some of your precious time to praying for this man who the majority of you have never met in person and never will; yet you prayed in faith believing. Your prayers have worked! After all, that's what this book is about— "Faith That Works!" I will be eternally grateful for your generosity and kindness. And that goes also for those who have contributed to my ministry financially to help keep the bills paid to keep it functioning and reaching out around the globe with the real truth of the Good News Gospel of Christ Jesus!

What more can I say, but that I thank you all, and I pray frequently that the Lord bless you all exceedingly abundantly above all you can ask or think in return for your graciousness extended toward me! Thank you!

Addendum

Saturday, October 21, 2023, I finally finished up the draft of the last chapter the Lord told me I needed to add to the book, The Shield of Faith. The writing was finished, but it would require a final copyedit, which I have since performed.

The following morning, Sunday October 22, 2023, approximately 4:45AM I stood outside my daughter's bedroom and whispered quietly, so as to not awaken my grandson, who was sleeping in his adjacent bedroom, "Angela, I need you to get up and come with me; I'm having pain in my jaw and shoulders, and I need you to pray for me." I didn't want to alarm her, but I knew these were signs of a heart attack.

Angela followed me into my bedroom as I, for whatever reason, explained to her that I had just awoken from a bad dream in which a whole bunch of men were gathered around me, gnashing their teeth at me, and saying they hated my father. I explained to her I knew it was not my natural but Heavenly Father they were talking about; they hated God. They all seemed to me to be men I actually knew who presented as Christians. The significance of that dream, if any, has not been made clear to me as yet.

We then proceeded to pray in tongues together as she laid hands on me. At some point she tells me I told her I was feeling a tiny bit of relief from the pain. I then got up and dressed, remarking that I was cold but not telling her it was also because I wanted to be dressed in the event we needed to go to the hospital. I then laid back down while she continued to pray for me. That's the last thing I remember! I don't remember anything of the events that ensued over the next few days after that until I came to on Wednesday, October 25.

Angela tells me after laying back down on my bed, I then suddenly began gasping for breath. Scared, she began screaming; "Daddy, Daddy, no NO, come back...JESUS HELP DADDY, JESUS, JESUS, JESUS!! She grabbed my cellphone and began trying to dial 911, all the while continuing to scream at the top of her lungs, "DADDY, DADDY...JESUS, JESUS, JESUS, JESUS," while she watched my eyes roll back, my mouth fall open, my breath leaving my body, my face turning red, then purple, then white, like Fourth of July fireworks exploding across a black sky.

Then, my grandson, Zachary, hearing the commotion, burst into the room, ran to the bed and immediately started CPR on me, while screaming at me to stay with him, and yelling out to Jesus also as he got some wheezing gasps out of my otherwise limp body!

Angela says she was still screaming Jesus' Name over me incessantly, decreeing that I would live and not die, commanding, "DADDY STAY HERE!" as the 911 operator is trying to get her to tell her if we wanted an ambulance or police. All she remembers being able to get out is, "HE's DYING, JESUS, SAVE HIM!" to which the operator sarcastically replied, "I guess that means you want an ambulance."

Angela said she could not stop invoking the Name of JESUS over me, so much so that the 911 operator kept telling her to calm down and began screaming at her to shut up and listen to her and kept telling her to start CPR. Finally, Angela yelled back that her son, Zachary, had been performing CPR the entire time. About that moment, she saw Zachary ball up his fist and press it deep into my chest while screaming at me to LIVE, and for JESUS to HELP me, saying to me outloud, "GRANDDAD DON'T LEAVE; STAY WITH ME AND MAMA!!"

The paramedics arrived within 12 minutes. Zachary kept performing CPR until they did. Right before the first responder entered the room, Angela saw Zachary blow a huge breath of air into my lungs. When the medic entered the room, he calmly and gently eased Zachary to the side and slid into place to take over the chest compressions. He immediately announced he was not finding a pulse. He hooked up and started the chest compression machine, as the other two medics began loading me into the ambulance.

There were two amazing aspects to Zachary's participation in the saving of my life that morning. One, he wasn't supposed to be there at all, in that he was on fall break from classes at Embry-Riddle Aeronautical University, where he is enrolled in the Astronautical Engineering Physics bachelors program, and had originally planned to return on Saturday, but we decided to move his return day to Sunday so that we could all share a Sunday breakfast before he returned. Because this event began at around 4:45 AM Sunday morning, we never made it to breakfast.

The second thing is, when he was in the ninth grade as a remote student attending Florida Virtual School, Zachary took a class on CPR, called, H.O.P.E. He not only mastered it, but made his own video of how to do it to share with his teachers for credit. His mastery of CPR is what saved my life. We have since watched that video of that fourteen year old boy multiple times in amazement and lots of weeping!

Another "irony" (or not) regarding Zachary's participation is that when he was four years old and his mother was in the shower, I heard him choking, ran to see what was going on, and immediately initiated the Heimlich Maneuver, propelling like a rifle shot a grape out of his throat he had accidentally swallowed! When his mother heard the commotion, she came running out of the shower, yelling, "What's wrong? What happened?" I calmly reported what happened and that everything was fine now. So that day, God used me to save Zachary's life; sixteen years later, God used Zachary to return the favor and save my life.

Picking back up with the event of Sunday, October 22, the medics rushed me, lights and sirens, to one of the nearest and newest hospitals in our area. Upon arrival the ER doctor gathered Angela and Zachary to ask what my symptoms were and apprise them of the dire situation, frankly telling them the risk of losing me was very high, and that I needed to be rushed into surgery ASAP, but that would require me being transported to an affiliated cardiac-specialty hospital about 45 minutes away. He said they would be going "lights and sirens" to get there ASAP.

At the same time, though, the ER doctor was expressing doubts about whether or not this was the right decision because I could very well die during the transport. He seemed to be equivocating about what to do. At that moment, my bold, prophet-in-training, grandson, asked the doctor if he could pray for him. After some stuttering and stammering, the ER doctor reluctantly said "Okay," and my grandson prayed a short powerful prayer over him concluding with: "Father God, we ask that you fill this doctor with the wisdom he needs to make the right decision for my grandfather, in the mighty Name of Jesus!"

The ER doctor then sprinted out of the room, returning less than five minutes later declaring: "We can move him to the cardiac hospital, because for some odd reason his blood Ph levels are surprisingly very good!" "We're loading him up and going lights and sirens all the way, you head there too, and we'll do everything we can to save his life!"

At the Cardiac hospital, all their tests and analysis indicated I had had a massive heart attack along with cardiac arrest, necessitating multiple shock treatments to restart my heart after coding (dying) "many times," according to the ER doctor. Finally, they were able to start and successfully complete an angioplasty procedure inserting a stent into my aorta.

Following all that, they said that while my physical response was good, I was not immediately responding to commands from a neurological standpoint, or that they were delayed, which were repeatedly attempted multiple times. A CAT scan was taken to make sure there was no brain bleed, and they decided to put me into a medically induced coma and begin hypothermia treatment for a period of 24 hours to prevent any neurological damage, also putting me on a respirator.

For the next two days, after being brought back from the coma, I was kept under heavy sedation as I began the road to recovery. Along the way, my daughter tells me that my team of doctors had told her that my progress was remarkable and even miraculous considering all I had been through, and they were all amazed!

Eight days after being hospitalized, on Tuesday, October 31st, I was discharged from the hospital! Of course, I am continuing to recover in many ways, though I won't be entering any marathons anytime soon! Through God's grace and mercy, His supernatural healing power, and the expert help of very skilled and knowledgeable medical people, I am on the road to recovery. I fully expect to fully recover! It will take a while, but it will happen!

I owe my life to my daughter, Angela, my grandson, Zachary, and all the medical personnel from the first responders to the ICU people. But, most of all to my Lord, Master, and Savior, Jesus Christ, King of kings, Lord of lords, and the exclusive Head of the Church He is building! They are all my heroes to whom I will be eternally grateful!

I believe I am still alive because the Lord has more work for me to do in His Kingdom and on His behalf! I will press on to continue all the labors He has assigned to me until my last breath!

As I write this, I am one day shy of seventy-five years old exactly! Tomorrow, Monday, November 6, 2023 is my 75th birthday. God is good! I plan to live until Jesus appears in the clouds in the air to call up His Church, which I believe cannot be many years away!

Like Abraham, I believe God shall reckon my faith in Him as righteousness! I am far from perfect in myself, but I **am forgiven** and **redeemed**! Let the redeemed of the Lord say so! Amen and Amen!

I'll see you in the morning!

My Blessing Over You

May the Lord bless you and keep you, make His face to shine upon you, be gracious to you and keep you in peace, in the name of the Father, the Son, and the Holy Spirit. I pray the Lord God heal and deliver you from the crown of your head to the soles of your feet. Amen!

No matter what, keep on believing in God with all you got! He will never fail or disappoint you! The battle is the Lord's; the only battle we are authorized to engage in is "the Good Fight of Faith!" Fight for Faith with all your might! In so doing, you cannot lose, because you've already been declared a *winner—**more than** a CONQUEROR through Christ who loved us*!

Other Books By Author

Charismatic Captivation

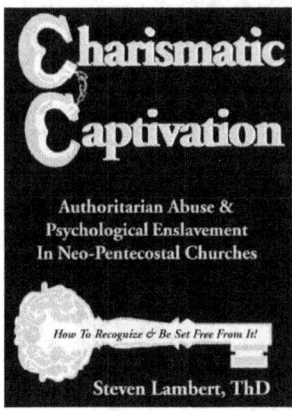

Charismatic Captivation exposes the widespread authoritarian abuse that was infused into the very fabric, foundation, and functions of the Charismatic/Neo-Pentecostal church during the Discipleship/Shepherding Movement (1970s). It identifies 33 signs of spiritual abuse and 15 steps of recovery from authoritarian abuse. The following is an overview of the book's contents.

- Introduction to the hyper-authoritarian doctrines, practices, and governmental structures that are accepted and instituted by many Neo-Pentecostal churches, groups, denominations, and networks today, plus biblical analysis showing why they are irrefutably:
  - unscriptural and thus patently false "doctrines of demons" by which many have been indoctrinated and duped;
  - illegitimate and unauthorized by God;
  - subtle but sophisticated scheme of religious enslavement;
  - in actuality it's witchcraft/sorcery, cultic, and occult;
  - idolatry and spiritual adultery;
  - masked mechanisms for private kingdom-building.
- The history of how these teachings and practices were introduced and infused into the fabric, foundation, and functions of the Neo-Pentecostal ecclesial stream, the firestorm of controversy they produced, identification of the leaders who propagated the teachings, the disrepute into which they fell, and their present status.
- How these doctrines/practices are identical to those of a First Century Christian cult whose deeds and doctrines Jesus Himself explicitly condemned and denounced in the Bible.
- The Signs of Authoritarian Abuse & Common Control Mechanisms used by self-aggrandizing leaders to captivate and control followers.
- The 15 R's of Recovery from Authoritarian Abuse—biblical steps victims must take to recover from the psychologically traumatizing and spiritually debilitating effects of authoritarian abuse.

To obtain or learn more about the print, PDF, and Kindle-book *Charismatic Captivation*, go to: https://www.charismatic-captivation.com.

Other Books By Author

Charismatic Control

Multitudes of sincere and trusting believers are caught unawares in the virtually invisible web of religious captivation in some Charismatic and Neo-Pentecostal churches. They are unwitting victims of spiritual abuse, psychological enslavement, and various forms of exploitation perpetrated under the heavy hand of hyper-authoritarianism. That is to say, the leadership of the church-group of which they are a part is dominating, controlling, manipulating, and exploiting adherents for personal gain and private kingdom-building.

High-profile incidences of authoritarian abuse and exploitation that emerge from time to time are only the tip of the iceberg! The truth is: ecclesial enslavement and exploitation is widespread in many sectors of Christendom, but the perpetrators, many of whom are prominent and respected church leaders, go to great lengths to disguise and conceal it.

Hyper-authoritarianism has especially flourished in the Charismatic and Neo-Pentecostal church-groups since it was infused into their fabric, foundation, and functions in the early-to mid-1970s via what became known as the "Discipleship/Shepherding Movement."

Charismatic Control shows readers how:
- to recognize unbiblical hyper-authoritarian doctrines and practices;
- how they became a widespread, integral part of the Neo-Pentecostal church;
- why these teachings and practices are outright witchcraft/sorcery authored by Satan himself;
- "The 33 Signs of Authoritarian Abuse"; and,
- "The Fifteen Common Control Mechanisms" employed by hyper-authoritarian groups and leaders.

To obtain or learn more about *Charismatic Control* book and audiobook, go to: https://www.charismatic-captivation.com.

Other Books By Author

The Mystery of the Kingdom

The Mystery of the Kingdom is a verse-by-verse exposition of what Jesus Himself identified as "The Paramount Parable"—The Parable of the Sower. Unpacked as it is by the author, this book is a virtual "Christianity 101," in that it puts the "big picture" of the Christian experience and life into proper perspective, unveils many insights into how the Kingdom of God operates on earth.

Its subtitle, Bearing Kingdom Fruit, reflects the book's and the Parable's ultimate message. The medium through which that message is conveyed—The Parable of the Sower—is what Jesus Himself indicated is the most important of all His Parables. In it, He delineates the four categories of hearers of the Word of God. Everyone who has ever heard the Word of God falls into one of these four categories, and thereby chooses their future and eternal destiny.

Dr. Lambert unveils the four-step path of progressive spiritual growth revealed in this "dark saying" of the Master. The most profound and intriguing "hidden pearl" inherent in the rich and ingenious Parable, however, is the "secret" of how the entire Kingdom of God operates and how every believer can bear Kingdom fruit in his/her own life. Indeed, as the book so clearly points out, the unequivocal message of Scripture is that bearing Kingdom fruit is not optional but absolutely imperative.

The *Mystery of the Kingdom* offers definitive and straightforward answers to many age-old questions—right out of the Word of God. By demystifying many of the conundrums of life, it will bring you new inward peace, rest, and faith, and in the process quench the psychological and emotional "fiery darts" with which the evil one assails all believers.

To obtain or learn more about *The Mystery of the Kingdom* book and audiobook, go to: https://realtruthpublications.com/catalog-store/mystery-of-the-kingdom/.

Other Books By Author

DUNAMIS! Power From On High!

Millions of believers around the world are earnestly, and in some cases, desperately, crying out for God's help in real overwhelming needs in their life on the premise that it is divine intervention they need to bring answers and resolution to those problems. But Jesus said, "The Kingdom of God is WITHIN you!"—which means the authority and power of the Kingdom of God is within every believer who has been regenerated, i.e., Born Again, by the infusion of the Holy Spirit in their human spirit!

Jesus Himself testified to the early disciples and every other disciple of every age, "You shall receive POWER after that the Holy Ghost has come UPON you to be my witnesses!" The ONLY WAY to be effective witnesses of the resurrected Christ is through the power believers receive with the BAPTISM IN THE HOLY SPIRIT AND FIRE!

Jesus was the Heavenly PROTOTYPE of the SONS OF GOD! As such, He received the power to perform the works of power, miracles, signs and wonders He performed throughout His earthly ministry when He Himself was baptized in the Holy Spirit. In so doing, He set the precedent for every other Son of God (Born Again Believer) to likewise receive the power He operated in through the Baptism In The Holy Spirit to fulfill His Word that the works He did and even greater works shall believers do!

Within every *Spirit-baptized* believer is the same AUTHORITY and POWER that raised Christ from the dead and that Jesus operated in to heal the sick, halt, and paralyzed; open blind eyes and deaf ears; cleanse lepers; cast out demons; raise the dead, feed the 5,000 and 3,000; and walk on water! The only way to receive that power and authority is by receiving the same Baptism in the Holy Spirit that Jesus received. *DUNAMIS! Power from on High!* is a step-by-step journey to receiving that power!

To obtain or learn more about this book and audiobook, go to: https://realtruthpublications.com/catalog-store/dunamis/.

Other Books By Author

Uncovering the Myth of Spiritual Covering

Uncovering the Myth of Spiritual Covering is adapted from a chapter of the widely disseminated book, **Charismatic Captivation**—*Authoritarian Abuse & Psychological Enslavement in Neo-Pentecostal Churches*. That book exposes the widespread problem of authoritarian abuse that has been flourishing virtually unabated since it was first infused into the very fabric, foundation, and functions of the Charismatic/Neo-Pentecostal church during the false movement known as the Discipleship/Shepherding Movement (1970-77).

Owing extensively to that movement and the teachings promulgated during it, hyper-authoritarian doctrines and practices are prevalant in many churches, major segments of some denominations, as well as many of the protodenominational "networks" that began emerging over primarily the last half of the 20th Century. The problem became so widespread that it reached pandemic proportions in Pentecostal/Neo-Pentecostal streams.

Uncovering the Myth of Spiritual Covering analyzes against the foundation-stone of Scripture the foundational theories of this hyper-authoritarian ecclesiastical culture, demonstrates their irrefutable incongruity with Scripture, and disabuses believers of acceptance of and adherence to them, thereby liberating them from the invisible chains of psychological enslavement that have been holding them in bondage to the illegitimate authority structures of men.

Ecclesial groups and ministries practicing the illegitimate predominance and psychological control of hyper-authoritarianism employ various means and degrees of psychological coercion to compel congregants/adherents to subject and conform their personal activities, behavior, and affairs of life to the leadership-prescribed standards, rules, expectations, and collective corporate goals of the ecclesiastical entity.

To obtain or learn more about the book and audiobook, go to: https://realtruthpublications.com/catalog-store/uncovering-spiritual-covering/.

Other Books By Author

Forty Healing Scriptures

As the title implies, *Forty Healing Scriptures*, is forty Scripture passages related to the matter of healing, compiled in the Kindle-book and read on the backdrop of melodious instrumental music in the audiobook by Prophet Steven Lambert, and is empowered with a discernible anointing.

God makes it abundantly clear repeatedly throughout His Word that it is His desire and will to effect healing in people's lives. In one place, He specifically states that healing people is an intrinsic part of His very nature: "I am the Lord who heals you!"

Moreover, He has also established the principal that faith is the key to obtaining all the spiritual blessings and benefits He desires to liberally pour out upon Mankind. He prescribes in His Word only one way to appropriate effective faith–faith that works–in one's life, which is through hearing the Word of Christ, who IS the Word of God. The Word of God heard produces effectual faith, and it is by that effectual faith that one receives all the spiritual blessings or benefits of the Kingdom of God.

Hebrews 1:3 speaks of "the WORD of His (God's) POWER!" This is alluding to the fact that all of God's POWER is resident or contained in His WORD! God created the entire creation by verbalizing, speaking, His WORD! And the Word of God is Jesus Himself. When the Rhema-Word is spoken, all of God's POWER is released, and God said His Word shall not return unto Him void without accomplishing the purpose for which it was sent; He also declared He is WATCHING OVER His Word to PERFORM it!

God has given us 66 books of His Word for us to speak it, verbalize it, declare and decree it, and thereby ACTIVATE it!

To obtain or learn more about the book and audiobook, go to: https://realtruthpublications.com/catalog-store/40-healing-scriptures/.

Other Books By Author

Let Us Pray!

 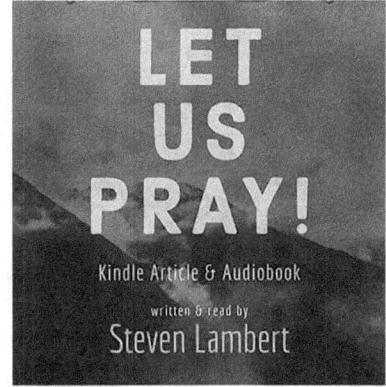

Prayer is one of the most vital keys to the Church and individual believers moving into the dimension of the spirit that God is calling her and them into! Unless we *pray*, we are going to *stay* where we have been! James, the half-brother of Jesus and author of the New Testament book of James, said that fervent and effectual prayer of the righteous availeth much!

Prayer changes things! Prayer brings about change! Prayer prepares the hearts of God's people for the manifestation and fulfillment of His purposes and plans!

There is no substitute for prayer. One great preacher on the subject of prayer once wrote, "It is as if God can do nothing unless and until someone first asks Him." Ask, seek, knock—this is the process the Lord has decreed that allows His intervention into the affairs of men. He has established forever the principle of free will, and it governs everything upon the Earth. He will not violate it, no matter what; He simply cannot! But when we ask in accordance with His will relative to our own life, He will do what we ask! "ALL things, WHATSOEVER things you ask IN PRAYER believing, you SHALL receive." Our asking gives Him the "permission" or "opportunity" to do it! But He cannot do it unless and until we ask!

A common detrimental presumption is that whatever God WANTS to do He CAN and therefore, presumeably, WILL do! After all, He can do whatever He wants, He's God! right? Wrong! Bad theology! He can only do what WE want and ASK Him to do! "The HEAVENS are the heavens of the Lord; But the EARTH He has given to the SONS OF MEN (sons of Adam, lit.)" (Psa. 115:16)! Human governmental authority in the affairs of men on this planet is sacrosanct!

So, saints of God, for this cause, let us pray!

To obtain or learn more about *Let Us Pray!* Kindle-book and audiobook, go to: https://amzn.to/3Xlaj2b.

Other Books By Author

The Prophetic Gifts & Office

In October 1987, 470 years almost to the day after the start of the Protestant Reformation, the Head of the Church publicly declared through the Spirit of prophecy the commencement of another restorational movement in the continuum of reformation by which the prophetic gifts and office would be restored to their proper place of function within the Church that Jesus is building.

Since that momentous event, the winds of reformation have been blowing to bring fresh revelation and illumination concerning this previously neglected and greatly misunderstood area of Truth, stirring new interest in the prophetic office and gifts. Lay believers and church leaders alike are being moved by a Spirit-inspired hunger to become more knowledgeable of and activated in this powerful realm of the Spirit—the prophetic realm.

The Prophetic Gifts and Office, by Dr. Steven Lambert, an Apostolic-Prophet, is the product of more than twenty-five years, at the time it was written in the late 1980s (now nearly 50 years), of exhaustive study, experience, and expertise in the operation of the prophetic gifts and office. The contents are based on many teaching outlines Dr. Lambert prepared to teach on the topic in some 300 seminars and prophetic meetings he conducted in meeting facilities, churches, and homes of people who hungerd to know more about the prophetic at a time when only a few prophets in the world were teaching on the topic and prophesying about a coming "prophetic movement" in which the prophetic gifts and office, in particular, would be restored to their rightful place of function in the church, followed by an "apostolic movment" that would restore the apostolic office to its rightful place of function as well.

The manual is a virtual encyclopedia of the prophetic realm, addressing a myriad of vital issues regarding the prophetic gifts and office, their function in the Church today, and the role of the prophetic in bringing about the purposes and plans of God in the End-time Church that Jesus is building. It is an excellent educational resource regarding the prophetic movement, gifts, and office, and has been used as a textbook for a bible college course also compiled by Dr. Lambert on the prophetic realm.

To obtain or learn more about *The Prophetic Gifts and Office*, go to: https://realtruthpublications.com/catalog-store/prophetic-book/.

Other Books By Author

The Dangerous Path of Doctrinal Deviation

Doctrinal deviation, degeneration, and denigration is a perilous path leading not to genuine unity of the Spirit, as posited by its propagators, but rather *disunity* with the Spirit, apostasy, perdition, and ultimately hell itself!

An oft recited slogan over the last few decades in some ecclesiastical streams is: "We must agree to disagree without being disagreeable." In itself, that pun's import has some merit. Even among the most sincerely congenial colleagues and cohorts, perfect and perpetual agreement is an unrealistic and impossible expectation. Honest and sincere people do sometimes have honest and sincere disagreements. Indeed, disagreement is inevitable, but disagreement need not be fraught with divisiveness or produce disharmony.

People working and walking together in whatever enterprise or relationship will not always be in perfect accord on every nuance of every issue, but that variance need not begat discord, particularly among those infused and immersed in the Spirit. *Disagreement* among reasoned individuals walking by the Spirit need not engender *disharmony*.

Regardless, believers must never yield to the temptation to deviate from established essential doctrines or compromise proper biblical principles in order to "keep the peace," or to "go along to get along." Yet, that is precisely what some have taken this slogan concerning disagreement to mean. A dangerous trend has developed among many ecclesiastical segments toward what they purport is "unity," but which really amounts to a "truce," by definition, based on doctrinal compromise. Though many of these alliances claim "unity," the truth is they are engaging in syncretism-based ecumenicism to institute a surreptitious agenda to ally with the Roman Catholic Church. These alliances ultimately will comprise the end-time one-world Babylonian Church signified in eschatological Scripture.

To obtain or learn more about *The Dangerous Path of Doctrinal Deviation* Kindle-book and audiobook, go to: https://amzn.to/3YlUAkX.

Other Books By Author

The Life Story of Lester Sumrall

To obtain or learn more about *The Dangerous Path of Doctrinal Deviation* Kindle-book and audiobook, go to: https://realtruthpublications.com/catalog-store/sumrall-story-audiobook/.

Other Books By Author

Exposing the Dangers of Martial Arts!

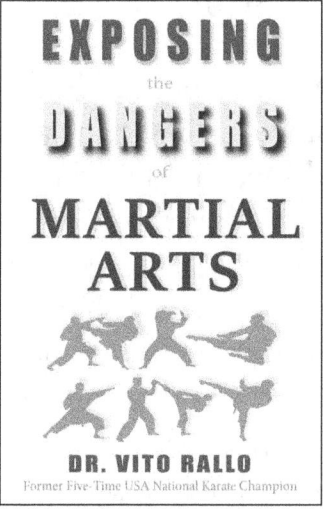

Follow former five-time USA National Karate Champion, Dr. Vito Rallo, as he takes you behind the veil of the martial arts rituals and reveals the closely guarded secret known only to the masters about the real power-source of the arts! Trained by the best Japanese instructors dispatched to America in the mid-60s, he rose to be among the best of the best in the world of martial arts. He owned and operated his own dojos (schools), taught karate in universities, mentored scores of other karate instructors and professional athletes, coached corporate business executives, and trained law enforcement agencies in martial arts skills.

A Born-Again Christian for many years now, former expert sensei, Vito Rallo steps out of the darkness of dimly-lit dojos, colored belts, gis, and barefooted martial arts devotees to expose the hidden demonic spiritual dangers of martial arts and yoga. The former karate master explains why a sprained ankle, loose tooth, bodily bruise, or bruised ego are the least of concerns for martial arts practitioners!

THE FACT IS: WHAT YOU DON'T KNOW AND CAN'T SEE <u>CAN</u> HURT YOU!

Among the truths Rallo uncovers in this easy-to-read book are:
- The true ancient religious origins of the martial arts.
- The clear and proven connection between yoga and the martial arts, and their occult roots.
- The hidden demonic forces behind these Eastern religion-based arts that empower the more advanced practitioners with near supernatural abilities.
- The history of the introduction of the martial arts and the intertwined practice of yoga in the West following WWII through returning soldiers.
- The promotion and glorification of these ancient fighting arts by Hollywood and television programmers as it came of age.
- The spiritual devastation martial arts and yoga wreak in the lives of individuals, Christians, and Christian churches.
- The many reasons martial arts and yoga are in no way compatible with genuine Christianity.
- Biblical advice to practitioners and those considering taking it up.

To obtain or learn more about the print or Kindle-book, go to: https://realtruthpublications.com/catalog-store/dangers-of-martial-arts/.

About The Author

DR. STEVEN LAMBERT has been ministering the Gospel of Jesus Christ as an ordained minister since 1976, serving as a pastor, prophet, teacher, Board Certified Doctoral Diplomate Christian counselor, deliverance minister, podcaster and radio broadcaster, narrator, and holds several theological degrees. He is the author of an ever-increasing number of books, published articles, other teaching materials, and is the publisher of Spirit Life Magazine (SpiritLifeMag.com). He is also the founder of Real Truth Publications (RealTruthPublications.com) that publishes Christian books and audiobooks. He also serves as the founding overseer of Ephesians Four Network of Churches & Ministers (EphesiansFour.net). More information and links to his various outreach media is available on his main ministry website at: SLM.org.

www.ingramcontent.com/pod-product-compliance
Lightning Source LLC
Chambersburg PA
CBHW071857110526
44591CB00011B/1443